北京市高等教育精品教材立项项目

英语国家概况

总主编　史宝辉
主　编　訾　缨
（按姓氏笔画排列）
副主编　吕丽塔　李　芝　高月琴
编　者　卢雨菁　卢晓敏　白雪莲　李　岩
　　　　朱红梅　芦　析　郭　陶　欧阳宏亮

北京大学出版社
PEKING UNIVERSITY PRESS

图书在版编目(CIP)数据

英语国家概况/訾缨主编. —北京:北京大学出版社,2010.8
(大学英语立体化网络化系列教材·拓展课程教材)
ISBN 978-7-301-13847-2

Ⅰ.英… Ⅱ.訾… Ⅲ.英语—阅读教学—高等学校—教材 Ⅳ.H319.4

中国版本图书馆CIP数据核字(2008)第068336号

书　　　名:	英语国家概况
著作责任者:	訾　缨　主编
责 任 编 辑:	李　颖
标 准 书 号:	ISBN 978-7-301-13847-2/H·2007
出 版 发 行:	北京大学出版社
地　　　址:	北京市海淀区成府路205号　100871
网　　　址:	http://www.pup.cn
电　　　话:	邮购部 62752015　发行部 62750672　编辑部 62755217　出版部 62754962
电 子 信 箱:	zbing@pup.pku.edu.cn
印　刷　者:	北京鑫海金澳胶印有限公司
经　销　者:	新华书店
	787毫米×1092毫米　16开本　17.25印张　480千字
	2010年8月第1版　**2021年8月第14次印刷**
定　　　价:	40.80元(含电子教程)

未经许可,不得以任何方式复制或抄袭本书之部分或全部内容。
版权所有,侵权必究　举报电话:010-62752024
　　　　　　　　　　　电子信箱:fd@pup.pku.edu.cn

前　言

《英语国家概况》是大学英语提高阶段的公共选修课教材。本书采用电子教程光盘与纸质版教材相结合的编写模式,配套使用。

一、整体框架

1. 电子教程光盘

电子教程光盘供拓展学习使用。光盘与纸质版教材基本框架结构相同,但内容更加丰富,为课堂教学内容的拓展与延伸,包含大量精美插图和音、视频教学资料;涵盖六大部分内容,第一至第五部分为美国、加拿大、英国和爱尔兰、澳大利亚和新西兰以及新加坡、南非和印度等九国的国家概况,分为十八单元进行介绍;第六部分为课程习题集和答案。具体框架如下:

1) 美国部分　　　　　　　　　（第 1—4 章　共 4 章）
2) 加拿大部分　　　　　　　　（第 5—8 章　共 4 章）
3) 英国/爱尔兰部分　　　　　（第 9—13 章　共 5 章）
4) 澳大利亚/新西兰部分　　　（第 14—17 章　共 4 章）
5) 其他英语国家部分(新加坡,南非,印度)(第 18 章,共 1 章)
6) 课程习题集与答案

2. 纸质版教材

纸质版教材供课堂教学使用。全书内容分为 15 章进行讲授,推荐学时为 30—40 学时;内容包括美国、加拿大、英国、爱尔兰、澳大利亚和新西兰等六个国家的概况,任课教师可根据教学要求和学生情况对上述国家进行选择性教学。

二、主要内容

每一国家的概况介绍编写体例基本相同,均涵盖以下四方面的内容:

1. 国家综述(General Survey)

包括国名、国土面积、人口、官方语言、国旗、国歌、国徽、国花、宗教和货币等。

2. 地理与历史(Geography and History)

包括地理特点、气候、山脉河流、区划、主要地区、城市简介;历史进程及重要历史事件介绍。

3. 政治与经济(Political System and National Economy)

政治概况包括政府、政体、政党、宪法、国王、国家元首和政府首脑介绍;经济概况包括工业、农业、旅游业、商业、金融业等情况的介绍。

4. 社会与文化(Culture and Society)

包括文化群体、价值观、中小学教育和高等教育、文学艺术、体育运动、社会习俗、衣食住行、重要节日和主要宗教的介绍。

三、教程特色

1. 本教程编写形式新颖。目前国内英语国家概况教材大多为纸质版教材，供大学英语使用的此类教材尚未见电子教程出版。本教程突破了传统模式，采用纸质教材与电子教程光盘相结合的编写模式，集知识性和趣味性于一体，在实现公共选修课教材立体化、网络化方面进行了有益的尝试，对激发学生学习兴趣、提高选修课大班教学效果具有良好的促进作用。

2. 本教程图文并茂，采用了插图式的讲授方法。在讲授过程中，充分利用电子教程的资源优势，根据所授内容插入相应人物、景物、事件等的图片、录像片断、演说录音、歌曲等等，使课程内容生动、直观，符合当代大学生的认知心理。电子教程丰富的图、文与音、视频教学资源可满足大学英语基础与提高阶段对文化背景知识的要求。

3. 本教程使用便捷。电子教程光盘字号大小，版式设计均已按照上课需要进行了设定，教师上课时可直接使用，不必自行调试，省时省力。学生课下可结合课堂教学内容，利用拓展内容进行复习，深化所学知识，完成所学章节的练习内容，并根据电子教程上所提供过的听力原文和答案进行自检。

四、习题形式

本教程附有配套习题集，含各类练习题七百余道。每节后附练习题 10 题(Section Exercises)，习题形式包括正误判断、多项选择和连线等客观题型；每章后附综合练习题 15-20 题(Chapter Exercises)，主要形式为填空、短语解释和简答等主观题型。练习题部分的设计可为学生通过四、六级考试和研究生英语入学考试提供帮助。

五、读者对象

本教程读者群宽泛，适用范围广阔。既可用于课堂教学，亦可用于学生课外拓展学习，同时它还是教师备课的优质资源库。

教程难度对应《大学英语教学要求》所规定的较高要求。对于英语专业本科生及研究生，教师可通过拓展内容提高教学难度。

六、编写队伍

本教程主要编写人员均有国外留学、访学经历，主讲过英美概况、美国历史、西方文化等本科和研究生课程，教学经验丰富，所编教材针对性、实用性强。

由于编写这样一部教材是一个新的尝试，时间紧、任务重，缺点错误在所难免，欢迎广大教师、学生和使用者提出宝贵意见，以便我们及时做出修改。

编者

Contents

Understanding the United States

A General Survey of the US ·· 1
Chapter 1   Geography ·· 4
Chapter 2   History ·· 20
Chapter 3   Political System ·· 41
Chapter 4   National Economy ·· 56
Chapter 5   Society and Culture ·· 66

Understanding Canada

A General Survey of Canada ·· 106
Chapter 6   Geography and History ·· 109
Chapter 7   Political System and National Economy ···································· 132
Chapter 8   Society and Culture ·· 139

Understanding U.K. & Ireland

A General Survey of UK ·· 150
Chapter 9   Geography and History of UK ·· 156
Chapter 10   Political System and Economy of UK ····································· 172
Chapter 11   Society and Culture of UK ·· 189
Chapter 12   Understanding the Republic of Ireland ···································· 206

Understanding Australia and New Zealand

A General Survey of Australia ·· 223
Chapter 13   History, Politics and Economy of Australia ······························ 233
Chapter 14   Culture and Society of Australia ·· 246
Chapter 15   Understanding New Zealand ·· 257

Understanding the United States

A General Survey of the US

Map of the United States

Covering the central part of North America, the United States is a vast country to explore. It is a federal republic consisting of 50 states with dazzling (耀眼的) landscape and variable geography, also an exciting mixture of cultural diversity and diplomatic controversy.

Country Name

The conventional official name is the United States of America, shortened as the United States, US, or USA. On July 4, 1776, *The Declaration of Independence* announced that the thirteen North American colonies would be the United States of America, free and independent of Great Britain. It has a nickname, "Uncle Sam." The image came from a meat provider named Samuel Wilson during the war of 1812. The American Congress officially recognized Uncle Sam as a national symbol in 1961.

Capital

Washington D. C. is the capital and political center of the United States. There are a number of important institutions in this city, such as the White House (residence of the President) and the Capitol Hill (home to the American Congress).

Language

English is the official language of the United States, also called American English in contrast with British English. According to the 2000 census (人口普查), English is spoken by 82.1% of its population, Spanish 10.7%, other Indo-European 3.8%, Asian and Pacific island 2.7%, and other 0.7%.

Note: Hawaiian is an official language in the state of Hawaii.

Religion

Most Americans are Christians, among them 52% are protestant and 24% Roman Catholic. For other religions, Mormon 2%, Jewish 1%, Muslim 1%, other 10%, and none 10%, according to a 2002 investigation.

Currency

The official currency of the United States is the United States dollar (USD $). In 1792 the newly independent United States chose the Spanish dollar, subdivided into 100 cents, as the unit of American currency in preference to the British pound. Now the US dollar is one of the most circulated currencies of the world.

National Flag

On June 14, 1777, at Philadelphia, the Marine Committee of the Second Continental Congress offered the resolution which resulted in the adoption of the Flag of the United States.

The flag of the US goes by many names: Stars and Stripes, Old Glory, Star-Spangled (星光灿烂的) Banner, or the Red, White, and Blue. It has 13 stripes—7 red stripes and 6 white stripes. A blue square in the upper corner contains 50 white stars. The stripes represent the 13 original American colonies. The 50 stars stand for the 50 US states. According to the Department of State, red stands for hardiness and courage, white is the symbol of purity and innocence, and blue is the color of vigilance, perseverance and justice.

The National Anthem

The "Star-Spangled Banner" is the national anthem of the United States. It was composed by Francis Scott Key in 1814. The United States Congress made the "Star-Spangled Banner" the national anthem of the United States in 1931.

The National Flower

Rose is the national flower of the United States. President Reagan signed Proclamation in 1986 that rose is named as the National Floral Emblem of the United States of America. The American people hold rose dear as the symbol of life, love and devotion, of beauty and eternity.

The National Bird

The bald eagle was chosen in 1782 as the emblem (象征) of the US because of its long life, great strength and majestic looks, and also because it was then believed to exist only on thes continent of North America.

The Great Seal (国玺)

The Seal of the United States depicts a bald eagle with a shield of 13 alternating red and white stripes representing the 13 original States on its breast. Across the top of the shield is a blue field that unites all the stripes into one. The blue chief represents the United States Congress. In his talons (爪) the eagle grasps an olive

A General Survey of the US

branch representing peace, and 13 arrows representing war. Above the eagle are thirteen stars inside a circular design, representing a "New Constellation." In his beak the eagle grasps a flowing ribbon bearing the first MOTTO of the United States: E Pluribus Unum. These Latin words are translated as "Out of many, One."

Population

The United States is home to about 301 million people. That makes it the world's third most populated country, after China and India, and the most populous of today's developed countries. It has also one of the highest population growth rates of the industrialized nations: about one percent annually. This adds some 2.5 million people every year. Most Americans are descended from immigrants. Immigration now contributes roughly a third of the annual U.S. population increase.

A Collection of Fast Facts of the United States

Official name	the United States of America
Capital	Washington, D.C.
Population	301,621,157 people
Rank among countries in population	3rd
Major cities	New York, Los Angeles, Chicago, Houston, Philadelphia
Total area	9,372,615 km^2
Rank in area worldwide	4th
Highest point	Mt. McKinley, 6,194 meters
Lowest point	Death Valley, 6 meters
Currency	United States dollar
Principal language	English
Major religion	Christianity
Literacy rate	97%
Largest state	Alaska, 1,720,000 km^2
Smallest state	Rhode Island, 4,000 km^2
Most populous state	California, 35,900,900 people
Least populous state	Wyoming, 507,000 people
Independence Day	July 4th

Chapter 1　Geography

I　Geographical Features

The United States is located in the central part of North America, bordering the North Atlantic Ocean in the east and the North Pacific Ocean in the west. With a total area of 9,372,615 square kilometers, the United States ranks the fourth largest country in area in the world, after Russia, Canada and China.

As far as geographical features are concerned, the country can be separated into three major divisions: the highlands in the east, the mountains in the west, and a vast plain region in between. In order to explain more clearly, we can begin by dividing the continent of North America into 7 regions. These regions are large areas where the landforms (地貌) or kinds of lands are similar. The 7 regions are:

- the Atlantic and Gulf coastal plain
- the Appalachian Mountains
- the Central Lowlands and the Great Plains
- the Rocky Mountains
- the Great Basin (山间高原盆地)
- the Pacific Coastal Ranges and Lowlands
- the Canadian Shield (also called the Laurentian Shield, 加拿大地盾,劳伦地盾)

The Coastal Plain

Along the east coast of North America is a narrow plain. This plain begins far up the coast and becomes wider as you travel south. The coastal plain extends all along the Atlantic and Gulf coasts of the United States. The coastal plain is low and flat. In some places, there are large areas where the land is covered with shallow water. These areas are called swamps or wet lands. The swamps are thick with plants, and there are many wild animals.

The Appalachian Mountains

In the west of the coastal plain are the Appalachian Mountains. The Appalachians are a chain of thickly wooded mountains that stretch from Maine all the way to Georgia and Alabama. The topography (地形学) of these mountains is different, and not many of them are nearly as tall as west-coast ranges. Much cultivation and urbanization has occurred in the Appalachians, but there are still many remote areas. The Appalachian Mountains are different from other ranges because most of their trees are deciduous (每年落叶的).

The Appalachians are old mountains. This means that they were formed millions of years ago. Since then, they have been worn down by the wind and the weather. Today, most of these mountains have rounded tops. The highest peak of the Appalachians is only a little over 2,000 meters. The valleys between them do not have steep sides. In parts of the Appalachians, the land is not good for farming. People have farmed thin strips of land in the valleys where it is flat. But farmers here barely grow enough for themselves to eat. Much coal is found in these mountains.

The Great Plains

In the west of the Appalachians, the land drops to the mighty Mississippi River. Still west is a vast open area called the Great Plains. The Great Plains is the broad expanse of prairie which lies east of the Rocky Mountains in the United States of America and Canada. As one of the largest areas of flatland in the world, it stretches from northern Canada to the Gulf of Mexico, covering the US states of New Mexico, Texas, Oklahoma, Colorado, Kansas, Nebraska, Wyoming, Montana, South Dakota and North Dakota, the Canadian provinces of Saskatchewan and Alberta. Much of Minnesota and Iowa and much of the Canadian province of Manitoba also lie in the Great Plains. It is usually divided by Missouri River into two regions: the Central Lowland in the east, and Great Plains in the west.

● *The Central Lowland*

The plains east of the Missouri River are called the Central Lowlands. It stretches from the five Great Lakes to central Texas. Here is some of the most fertile land in the world. On these plains, the farmers grow corn, soybeans, and wheat. The Central Lowlands are also rich in oil and natural gas. Many of the large cities in the US are located in the Central Lowlands.

● *The Great Plains*

To the west of the Missouri River is the Great Plains. Most of the area is treeless grassland. Wheat and corn fields cover much of the plains. Great herds of cattle and sheep feed on its grasses. Places such as South Dakota's Ordway Prairie Preserve ensure that some of the natural prairie land survives.

Rocky Mountains

West of the Great Plains are the Rocky Mountains, spanning the country from Alaska to Mexico. High with rugged peaks and steep valleys, the Rocky Mountains rise over 4,260 meters above sea levels and form the continental divide of the United States. On one side of this great divide, all rivers flow west to the Pacific Ocean. On the other side, the rivers flow east. Rocky Mountains are younger than the Appalachians. Some of the people living in the Rocky Mountains earn their living by mining and logging. Rocky Mountains also attract visitors who come for sports and vacations. The Breathtaking sunsets, glaciated valleys (冰川谷), pristine (原始的) forests, and snow-crested peaks—this is nature of drama.

Plateaus and the Great Basin

West of the Rockies are the two great plateaus: the Columbia Plateau in the north and the Colorado Plateau in the south, with the Great Basin in between. The Columbia Plateau is largely underlain by ancient lava (熔岩) flows, while Colorado Plateau includes spectacular canyons, high plateaus, and mountains.

A number of ancient salty lakes are found in the basin, including the famous Great Salt Lake of Utah. The rivers here do not flow toward the sea and most of them are shallow and salty. Many flow into the Great Salt Lake. This land receives little rainfall. Much of it is desert. Death Valley is on the western edge of this region. This valley, 200 kilometers long and 86 kilometers below the sea level, is the lowest point and hottest place in the US. There are few big cities in this part .The land near the Rocky Mountains is good for grazing cattle.

The Pacific Coastal Ranges

Farther west, along the coast, stands another great system of mountains, the Pacific Coastal ranges including the Sierra Nevada (内华达山脉) and Cascade ranges (喀斯喀特山脉). It is truly a unique landscape consisting of various physiographic regions. With dynamic landforms such as California's white sand beaches in the south and the rugged and rocky coasts of Washington in the north, the Pacific Coast is very different from other coastal regions in the US. Another unique feature running along the Pacific Ocean is the Coast Ranges, which have peak elevations of about 1,200 meters in the state of Oregon.

The Canadian Shield

The last main region of North America is called the Canadian Shield, also known as the Laurentian Plateau (or Laurentian Highlands), which covers an area of 4,790,000 km² and has the shape of a giant shield. It stands mainly in Canada, extending from Newfoundland in the east, to the Beaufort Sea in the northwest, and south through Wisconsin and Minnesota in the US. This is a large area of rocky hills covered with forests. It forms the central land mass of North America. Few people live in the northern region. But the land is rich in minerals such as nickel, copper, and silver. There are many streams and lakes in the Canadian Shield. These waters attract many Canadians and Americans from farther south for vacations.

Alaska and Hawaii

Alaska lies in the northwestern corner of North America, still mostly a rugged wilderness. Alaska covers 656,425 square miles, making it the largest of the 50 states and more than twice the size of Texas, the second largest state. Juneau (朱诺) is the capital of Alaska. Most of Alaska is surrounded by water. To the north is the Arctic Ocean; to the south is the Gulf of Alaska and Pacific Ocean; to the west is the Bering Sea. Alaska's land borders Canada to the east and south. The geography can be categorized into four main areas including two mountain ranges, a central plateau, and the Arctic slope or coastal plain. It also includes the fertile farmland known as the Matanuska (马塔努斯卡河) Valley. Alaska contains 375 million acres of land and thousands of lakes. Permafrost (永久冻结带) is a major factor in the geography of Alaska. It covers most of the northern part of the State. Discontinuous or isolated patches also exist over the central portions in an overall area covering nearly a third of the State. The highest point in Alaska is Mt. McKinley at 20,320 feet above sea level (麦金利山). In fact, Mt. McKinley is the highest point in North America. Yukon River (3,185 km long, of which 1,149 km lie in Canada) is the longest river in Alaska and the fifth-longest river in North America.

About 3,680 kilometers across the Pacific Ocean is Hawaii, a long chain of tropical islands including 8 main islands and over a hundred atolls (环状珊瑚岛) and islets. The Hawaiian Islands were formed by volcanoes that pushed up from the seafloor millions of years ago. Hawaii is the largest of the habitable Hawaiian islands and covers 4,038 square miles. This island was formed by five volcanoes, two of which are still active and erupt intermittently (间歇地). Waikiki Beach(威基基海滩), located in Honolulu (火奴鲁鲁, 即"檀香山", 美国夏威夷州首府和最大的城市), is one of Hawaii's most popular attractions. Millions of tourists visit Hawaii to bask in the sun on its beautiful beaches.

II   Major Rivers, Lakes and Mountains

Rivers

- ***Mississippi River***

The Mississippi River, lying between the Appalachian Mountains and the Rocky Mountains, is the most important river in the United States and one of the great continental rivers in the world. It flows 3,770 kilometers from its source in northwestern Minnesota to its mouth in the Gulf of Mexico.

The Mississippi is the largest river in North America. This means that it carries a greater volume of water than any other North American river. But the Mississippi is not the longest river. That honor goes to the Missouri. The Missouri is 320 kilometers longer. But if Mississippi is measured from the source of its chief headstream (the main branch), the Missouri River, it is over 6,000 kilometers with more than 40 tributaries. The two major tributaries are the Missouri River and Ohio River. The Illinois and Arkansas are other major rivers that flow into the Mississippi. Along the way, the Mississippi borders ten states. It is known as the Father of Waters.

● *Missouri River*

The Missouri River is the longest river system in the United States. It flows about 4,090 kilometers from southwest Montana among the Rocky Mountains to just north of St. Louis, Missouri, where it joins the Mississippi River. The river is nicknamed "The Big Muddy" as it has a great deal of mud in it. On its way to the Mississippi, the Missouri forms part of the border of seven states. The three largest cities along the Missouri are Omaha in Nebraska, and Kansas City and St. Louis in Missouri.

● *Ohio River*

Another main tributary of the Mississippi is Ohio River (1,500 kilometers), which rises from the rainy east at Pittsburgh, Penn. and joins the Mississippi at Cairo, Illinois. It served as the gateway to the West at the beginning of the 1800s for the early settlers moving west from the Appalachians. By the 1820s, steamboats had arrived on the Ohio River. Steamboats moved a lot faster than flatboats. Traffic on the Ohio rapidly increased as steamboats carried goods and people up and down the river. Three cities became important centers of trade because of

their locations on the busy waterway: Pittsburgh, Cincinnati (in Ohio), and Louisville (in Kentucky). Traffic on the river lessened in the late 1800s after the railroads were built.

By the mid-1900s, the Ohio River had become severely polluted. Sewage and industrial wastes had been dumped in it for many years. No one wanted to swim in the river. Cleanup efforts have helped make the river a place where people can once again enjoy fishing, swimming, and boating.

● *St. Laurence River*

Another important river is the St. Laurence, which forms part of the boundary between Canada and the United States. The St. Lawrence River is the chief outlet of the Great Lakes, flowing northeast from Lake Ontario to the Gulf of St. Lawrence on the North Atlantic Ocean, a distance of 1,300 km. It serves as a major water route to the interior of the United States and Canada, linking the Great Lakes with the Atlantic Ocean.

● *Colorado River and Columbia River*

On the Pacific side there are two great rivers: the Colorado River and the Columbia River. The Colorado River begins in the Rocky Mountains. It flows southwest for some 2,300 kilometers and empties into the Gulf of California. For 342 of these kilometers the Colorado flows through the magnificent Grand Canyon in Arizona, which is one of the most beautiful places in the United States. The Colorado drains an enormous area. All the farms and cities of the southwestern corner of the country depend on its water. Many Dams have been built in the Colorado River system. Hoover Dam, built in 1936 by the federal government, is the largest of the dams located on the Colorado River.

The Columbia River rises in western Canada and continues in the US for about 1,900 kilometers. It flows into the Pacific Ocean. The volume of the Columbia's flow is second only to that of the Mississippi. among the US rivers.

the Grand Canyon

● *Rio Grande River*

Another important river in the southwest America is the Rio Grande River. It runs about 3,000 kilometers from the southern Rocky Mountains to the Gulf of Mexico and forms part of the United States-Mexico border.

● *Rivers East of the Appalachians*

The rivers east of the Appalachians are usually short. All of them run to the Atlantic Ocean. The Potomac River is famous not only because Washington D.C. is located on its band but also because it is the dividing line between the South and the North. The Hudson River is famous because New York City stands at the river mouth. It is there (at New York City) that the Hudson river meets the Atlantic Ocean. Linked by canals with the five Great Lakes, the Hudson River serves as an important route for inland waterway traffic.

Great Lakes and Niagara Falls

● *Great Lakes*

Along the United States-Canadian border lie the world's largest group of freshwater lakes— the five connected Great Lakes, including (from largest to smallest) Lake Superior, Lake Huron, Lake Michigan, Lake Erie, and Lake Ontario. The lakes are a part of both countries and are shared by both. Only Lake Michigan lies entirely within the United States.

Covering an area of 244,100 square kilometers, the Great Lakes are so large that they could be easily seen from the Moon! All together, the lakes hold about 20 percent of all the fresh water on the Earth's surface. The Great lakes are connected to the Atlantic Ocean by the St. Lawrence River. Four of North America's largest cities are located on the edge of the Great Lakes. They are Chicago, Detroit, Toronto (Canada), and Cleveland. These lakes are joined together by canals and linked to the Mississippi. and its tributaries. They are the economic lifeline of the Midwest.

● *Niagara Falls* (尼亚加拉瀑布)

Niagara Falls is the most spectacular falls in the United States because of its great beauty and immense size. It is part of the Niagara River, which connects Lake Erie and Lake Ontario. East of the river is the United States. West of the river is Canada. About halfway between the two lakes, a sharp drop in the river makes Niagara Falls.

Niagara Falls consists of two giant waterfalls and one smaller one. One big waterfall, called American Falls, is on the US side of the river. The waterfall is 328 meters wide and 55 meters high. The biggest of the two giant waterfalls is in Canada and is known as the Canadian Falls, also called the Horseshoe Falls because of its horseshoe shape. The curved edge of the Canadian Falls measures 670 meters wide and the water drops 57 meters. The Canadian Falls carries nine times more water than the American Falls! A great tourist attraction, Niagara Falls makes an enormous, ground-shaking roar and a huge cloud of water mist. Rainbows shine through the mist. At night, the falls are lit with colored lights, creating a brilliant display!

● *Great Salt Lake*

In northwest Utah lies the Great Salt Lake. Its maximum depth is 8 meters. As a terminal lake, the Great Salt Lake is several times more saline than seawater, making it easy to float in. It contains about 4.4 billion tons of minerals. About three fourths of this total is common table salt. Surrounded by stretches of sand, salt land and marsh, the lake remains isolated, though in recent years it has become important as a source of minerals, as a beach and water-sports attraction, and as a wildlife preserve. Near Great Salt Lake lies the capital and largest city of Utah—Salt Lake City. The marshlands on the lake's eastern and northern shores are the habitat for millions of migratory shorebirds and waterfowl.

Mountains

Beside the Appalachian Mountains and the Rocky Mountains, there are still a few more worth mentioning in this part. Mount McKinley in Alaska is the tallest mountain in the United States. It rises 6,194 meters above sea level. In the Sierra Nevada of eastern California, Mount Whitney, at 4,418 meters, is the highest peak in the United States outside of Alaska. The Sawatch Mountains form part of the Continental Divide, which runs through western Colorado. The divide, the main watershed boundary of the North American continent, weave (迂回通过) through the continent along the tops of the Rocky Mountains. It marks the point at which all rivers to the east flow toward the Atlantic Ocean and all rivers to the west flow toward the Pacific Ocean. The Cascade Range is a major mountain range extending from northern California through Oregon and Washington into British Columbia, Canada.

10 | Understanding the United States

III Natural Resources and Climate

Natural Resources
● *Minerals and Metals*

The United States is a land rich in natural resources. Many minerals are found in North America. Iron, nickel(镍), copper, gold, and many other metals are found in the North of the Great Lakes. Coal is found in eastern United States. Oil is found near the Gulf of Mexico. More metals—including lead, zinc(锌), and silver—are found in the western mountains. The US ranks first in the world in coal and natural gas deposits, and ranks second in the oil deposits.

● *Forests*

Before European settlement, forests covered nearly one billion acres of what is now the United States. Since the mid-1600's, about 300 million acres of forest have been cleared, primarily for agriculture during the 19th century. Today about one-third of the nation is forested. Total forest area has been relatively stable for the last 100 years (currently about 747 million acres). Forests are chiefly found in the eastern and western highlands of the country. Along the Pacific coast there are more thick forests. The heavy rainfall there helps the trees to grow very large. This is the home of giant trees like the redwoods of California. Redwood trees often grow to be 61—91 meters tall. But in the Southwest, there are deserts where only small shrubs and cacti can grow.

Climate

Climates throughout the United States are as varied as its geographical features. It is mostly temperate, but tropical in Hawaii and Florida, arctic in Alaska, semiarid (半干旱的) in the great plains west of the Mississippi River, and arid in the Great Basin of the southwest. Most of the nation experiences all four seasons, with cold and snow winters and warm summers. The southwest and southeast experience fewer variations in climate and rarely receive snow in the winter.

The United States are exposed to various natural hazards: tsunamis (海啸), volcanoes, and earthquake activity around Pacific Basin; hurricanes along the Atlantic and Gulf of Mexico coasts; tornadoes(龙卷风) in the Midwest and southeast; mud slides in California; forest fires in the west; flooding; permafrost in northern Alaska.

IV State Regions

Map of State Regions

Chapter 1 Geography | 11

According to their climate, geography, traditions, and history, the 50 states of the United States are divided into six regions as shown in the following table.

New England	Connecticut, Maine, Massachusetts, New Hampshire, Rhode Island, Vermont
Middle Atlantic	Delaware, Maryland, New Jersey, New York, Pennsylvania
South	Alabama, Arkansas, Florida, Georgia, Kentucky, Louisiana, Mississippi, Missouri, North Carolina, South Carolina, Tennessee, Virginia, West Virginia
Midwest	Illinois, Indiana, Iowa, Kansas, Michigan, Minnesota, Nebraska, North Dakota, Ohio, South Dakota, Wisconsin
Southwest	Arizona, New Mexico, Oklahoma, Texas
West	Alaska, California, Colorado, Hawaii, Idaho, Montana, Nevada, Oregon, Utah, Washington, Wyoming

New England

New England is the smallest of all six regions. Yet it played a dominant role in American development. From the 17th century until well into the 19th, New England was the country's cultural and economic center.

The earliest European settlers of New England were English. They found it difficult to farm the land in large lots, as was common in the South. By 1750, many settlers had turned to other pursuits. The mainstays(支柱) of the region became shipbuilding, fishing, and trade.

New Englanders gained a reputation for hard work, shrewdness, thrift, and ingenuity. These traits came in handy as the Industrial Revolution reached America in the first half of the 19th century and new factories sprang up in this region. Boston had become the financial heart of the nation.

New England also supported a vibrant (充满活力的) cultural life. Education is the region's strongest legacies. There are such top-ranking universities and colleges as Harvard, Yale, Brown, Dartmouth, Smith, Wellesley, Mt. Holyoke, Williams, Amherst, and Wesleyan, unequaled by any other region. In the 20th century, most of New England's traditional industries have relocated (重新部署) to states or foreign countries where goods can be made more cheaply. The gap has been partly filled by the microelectronics and computer industry.

Map of New England

The Middle Atlantic States

If New England provided the brains and dollars for 19th century American expansion, the Middle Atlantic States provided the muscle. The region's largest states, New York and Pennsylvania, became centers of heavy industry (iron, glass, and steel).

The Middle Atlantic region was settled by a wider range of people than New England. Early settlers were mostly farmers and traders, and the region served as a bridge between North and South. Philadelphia was home to the Continental Congress that organized the American Revolution and the birthplace of the

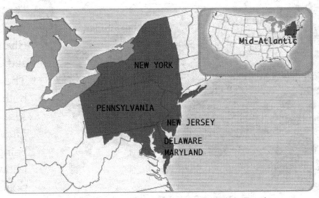

Map of the Middle Region Atlantick Region

12 | Understanding the United States

Declaration of Independence in 1776 and the US Constitution in 1787.

As heavy industry spread throughout the region, rivers such as the Hudson and Delaware were transformed into vital shipping lanes. Cities on waterways—New York on the Hudson, Philadelphia on the Delaware, Baltimore on Chesapeake Bay—grew dramatically. Now New York is the nation's largest city, its financial hub and cultural center. Like New England, the Middle Atlantic region has seen much of its heavy industry relocate elsewhere. Other industries, such as drug manufacturing and communications, have taken up the slack.

The South

The South is perhaps the most distinctive and colorful American region. The American Civil War (1861—1865) devastated the South socially and economically. Nevertheless, it retained its unmistakable identity.

Southern settlers grew wealthy by raising and selling cotton and tobacco on plantations, which required the work of many laborers. To supply this need, plantation owners relied on slaves brought from Africa, and slavery spread throughout the South. As slavery was disapproved

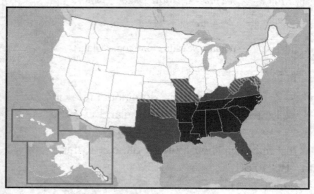
Map of the South

by the Northerners in 1860, 11 southern states left the Union intending to form a separate nation, the Confederate States of America. This rupture (决裂) led to the Civil War, the Confederacy's defeat and the end of slavery.

The scars left by the war took decades to heal. However, a new regional pride expressed itself under the banner of "the New South." Today the South has evolved into a manufacturing region, and high-rise buildings crowd the skylines of such cities as Atlanta and Little Rock, Arkansas. Owing to its mild weather, the South has become very popular with retirees from other US regions and from Canada.

The Midwest

The Midwestern United States (or Midwest or Middle West) is an informal name for a group of north-central states of the United States of America, usually including Illinois, Indiana, Iowa, Kansas, Michigan, Minnesota, Missouri, Ohio, Nebraska, North Dakota, South Dakota and Wisconsin. A 2006 Census Bureau estimate put the population at 66,217,736. Chicago is the largest city in the region, followed by Detroit and Indianapolis. The region's fertile soil made it possible for farmers to produce abundant harvests of cereal crops such as wheat, oats, and corn.

The region was soon known as the nation's "breadbasket."

Most of the Midwest is flat. The Mississippi River has acted as a regional lifeline, moving settlers to new homes and foodstuffs to market. The river inspired two classic American books, both written by a native Missourian, Mark Twain: *Life on the Mississippi* and *The Adventures of Huckleberry Finn*. Midwesterners are praised as being open, friendly, and straightforward. The Midwest gave birth to one of America's two major political parties, the Republican Party, which was formed in the 1850s to oppose the spread of

Map of the Midwest

slavery into new states. Perhaps because of their geographic location, many mid-westerners have been strong adherents of isolationism, the belief that Americans should not concern themselves with foreign wars and problems.

The Southwest

The Southwestern United States is a region of the western United States, and home to over 50 million residents. The United States Geological Survey (USGS) does not define regions, so regional definitions vary from source to source. The Southwest always includes New Mexico and Arizona, but often takes in western Texas. Parts of the Southwest once belonged to Mexico. The United States obtained this land following the Mexican-American War of 1846—1848. Its Mexican heritage continues to exert a strong influence on the region.

Map of the Southwest

The population density of the region is less than three people per square mile. The Southwest is also more ethnically varied than neighboring regions, with significant European American, Mexican American, and American Indian populations. The Southwest contains many large cities and metropolitan areas of the country, despite the low population density of the region as a whole. Phoenix, Los Angeles, Dallas, San Antonio, San Diego and Houston all rank among the top ten most populous cities in the country. Many of the states in this region, such as Nevada, New Mexico and Arizona, have witnessed some of the highest population growth in the United States, with Arizona in particular as a destination for retired Americans in search of a warm climate. Urban areas in this region, like Albuquerque (阿尔伯克基：新墨西哥州中部格兰德河上游的一个城市) and Phoenix, are some of the fastest growing cities in the country. Las Vegas is renowned as one of the world's centers for gambling. Outside the cities, the region is a land of open spaces, much of which is desert. The magnificent Grand Canyon is located in this region, as is Monument Valley, home of the most populous American Indian tribe. Compared with the adjoining Midwest, the Southwest is drier in weather, less densely populated, and has strong Spanish-American and Native-American components.

The West

The Western United States—commonly referred to as the American West or simply The West—traditionally refers to the region comprising the westernmost states of the United States. Because the United States expanded westward after its founding, the meaning of the West has evolved over time. The Mississippi River is often referenced as the easternmost possible boundary of the West. As defined by the Census Bureau, the western United States includes 13 states: Alaska, Arizona, California, Colorado, Hawaii, Idaho, Montana, Nevada, New Mexico, Oregon, Utah, Washington, and Wyoming.

Map of the West

The "West" had played an important part in American history. The Old West is embedded in America's folklore.The West is a region of scenic beauty on a grand scale. All of its states are partly mountainous, and the ranges are the sources of startling contrasts. To the west of the peaks, winds from the Pacific Ocean carry enough moisture to keep the land well-watered. To the east, however, the land is very dry. Parts of western Washington State, for example, receive 20 times the amount of rain that falls on the eastern side of the state's Cascade Range.

In much of the West the population is sparse, and the federal government owns and manages millions of hectares of undeveloped land. Americans use these areas for recreational and

14 | Understanding the United States

commercial activities, such as fishing, camping, hiking, boating, grazing, lumbering, and mining.

Alaska, the northernmost state in the Union, is a vast land of few people and great stretches of wilderness, protected in national parks and wildlife refuges. Hawaii is the only state in the union in which Asian Americans outnumber residents of European stock

V Major Cities

Washington, D.C.

Washington D.C. is the capital of the United States. D.C. stands for District of Columbia, the name of the capital territory. Washington is the name of the city that fills the entire District of Columbia.

● *The White House*

The White House is a grand mansion with 132 rooms at 1600 Pennsylvania Avenue in the middle of Washington, D.C. It is the America's oldest federal building, where the president of the United States works and lives. Philadelphia architect James Hoban designed the Georgian-style gray sandstone building. George Washington, the first US president, helped lay the building's first stone in 1792. John Adams, the second president, was the first president to live in the White House.

● *Capitol Hill*

The United States Capitol is located in Washington, D.C. It has been the seat of the US Senate and House of Representatives since 1800. William Thornton, a man with no formal training in architecture won the competition for design of a new United States Capitol in the early 1790s. George Washington laid the cornerstone for the new Capitol on 18 September 1793, and it was completed over a period of decades under the supervision of many architects. The building is situated on Capitol Hill, overlooking the Potomac River.

● *The Smithsonian Institution*

The Smithsonian Institution is the largest museum complex (综合建筑) in the world. Built in 1846, it was a bequest (遗赠) from British scientist James Smithson. The Smithsonian owns dinosaur bones, historic airplanes, a zoo full of wild animals, famous paintings, and so on. At the Air and Space Museum you can see the first airplane. The Wright brothers flew it in 1903 and the command module (太空船驾驶舱) from Apollo 11, which was the first human mission to land on the Moon.

● *Washington Monument*

Washington, D.C. is well known for its monuments. No building in the District of Columbia is taller than the Washington Monument. It's 169 meters high. That is taller than a 50-story building. The Washington Monument was constructed to honor the memory of George Washington.

- *Thomas Jefferson Memorial*

The Thomas Jefferson Memorial, completed in 1943, honors the man who was principal author of the Declaration of Independence, the nation's third president, and the first US Secretary of State. The memorial's walls are inscribed with some of Jefferson's most famous quotations. Inside the round building of the Jefferson Memorial stands a bronze statue of America's third president, Thomas Jefferson.

- *Lincoln Memorial*

The Lincoln Memorial, a monument dedicated to President Abraham Lincoln (1861—1865), stands in Potomac Park in Washington, D.C. The structure was inspired by classical Greek architecture, and it houses a grand, marble statue of Lincoln. His short Gettysburg Address is inscribed on a marble wall. He delivered this speech in 1863 during the Civil War. The Lincoln Memorial is where 200,000 people in 1963 heard Martin Luther King, Jr., give his famous "I Have a Dream" speech, which expressed the hopes of the civil rights movement in moving words.

- *Roosevelt Memorial*

The Franklin Delano Roosevelt Memorial consists of four outdoor rooms with waterfalls, pools, and gardens. A quotation from Roosevelt is engraved on the wall. Roosevelt was the 32nd president of the United States. He led the nation through the difficult years of the Great Depression (1930s) and World War II (1939—1945).

There is only one statue of Roosevelt in the memorial, sitting in a chair with his faithful dog, Fala. There is a statue of First Lady Eleanor Roosevelt, the first wife of a president to be honored in a national memorial. She is shown before the seal of the United Nations (UN) to which she was the first US delegate in 1948.

New York City

A financial, commercial and cultural center, New York City is the most populous city in the United States and the fourth largest in the world (after Tokyo in Japan, Mexico City in Mexico and São Paulo in Brazil). About 8.1 million people live in New York City, and 18.3 million live in the city and its surrounding urban area.

In 1626, Manhattan Island was purchased from the Indians by Peter Minuit. It cost about 2,400 dollars. At first, it was called New Amsterdam by the Dutch settlers and later was renamed New York by the English. The city grew rapidly from a deserted island into now a great metropolis. The fast expansion of New York is largely due to its location. It is situated on the best American harbor on the Atlantic Ocean. It also lies on the Hudson River, which allows water transportation into the middle of the United States.

The city has five boroughs: Manhattan, Queens, Brooklyn, the Bronx, and Staten Island. As a city of islands, the Bronx is the only borough on the mainland. The other boroughs are on islands. Brooklyn and Queens occupy the western end of Long Island. Water surrounds Staten Island and Manhattan. These two boroughs face each other across New York Harbor.

New York is the world's most ethnically diverse city. About one third of New York's residents, over 2.6 million people, were born in other countries. It is famous for its Chinatown. It also has the largest Jewish population of any city outside Israel. After the blacks were released from slavery, a large number of them moved into cities like New York, Philadelphia, and Washington.

Understanding the United States

New York City is a constellation of famous buildings. The most outstanding ones include the Empire State Building, United Nations headquarters, Rockefeller Center, and the destroyed twin towers of World Trade Center.

● *Empire State Building*

The Empire State Building is a 102-story landmark in New York City and one of the Seven Wonders of the Modern World. Its name is derived from the nickname for the state of New York (the Empire State). It stood as the world's tallest building for more than forty years, from its completion in 1931 until the construction of the World Trade Center's North Tower was completed in 1972. Following the destruction of the World Trade Center in 2001, the Empire State Building once again became the tallest building in New York City and New York State, the third tallest skyscraper in the Americas (after Chicago's Willis Tower and Trump International Hotel and Tower) and the 15th tallest in the world.

The Empire State Building was designated as a National Historic Landmark in 1986. In 2007, it was ranked number one on the List of America's Favorite Architecture according to the AIA.

● *United Nations Headquarters*

The landmark buildings of the United Nations (UN) stand in Manhattan, alongside the East River in New York City. Established in 1945, the UN moved into its New York headquarters in the fall of 1952, and the majority of the world's nations are now members. Each country displays its flag near the entryway.

● *Rockefeller Center*

Rockefeller Center is a vast complex of 19 commercial buildings covering 89,000 m² in the center of Midtown Manhattan. It is entertainment and shopping center, and home to NBC—TV and radio and other media. Built by the Rockefeller family, it was declared a National Historic Landmark in 1987.

● *The Statue of Liberty*

Standing on Staten Island in New York Harbor, the Statue of Liberty was a gift of friendship from the people of France to the people of the United States and is a universal symbol of freedom and democracy. The Statue of Liberty was dedicated on October 28,1886, designated as a National Monument in 1924 and restored for her centennial on July 4,1986.

● *World Trade Center*

The World Trade Center (WTC) was a complex located in the heart of New York City's downtown financial district whose seven buildings were destroyed in 2001 in the September 11 terrorist attacks. The most notable were the main two towers, which were 110 stories tall each, stood over 410 meters high, and occupied about one acre of the total 16 acre of the site's land.

The complex contained 1.24 million m² of office space. When completed in 1972, the North Tower became the tallest building in the world for two years, surpassing the Empire State Building after a 40-year reign. The North Tower stood 417 meters tall and featured telecommunications antenna that was added at the top of the roof in 1978 and stood 110 meters tall.

On the morning of September 11, 2001, hijackers (劫持犯) flew two 767 jets into the complex, one into each tower, in a coordinated suicide attack. After burning for 56 minutes, the South Tower collapsed, followed a half-hour later by the North Tower, with the attacks on the World Trade Center resulting in 2,750 deaths. The process of cleanup and recovery at the World Trade Center site took eight months. The first new building at the site was 7 World Trade Center which opened in May 2006. The site is currently being rebuilt with six new skyscrapers

and a memorial to the casualties of the attacks.
- *Central Park*

Central Park is a large park in the middle of New York City. It offers a zoo, a nature center, playgrounds, paths for running and bicycling, and places for ice skating, roller skating, and playing sports. Horse-drawn carriages are popular with both tourists and New Yorkers.

- *Wall Street*

Wall Street is a street in Lower Manhattan, running through the historical center of the Financial District. It is the first permanent home of the New York Stock Exchange, New York's financial center and the leading financial center for the world; over time Wall Street became the name of the surrounding geographic neighborhood. You can find many banks, stock markets, stockbrokers, and other financial institutions along this famous street and in the Financial District.

Landmark buildings on Wall Street include Federal Hall, 14 Wall Street, 40 Wall Street, and the New York Stock Exchange at the corner of Broad Street. In 1789, Federal Hall and Wall Street was the scene of the United States' first presidential inauguration. George Washington took the oath of office on the balcony of Federal Hall overlooking Wall Street on April 30, 1789. This was also the location of the passing of the *Bill of Rights*.

- *Broadway Theater District*

New York City's Broadway theater district is considered by many to be the epitome (典范,缩影) of world-class stage talent and entertainment and Broadway shows in New York have included famous productions over the years. Broadway is a generic (总称的) term that has grown to include more than just Broadway Street in New York City. It is an entire area on and adjacent to Broadway Street in midtown Manhattan, in and around Times Square, and includes several theaters of varying sizes and popularity. Times Square is a major intersection in Manhattan and a symbol of New York City. It is the site of the annual New Year's Eve ball drop; about 1 million revelers crowd Times Square for the New Year's Eve celebrations. Times Square has achieved the status of an iconic world landmark which is principally defined by its spectacular, animated digital advertisements. The theater district runs from about 40th Street to the mid-fifties. The majority of the theatres are between 7th and 8th Avenue.

- *Greenwich Village*

Greenwich Village is a largely residential neighborhood on the west side of Lower Manhattan. A large majority of the district is home to upper middle class families. Greenwich Village, however, was known in the late 19th—to earlier mid 20th centuries as the bohemian (放荡不羁的文化人) capital and the birthplace of the Beat movement (披头族,20世纪50年代末出现于美国知识阶层中的一颓废流派). Greenwich Village was better known as Washington Square—based on the major landmark Washington Square Parkor in the 19th century.

Currently, artists and local historians bemoan the fact that the bohemian days of Greenwich Village are long gone, because of the extraordinarily high housing costs in the neighborhood. The artists have fled to otherplaces. Nevertheless, residents of Greenwich Village still possess a strong community identity and are proud of their neighborhood's unique history and fame, and its well-known liberal live-and-let-live attitude.

- *Fifth Avenue*

Fifth Avenue is a major thoroughfare in the center of the borough of Manhattan. Fifth Avenue serves as a symbol of wealthy New York and is consistently ranked as one of the most expensive streets in the world. For several years starting in the mid-1990s, the shopping district between 49th and 57th Streets was ranked as having the world's most expensive retail spaces on a cost per square foot basis. The average rent on Fifth Avenue in Manhattan is $10,226 per square meter per year. In 2008, *Forbes* (《福布斯》) magazine ranked Fifth Avenue as being the most expensive street in the world.

Los Angeles

Located along the Pacific Ocean, Los Angeles is the largest city in the state of California and the second largest in the United States. Often abbreviated as L.A. and nicknamed the City of Angels, Los Angeles has an estimated population of 3.8 million and the Los Angeles Metropolitan Area is home to nearly 12.9 million residents. Its inhabitants are known as "Angelenos." In 2008, Los Angeles was named the world's eighth most economically powerful city by *Forbes.com*, ahead of Shanghai and Toronto but behind Chicago and Paris.

● *Location*

Los Angeles sprawls over 1,290.6 km^2 in Southern California between the San Gabriel Mountains and the ocean. People depend on cars to get around this large area. As a result, the city develops powerful roads and freeways, and at the same time suffers from air pollution and traffic jams.

● *History*

Los Angeles was founded in 1781 by Spanish governor. It became a part of Mexico in 1821, following its independence from Spain. In 1848, at the end of the Mexican-American War, Los Angeles and California were purchased as part of the *Treaty of Guadalupe Hidalgo*, thereby becoming part of the United States. It grew rapidly after railroads linked it to the Midwest and Eastern United States. Between 1880 and 1920, the population jumped from 11,000 to 1 million people. In 1970, California became the US state with the largest population and in 1982, it surpassed Chicago to become the second largest US city and it is still growing.

Los Angeles is one of the world's centers of business, international trade, entertainment, culture, media, fashion, science, technology, and education. It is home to renowned institutions covering a broad range of professional and cultural fields, and is one of the most substantial economic engines within the United States. As the home base of Hollywood, it is known as the "Entertainment Capital of the World," leading the world in the creation of motion pictures, television production and recorded music. The importance of the entertainment business to the city has led many celebrities to call Los Angeles and its surrounding suburbs home.

● *People*

Los Angeles is home to a large number of people from China, Japan, Vietnam, and other places around the globe. Nearly half of the city's people are Hispanics. Most of the Hispanics are of Mexican ancestry. More Mexicans live in Los Angeles than in any other city except Mexico City. The city is also renowned for its great population of Chinese immigrants and displays of Chinese tradition and culture. Here you can find the famous Chinese American Museum, where materials and photographs that depict the experiences of Chinese Americans living in Southern California from 1850 to 2000 are collected. Los Angeles also has one of the largest Chinatowns in the United States.

● *Capital of Movies*

Los Angeles is called the capital of movies. Early in the 1900s, the movie industry moved from New York City to Los Angeles. Most of the movie studios were located in a part of Los Angeles called Hollywood. In 1923, a real estate agency put up a huge sign on a hilltop to advertise the area. The letters of the sign, which spell Hollywood, stand 14 meters tall. It is a city landmark.

Beverly Hills is a city in the western part of Los Angeles County. It is home to countless Hollywood celebrities and the wealthy. Beverly Hills and the neighboring city of West Hollywood are entirely surrounded by the city of Los Angeles. The area is called "Golden Triangle" with a population of 34,980 as of the 2006 census. Beverly Hills contains some of the largest homes in Los Angeles County and the nation. These homes range from the extravagant and luxurious in size, to the more elegant and modern homes, and then to the many small duplex (联式房屋) rental units and detached (独立的) homes with less than 280 square meters. The city's average household income is just over $87,000.

Movies are big business in Los Angeles. But there is a lot more going on than moviemaking. The city's seaport is one of the busiest in the United States. Los Angeles is a leading producer of aircraft and military equipment. It is also an important banking center.

Chapter 2 History

United States History is the story of how the republic developed from colonial beginnings in the 16th century when the first European explorers arrived, until modern times. As the nation developed, it expanded westward from small settlements along the Atlantic Coast, eventually including all the territory between the Atlantic and Pacific oceans across the middle of the North American continent, as well as two noncontiguous states and a number of territories. At the same time, the population and the economy of the United States grew and changed dramatically. The population diversified as immigrants arrived from all countries of the world. From its beginnings as a remote English colony, the United States has developed the largest economy in the world. Throughout its history, the United States has faced struggles, both within the country—between various ethnic, religious, political, and economic groups—and with other nations. The efforts to deal with and resolve these struggles have shaped the United States of America into the 21st century

I The First Inhabitants

For a great many years, anthropologists have debated the origins of the first Americans. Today most agree that America's first settlers came from northeast Asia and entered the New World in the general area of Bering Strait(白令海峡,为丹麦航海家 Bering〔1680—1741〕发现), during the last Ice Age. During that period, which began about 70,000 B.C and ended about 10000BC, the weather in the northern half of the earth changed greatly. It grew colder. Much of the land was covered with huge glaciers. Sea water froze, and the water level in the sea dropped. There is a narrow strait between the Bering Sea (白令海,太平洋之最北部分)and Chukchi Sea (楚克其海,在西伯利亚东北端与阿拉斯加之间). During the Ice Age this strait probably became very shallow. In some places it dried up completely and formed a land bridge from Asia to North America. At its widest points, the land bridge, known today as Beringia (an area covering easternmost Siberia and western Alaska), was about 1600 kilometers across. The earliest Americans must have crossed the bridge from Siberia into Alaska as bands of hunters followed big animals such as giant buffalos and mammoths(猛犸象,已绝种).

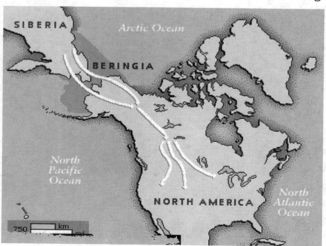

The scientists think that the people of Asia found this land bridge between 15,000 and 40,000 years ago. Group after group moved across the bridge to the unexplored continent of North America. They passed through what is now Alaska and western Canada. This crossing took place over hundreds of years. Because the people migrated in separate waves over such a long period of time, they were very different from one another in physical characteristics, skills, and talents. By the time the first Europeans came to shores of America, the early immigrants had spread throughout the Western hemisphere and developed cultures in keeping with the different terrains (地形) and climates in which they had settled.

Although the first explorers came to America by accident, they opened up two continents—North and South America—to European settlement. On the one hand, the settlers largely destroyed Native American cultures, but on the other hand, they laid the foundations for many new nations, including the United States.

II Colonial Period

History of Colonial America was formed by European nations. After Christopher Columbus explored the Americas in 1492, the nations of Western Europe—Spain, Portugal, France, the Netherlands, and England—created vast colonial empires in the western hemisphere. European countries developed colonies for many reasons, but primarily to generate income. They used colonies to provide raw materials for trade and to serve as markets for finished products. English colonies eventually became dominant in North America because many settlers were drawn to their political systems. These systems encouraged representative government, religious toleration, economic growth, and cultural diversity.

European Colonial Ventures

The discovery of the Americas was made accidentally as a result of Europeans' desire to establish new trade routes with the Far East. During the 1500's and 1600's several European nations sponsored explorations in the New World and made claims based on those explorations. The Portuguese took the lead in explorations by rounding the tip of Africa and opening an eastern sea route to India. Beginning in 1519, Spain, Portugal, France, the Netherlands, and England established colonies in the Americas. The colonial holdings of each European country developed in a different way. Spain made a great mining and agricultural empire in Mexico, South America, and the Caribbean. Great wealth sent to Spain in the form of gold and silver were envied by others. Portugal created a slave-based agricultural colony in Brazil. The French, who had the largest empire in North America, made profitable business of fishing and fur trading. The Dutch and the Swedes established successful colonies in the northeastern part of North America. Among the European invaders of North America, only the English established colonies of agricultural settlers, whose interests in Native Americans was less about trade than about the acquisition of land. That fact would have huge implications in the long struggle for control of North America.

The First European Settlements in North America

Country	Name of Settlement	Present-Day Location	Year First Settled
Spain	St. Augustine	Florida	1565
France	Quebec	Canada	1603
England	Jamestown	Virginia	1607
Holland	New Amsterdam	New York	1624
Sweden	New Sweden	New Jersey	1638

Early English Settlement

During the 16th century, some English adventurers were exploring the east coast of North America. In 1588, the English navy destroyed the Spanish Armada and controlled some of the sea routes leading to America. This marked a turning point in the course of American history, for the English immigrants started to become the most important colonists in North America. This led to the establishment of the 13 English-American colonies.

● *The Lost Colony of 1587*

In 1585, the Queen of England had given Sir Walter Raliegh permission to start a colony in the New World. He sent 100 colonists with food and supplies to Roanoke Island off the coast of present-day North Carolina. As governor, White hoped to establish the first permanent English settlement in the New World by developing a self-sufficient economy and agriculture. However, within three years, the group disappeared without any signs. All that was found was a deserted settlement and the letters "CRO" carved on a tree and the word "CROATOAN" carved on one of the palisade's entrance posts. The Croatoans were a group of nearby Indians. No one knows what happened to them and Roanoke came to be known as *the Lost Colony*. Although the first English attempts at colonization were unsuccessful and the fate of these settlers remains unknown, their dreams, courage and ideals are symbols of the birthplace of America.

Development of 13 English Colonies

The first colonies in North America were along the eastern coast. Settlers from Spain, France, Sweden, Holland, and England claimed land beginning in the 17th century. But it was the English who eventually dominated the continent. By 1733, there were 13 colonies along the eastern seaboard under English control. They were Massachusetts, New Hampshire, Connecticut, Rhode Island, New York, New Jersey, Pennsylvania, Maryland, Delaware, Virginia, North Carolina, South Carolina, and Georgia. These colonies had been founded in a variety of ways and for a variety of reasons. Regional differences had developed in their cultures and economies. All, however, had their English heritage in common.

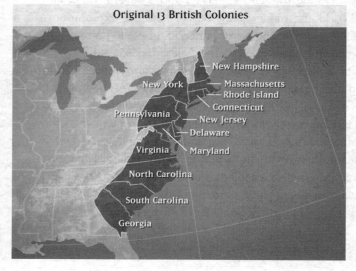

Original 13 British Colonies

The historians lump the colonies into three groups based on where they were, why they were founded, and what kinds of industry they had: New England colonies, mid-Atlantic colonies, and Southern colonies. By the 18th century regional differences among the New England colonies, the middle colonies, and southern colonies, had already developed. The colonial economy was mainly agricultural with some industry and commerce.

New England Colonies	Middle Colonies	Southern Colonies
Rhode Island	Delaware	Maryland
Connecticut	Pennsylvania	Virginia
Massachusetts	New York	North Carolina
New Hampshire	New Jersey	South Carolina
		Georgia

● *The New England Colonies*

Massachusetts （马萨诸塞 1620)was settled by the Pilgrims and later by the Puritans
◆ Great Migration over 20,000 came in a 10 year period between 1630—1640
◆ Believed in Christian Education
New Hampshire (新罕布什尔,1623)was founded by John Mason
Rhode Island （罗得岛,1636)was founded by Roger Williams; offered complete religious freedom
Connecticut（康涅狄格,1636) was founded by Thomas Hooker. Religious dissension in Massachusetts led to the founding of settlements in Rhode Island and Connecticut.

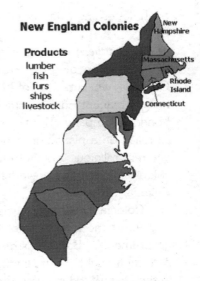

A group of people called Puritans came to America to seek freedom of religion and founded the New England colonies of Massachusetts, New Hampshire, Rhode Island, and Connecticut. By and large, the people who settled in the New England Colonies wanted to keep their family unit together and practice their own religion. They were used to doing many things themselves and not depending on other people for much. Some of these people came to New England to make money, but they were not the majority. The people living in the colonies made a living by fishing and building ships. They also carried on much of the slave trade.

● *The Mid-Atlantic Colonies*

The Mid-Atlantic Colonies, composed of Pennsylvania (1682), Delaware (1638), New York(1624), and New Jersey (1623), were a mix of both northern and southern features, creating a unique environment of early settlement by non-English Europeans, mostly Dutch and German. A combination of both urban and rural lifestyles made it more cosmopolitan, religiously pluralistic, and socially tolerant within a commercial atmosphere. From early colonial times, the Mid-Atlantic region was settled by a wider range of European people than in New England or the South. The people who founded the Middle Colonies were looking to practice their own religion (Pennsylvania mainly) or to make money. Many of these people didn't bring their families with them from England and were the perfect workers for the hard work required in ironworks and shipyards.

The Mid-Atlantic had rich farmland and a moderate climate which made farming much easier than it was in New England. Due to the ease of farming these colonies were able to provide food for their own people and to send to the other colonies; the Middle colonies became known as the breadbasket colonies. Market towns were extremely important in the colonies because people needed to go to town to trade the products they grew or made. Cities grew along major shipping routes and waterways.

Such flourishing cities included New York City on the Hudson River, Philadelphia on the Delaware River.

● ***The Southern Colonies***

The hope of gold, resources, and virgin lands drew English colonists to the Southern Colonies, which consist of Maryland, Virginia, North Carolina, South Carolina, and Georgia. The first permanent English settlement in the New World was Jamestown, Virginia, founded by the London Company. The five southern English colonies displayed many similar characteristics. They all relied on a plantation economy and a staple crop, provided some religious toleration, allowing different religious groups to flourish. Slavery was also permitted and accepted in all the southern colonies. A rich and powerful aristocracy was dominant in the southern colonies.

Colonial Government

Colonial government was modeled on English government.

All of the English colonies, no matter how they were founded or by whom, had similar governments. Both the structure and philosophy of American government evolved out of English political thought and tradition. The concept of representative government, for example, developed in the New World in much the same way as it developed in England.

In the colonies, representative government was put into practice with the colonial assemblies (议会). In both England and America, government was representative only to the extent that people had the right to vote. In both cases, only free adult white males had the privilege. Sometimes there were religious requirements, as with the Puritans of Massachusetts. Almost always there were property requirements.

The organization of government was also modeled after the familiar English system. By the 1760's, there were three types of colonies in America—charter colonies (自治殖民地, self-governing), proprietary colonies (业主殖民地), and royal colonies (王室殖民地). In all three types, government had basically the same structure as government in England. Each colony had an executive branch, a legislative branch, and a judicial branch. The governor was the chief executive in the colonies, as the king was in England.

Education in Colonial Period

Education was most emphasized in New England. Puritans believed all people should know how to read so they could study the Bible and save themselves. They passed laws to establish necessary schools for their children. The first college, Harvard, was set up in Massachusetts in 1636. By the mid-eighteenth century several well-known colleges were founded, including Yale in Connecticut, Columbia in New York and Princeton in New Jersey. Colonial schools laid the foundation of the American educational system in which all the American schools were left to the care of communities or the local authority.

End of the Colonial Period

The colonies began in the early 1600s. As decades passed, people from other countries brought new ideas and different religions to the colonies. By the time America declared its independence from Britain in 1776, the differences had become one of the most notable characteristics of the new people. They were no longer British colonists, but American citizens.

III The Struggle for Independence

French and Indian War

In the 17th and 18th centuries, England and France emerged as the world's most powerful nations. Between the 1680's and 1750's, colonial rivalry led to struggle for empire between Great Britain and France. The two fought four major wars in various parts of the globe. The last of these wars was known in Europe as the Seven Years' War (1756—1763) and in North America as the French and Indian War (1754—1760), which was regarded by some historians as the first truly world war and resulted in British domination of that continent.

Victory had brought Great Britain vast new territories but also a number of new problems. One of these was the disposal of western lands. The British government faced the problem of Indian resistance to westward expansion. In the spring of 1763, Pontiac, an Ottawa chief, led a rebellion against the British. Pontiac's rebellion forced the British government to act. The attempted solution was the *Proclamation of 1763*, which established the crest (顶部) of the Appalachians as a boundary line between white and Indian lands. Although this was a temporary measure, the colonists resented both the line and the presence of British troops sent to enforce the new law.

The British government's attempts to raise revenue through direct taxation to pay for the huge debt left by the war aroused even greater resentment in the colonies. Colonial protests and British determination to force the colonies to submit to parliamentary authority led to open warfare that eventually split the two apart.

The Declaration of Independence

On June 7, Richard Henry Lee of Virginia introduced a resolution in the Second Continental Congress declaring "That these United Colonies are, and of right ought to be, free and independent states..." Immediately, a committee of five was appointed to prepare a formal declaration of Independence. This committee included Benjamin Franklin of Pennsylvania, John Adams of Massachusetts, Robert Livingston of New York, Roger Sherman of Connecticut and Thomas Jefferson of Virginia, Jefferson was chosen to do the writing.

On July 4,1776, the Second Continental Congress adopted the Declaration of Independence, in which the 13 Colonies officially broke away from Britain and formally declared their independence as the United States of America. The pronouncement of independence on the part of the new United States had far-reaching effects. It transformed the rebellion into a revolution and committed the mass of patriots to separation. The Declaration also led to increased foreign aid for the revolution and prepared the way for French intervention on the American side. In order to achieve and maintain independence, however, the new nation had to face full-scale war with Britain.

Four Phases of the War

In total, the war lasted for eight years and had four phases, each with a distinct strategy and character. Despite early American losses, the tides of battle changed when the French entered the war on the side of the United States. Backed by the French, the Americans achieved ultimate victory over the British at Yorktown in 1781. By the terms of the Treaty of Paris, England recognized American independence and surrendered to the United States its territories east of the Mississippi River between the Great Lakes and Florida.

Phase One: The Opening Campaigns   (April 1775—July1776)
Phase Two: The British Northern Offensive   (July 1776—Oct. 1777)
Phase Three: The War in the South   (early 1778—Oct. 1781)
Phase Four: Peace Negotiations   (Oct.1781—Sept.1783)

During the first phase, from April 1775 to July 1776, the Patriots' goal was to turn the revolt into an organized rebellion, while British governors and armed Loyalists tried to suppress the uprising. The second phase of the war began with a major British invasion of New York in July 1776 and ended with the American victory at Saratoga in October 1777. During the third phase of the war Britain tried to subdue the South. Beginning in early 1778 it used regular troops to take territory and local Loyalists to hold it. Patriots used guerrilla warfare to weaken British forces, and then used French assistance to achieved ultimate victory over the British at Yorktown, Virginia in October, 1781. The final phase of the war came when astute Patriot diplomacy won a treaty recognizing the independence of the United States in September 1783. By the terms of the Treaty of Paris, England recognized American independence and surrendered to the United States its territories east of the Mississippi River between the Great Lakes and Florida.

Surrender of General John Burgoyne at Old Saratoga (now Schuylerville), NY, October 17, 1777

Washington in his headquarters at Yorktown, receiving a letter through Cornwallis's emissary on October 17, 1781. The formal British surrender ceremony occurred on October 19, 1781.

IV The Westward Movement

American development involved moving toward the west. The Westward Movement referred to the movement of people from the settled regions of the United States to lands farther west. It began soon after the first English colonists reached North America in the early 1600's. In a little over 200 years, American settlers moved west across what was called the frontier. By 1848 the United States stretched unchallenged from sea to sea, a distance of nearly 5,000 kilometers. This westward movement was one of the most influential forces to shape North American history and had an important impact on American institutions and American characters.

Louisiana Purchase of 1803

People from France settled in the Louisiana Territory in the early 1700s. In a secret treaty in 1762, France gave part of the land to Spain. In 1800, France and Spain signed another secret treaty. Spain agreed to give the Louisiana Territory back to France. By this time, the United States had won its independence from Great Britain. The Mississippi River formed the western boundary of the United States. Only Florida in the east belonged to Spain. The United States, led by President Thomas Jefferson, nervously watched the dealings of Spain and France. America's main concern was the port city of New Orleans which stood at the mouth of the Mississippi on the Gulf of Mexico. Whoever controlled New Orleans controlled trade on the river.

President Thomas Jefferson determined to gain control of New Orleans. In 1803, he sent

James Monroe to France to negotiate the purchase of the port city. At that time, France faced a series of troubles, including the threat of war with Great Britain. The French leader, Napoleon Bonaparte, worried that Britain might seize Louisiana if war broke out, so he decided to sell it to the Americans. In April 1803, the French made an astonishing offer to the American officials in Paris. France would sell to the United States not just New Orleans but all of the Louisiana Territory which was about 2,100,000 square kilometers of land, stretching

west of the Mississippi River all the way to the Rocky Mountains. France's price for the Louisiana Territory was $15 million dollars. In December 1803, the United States took control of Louisiana and raised the American flag in New Orleans.

The Louisiana Purchase was the most important accomplishment of Jefferson's presidency and was the biggest land deal in American history. It doubled the size of the United States and opened the door for America's westward expansion. Later, all or parts of 15 states were carved from this vast region.

Indian Removal—The Trail of Tears

In 1830 with the encouragement of President Andrew Jackson, Congress passed a law called the Indian Removal Act, which required that the Indians living east of the Mississippi River should move to Indian Territory west of the Mississippi. This territory later became part of the state of Oklahoma.

Most Indian tribes did not want to leave their land. It was their spiritual and physical home. But the

The Forced March

government sent in the army to force tribes to move. The plight of the Cherokees (切罗基人) of Georgia is a case in point. Under several treaties with the United States, the Cherokees had been recognized as a nation. They had developed a written language, adopted a constitution, and elected a legislature. In 1828, however, gold was discovered in Cherokee territory. The Georgia legislature ordered the seizure of their lands. The Cherokee resisted through legal action and took their case to the US Supreme Court. And they won! But President Jackson ignored the Supreme Court ruling. He directed the U.S Army to capture all the Cherokee they could find and force them to move. The US Army followed the president's direction. The Supreme Court did nothing.

This was an incredibly sad time in American history. During the winter of 1838—39, the Cherokees, along with some other Indian groups of the region, were forced to leave their homelands in Tennessee, Alabama, North Carolina, and Georgia and marched more than 1,600 kilometers to their new home in the Indian Territory that is today known as Oklahoma. The impact was devastating—an estimated 4,000 of the 15,000 Cherokees died during this forced migration. This tragic chapter in American and Cherokee history became known as the "Trail of Tears." This process of uprooting had been going on for a long time. By 1840, most Indians had been forced from their lands east of the Mississippi River.

The Forced March

Moving West—Addition of Territory

Between 1845 and 1848 the United States rapidly pushed the national border to the Pacific Ocean, increasing its territory by more than 3.1 million square kilometers, more land than was added by the Louisiana Purchase. It acquired these lands in three great chunks, through annexation (合并), diplomacy, and a war. This acquisition of land was probably the most important step taken by the U.S. government in encouraging westward expansion.

Many Americans believed it was the destiny of the United States to control all the land from the Atlantic to the Pacific. In 1845 the United States annexed Texas, which had been an independent republic since winning its independence from Mexico in1836. In 1846 Britain handed over the Oregon Territory in a treaty. Also in that year, the United States went to war with Mexico. The war aims of the United States were to gain the Mexican provinces of New Mexico and California and to keep the war as short as possible.

■ Guadalupe Hidalgo
■ Gadsden Purchase

After almost two years of fighting, the Mexican Government agreed to sign the *American-Mexican Treaty of Guadalupe-Hidalgo* on February 2,1848. Out of this important treaty came the newly created territory, which later became the states of California, Nevada, and Utah, and parts of Colorado, Arizona, New Mexico, and Wyoming. Mexico also relinquished its claims to Texas. With the addition of California and New Mexico, the United States stretched from ocean to ocean.

On December 30, 1853 James Gadsden, U.S. Minister to Mexico, and Santa Anna (1794—1876), president of Mexico, signed the *Gadsden Purchase* in Mexico City. The treaty settled the dispute over the exact location of the Mexican border west of El Paso, Texas, giving the U.S. claim to approximately 76,800 km² of land, which is almost as large as Pennsylvania, in what is now southern Arizona and southwestern New Mexico, for the price of $10 million, about thirty-three cents an acre. With the acquisition of this territory, the United States had reached its present continental boundaries. The nation had fulfilled its manifest destiny.

The Gold Rush of 1849

Victory in war with Mexico, along with purchases and treaty agreements, expanded the United States from the Atlantic Ocean to the Pacific Ocean. Once the United States gained control over large areas of the West, Americans began moving into these lands in ever increasing numbers.

One event which drew people to the West was the discovery of gold in California. This discovery was made in January 1848 by James Marshall, a worker at John Sutter's sawmill in California's Sacramento Valley. News of Marshall's find quickly spread throughout the nation.

Gold fever brought a huge wave of people into the West. In 1849 over 80,000 people, known as "Forty-Niners", traveled west to the California gold fields. New Western settlements sprang up almost overnight. Although many of the newcomers returned home after the uproar died down, enough stayed to establish California as a state just two years after the gold rush began. More than $1 billion in gold was mined in California. This money helped build railroads and factories, establishing America as a nation of industry.

The Transcontinental Railroads

With explosive growth in population on the Pacific Coast, there was a need to connect these distant communities with the eastern states. The answer seemed to be a railroad linking the two parts of the continent.

In 1862 Congress agreed to loan hundreds of millions of dollars to two corporations to construct the railroad. These companies were also given millions of acres of Western land to sell in order to pay back the loan. With the help of thousands of Irish immigrant laborers, the Union Pacific Railroad was built westward from Omaha, Nebraska. At the same time, the Central Pacific was built eastward from northern California, edging(逐渐推进) over the Sierra Nevada through the efforts of Chinese workers imported for the job. In 1869 the two railroads joined at Promontory Summit, Utah.

Over the next 20 years, other transcontinental railroads were built. By the 1890s a web of steel rails covered much of the West. The growth of railroads encouraged westward expansion more than any other single development.

The Significance of the Westward Movement

The westward movement is of great significance in the American history. It added more than three million square miles to the nation's territory. For many Americans, the West represented freedom, hope, and a fresh start. It has produced great wealth and has supplied enormous resources to others in the nation and the world. The westward movement helped turn the United States into a large, powerful and wealthy nation. Many of the trends set in motion by westward expansion continue.

V The American Civil War

Brief Introduction

The American Civil War (1861—1865), also known as the War Between the States, was a civil war in the United States of America. Eleven Southern slave states declared their secession(脱离) from the U.S. and formed the Confederate States of America (the Confederacy, 美国南部邦联). Led by Jefferson Davis, they fought against the U.S. federal government (the Union), which was supported by all the free states and the five border states (Delaware, Kentucky, Maryland, Missouri, and West Virginia) in the north. The Union won a decisive victory. The American Civil War was the deadliest war in American history, producing more than 970,000 casualties (人员伤亡),3% of the population, including 620,000 soldier deaths. The war ended slavery in the United States, restored the Union, and strengthened the role of the federal government. The social, political, economic and racial issues of the war brought changes that helped make the country a united superpower.

Causes of the Civil War

● *Economic factors*

In the days of the American Revolution and of the adoption of the Constitution, differences between the North and the South were small under their common interest in establishing a new nation. But in the 19th century the south and north developed in different directions. Before the Civil War began in 1861, the South remained almost completely agricultural and was dominated by a settled plantation system based on slavery. There was very little urbanization or industrialization. Slave owners controlled politics and economics.

On the other hand, The North was by then firmly established as an industrial society and had a rapidly growing economy based on family farms, industry, mining, commerce and transportation, with a large and rapidly growing urban areas and population and no slavery outside the Border States.

The South manufactured little. Almost all manufactured goods had to be imported. Southerners therefore opposed high tariffs. The manufacturing economy of the North, on the other hand, demanded high tariffs to protect its own products from cheap foreign competition.

● *Political factors*

Different economic needs sharpened sectional differences, adding to the interregional hostility. As Northern and Southern patterns of living differed, their political ideas also developed marked differences. The North needed a central government to build an infrastructure of roads and railways, protect its complex trading and financial interests, and control the national currency. The South depended much less on the federal government than did other regions, and Southerners therefore felt no need to strengthen it. In addition, Southern patriots feared that a strong central government might interfere with slavery.

● *The issue of slavery*

The chief and immediate cause of the war was slavery. After the Mexican War, the dominant political issue was the spread of slavery into the western territories. The South wanted to expand slavery into the new territories. But the North opposed to this because slavery was regarded as violation of human rights as a free person. The government balanced the disagreement with the passage of Compromise of 1850 and the Kansas-Nebraska Act in 1854. The Compromise of 1850 provided a temporary respite (缓解) from sectional strife, but the passage of Kansas-Nebraska Act had an extremely divisive effect on the nation and spurred the creation of the Republican Party, formed largely to keep slavery out of the western territories. Soon the Republican Party emerged as the dominant force throughout the North.

● *Secession*

The election of Lincoln as a Republican President in 1860 resulted in the secession of seven southern states in February 1861. As an outspoken opponent of the expansion of slavery in the United States, Abraham Lincoln had long regarded slavery as an evil; therefore, the election of Lincoln as president was viewed by the South as a threat to slavery which was such an important part of Southern society and without which the South felt that they could not survive. During the campaign many Southerners had threatened that their states would secede from the Union if Lincoln was elected.

South Carolina led the way in secession in December, 1860. This was even before Lincoln took office in March 1861. Within six weeks South Carolina was followed by six other cotton-growing states: Mississippi, Florida, Georgia, Alabama, Louisiana, and Texas. The seven seceding states met in Montgomery, Alabama and formed the Confederate States of America in February 9,1861. They chose Jefferson Davis as president and picked Richmond, Virginia, as their capital. The constitution of the Confederate States was similar to that of the United States, except the power of the central government was much more limited. Slavery was explicitly protected.

Chapter 2 History | 31

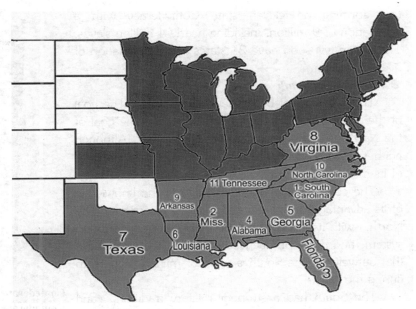

Map of the Confederacy, showing the order in which the states of the Confederacy left the Union. Areas in white were not states during the Secession Crisis.

- *Lincoln's Position*

Lincoln took the oath of office on March 4, 1861. In his inaugural address Lincoln eloquently called for the preservation of the Union. To the south he was both conciliatory and firm. He promised that he would not interfere with slavery where it already existed. But he also said that the Union was perpetual and that secession was illegal. Lincoln hoped that the seceded states would return to the Union with time, and without force.

- *Fort Sumter*

After Lincoln's inauguration, attention was drawn to the federal forts in the South, especially Fort Sumter in Charleston harbor. Fort Sumter was lightly garrisoned (守卫) and had provisions for only six weeks. As supplies dwindled, Lincoln informed the Confederate authorities that he was sending a ship with supplies to the fort. He promised he would not send troops without notice.

The Confederates had thousands of troops encamped around Charleston and cannons placed so that they could bomb Fort Sumter. When Lincoln's message arrived, Jefferson Davis ordered Confederate General Pierre G. T. Beauregard to demand the fort's surrender. When the commander of the fort, refused, Confederate shore cannons began firing at the fort on April 12. The American Civil War had begun. In the spring of 1861, each side expected a brief war and an early victory. Few people foresaw that four years of bloody struggle lay ahead. The Union would survive, and slavery issue would be settled, but at great cost.

Civil War

The attack on Fort Sumter outraged people in the North. President Lincoln issues a Proclamation calling for 75,000 militiamen, and summoning a special session of Congress for July 4. On April 19, 1861, he ordered a blockade against Southern ports

The South, regarding this as declaration of war, also called for volunteers to fight. At this point, four more slave states—Virginia, Arkansas, Tennessee, and North Carolina— seceded from the Union,

Union general holding US flag

Confederate general holding Confederate battle flag

thus forming an eleven state Confederacy with a population of 9 million, including nearly 4 million slaves. The Union will soon have 21 states and a population of over 20 million.

● *North versus South*

The war aims of both sides were simple. The goal of the South was to defend independence. The goal of the North was to restore the Union by force. Although neither side was prepared for war, each was confident of its military superiority.

The confidence of the North lied in the knowledge of its advantages in human and material resources. The North, with its larger population, better transportation system, and more productive economy, had advantages that outweighed the South's superior military leadership during the war.

The South had a stronger military tradition, and many of the nation's outstanding military leaders were southerners. In addition, the South had the popular support of the southern people in their quest for independence. More importantly, they had the advantage of being able to fight a defensive war on familiar home ground, and, therefore, their lines of communication and supply would be shorter. Anther advantage of the South was that it had the sympathy of many Europeans.

Comparison of Union and CSA		
	Union	**CSA**
Total population	22,100,000 (71%)	9,100,000 (29%)
Free population	21,700,000	5,600,000
Soldiers	2,100,000 (67%)	1,064,000 (33%)
Railroad miles	21,788 (71%)	8,838 (29%)
Manufactured items	90%	10%
Firearm production	97%	3%
Bales(大包)of cotton in 1860	Negligible(微不足道的)	4,500,000
Bales of cotton in 1864	Negligible	300,000
Pre-war U.S. exports	30%	70%

The table shows the relative advantage of the Union over the Confederate States of America (CSA) at the start of the war. The advantages widened rapidly during the war, as the Northern economy grew, and Confederate territory shrank and its economy weakened. The Union population was 22 million and the South 9 million in 1861; the Southern population included more than 3.5 million slaves and about 5.5 million whites, thus leaving the South's white population outnumbered by a ratio of more than four to one compared with that of the North.

● *The War*

The South's strategy was to fight a defensive war, whereas the North, on the other hand, had to invade Confederate territory and subdue the South completely.

At the outset of the Civil War, neither side possessed the material nor manpower required for what would prove to be the first modern industrialized war. The North at least had a navy and the Union's naval superiority was a significant factor contributing to the defeat of confederate forces. In the early stage of the war, the Union forces were successful in the west, but the Confederate forces held out against Union attacks in the East. Confederate General Robert E. Lee's first invasion of the North was repulsed (击退) at the strategic battle of Antietam in September 1862.

The Union victory at Anteitam gave Lincoln an opportunity to make the announcement of freeing the slaves. He issued the Emancipation Proclamation on January 1,1863.The proclamation declared that "all persons held as slaves" within the rebellious states "are, and henceforward shall be free." The Emancipation Proclamation had a great long-range effect. It reflected a shift in the war objectives of the North—reuniting the nation was no longer the only goal, and represented a major step toward the ultimate abolition of slavery in the United States and a "new birth of freedom". It gave a high moral purpose to the struggle and strengthened the Union both militarily and politically. As a milestone along the road to slavery's final destruction, the Emancipation Proclamation has assumed a place among the great documents of human freedom.

The Union victory at Gettysburg in July of 1863 ended the South's last chance for military victory. The Battle of Gettysburg was one of the most critical battles of the Civil War. The cost of the battle was high—the North had 23,000 casualties and the South, 28,000. No more men fought and died in any other battle before or since on the land of North America. The battle ended Confederate hopes of formal recognition by foreign governments. The tide of war began to turn against the South. On November 19, 1863, President Lincoln dedicated a portion of the Gettysburg battlefield as a national cemetery, and delivered "Gettysburg Address" to the throng of fifteen thousand for two minutes. The short speech has come to be regarded as the best remembered speech of the Civil War and one of the best speeches in American history.

In March 1864 Lincoln made Ulysses S. Grant commander of all the Union armies. The President had finally found a military genius to match Lee. Under Ulysses S. Grant, the Union armies used tactics of attrition (消耗) and total war to deplete Confederate forces. Lee's army surrender to Grant at Appomattox, Virginia on April 9, 1865 and within a few weeks, the remaining southern armies also capitulated (投降). Jefferson Davis was captured on May 10. The last important Confederate force, under General Edmond Kirby-Smith, laid down its arms at New Orleans on May 26. The war was over.

The Civil War resulted in the defeat of the South and the emancipation of the slaves. The war left the South physically and economically devastated.

General Ulysses S.Grant

Confederate Gen. Robert E. Lee surrendering to Union Gen. Ulysses S. Grant at Appomattox Court House, Virginia, April 9, 1865

VI America in the First World War

In 1914 the United States found itself in the midst of a European crisis. World War I broke out in Europe with the Allied Powers of Great Britain, France, and Russia facing the central powers of Germany and Austria-Hungary. Over the next few years the war involved 28 countries including the United States. Although the principal campaigns were fought in Europe, armies also fought in the Middle East, Africa, and China, and navies clashed on all the oceans. The direct cause of the World War I was the assassination of Archduke Francis Ferdinand, heir to the throne of Austria-Hungary, on June 28,1914.

When the war broke out, most Americans wanted no part of a European war and the US government adopted neutral policy. American neutral policy was aimed at making a profit, for it enabled America to continue its trade with the warring countries.

Many factors contributed to America's final entry into the War. Soon after the War broke out, Britain and Germany tried to blockade each other. In May 1915, a German submarine sank the British luxury liner Lusitania liner and killed 128 American passengers. Then German submarines sank five American merchant ships bound for or leaving Allied seaports. The Germany foreign minister promised to help Mexico to recover the territory it lost during the war with America in 1848. In addition, American business men feared that German winning of the war would make them suffer a big loss because they sold their products to Britain and France and provided large loans to the English government to finance the War. All these factors made America to support Britain and helped to draw the United States into the First World War. In April 1917, the Congress of the United States declared war against the Central Powers.

American troops did not reach Europe in large numbers until 1918, when about 2 million American soldiers were sent to fight in Europe. They soon turned the tide of battle. In July, Americans joined a huge Allied attack. By late summer, the Central Powers were in retreat. On November 11,1918, the War was over.

The war had caused terrible destruction and death. More than 125,000 American lives were lost during the brief period the United States was engaged militarily in the war. This loss was small, however, when compared to the 900,000 British, 1,385,000 French, and 1,700,000 Russian lives lost in battle. In all, nearly 9 million soldiers and more than 13 million civilians died within a span of 4 years.

At a peace conference in Paris, 27 countries took part in drawing up the Treaty of Versailles, which imposed harsh measures against Germany and included an agreement to form a League of Nations. The U.S. Senate never ratified this treaty and the U.S. did not join the League, despite President Woodrow Wilson's active campaigning in support of the League. The United States negotiated a separate peace with Germany, finalized in August 1921.

In the aftermath of the war, the political, cultural, and social order of the world was drastically changed in many places. The map of Europe was redrawn. New countries were formed, old ones were abolished. The Austro-Hungarian and Ottoman empires were broken up. Germany lost some of its territory. It was forced to pay huge amounts of money for war damage. France and Britain took over Germany's colonies.

Yanks (美国兵) & Tommies(英国兵) waving American, British & French flags during Armistice celebration, at end of WWI. Date taken: November 1918

VII Great Depression and New Deal

The Great Depression

Although Americans enjoyed prosperity during the 1920's, the nation's economy was slowing down as a result of overproduction, reduced purchasing power, and government policies on taxes and tariffs (政府向进出口商品所征收的关税). The weakened economy could not sustain the stock market boom, and the market crashed in the fall of 1929.

The stock market crash was the beginning of the Great Depression, the worst and longest economic decline in the history of the United States, lasting from the end of 1929 until the early 1940s. Unemployment, low wages, and the collapse of farm prices resulted hard times for millions of Americans. Countless factories got bankrupt and closed down. Many farmers lost their farms because they had no money. A large number of unemployed workers wandered all over the country looking for jobs. People stopped spending money. Demand for durable goods and luxuries declined, and production faltered. By 1932 the gross national product had been cut by almost one-third. By 1933 over 5,000 banks had failed, and more than 85,000 businesses had gone under (破产), more than 15 million Americans—one-quarter of the nation's workforce—were unemployed. The whole country was in the economic collapse.

President Roosevelt and His "New Deal"

President Hoover, following his personal and political beliefs concerning the role of government, took limited steps to improve the nation's economy. In 1932 the American people elected a new President, Democrat Franklin D. Roosevelt, who promised action to help victims of the Great Depression. President Roosevelt set to work immediately after taking office. Declaring in his inaugural speech that "the only thing we have to fear is fear itself," Roosevelt quickly lifted the nation's spirits. He attacked the Great Depression and presented an unprecedented number of new government programs called the New Deal, which aimed to restore the nation's economy, reduce unemployment, assist businesses and agriculture, regulate banking and the stock market, and provide security for the needy, elderly, and disabled. Under the New Deal, the federal government became involved in direct public relief for the first time.

The New Deal had a strong influence on American life and culture. It was based on the concept that the government was responsible for the healthy development of national economy and social security, and that the growth of production could be maintained only if the great body of the consumers could continue to purchase its output. The New Deal increased government interference in the nation's economic life. As a result of Roosevelt's New Deal, the responsibilities of the federal government for economic and social welfare increased to new level.

VIII America in the Second World War

World War II was a global military conflict which involved more than two hundred countries all over the world. The great powers were organized into two opposing military alliances: the Allies and the Axis. The war fought in the Soviet Union, North Africa and the Mediterranean, Western Europe and the Far East. It was the most widespread and devastating war

36 Understanding the United States

in human history in terms of lives lost and material destruction.

Causes of the War

● **The Failure of Peace Efforts**

During the 1920s, attempts were made to achieve a stable peace. The establishment of the League of Nations in 1920 was the first action intended for this goal. But it turned out to be a failure.

During the 1930s, Britain and France followed the Appeasement policy(绥靖政策).They were not ready to help the League take decisive measures to prevent the expansion of Germany and Italy. And the League failed to foster a sense of co-operation among the member states. After France and Britain adopted the policy of appeasement, Germany and Italy became more aggressive. They defied(蔑视)the League.

● **The Rise of Fascism**

During the first twenty years of the twentieth century, there were frequent riots and strikes in Italy. The Italian government of the time was unable to maintain order and control these upheavals. The state of affairs gave Benito Mussolini the opportunity to rise to power. In 1919, Benito Mussolini founded the fascist Party in Milan, Italy. After the Fascists had marched on Rome in October 1922, King Victor Emmanuel III named Mussolini prime minister. In the following four years, Mussolini established the first Fascist dictatorship by destroying civil liberties, outlawing all other political parties, and imposing a totalitarian regime on the country by means of terror.

● **Hitler as a Dictator**

Throughout the early 1920's, Germany was trapped in a series of troubles, such as high unemployment, inflation, and political turmoil. Many Germans were not satisfied with the German government especially because it had agreed to the terms of the Treaty of Versailles. Extremist groups and political parties often used violent actions to compete for the control of the country. One of these groups was Adolf Hitler's National Socialist German Workers' party, or Nazi party founded in 1918. Hitler joined the party in 1919 and soon became prominent by his eloquent emotion-arousing oration. He designed the Nazi program, which held that only true Germans were a "master race."

In 1933 Hitler was appointed chancellor and soon demanded and received absolute power from the legislature. He became the dictator of Germany. Hitler withdrew Germany from the League of Nations immediately after he gained the power. He also undertook large-scale rearmament and began to demand more territory. He annexed Austria in March 1938 with the support of Mussolini and benefited from the appeasement policy of Britain and France. The United States at that time took the neutral position, refusing to provide any material assistance to all parties in foreign conflicts.

● **Formation of the Axis Coalition**

In October, 1935, Mussolini invaded Ethiopia. The world denounced Italy's invasion of Ethiopia. However, Germany fully supported it. In 1936 the two countries signed a political and commercial agreement that signified the formation of German-Italian Alliance.

Totalitarianism (极权主义)also emerged in Japan because the armed forces occupied a powerful position in the government. They proclaimed the puppet state of Manchukuo in northeast China in 1932 and occupied the main Chinese ports in 1937—1938.

Treaties between Germany, Italy, and Japan from 1936 to 1940 brought about the formation of Rome-Berlin-Tokyo Axis. The Axis thereafter became the collective term for those countries and their allies.

On 1 September, 1939, Hitler invaded Poland. Britain and France declared war on Germany two days later. World War II broke out.

The United States at War

At the beginning of World War II, the United States was determined not to be involved in the war. However, with the fall of France and the air war against Britain in 1940, public sentiment increasingly favored the Allied powers that opposed German expansion.

The Big Three: Franklin D. Roosevelt, Stalin, and Churchill in Teheran, Iran (November 29, 1943).

On the morning of December 7, Japanese carrier-based planes launched a devastating, surprise attack to the U.S. Pacific fleet at Pearl Harbor, Hawaii. Nineteen ships, including five battleships, and about 150 U.S. planes were destroyed; more than 2,300 soldiers, sailors and civilians were killed. On December 8, U.S. Congress declared a state of war with Japan; three days later Germany and Italy declared war on the United States.

Countries and organizations that opposed to the Axis powers formed the Allies of World War II. The leaders of the United Kingdom, Soviet Union and the United States were known as "The Big Three." On November 28 at Tehran(德黑兰,伊朗首都和最大城市), Roosevelt, Churchill and Joseph Stalin agreed to establish a new international organization, the United Nations.

The Normandy Landing

Under the command of General Eisenhower, the first contingents (队伍) of Allied Expeditionary Force (AEF), including U.S., British and Canadian troops, landed on the beaches of Normandy in northern France on June 6, 1944. The day was named D-Day, the term used for the day of actual landing. The landing took place along a 80-kilometer stretch of the Normandy coast.

The landing was the largest amphibious operation (两栖作战) in history, involving 175,000 troops landing on D-Day, 195,700 Allied naval and merchant navy personnel in over 5,000 ships. The subsequent battle of Normandy involved over a million men from America, Canada, Britain, France, Poland, and Germany. The Allied armies continued to move across France toward Germany and helped seal the fate of Hitler's. On August 25 Paris was liberated.

Japan Surrender

In the central Pacific Ocean, the Battle of Midway became the turning point for the Allies, resulting in the first major defeat of the Japanese navy, ending the Japanese advance across the central Pacific.

From July 17, to August 2, 1945, the heads of the U.S., Britain and Soviet Union met at Potsdam, a suburb outside Berlin, to discuss operations against Japan, the peace settlement in Europe, and a policy for the future of Germany. They issued the Potsdam Declaration on July 26, in which Japan was urged to surrender immediately. On August 6, U.S. dropped an atomic bomb on the city of Hiroshima (广岛,日本本州岛西南部一城市), Japan. A second atomic bomb was dropped on Nagasaki (长崎,日本九州岛西岸港市)on August 8. Japan formally surrendered on September 2, 1945.

On April 25, 1945, Representatives of 50 nations met in San Francisco, California, to discuss the framework of the United Nations. It was also a signal that the United States intended to play a major role in international affairs.

38 | Understanding the United States

Mushroom Cloud of Atomic Bomb

Japanese Foreign Minister Mamoru Shigemitsu signs the final documents for the surrender of Japan on September 2, 1945 aboard the USS Missouri.

Effect of World War II

Lasting six years, World War II involved a majority of countries all over the world and caused millions of people to suffer, costing 55 million lives and material damage of some 3 billion dollars. It was a war that was more cruel, bitter and extensive than any other war in history.

After World War II the United States and the Soviet Union became the two leading world powers. They set the stage for the Cold War, which lasted for the next 46 years.

The economy of the United States benefits greatly from World War II. The depression was brought to an end, and new industrial complexes were built all over the United States. After 4 years of military buildup, the U.S. had also become the leading military power in the world.

Year	Events
1939	On 1 September, Hitler invaded Poland. Britain and France declared war on Germany two days later.
1940	German "Blitzkrieg" (闪电战) occupied Belgium, Holland and France.
	Churchill became Prime Minister of Britain.
	British Expeditionary Force withdrew from Dunkirk.
	British victory in Battle of Britain forced Hitler to delay invasion plans.
1941	Hitler invaded Russia by launching Operation Barbarossa(巴巴罗萨行动)
	The Blitz (闪电战) continued against Britain's major cities.
	Allies took Tobruk (托布鲁克,利比亚东北部港市) in North Africa, and resisted German attacks.
	Japan attacked Pearl Harbor, and the US entered the war.
1942	Germany suffered setbacks at Stalingrad and El Alamein (阿拉曼,埃及北部一村庄).
	Singapore was defeated by Japan in February.
	American naval victory at the Battle of Midway, in June, marked the turning point in Pacific War.
	Massive slaughter of Jewish people at Auschwitz began.

1943	Germany's first major defeat occurred at Stalingrad.
	Allied victory in North Africa enabled invasion of Italy to be started.
	Italy surrendered, but Germany took over the battle.
	British and Indian troops fought Japan in Burma(缅甸).
1944	Allies landed at Anzio and bombed monastery at Monte Cassino.
	Soviet Union took a faster offensive step in Eastern Europe.
	D-Day: The Allied invasion of France. Paris was liberated in August.
	Guam（关岛,位于西太平洋）was liberated by the U.S.
1945	Soviet forces liberated Auschwitz.
	Russian troops arrived at Berlin. Hitler committed suicide and Germany surrendered on 7 May.
	Truman became President of the U.S.
	After atomic bombs were dropped on Hiroshima and Nagasaki, Japan surrendered on 14 August.

IX Cold War

The world entered the Cold War period after the ending of the Second World War. The Cold War (1945—1991) was the continuing state of political conflict, military tension, and economic competition existing after World War II (1939—1945), between the USSR and its satellite states, and the powers of the Western world, primarily the United States. The main features of this period were international tension and conflict without bloody "hot war" between the two sides. Although the primary participants' military forces never officially clashed directly, they expressed the conflict through military coalitions, strategic conventional force deployments (部署), a nuclear arms race, espionage (间谍活动), propaganda, and technological competition, e.g. the space race.

The Soviet Union created the Eastern Bloc (集团), the former Communist states of Eastern and Central Europe, including the member states of the Warsaw Pact (华沙条约组织 1955—1991) Poland, East Germany, Czechoslovakia, Hungary, Romania, Bulgaria, along with Yugoslavia(南斯拉夫) and Albania, which were not aligned with the Soviet Union after 1948 and 1960 respectively.

The US and some western European countries established containment (牵制政策) of communism as a defensive policy, establishing alliances (e.g. NATO, 1949) to that end. Several such countries also coordinated the rebuilding of Western Europe, especially western Germany, which the USSR opposed.

Elsewhere, in Latin America and Southeast Asia, the USSR fostered communist revolutions, opposed by several western countries and their regional allies. Some countries aligned with NATO and the Warsaw Pact, yet non-aligned country blocs also emerged.

The Cold War featured periods of relative calm and of international high tension— the Berlin Blockade (1948—1949), the Korean War (1950—1953), the Berlin Crisis of 1961, the Vietnam War (1959—1975), the Cuban Missile Crisis (1962), the Soviet War in Afghanistan (1979—1989), and the Able Archer 83 NATO exercises in November 1983. Both sides sought détente (国际关系的缓和) to relieve political tensions and deter (阻止) direct military attack, which would likely guarantee their mutual assured destruction with nuclear weapons.

The early 1980s witnessed a final period of friction between the United States and the

Understanding the United States

The most visible symbol of the Cold War, the Berlin Wall was torn down.

USSR. In 1980, Ronald Reagan became the U.S. president and he set about strengthening American military capabilities.

In the mid-1980s Mikhail Gorbachev came to power in the USSR. He brought a revolution to Soviet foreign policy, seeking new and far-reaching agreements with the West. From 1985, Gorbachev and Reagan held a series of summit talks, and in 1987 the two leaders agreed to eliminate a whole class of their countries' nuclear missiles. The USSR agreed to reduce its forces in Eastern Europe, and in 1989 it pulled its troops out of Afghanistan. That year the Berlin wall that had divided East and West Germany since 1961 was torn down. In 1991 the USSR dissolved, and Russia and the other Soviet republics emerged as independent states. The Soviet power in Eastern Europe collapsed, which led to the end of the Cold War period.

Chapter 3 Political System

I A Brief Introduction to the Political System

The United States is an indirect democracy — that is, the people rule through the representatives they elect. In the beginning, only white men with property could vote. Over time, the vote has been given to more and more people. Today any citizen who is at least 18 years old can vote.

The Constitution

The United States Constitution, written in 1787, established the country's political system and is the basis for its laws. Over the 200 years of its history, the United States has greatly grown and changed. Yet the Constitution works as well today as when it was written. One reason is that the Constitution can be amended (for example, the *Fifteenth Amendment* gave black Americans the right to vote and the *Nineteenth Amendment* gave women the right to vote). Another reason is that the Constitution is flexible: its basic principles can be applied and interpreted differently at different times.

Federalism (联邦制)

The United States has a federalist system. It means that there are individual states, each with its own government, and there is a federal, or national, government. The US Constitution gives certain powers to the federal government, other powers to the state governments, and yet other powers to both. For example, only the national government can print money; the states establish their own school systems; and both the national and the state governments can collect taxes.

Three Branches of Government

Within the national government, power is divided among three branches: the legislative(立法的) branch, the executive (行政的) branch, and the judicial(司法的) branch.

The legislative branch is represented by Congress, which consists of two parts — the House of Representatives and the Senate. Congress's main function is to make laws. There are 100 senators (two from each state) and 435 representatives (the number from each state depends on the size of the state's population).

The executive branch is headed by the President, who is also head of the country. The executive branch administers (执行) the laws. In addition to the President and the Vice-President, the executive branch consists of departments and agencies. The President appoints the department heads, or advisers, who together make up the President's Cabinet (内阁). There are 15 major departments in the executive branch. They employ about 1.6 million civilian employees.

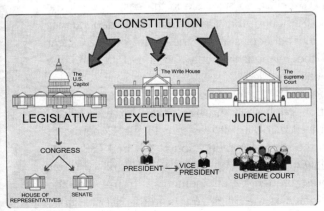

The judicial branch interprets the laws and makes sure that new laws are in keeping with the Constitution. The judicial branch is represented by several levels of federal courts. The Supreme Court is the most important body. It has nine members, who are appointed for life.

There is a system of checks and balances established by the Constitution, which is meant to prevent any of the three branches from having too much power. Each branch has certain controls over the other branches. For example, Congress makes the laws, but the President can veto (否决) a law, and the Supreme Court can decide that the law is unconstitutional.

State and Local Governments

Each state has its own constitution. Like the national government, state governments are divided into legislative, executive and judicial branches. In each state there are state senators and representatives, state court systems, and, like the President of the country, a governor of the state. Below the state level of government, there are county and city governments.

Two-Party System

The United States has two main political parties — the Democratic Party and the Republican Party. There are other much smaller parties, which play little, if any, role. There are no clear differences between the Republican and Democratic parties. In general, the Republicans tend to be more conservative and to have more support among the upper classes, while the Democrats tend to be more liberal and to have more support among the working class and the poor.

II Constitution of the United States

What Is a Constitution?

A constitution is a set of rules for a country. It defines how the country should be run and how new rules should be made. Constitution of the United States has been the supreme law of the nation since 1788. It is the oldest constitution still in effect in the world and created the American system of government. Drafted at the Constitutional Convention in Philadelphia, the Constitution calls for a government of limited and delegated powers. It opens with these three words: "We, the people ..."

US Constitution

How Was the Constitution Born?

The peace treaty of 1783 recognized the independence of the United States and the former 13 British colonies along the east coast of the Atlantic became 13 states of the new nation. Although the *Declaration of Independence* proclaimed that 13 united colonies were free and independent states, they were not very clear about the future political system of the US and the relationships between the states and the government of the new nation. A constitution was badly needed.

The United States Constitution was written in 1787, four years after America won its independence from Great Britain. The Constitution established the framework for the Federal Government and guarantees rights, freedom and justice to all. It was sent to the Congress of Confederation (邦联) for approval and then sent to the states for ratification(批准). In 1788, after nine states ratified it, the Constitution became the law of the land. By May 29, 1790, all 13 states had ratified the Constitution. The First US Congress drafted 12 amendments, from which the states ratified 10. Those 10 amendments became known as the *Bill of Rights*. In the *Bill of Rights*,

Americans are guaranteed freedom of religion, of speech, of the press and freedom to protest against government policies. They have the right to assemble in public places, to protest government actions and to demand change. They have the right to own weapons if they wish. The *Bill of Rights* guarantees Americans the right to a fair and speedy trial if accused of a crime.

Before the ratification of the Constitution, the states were governed under the Articles of Confederation (邦联条例), which served as a constitution. Under the articles, the central government was much weaker than the state governments. The men who drafted the Constitution favored a stronger central government. In the preamble (导言) to the Constitution, in which they stated their principles and purposes, the Founders recognized the United States as a government of the people, not of the states. They saw their purpose as forming "a more perfect Union," which, along with promoting the "general welfare," would secure "the Blessings of Liberty to ourselves and our Posterity (后代)."

The Contents of the Constitution

The Constitution defines the powers of the US Congress, President, and federal courts. Just as important, the Constitution lays out the rights and freedoms of all American citizens in the *Bill of Rights.*

The Constitution gives the LEGISLATIVE (立法) power to the Congress, which consists of the Senate (参议院) and the House of Representatives (众议院). The Congress has the power to make any laws that are considered "necessary and proper." The Constitution gives the EXECUTIVE (行政) power to the President alone. All the executive departments and independent agencies are responsible to the President. And the federal courts have the JUDICIAL (司法) power. Each branch can limit the other branches from gaining too much power. This division of authority is known as a system of checks and balances (制衡), and it ensures that none of the branches of government can dominate the others. The Constitution also establishes and limits the authority of the federal government over the states and spells out freedoms and liberties for US citizens.

Two overall ideas shape the Constitution. First, America is a democracy. In a democracy, the people have the ultimate power over government because they elect the leaders. Second, no government official is above the law. There are mainly four parts of the constitution spirit. They are the authority power of the law; the separation of the power; the check and balance of each branch; and the right of the people. Under the Constitution, each state has its own government. There is also a federal government for the whole country. The Constitution states what powers each one has.

The ultimate strength of the US Constitution is that it not only establishes a government, but it establishes a government which, to use Thomas Jefferson's words, can "govern itself." In other words, the document not only lets all people know the limits of the government's power, but, the system of checks and balances that it has created ensures that these limits will be obeyed. The Constitution plays a role in virtually every aspect of life in the United States.

How Is the Constitution Changed?

The Constitution can be changed, but not easily. Each change is called an amendment (修正案). Congress generally suggests amendments, though states can suggest them, too. Two-thirds of Congress must approve an amendment. After that, three-fourths of the states must say yes to it. Only then is an amendment added to the Constitution. The Constitution now has 27 amendments, of which only 25 are active and new ones may still be added. That is why people sometimes call the Constitution a "living document."

III Government

Functions of a Government

Every country has its own government. The basic function of a government is to provide stability. It does so by maintaining order within a country and by protecting the country's borders from outside attack. The government makes laws, collects and spends tax money, and provides services. Services provided by the government include education, law courts, transportation, police forces and armed forces.

Types of Government

There are several different types of government. One is monarchy(君主政体). In this type of government, one person is the monarch. When a monarch dies, the power of ruling the country passes to one of the monarch's children or, if there are no children, to another family member. In the past, monarchs were completely in charge of their countries. They chose all other officials. Today, most monarchs have much less power. Queen Elizabeth II of the United Kingdom, for example, has very limited powers. Actually she is only a symbol of the country, which is now run by the Parliament.

A second type of government is the republic. In a republic, the rulers and top officials are all elected by the people. Unlike the monarchs, these rulers and officials do not hold power for life. They are only elected for a specific period of time and they are only entitled to execute the power on behalf of the people within this term. After that term is up, the group chooses another ruler. In a democratic republic, the people have rights that no ruler may cut off(剥夺). The people can also replace their rulers.

Republics can turn into dictatorships. In a dictatorship, one person — the dictator — has total power. Dictators can usually do whatever they want. Everyone must obey a dictator. In a military dictatorship, the ruling officials are military officers.

A Federal Government

Many countries have a federal system(联邦制). In a federal system, power is shared between a central government and smaller government units. The United States, for example, is a federalist system as defined in the Tenth Amendment of its constitution. There is a federal, or central, government for the entire country. In addition, each of the 50 states has its own government. In some matters, the state governments have final say. In other matters, the federal government rules. However, only the federal government, can mint money or declare war.

Government of the United States

President Obama held his first full cabinet meeting at the White House

Chapter 3　Political System

Form of government	Federal republic
Head of state	President
Head of government	President
Legislature	Bicameral（两院制的） legislature: House of Representative（435 representatives） Senate（100 senators）
Voting qualifications	Universal at age 18
Constitution	17 September 1787, effective 4 March 1789
Highest court	Supreme Court of the United States

Four Elements（原理）to Build the Government on

　　Every government has a source of its sovereignty or authority, and most of the political structures of the US Government apply the doctrine of popular sovereignty（人民权利至上论）, meaning that the ultimate political authority rests with the people. In other words, government is based upon the consent of the governed. If the government fails in its obligations（职责）, the people have the power to create, change, or even abolish government. In this idea, the citizens collectively represent the nation's authority. They then express that authority individually by voting to elect leaders to represent them in government.

　　The second principle of US democracy is representative government. In a representative government, the people delegate their powers to elected officials. In the United States, candidates compete for the presidency, the Senate, and the House of Representatives, as well as for many state and local positions. In turn these elected officials represent the will of the people and ensure that the government is accountable(有责任的) to its citizens. In a democracy, the people exercise power through elections, which allow adult citizens of the United States the chance to have their voices heard and to influence government. With their vote, they can remove officials who ignore their intentions or who betray their trust. Political leaders are accountable as agents of the people; this accountability is an important feature of the American system of representative government.

　　In order to truly work, however, representative government must represent all people. Originally, the only people allowed to vote, and thus to be represented, were white men who owned property — a small percentage of the population. Gradually, voting rights were broadened to include white men without property, blacks, Native Americans, naturalized immigrants, and women.

　　The third principle of American democracy is the system of checks and balances （立法权、行政权和司法权相互独立，互相制衡）. The three branches of government — the legislative, the executive, and the judicial — restrain and stabilize one another through their separated functions. The legislative branch, represented by Congress, must pass bills before they can become law. The executive branch — namely, the president — can veto bills passed by Congress, thus preventing them from becoming law. In turn, by a two-thirds vote, Congress can override the president's veto. The Supreme Court may invalidate（使无效）acts of Congress by declaring them contrary to the Constitution of the United States, but Congress can change the Constitution through the amendment process.

　　The fourth principle of democracy in the United States is federalism. In the American federal system, the states and the national government divide authority. This division of power helps curb (抑制) abuses by either the national or the state governments.

Division of Powers

　　The federalist system set up by the Constitution, granted certain powers to the national government, reserved others to the states, and allowed some to exist on both level. This arrangement is an embodiment(体现) of the American political principle of division of power.

Division of Powers

Exclusive Powers of the National Government	Concurrent Powers	Reserved Powers of the State Governments
Declare war and conduct foreign affairs	Levy taxes	Maintain a system of public education
Coin money	Borrow money	Create local governments
Manage a postal system	Define and punish crimes	Provide public education
Establish lower courts	Charter banks	Direct traffic laws
Raise and support armed forces		
Powers Denied to the National Governments	**Powers Denied to the National and State Governments**	**Powers Denied to the State Government**
Tax exports	Deny due process of law	Coin money
Suspend writ(正式文件) of *habeas corpus*(人身保护权)	Pass ex post facto laws (有追溯效力的法令)	Enter into treaties
Grant titles of nobility	Pass bills of attainder (被剥夺财产和公民权)	Void(使无效) contracts

American Democracy

The United States is a democracy. This means that American citizens choose their government, rather than having one forced on them. Americans choose their government by voting. American elections seem rather democratic, but the American people have only a small area of choice in elections. There are only two major parties in the country and they are almost the same in nature. American voters have no alternative but to give their votes to one party or the other.

Democracy in America is based on six essential ideals: 1) People must accept the principle of majority rule(多数决定原则). 2) The political rights of minorities must be protected. 3) Citizens must agree to a system of rule by law. 4) The free exchange of opinions and ideas must not be restricted. 5) All citizens must be equal before the law. 6) Government exists to serve the people, because it derives its power from the people. These ideals form the basis of the democratic system in the United States, which seeks to create a union of diverse peoples, places, and interests.

Election Day

Every four years, on Election Day, (Tuesday after the first Monday in November), registered voters in the United States cast their votes for presidential electors. Collectively, these electors form the Electoral College. The number of electors per state is equal to the number in its Congressional delegation. Thus, each state has at least three electors. Kansas has six electors and Missouri has eleven. These electors meet on the first Tuesday after the second Wednesday in December to elect the President and Vice-President.

IV Major Political Parties

The Democratic Party

The Democratic Party is almost as old as the United States and traces its origins to the

Democratic-Republican Party, founded by Thomas Jefferson, James Madison, and other influential opponents of the Federalists in 1792.

Its history started with a feud between Alexander Hamilton and Thomas Jefferson, America's third president. In the 1790's, Hamilton was appointed Secretary of the Treasury and felt that the federal government should have the power to direct the economy, and a society built on industrial interests. Thomas Jefferson, who was at that time the first Secretary of the State, disagreed with Hamilton. He felt the national government should have limited powers and a society with independent farming. Thomas Jefferson, with the help of James Madison then formed what was then called the Democratic-Republic Party, fighting strongly against the Federalist Party of which Hamilton helped form. Thus, Thomas Jefferson was known as the Founding Father of the Democratic Party, which became the dominant political party in the United States from 1800 until the 1820s. When it split into competing factions, one of the factions became the modern-day Democratic Party. In 1800 Jefferson was elected as the first Democratic President of the United States. Five of the country's first eight presidents were Democrats.

The Republican Party

The Republican Party is one of the two major contemporary political parties in the United States of America, along with the Democratic Party. It is often referred to as the Grand Old Party or the GOP. When the Republican Party was created, the two major parties in the United States were the Democratic Party and the Whig Party.

Founded in 1854 by people who wanted to keep slavery from spreading to other parts of the country, the Republican Party rose to prominence with the election of Abraham Lincoln, the first Republican president. The party presided over the American Civil War and Reconstruction and was harried by internal factions and scandals towards the end of the 19th century. Today, the Republican Party supports a conservative platform, with further foundations in economic liberalism, fiscal conservatism, and social conservatism.

Abraham Lincoln

The Democratic Donkey and the Republican Elephant

Did you ever wonder what the story was behind these two famous party animals? The now-famous Democratic donkey was first associated with Democrat Andrew Jackson's 1828 presidential campaign. His opponents called him a jackass (a donkey), and Jackson decided to use the image of the strong-willed animal on his campaign posters. Later, cartoonist Thomas Nast used the Democratic donkey in newspaper cartoons and made the symbol famous.

Nast invented another famous symbol — the Republican elephant. In a cartoon that appeared in Harper's Weekly in 1874, Nast drew a donkey clothed in lion's skin, scaring away all the animals at the zoo. One of those animals, the elephant, was labeled "The Republican Vote." The elephant characterized the Republican vote — not the party — which had been scared by the possibility of the Democratic Party seeking a third term for President Ulysses S. Grant. In time, other cartoonists used the elephant, which came to define the party. Democrats today say the donkey is smart and brave, while Republicans say the elephant is strong and dignified.

V Presidents of the United States

This photo shows the official seal of the president of the United States. The official US motto, E pluribus unum, appears in the center of the seal. It means "From many, one."

The U.S. President is the head of its Administration. Chosen through a general or presidential election, the president is the most prominent figure in the United States. He is known as the First Citizen and his wife, the First Lady. Of all the federal officials he is the only one to have an official residence, the White House.

The Job of the President

Although presidents are entitled to a lot of power, they also shoulder quite a heavy burden. The president heads up the executive branch of the US government. The executive branch is in charge of running the country and defending it from enemies. The president takes an oath to uphold the Constitution. The president is commanded by the Constitution to "preserve, protect and defend the Constitution of the United States" and to "take care that the laws be faithfully executed." He can issue rules, regulations and instructions which, known as executive orders, have the binding force of laws upon federal agencies.

Presidents suggest new laws. They appoint most of the country's judges, including the judges of the Supreme Court and appoint ambassadors. The president also serves as commander-in-chief of the country's military forces — the Army, Navy, Air Force, and Marines, and has the power to raise, train, supervise, and deploy American armed forces, provided Congress shows no disagreement. Presidents cannot declare war — only Congress can do that. Once a war has started, however, the president gives the orders.

Every president has a group of advisers called the Cabinet. Each Cabinet member, except the attorney general, is called a secretary and heads a different department. The Secretary of the Treasury, for example, handles the country's money supply. The attorney general is the chief law officer of the United States and heads the Department of Justice. Other secretaries deal with defense, schools, cities, and so on. There are 15 Cabinet posts in all.

How Long Do Presidents Serve?

A president is elected to serve for four years. The president may then run for one more term. When the nation was born, no law limited how many times a president could serve. By custom, however, no president ran more than twice. Then, in the 20th century, Franklin Delano Roosevelt ran and won four times. After Roosevelt died, a new law was added to the Constitution. It said presidents could serve no more than two terms.

Five presidents have died in office. William Henry Harrison died of pneumonia one month into his first term. The other four — Abraham Lincoln, James Garfield, William McKinley, and John F. Kennedy — were killed by assassins.

Presidential Impeachment

If the president is accused of a serious crime, Congress can bring charges against the president. This is called impeachment. The House of Representatives draws up the charges. Representatives can impeach the president if a majority in the House vote to do so. The Senate then sits as a court to hear the charges. Afterward, the Senate may vote to remove the president from office.

Congress has never removed a president from office. It did impeach President Andrew Johnson in 1868. Johnson kept his job by one vote in the Senate. Congress investigated President Richard Nixon for possible crimes in 1974. Nixon resigned before he could be

Chapter 3　Political System

impeached. In 1998, President Clinton was impeached in the House. But he won his trial in the Senate and kept his job.

The Royal Road to Presidency

To become president, it's best to become the candidate of a big political party. No law says presidents must belong to a party. It's just that it's hard to win such a job without help. The United States has two major political parties, the Democrats and the Republicans. Every president since 1853 has belonged to one of these two parties.

Most people who run for president have first served as governor of a state or as a member of the United States Congress. Some have come from the military.

At one time, political parties chose their candidates at big meetings called conventions. Leading members of the party would get together and decide who should run. Now, most states hold primary elections before the presidential election. Citizens decide who should run from their party by voting in the primary.

Introduction of Some American Presidents

● *George Washington (1732—1799)*

George Washington was the first president of the United States (1789—1797) and one of the most important leaders in United States history. His role in gaining independence for the American colonies and later in unifying them under the new US federal government cannot be overestimated. Laboring against great difficulties, he created the Continental Army, which fought and won the American Revolution (1775—1783). After an eight-year struggle, his design for victory brought final defeat to the British at Yorktown, Virginia, and forced Great Britain to grant independence to its overseas possession. After his second term, many Americans wanted to make Washington king. He refused. In doing so, he kept American democracy going.

Shortly after resigning his military commission, George Washington wed Martha Dandridge Custis, a wealthy young widow, on January 6, 1759. The Washingtons had no children of their own, but they raised Martha's children from her previous marriage. The marriage began the relatively peaceful inter-war(两次战争之间的) period in Washington's life, during which he farmed tobacco and served on the House of Burgesses, the popularly elected chamber of the Virginia colonial legislature. In later years, the Washingtons also adopted two of their grandchildren. George Washington and his wife, Martha, lived on a large farm in Virginia called Mount Vernon. Apart from very pretty location on a hill by the Potomac River, the estate offers great educational value.

> *Did you know these facts?*
> 1. George Washington was a passionate farmer and gardener.
> 2. He introduced the mule to American agriculture.
> 3. There are 13 trees planted personally by Washington in the estate.
> 4. He was horse lover, avid rider and fox hunter.
> 5. He was buried in Mount Vernon, not at famous Arlington cemetery.
> 6. He treated his over 300 slaves far more humanely than did his fellow citizens of Virginia.

● *Thomas Jefferson (1743—1826)*

Thomas Jefferson was the third president of the United States (1801—1809) and author of the *Declaration of Independence*. He was regarded as one of the most brilliant individuals in history. His interests were boundless, and his accomplishments were great and varied. He was a philosopher, educator, naturalist, politician, scientist, architect, inventor, pioneer in scientific farming, musician, and writer, and he was the foremost spokesman for democracy of his day. Jefferson is also regarded as a great political thinker and diplomat. The US doubled its area in

50 | Understanding the United States

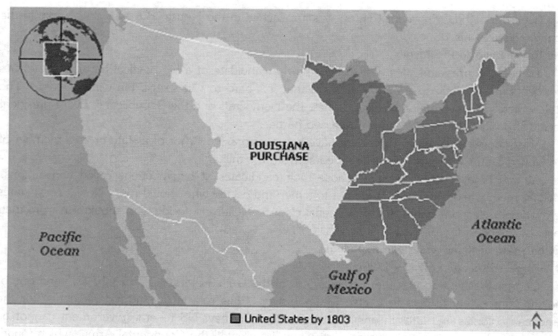

Louisiana Purchase has double the size of the United States. In 1803 United States President Thomas Jefferson paid Napoleon Bonaparte of France $15 million for about 2.1 million sq km of land west of the Mississippi River.

1803 when he bought territory west of the Mississippi called the Louisiana Purchase.

- *James Madison*

James Madison was the fourth president of the United States. He served two terms from 1809 to 1817. In 1808, Madison was elected the fourth president of the United States. Even more importantly, Madison played a leading role in the creation of the Constitution of the United States. He helped design the system of government under which the American people still live today. He is often called the Father of the Constitution.

- *Abraham Lincoln (1861—1865)*

Abraham Lincoln served as the 16th President of the United States from March 1861 until his assassination in April 1865. He successfully led his country during the Civil War (1861—1865), preserving the Union and ending slavery.

Before his election in 1860 as the first Republican president, Lincoln had been a country lawyer, an Illinois state legislator, a member of the United States House of Representatives, and twice an unsuccessful candidate for election to the US Senate. As an outspoken opponent of the  expansion of slavery in the United States, Lincoln won the Republican Party nomination in 1860 and was elected president later that year. His tenure in office was occupied primarily with the defeat of the secessionist Confederate States of America in the American Civil War. He introduced measures that resulted in the abolition of slavery, issuing his *Emancipation Proclamation* in 1863 and promoting the passage of the *Thirteenth Amendment* to the Constitution. His Gettysburg Address (1863) became an iconic symbol of the nation's duty. At the close of the war, Lincoln held a moderate view of Reconstruction, seeking to speedily reunite the nation through a policy of generous reconciliation. Lincoln has consistently been ranked by scholars as one of the greatest of all US Presidents.

Six days after the large-scale surrender of Confederate forces under General Robert E. Lee, Lincoln became the first American president to be assassinated.

● *Franklin Delano Roosevelt (1882—1945)*

Franklin Delano Roosevelt, the 32nd President of the United States, was a central figure in world events during the mid-20th century, leading the United States during a time of worldwide economic crisis and world war. The only American president elected to more than two terms, Roosevelt won his first of four presidential elections in 1932, while the United States was in the depths of the Great Depression. This was a time when banks and businesses were failing and many people lost their jobs. Roosevelt used the government to create jobs and help the needy. His combination of optimism and economic activism is often credited with keeping the country's economic crisis from developing into a political crisis.

Roosevelt dominated the American political scene, not only during the twelve years of his presidency, but for decades afterwards. His presidency created a realignment that dominated American politics until the election of Richard Nixon in 1968. Roosevelt's political impact also resonated (反响) on the world stage long after his death, with the United Nations as examples of his administration's wide ranging impact. Roosevelt greatly increased the powers of the presidency and is rated by historians as one of the greatest US Presidents. He died in office of a cerebral hemorrhage (脑出血), shortly before the war ended.

Roosevelt named his approach to the economic situation the New Deal; it consisted of legislation pushed through Congress as well as executive orders. Executive orders included the bank holiday declared when he first came to office; legislation created new government agencies, such as the Works Progress Administration and the National Recovery Administration, with the intent of creating new jobs for the unemployed. Other legislation provided direct assistance to individuals, such as the *Social Security Act.*

During the 1940s, he led America to victory in World War II. As World War II began in 1939, with Japanese occupation of countries on the western Pacific rim and the rise of Hitler in Germany, Roosevelt kept the US on an ostensibly neutral course. Once war broke out in Europe, however, Roosevelt provided Lend-Lease (由租借法批准的) aid to the countries fighting against Nazi Germany, with Great Britain the recipient of the most assistance. With the Japanese attack on Pearl Harbor on December 7, 1941, Roosevelt immediately asked for and received a declaration of war against Japan. Germany subsequently declared war on the United States on December 11, 1941. The nearly total mobilization of the US economy to support the war effort caused a rapid economic recovery.

Roosevelt's Marriage and Family

Franklin Roosevelt married his distant cousin, Eleanor Roosevelt, in 1905. For their personal lives, Franklin was a charismatic (超凡魅力的), handsome, and socially active man. In contrast, Eleanor was shy and disliked social life, and at first stayed at home to raise their children. They had six children but one died as an infant.

Roosevelt had affairs outside his marriage, including one with Eleanor's social secretary Lucy Mercer which began soon after she was hired in early 1914. In September 1918, Eleanor found letters revealing the affair in Roosevelt's luggage, when he returned from World War I. According to the Roosevelt family, Eleanor offered Franklin a divorce so that he could be with the woman he loved, but Lucy, being Catholic, could not bring herself to marry a divorced man with five children. They reconciled after a fashion (勉强) with the informal mediation of Roosevelt's adviser Louis McHenry Howe, and Franklin Roosevelt promised never to see Lucy

President Franklin D. Roosevelt and his family on December 24, 1943

again. However, Franklin broke his promise. He and Lucy maintained a formal correspondence, and began seeing each other again in 1941 — and perhaps earlier. Lucy was with him on April 12, 1945 — the day he died. Despite this, his affair was not widely known of until the 1960s. The effect of this affair upon Eleanor Roosevelt is difficult to estimate. Eleanor soon thereafter established a separate house in Hyde Park at Valkill, and increasingly devoted herself to a various social and political causes. For the rest of their lives, the Roosevelts' marriage was more of political partnership than an intimate relationship. The emotional break in their marriage was so severe that when Roosevelt asked Eleanor in 1942 — in light of his failing health — to come back home and live with him again, she refused.

- *John F. Kennedy (1917—1963)*

John F.Kennedy

John F. Kennedy, the 35th President of the United States and the youngest man ever elected to the United States presidency, assumed the office in 1961 and served until his assassination in 1963. As president, Kennedy directed his initial policies toward invigorating the country, attempting to release it from the grip of economic recession. He made direct appeals for public service and public commitment, paying particular attention to civil rights. The energy and possibility of his message was cut short when Kennedy was killed by an assassin's bullets as his motorcade wound through Dallas, Texas on November 22, 1963. Kennedy was the youngest man elected President; he was the youngest to die.

Facts about John F. Kennedy

Kennedy was the youngest elected president at 43 years old, and the youngest to die in office at 46 years old.
Kennedy was the only president to win a Pulitzer Prize — for his biography *Profiles in Courage*.
First President born in the 1900's.
He was the only president to appoint his brother to a cabinet post.
He was the first president who had served in the US Navy.
Nicknames: "JFK" ; "Jack".

- *Richard M. Nixon (1969—1974)*

Nixon opened diplomatic channels with the People's Republic of China as part of a policy to balance the growing military strength of the Union of Soviet Socialist Republics. Chairman Mao Zedong greeted United States president Richard Nixon in February 1972. Nixon's visit to China improved relations between the two countries and helped reestablish trade that had ceased two decades earlier.

The Watergate Scandal

Early in Nixon's second term, a scandal began to hound him. In 1972, a group of burglars was caught in the Watergate Hotel in Washington, D.C. They were stealing papers from a Democratic Party office. The burglars, it turned out, worked for President Nixon's campaign team. Reporters dug into the story further. They found that Nixon's team may have committed a number of crimes to get Nixon elected. Congress decided to investigate. Nixon denied any role in the burglary. Congress then learned that Nixon had secretly recorded many of his conversations. These recordings could show if Nixon was involved. There was talk of putting Nixon on trial.

On August 9, 1974, Nixon resigned before he could be charged with any crime. His vice president, Gerald Ford, took over. Ford pardoned Nixon for any crimes he may have committed. The next day, he became emotional, as he said goodbye to staff members. He then boarded a helicopter, on the White House lawn, stopping to give a two-armed victory salute in farewell.

● *Bill Clinton(1946—)*

In 1978, at the age of 32, Bill Clinton was elected governor of Arkansas, becoming the youngest citizen of the United States to win a gubernatorial election. He governed the state for more than 10 years, concentrating on education and social reforms. Clinton headed the 1992 Democratic campaign ticket and defeated President George Bush to become the 42nd President of the United States.

Bill Clinton and Hillary Rodham's Love Story

Bill and Hillary met in 1970 at the Yale University law school library. Hillary noticed Bill looking over at her, and eventually she walked up to him and said, "If you're going to keep looking at me, and I'm going to keep looking back, we might as well be introduced." Bill was so nervous at the time, he forgot his own name. A few days later, the couple went on their first date — to an art gallery exhibiting Mark Rothko.

After graduating from law school in 1973, Bill took Hillary on her first trip to Europe. While vacationing in England, Bill proposed on the shores of Ennerdale. Hillary declined the proposal saying she loved him but needed time. Bill proposed again but Hillary said no. When they returned from Europe, Hillary moved to Arkansas to find a job. She didn't have much luck and decided to go home to visit family. On the way to the airport, the couple passed a modest brick house in the university district with a for-sale sign. Hillary mentioned she liked the house. When she returned a few weeks later, Bill told her he had bought it. He said that he couldn't live in it by himself, and that he hoped she would marry him. That time Hillary said yes.

The couple were married at their new home in Fayetteville, Arkansas on October 11, 1975. The small, intimate ceremony was attended by 15 guests. Hillary wore a lace gown by Jessica McClintock that she purchased at Dillard's. The vows were officiated by a local Methodist minister. Following the wedding, several hundred friends joined the newlyweds for a backyard reception held at the home of Morris and Ann Henry. The couple enjoyed a honeymoon in Acapulco, Mexico.

● *George W. Bush(1946—)*

George W. Bush was the 43rd President of the United States from 2001 to 2009 and the 46th Governor of Texas from 1995 to 2000.

54 | Understanding the United States

George W. Bush is the eldest son of George H. W. Bush (the 41st President) and Barbara Bush, making him one of only two American presidents to be the son of a preceding president. After graduating from Yale University in 1968, and Harvard Business School in 1975, Bush worked in his family's oil businesses. He married Laura Welch in 1977 and unsuccessfully ran for the United States House of Representatives shortly thereafter. Bush was elected President in 2000 as the Republican candidate.

Eight months into Bush's first term as president, the September 11, 2001, terrorist attacks occurred. In response, Bush announced a global War on Terrorism, ordered an invasion of Afghanistan that same year and an invasion of Iraq in 2003. In addition to national security issues, Bush promoted policies on the economy, health care, education, and social security reform.

Bush successfully ran for re-election against Democratic Senator John Kerry in 2004. After his re-election, Bush received increasingly heated criticism from conservatives. In 2005, the Bush Administration dealt with widespread criticism over its handling of Hurricane Katrina. In December 2007, the United States entered the longest post-World War II recession. That prompted the Bush Administration to take more direct control of the economy, enacting multiple economic programs intended to preserve the country's financial structure. Though Bush was a popular president for much of his first term, his popularity declined sharply during his second term. After leaving office, Bush returned to Texas. He is currently a public speaker and is writing a book about his presidency.

● *Barack Obama (1961—)*

Obama is the 44th and current President of the United States. He is the first African-American to be nominated by a major American political party for president and is the first African American to hold the office, as well as the first president born in Hawaii. Obama previously served as the junior United States Senator from Illinois from January 2005 until he resigned after his election to the presidency in November 2008.

Obama is a graduate of Columbia University and Harvard Law School, where he became the first black person to serve as president of the *Harvard Law Review*. He was a community organizer in Chicago before earning his law degree. He worked as a civil rights attorney in Chicago before serving three terms in the Illinois Senate from 1997 to 2004 and taught constitutional law at the University of Chicago Law School from 1992 to 2004. Obama began his run for the presidency in February 2007. After a close campaign in the 2008 Democratic Party presidential primaries against Hillary Clinton, he won his party's nomination. In the 2008 general election, he defeated Republican nominee John McCain and was inaugurated as president on January 20, 2009. On October 9, 2009, he was awarded the 2009 Nobel Peace Prize.

Official portrait of Barack Obama

Marriage and Family

Obama met his wife, Michelle Robinson, in June 1989 when he was employed as a summer associate at the Chicago law firm of Sidley Austin. Assigned for three months as Obama's adviser at the firm, Robinson joined him at group social functions, but declined his initial offers to date. They began dating later that summer, became engaged in 1991, and were married on October 3, 1992. The couple's first daughter, Malia Ann, was born in 1998, followed by a second daughter, Natasha ("Sasha"), in 2001.

President Barack Obama and First Lady Michelle Obama are joined by their daughters, Sasha and Malia, and Michelle Obama's mother, Marian Robinson, April 13, 2009, as they wave from the South Portico of the White House to guests attending the White House Easter Egg Roll.

(right to left) Barack Obama and half-sister Maya Soetoro, with their mother Ann Dunham and grandfather Stanley Dunham, in Hawaii (early 1970s)

Chapter 4 National Economy

I An Overview

For the most part, the United States has a market economy in which individual producers and consumers determine the kinds of goods and services produced and the prices of those products. A guiding principle of the U.S. economy, dating back to the colonial period, has been that individuals own the goods and services they make for themselves or purchase to consume.

The United States emerges as a world leader in producing various goods and services and generates more than 20% of worldwide gross domestic product (GDP 国内生产总值). The economy is marked by steady growth, low unemployment and inflation, and rapid advances in technology.

Major Economic Sectors

From colonization till the beginning of the 20th century the United States was largely an agricultural nation with the majority of Americans working on farms.

The Industrial Revolution that started in England in the 18th century, along with a lot more factors, including the introduction of the factory system, mass production, technological advancement and the emergence of the bank and the corporation, contributed to the rapid growth of American industry. In 1890, for the first time, the output of American factories exceeded that of American farms. By 1913 more than 1/3 of the world's industrial production came from the United States.

New technologies and computerization enabled many of the newly rising industries to be highly automated. Fewer workers were needed in traditional industries and entirely new kinds of jobs and businesses are created. Since the mid-20th century, services (such as health care, entertainment, and finance) have grown faster than any other sector of the economy. A large proportion of the workforce entered service industry in recent years.

Free Enterprise & Government Role

U.S. economy is mainly a free enterprise system, in which the person whose money is at risk is the person who gets to decide. Wrong or right, foolish or wise, whoever has the gold makes the rules. Government plays a limited role in economic decision making in the open, market economy; the initiative for production and consumption decisions lies with individuals or companies.

However, business in this free enterprise system is not purely free. The consolidation of small businesses into increasingly powerful corporations in the 20th century spurred government intervention to protect small industries and consumers. Every year, the government produces thousands of pages of new laws and regulations, often spelling out in painstaking detail what businesses can do and cannot.

The federal government provides services and goods that the market cannot provide effectively, such as national defense, assistance programs for low-income families, and interstate highways and airports. It regulates private industry in two ways — economic regulation and social regulation. Economic regulation seeks primarily to control prices. Social regulation, on the other hand, promotes objectives that are not economic — such as workplace safety or environmental protection.

Business Forms

Most businesses in the United States operate under one of three different legal forms: sole proprietorships, partnerships, or corporations.

In a sole proprietorship, the proprietor owns and operates the business and collects all profits. Most small businesses in the United States are individual proprietorships. They are flexible and respond quickly to changing economic conditions, since owners can make decisions quickly without having to consult others.

Another kind of business is the partnership. According to the Census Bureau, there are more than one million American partnerships. Two or more people operate a partnership. They generally reach a legal agreement to specify each member's rights and duties. Partnerships can end at any time and exist only as long as the owners are alive. They enable entrepreneurs to pool their talents, but serious disagreements constantly arise.

In the United States, most large businesses are organized as corporations. A corporation has legal standing itself. It is treated under the law as a distinct person, separated from its owners. Ownership in a corporation is divided into shares. The owner can trade his shares or keep them as long as the company is in business. A corporation may have a few major shareholders. Or ownership may be spread among the general public. As a result, corporations may survive the death of any particular owners and, thus, have an unlimited lifetime. Shareholders are paid in the form of dividends （股息） in return for their investments. A board of directors makes major corporate decisions and appoints top company executives. The directors might or might not hold shares in the corporation.

Facts

- New York City is the center of American financial, publishing, broadcasting, and advertising industries.
- Los Angeles is the most important center for film and television production.
- Detroit, known as the Motor City, serves as the historic center of the American automotive industry.
- Chicago is the world's most celebrated center of architecture innovation and a significant transportation hub.
- The San Francisco Bay Area and the Pacific Northwest are major centers for technology.
- The Midwest is a major area for manufacturing and heavy industry.
- The Southeast is known for its reliance on agriculture, tourism and lumber industry.

II Agriculture

American agriculture represents about 1% of annual GDP and feeds nearly 60% of the world's production. It assumes a vastness and diversity unmatched in most other parts of the world. American farmers have generally been successful in producing crops cheaply and in quantity. Although farm workers make up a small percentage of American workforce, less than 2 percent in 2004, the nation produces as much as half of the world's soybeans and corn for grain, and from 10 to 25 percent of its cotton, wheat, tobacco and vegetable oil.

Agricultural Regions

Nature is generous in giving the nation plenty of fertile soil, along with a moderate climate. Cultivated farmland accounts for 19 percent of the land area. Large areas of gently rolling land — especially in the eastern Great Plains — provide ideal conditions for large-scale agriculture. Rainfall is abundant over most areas of the country; rivers and underground water permit extensive irrigation where rainfall is not abundant.

The Central Plain of the Mississippi River system is the chief agricultural region, the "Barn of America." Each year this region produces a large quantity of corn, wheat, soybean, and to the south, rice and cotton.

Prune "Fruit of Life"
More than 70% of the world's Prune production is grown in California.

On the Atlantic Coast and in the Great Lake region, many of the farms, known as truck farms, are devoted to dairying, poultry and the growing of vegetables. Dairy farmers grow hay and corn as fodder (饲料) crops. Fruit farming in this region is also very popular.

The states to the west of Rockies now grow some wheat, barley, and sugar beets (甜菜). California is well-known for its large variety and huge quantity of fruits. The Great Central Valley of California is one of the most beautiful and productive agricultural regions of the world. It produces a full quarter of the nation's food supplies. Another important industry in the west is cattle ranching and sheep-raising.

Crops & Livestock

The United States is the world's largest producer of corn, soybeans, and sorghum. Corn is the most important of all American crops. "You cannot buy anything at all in a North American supermarket which has been untouched by corn…" Its annual product constitutes more than half the total grain output. It is mainly used for fodder and exportation, only a small fraction is used for food.

Soybean, the nation's second most valuable crop after corn, was discovered in China about 13,000 years ago. Not until the 18th century did the first American plant a soybean from China in American soil. During the 19th century, American farmers began cultivating the soybean, and now the US is the world's number one producer of the vegetable. American farmers grow soybeans for high-protein animal feed and for vegetable oil. Much of the soybean production goes to exports.

The United States ranks second in the production of wheat, oats, citrus fruits, and tobacco. It is also a major producer of sugar cane, potatoes, peanuts, cotton and beet sugar. Vegetables are grown widely in the United States. California is the leading vegetable producing state. Nuts grow on irrigated land in the Central Valley of California and in parts of southern California.

The United States ranks fourth in the world in cattle production and second in hogs.

Forestry

About 1/3 of the land area of the United States is covered with forests, and more than 240 million hectares is commercial forestland. There are mainly three forest areas: the Pacific Northwest; the South Atlantic and Gulf states; the Appalachian Highland and parts of the Great Lakes.

The United States leads the world in lumber production and is second in the production of wood for pulp and paper manufacture. These high production levels, however, do not satisfy all of the U.S. demand for forest products. It is the world's largest importer of lumber, most of which comes from Canada.

At the beginning of the 21st century, forestry accounted for less than 0.5 percent of the nation's gross domestic product (GDP), and less than 1 percent of the country's workforce was involved in the lumber industry. Nevertheless, forests represent a crucial resource for U.S. industry.

The state of Oregon is a leading manufacturer of lumber, wood, and pulp(纸浆) and paper products.

Fishing

In 2003 the United States had a commercial fish catch of 4.3 million metric tons. In most years, the United States ranks fifth among the nations of the world in weight of total catch, behind China, Peru, Chile, and Japan.

Marine species dominate U.S. commercial catches, with freshwater fish representing only a small portion of the total catch. Shellfish account for only one-sixth of the weight of the total catch but nearly one-half of the value; finfish represent the remaining share of weight and value. Alaska leads all states in both volume and value of the catch. Other leading fishing states, ranked by value, are Louisiana, Massachusetts, Texas, Maine, California, Florida, Washington, and Virginia.

Commercial fishing is often rough, dangerous, and physically demanding.

Important species caught in the New England region include lobsters, scallops, clams, oysters, and cod; in the Chesapeake Bay, crabs; and in the Gulf of Mexico, menhaden and shrimp.

Much of the annual U.S. tonnage of commercial freshwater fish comes from aquatic farms. The most important species raised on farms are catfish, trout, salmon, oysters, and crawfish. Mississippi leads all states in the production of catfish on farms.

III Mining & Manufacturing

Mining Industry and Major Mineral Products

The United States enjoys rich mineral deposits and abundant energy resources within its borders. Mining industry employs over 3 million people directly and indirectly and accounts for about 2 percent of annual GDP. The nation exports $26 billion worth of minerals and material produced from minerals each year. California is the largest producer of non-fuel minerals of any U.S. states.

The nation's three chief mineral products are fuels. In order of value, they are natural gas, petroleum, and coal.

American petroleum industry has been greatly influenced by Standard Oil founded by John D. Rockefeller in 1870. His company became the leading oil manufacturer in the United States during the late 1800s and early 1900s.

The US was the world's second largest coal producer after China, as of year 2004, and the third highest producer of copper and gold in 2005. The principal mining states of copper are Arizona, Utah, New Mexico, Nevada, and Montana. Other metals and minerals mined on a large scale in the U.S. include phosphate (磷酸盐), an important ingredient in fertilizers, silver, zinc (锌) and lead.

Manufacturing

The United States has large manufacturing industries, which employ about 12 percent of the nation's workforce and account for 14 percent of annual GDP. In 2003 the total value added by manufacturing was $1.9 trillion. Significant economic productivity occurs in a wide range of industries. The manufacture of machinery and transportation equipment (including motor vehicles, aircraft, and space equipment) represents a leading sector. Computer and telecommunications firms (including software and hardware) remain strong, despite a downturn in the early 21st century.

The Northeast, including the Great Lakes region and New England, was the nation's industrial core after independence. Though this area still has the greatest number of industrial firms, manufacturing has grown rapidly in other regions. Since 1947, the South's share of the nation's manufacturing workers increased from 19 to 32 percent, and the West's share grew from 7 to 18 percent.

In the North, manufacturing clusters in the Middle Atlantic and Northeast Central states. Located in this area are five of the top seven manufacturing states — New York, Ohio, Illinois, Pennsylvania and Michigan. Important products in this region include motor vehicles, fabricated metal products, and industrial equipment.

In the South, the greatest gains in manufacturing have been in Texas. In the west California was the leading manufacturing state in the late 1990s. It dominates the Pacific region which specializes in the production of transportation equipment, food products, and electrical and electronic equipment.

High-tech Industry

High-tech industry has been the fastest growing sector of American manufacturing. The largest component is electronics industry, especially the manufacture of computers, microchips, and telecommunications equipment.

The revenues generated by the overall U.S. electronics industry today exceed the combined revenues of all U.S. automobile, steel and chemical manufacturers. Most of these revenues are produced by less than ten companies, with IBM as the leader.

Silicon Valley has become a metaphor for all high tech businesses in the area. It is the southern part of the San Francisco Bay Area in Northern California, an area that radiates outward from Stanford University. Silicon refers to the high concentration of semiconductor and computer-related industries in the area; Valley refers to the Santa Clara Valley.

IV Finance & Insurance

Federal Reserve System

The Federal Reserve System, established by Congress in 1913, functions as a central bank for other banks and for the federal government.

All nationally chartered commercial banks are required by law to be members of the Federal Reserve System; membership is optional for state-chartered banks. In general, a bank that is a member of the Federal Reserve System uses the Reserve Bank in its region in the same way that a person uses a bank in his or her community. The Federal Reserve has the legal authority to make banks hold some of their deposits as reserves. These reserve funds are held in the Federal Reserve Bank.

The Federal Reserve System performs several important functions in the national economy.

- First, the branches of the Federal Reserve distribute paper currency in their regions. Dollar bills are actually Federal Reserve notes.
- Second, the regional Federal Reserve banks transfer funds for checks that are deposited by a bank in one part of the country but were written by someone who has a checking account with a bank in another part of the country.
- Third, the regional Federal Reserve Banks collect and analyze data on the economic performance of their regions, and provide the information for the national Federal Reserve System.

Federal Reserve Bank of New York on Liberty Street

Because the Federal Reserve System exercises so much influence over the U.S. economy, the chairman of the Federal Reserve Board is often considered one of the world's most powerful individuals. Ben S. Bernanke was sworn in on February 1, 2006, as Chairman and a member of the Board of Governors of the Federal Reserve System.

By far the most important function of the Federal Reserve System is controlling the nation's money supply and the overall availability of credit in the economy. It can increase the supply of money and the availability of credit by lowering the percentage of deposits that banks must hold as reserves at the Federal Reserve System, by lowering the discount rate, or by purchasing government bonds through open market operations. The Federal Reserve System can decrease the supply of money and the availability of credit by raising reserve ratios, raising the discount rate, or by selling government bonds.

Currency

More than 99 percent of the total dollar amount of paper money in circulation in the U.S. today is made up of Federal Reserve notes. The other small part of circulating currency consists of U.S. notes or legal tender notes still in circulation but no longer issued. The Federal Reserve System issues Federal Reserve notes through its 12 Federal Reserve Districts. The U.S. Mint, which makes all U.S. coins, was established by Congress in 1792 and became an operating bureau of the Treasury Department in 1873.

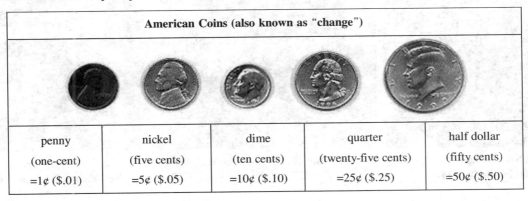

American Coins (also known as "change")				
penny	nickel	dime	quarter	half dollar
(one-cent)	(five cents)	(ten cents)	(twenty-five cents)	(fifty cents)
=1¢ ($.01)	=5¢ ($.05)	=10¢ ($.10)	=25¢ ($.25)	=50¢ ($.50)

62 | Understanding the United States

This is the First Bank of the United States, completed in 1797. Alexander Hamilton was the person behind starting it, back in 1791.

Banks

Banks safeguard money and valuables and perform their primary role in the financial system — provide loans, credit, and payment services. With the passage of the Financial Modernization Act in 1999, banks may also offer investment and insurance products.

Commercial banks, which dominate this industry, offer a full range of services for individuals, businesses, and governments. These banks come in a wide range of sizes, from large global banks to regional and community banks.

- Global banks are involved in international lending and foreign currency trading.
- Regional banks have numerous branches and automated teller machine (ATM) locations throughout a multi-state area that provide banking services to individuals.
- Community banks are based locally and offer more personal attention.
- In recent years, online banks have entered the market, with some success. However, many traditional banks have also expanded to offer online banking.

Banking in the 1980s and 1990s was a highly competitive business. Because of mergers and closures, the number of banks steadily declined while the number of bank offices increased.

Large banks in the U.S., in terms of assets, include Citibank and J.P. Morgan Chase & Co., headquartered in New York City; Bank of America and Wachovia/First Union, headquartered in Charlotte, North Carolina; and Wells Fargo, headquartered in San Francisco, California.

Citibank is the consumer and corporate banking arm of Citigroup. According to Forbes Global 2000, Citigroup is the world's largest company and the most profitable financial services firm.

JP Morgan Chase is a leader in investment banking and financial services for consumers, small business and commercial banking. JP Morgan Chase has its corporate headquarters in New York and its U.S. retail financial services and commercial banking headquarters in Chicago.

Stock Exchanges

A stock exchange is a corporation or mutual organization providing facilities for stock brokers to trade company stocks and other security. Stock exchanges also provide facilities for the issue and redemption of securities, as well as other financial instruments and capital events including the payment of income and dividends. The American Stock Exchange, located in Manhattan, is one

NYSE is housed in a 17-story building built in 1903

Bronze Bull, Symbol of Wall Street

The NASDAQ Screen in New York's Times Square

of the major exchange houses in the U.S.

The securities traded on a stock exchange include shares issued by companies, unit trusts (基金) and other pooled investment products as well as bonds. To be able to trade a security on a certain stock exchange, it has to be listed there. All of the companies in the list are large publicly-held companies which trade on major US stock exchanges such as the New York Stock Exchange and NASDAQ. The New York Stock Exchange (NYSE) is the largest in the world. By the late 1990s, it listed some 3,600 different stocks. The exchange has 1,366 members, or "seats," for buying and selling stocks for the public. NASDAQ is the largest electronic screen-based equity securities in the United States and the primary market for trading NASDAQ-listed stocks.

Insurance

Consisting of approximately 1600 life (life/health) and 3000 non-life (property/casualty) insurance and reinsurance companies (Reinsurance companies provide insurance for carriers 承保公司), the U.S. insurance industry is the world's largest insurance market, accounting for $736 billion or 34 percent of 1998's worldwide premiums (保险费) of $2.2 trillion. Over two million Americans work in the industry.

Insurance is sold either directly by insurers (direct insurers) or through the independent agency system, exclusive agencies, and brokers. According to the Insurance Information Institute, Americans paid 39,000 million dollars for homeowners insurance in 2003. Premiums for car insurance totaled 65,000 million.

In the United States, private insurers pay for about 40 percent of all health care costs. Medicare (医疗保险) is federal health insurance for people above the retirement age of 65. Medicaid (医疗补助) is federal and state health insurance for the poor. Workers who are injured on the job can receive workers compensation. States require employers to pay into this form of insurance. And workers who lose their jobs may collect unemployment insurance, for up to twenty-six weeks.

V Transportation, Tourism & Commerce

Transportation

Transportation-related businesses are an important part of the service industry. The U.S. is a nation on the move. Trucks, railroads, and ships carry goods to markets across the country. Commercial airlines, railroads, bus companies, and taxis transport tourists and commuters to their destinations. The U.S. transportation network spreads into all sections of the country, but the web of railroads and highways is much denser in the eastern half of the United States, where it serves the nation's largest urban, industrial, and population concentrations.

● *Travel by Road*

The backbone of the nation's transportation infrastructure is a network of high-capacity highways that connects the nation's principal cities. Over six million km of paved roads, the most in the world, are open to the public. Driving is the primary form of transportation in the U.S. The fastest and most convenient part of the U.S. highway system is the Interstate Highway, a high-speed, limited-access highway. Accounting for just one percent of U.S. highway mileage, the interstate system carries 21 percent of highway travel. While Interstate Highways usually receive substantial federal funding and comply with federal standards, they are owned, built, and operated by the states in which they are located.

- *Travel by Air*

Air travel is the preferred means of passenger travel for distances over 300 miles. The air transportation network in the U.S. includes over 200 domestic passenger and cargo airlines, a number of international carriers and approximately 15 thousand airports. In terms of passengers, 17 of the world's 30 busiest airports in 2004 were in the U.S., including the world's busiest, Hartsfield-Jackson Atlanta International Airport (ATL). In terms of cargo, in the same year, 12 of the world's 30 busiest airports were in the U.S., including the world's busiest, Memphis International Airport.

- *Travel by Train*

Americans often complain about the limited network and inconvenient schedules of train rides. Rail passenger travel has declined in importance since air transport dominates long-distance travel and the Interstate Highway makes intercity driving fast. Rail system has shifted emphasis toward freight.

- *Other Transportations*

Buses are a good option for urban or suburban transportation. The nation-wide carrier Greyhound Lines is the sole national provider of intercity bus service in the U.S.

Some U.S. cities still maintain extensive subways or commuter railways, including New York City, Washington, D.C., Chicago, and the San Francisco-Oakland area of California.

Several major seaports are in the United States; the three busiest are California's Port of Los Angeles and Port of Long Beach, and the Port of New York and New Jersey, all among the world's busiest. The interior of the U.S. also has major shipping channels, via the St. Lawrence Seaway and the Mississippi River.

Tourism

The United States has a large and lucrative (获利多的) tourism industry serving millions of international and domestic tourists. Tourists visit the U.S. to see natural wonders, cities, historic landmarks, and gambling venues (场所). Americans seek similar attractions, but also are attracted to recreation and vacation areas.

Congress laid the foundation of the National Park System in 1872 when it established

Castle Geyser Erupting — Yellowstone National Park

Castle Geyser major eruptions occur at intervals of nine to eleven hours apart. During the twenty minute water phase of the two-phase eruption, the water plume reaches heights of sixty to ninety feet. The water phase is followed by a forty minute steam phase. Occasionally Castle Geyser has a minor eruption, lasting only a few minutes. Following a minor eruption Castle Geyser does not become predicable again until after the next major eruption.

Yellowstone National Park, which is located primarily in the state of Wyoming, though it also extends into Montana and Idaho. The system now comprises some 380 areas of scenic, historic, or scientific interest totaling more than 84 million acres. Most national parks have a full range of facilities and offer a variety of outdoor activities.

Commerce

- *Retail Industry*

Retail is the second largest industry in the United States in terms of the number of establishments and the number of employees. The U.S. retail industry generates $3.8 trillion in retail sales annually, approximately $11,993 per capita (人均). The retail sector is also one of the largest worldwide.

● *Export & Import*

The United States believes in a system of open trade subject to the rule of law. Government refrains from actions specifically designed to hinder imports.

Trade balances were generally positive in most of the years after WWII. But under the influence of oil price shocks and the global recession in the 1970s, the United States experienced its first trade deficit of the 20th century in 1971. The U.S. trade deficit has continued to increase and reached a record $750 billion in 2006.

The United States mainly exports transportation equipment and electronic products and imports equipment goods, manufactured products and consumer goods. The country's five top export partners are Canada, Mexico, Japan, China and the United Kingdom. Its five top import partners are Canada, China, Mexico, Japan and Germany.

Wal-Mart, the world's largest retailer, was first on the 2008 Fortune five hundred list by revenue, with more than $378 billion (USD) in sales annually.

Chapter 5 Society and Culture

I Cultural Groups

What Is a Cultural Group?

A cultural group is made up of people who share the same behavior, belief, and language (people who share the same culture). In the United States, there are many cultural groups. Because they live in one country and are subject (服从于……的) to the same laws, together they form a society. The dominant or major culture group is British American. It is the most powerful and influential group whose people make up about 45% of the American population and control most of the national wealth and political powering of the nation. The minor groups are called subcultures (亚文化群体). Among them are Hispanic Americans (Spanish-speaking Americans), Native Americans, African Americans, Italian Americans, Asian-Americans, etc.

People in cultural groups do things in ways that are alike or similar. These are all kinds of behavior. People's behavior is how they act or what they do. The kinds of behavior a cultural group shares make a long list. Examples include how they dress, what they eat, where they live, and what entertainment they seek. You share many kinds of behavior with others in your culture group. Suppose you are talking to someone you don't know very well, how close would you stand to that person?

People in culture groups also share a common language. Language shows what is important in a culture. It shows how the people of a cultural group think. Languages most used in the United States other than English are listed below:

1. Spanish	2. German	3. Italian
4. polish	5. French	6. Yiddish 意第绪语(犹太人使用的国际语)
7. Swedish	8. Norwegian	9. Slovak 斯洛伐克语
10. Greek	11. Czech 捷克语	12. Hungarian 匈牙利语
13. Japanese	14. Portuguese	15. Dutch
16. Chinese	17. Russian	18. Lithuanian 立陶宛语
19. Native American languages	20. Ukranian 乌克兰语	

To get the idea of the number of people who speak these languages, look at the top three. Spanish is spoken as a first of second language by about 11 million Americans. German is spoken by about 4 million Americans. Italian is also spoken by about 4 million people in the US. At the bottom of the list, about 300,000 people speak different Native American languages. About 200,000 Americans speak Ukrainian.

Sharing belief represents an important aspect of culture. People in cultural groups share many beliefs. Different cultures often have different values. Many people in the United States consider freedom of religion an important value. They also value equality, the right to peaceful protest and the right of each person to get an education.

Social Theories of Immigration

Sociologists have identified a few major theories on how newly arrived immigrants integrate themselves into American society. Over time all new immigrants adopt some aspects of American culture and add something new.

- **Melting Pot Theory**

According to the Melting Pot Theory, peoples from various cultures come to America and contribute aspects of their culture to create a new, and unique (独特的) American culture. The result is that contributions from many cultures are indistinguishable (不能区别的) from one another and are effectively "melted" together.

- **Salad Bowl Theory**

According to the Salad Bowl Theory, there are times when newly arrived immigrants do not lose the unique aspects of their cultures like in the melting pot model; instead they retain them. Much like the ingredients (成分) in a salad, the unique characteristics of each culture are still identifiable (可以确认的) within the larger American society, yet contribute to the overall makeup of the salad bowl. This theory is also referred to as pluralism (多元化的社会形态).

- **Assimilation** (同化)

Assimilation is the concept that eventually immigrants or their descendants adopt enough of the American culture, while they may retain aspects or traditions of their cultural heritage, and they are uniquely identifiable as "American."

Introduction of Some Cultural Minority Groups

1. Hispanics

Hispanic Americans, also called Latinos, are Americans of Spanish-speaking descent. Many Hispanic Americans are the descendants of Mexican people who lived in the Southwest when it became part of the United States. Almost all other Hispanic Americans or their ancestors migrated to the United States from Latin America. Hispanics can be white, black or Latin-American Indian, or a mixture of races. Experts who study communities point out that Hispanics from different countries often have different cultures.

Today, more than 35 million people of Hispanic descent live in the United States. They make up the largest minority group in the country. Hispanics are also the fastest-growing U.S. minority, as a result of a high birth rate and continuing immigration. Most Hispanic Americans speak English but continue to use Spanish as well. As Spanish-speakers, they form the largest language minority in the United States. In addition to their language, Hispanic Americans have preserved many other traditions of their homelands. The foods, music, clothing styles, and architecture of these countries have greatly influenced U.S. culture.

Like other minorities, Hispanic Americans have suffered from discrimination in jobs, housing, and education. Many Hispanics are in lower-paid jobs. The most important obstacle to Hispanic success in the labor market is their low education. Hispanics have the highest school dropout rate of any major racial and ethnic group. One of the reasons is that for many Hispanic American children, Spanish is the only language spoken at home. When children reach school age, they speak and understand only Spanish, but the language in their school is English.

Today, especially in the southwest, this is changing. More and more lessons are taught in both Spanish and English. This means that children can learn in their first language. In this way, they won't fall behind in their lessons. Then, little by little, they can learn English as their second language. When this happens, they will become bilingual.

Most Hispanic Americans are members of the Roman Catholic Church. Many of the cities in the American Southwest are named after Catholic Saints. San Francisco, Santa Barbara, and San Antonio are examples.

Hispanic families tend to have large numbers of children, who typically occupy the center of family life. They are taught to respect the elders, to appreciate family unit, and to assume family responsibilities. Imbued (被灌输) with strong family values, Hispanics generally have lower divorce rates compared with Anglos. The exception is Puerto Ricans, who have a much higher rate as a result of a greater prevalence of poverty. Hispanics are also likely to marry outside their group, especially among those with a higher socioeconomic status. Generally, the longer their families have been in the United States, the higher their rates of interethnic (不同种族间的) marriage.

The three largest Hispanic groups in the United States are Mexican Americans, Puerto Ricans and Cuban Americans.

Mexican Americans, or Chicanos (奇卡诺人) are the largest Hispanic group in the United States today, comprising approximately 66% of the U.S. Hispanic population. They live in the Southwest, such as New Mexico, California, and Texas. Puerto Rican Americans are the second largest Spanish-speaking group. They live in the Eastern states, such as New York (Puerto Rico is an island southwest of Florida. All Puerto Ricans have been United States citizens since 1917). Cuban Americans are in Florida. Cubans came to the United States in large numbers in the 1960s. Many Cubans settled in Florida. Most of them have become United States citizens.

Educational Attainment by Hispanic Origin in 2000
(Population 25 years and over)

Hispanic Origin	Educational Attainment			
	Less than 9th grade	9th to 12th grade (no diploma)	High school graduate	More than high school
Hispanic	27.3%	15.7%	27.9%	29.1%
Non-Hispanic White	4.2%	7.3%	34.1%	54.4%

2. African Americans

The most numerous minority in America is the black people whose ancestors were from Africa. The first blacks arrived in Jamestown Va. in 1619, a year before the Pilgrims arrived on the Mayflower, as indentured servants (契约佣工). But very soon after 1619 blacks were brought to colonies as slaves.

The African American population is represented throughout the country, with the greatest concentrations in the Southeast and mid-Atlantic regions, especially Louisiana, Mississippi, Alabama, Georgia, South Carolina, and Maryland. African Americans have a long history in the United States. Some African American families have been in the United States for many generations; others are recent immigrants from places such as Africa, the Caribbean, or the West

Indies.

Today African Americans make up about 12% percent of the American population—almost 35 million individuals, according to the 2000 U.S. Census. The Census Bureau projects that by the year 2035 there will be more than 50 million African American individuals in the United States, comprising 14.3 percent of the population.

African Americans' Contribution to America and to the World

Memory of Indigo

From their earliest presence in North America, Africans and African Americans have contributed literature, art, agricultural skills, foods, clothing styles, music, language, social and technological innovation to American culture. The cultivation and use of many agricultural products in the U.S., such as yams, peanuts, rice, okra (秋葵), sorghum (高粱), grits (粗玉米粉), watermelon, indigo dyes (a blue dye obtained from plants or made synthetically 靛青), and cotton, can be traced to African and African American influences.

African American music is one of the most pervasive cultural influences in the United States today. Blues, jazz, gospel (黑人福音音乐), hip-hop, R&B (Rhythm and Blues 蓝调音乐), funk (乡土音乐), rock-and-roll, soul (爵士灵歌), techno and many other contemporary American musical forms originated in black communities and have been incorporated into the popular music of almost every culture in the world. The names of famous and influential African American musicians are too numerous to mention. African Americans have also had an important role in the world of dance.

In 1967, civil rights attorney Thurgood Marshall became the first black Supreme Court Justice. In 1989, Douglas Wilder became the nation's first black Governor. In 2001, General Colin Powell became the first black Secretary of State, and his successor, Condoleezza Rice, became the first black woman Secretary of State in 2005. Obama is the first African-American to be nominated by a major American political party for president and is the first African American to hold the office in 2008.

African Americans made great contribution during the wars. In the Revolutionary War (1776—1783), 10,000 African Americans—some of them slaves—served in the continental armies, participating in the defeat of the British at several famous battles. In the American Civil War (1861—1865) 186,000 soldiers of African descent served in 150 regiments of the Union army, making up about almost 13% of the Union army's combat manpower. Another 30,000 were in the Navy. In four years of fighting, it is believed that 37,000 African Americans died in battle or from disease. Twenty Black soldiers were awarded the Congressional Medal of Honor for their services in the Civil War. During America's participation in World War I (1914—1918), 367,000 Black Americans served their country both at home and overseas. Eventually they would comprise 11% of the troops that went overseas. In World War II, 1,154,720 black soldiers served in the armed forces, 3,902 African-American women answered the call of their country and enrolled in the Women's Army Auxiliary Corps.

3. Native Americans

Native American inhabitants were incorrectly called Indians by early European explorers who mistakenly believed that they had reached India. Unfortunately, the mistake persists to this day, and many people still refer to all Native Americans as Indians. Even some Native Americans call themselves Indians, but most of them prefer using their legitimate tribal names.

How many Native Americans are there in the USA?

The Bureau of the Census counts anyone an Indian who declares himself or herself to be an Indian. According to the 2000 US Census, those who identify only as American Indians and Alaska Natives (AI/AN) constitute 0.9 percent of the United States population, or approximately 2.5 million individuals, up from 1.8 million in 1990. The Census Bureau projects (预计) modest growth by AI/AN communities in the next few decades, topping 5 million individuals by the year 2065 and comprising 1.1 percent of the population. The greatest concentrations of AI/AN populations are in the West, Southwest, and Midwest, especially in Alaska, Arizona, Montana, New Mexico, Oklahoma, and South Dakota. There are 569 federally recognized AI/AN tribes, plus an unknown number of tribes that are not federally recognized. Each tribe has its own culture, beliefs, and practices.

Five Groups of Indians

The American Indians can be divided into five groups, according to where they lived.

★ The Pacific Northwest Indians lived near the forests along 2,000 miles of coastline from southern Alaska to northern California. Basically, the Indians of this region were maritime people.

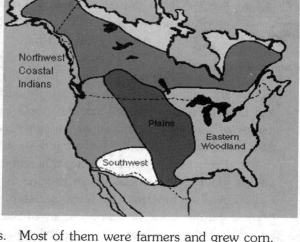

★ The Great Basin / California Indians settled between the Rocky Mountains and the California coast.

★ The Plains Indians came from other areas after being pushed out by other tribes. In their old lands, they had been farmers. In the plains they became buffalo hunters.

★ The Southwest Indians live in a hot, dry region, partly desert and partly canyons and cliffs. Most of them were farmers and grew corn, beans and squash, which they called the "Three Sisters." There were two groups of Native Americans in the southwest region. One group was the Pueblo, Hopi and Zuni ; another group was the Navajo (纳瓦霍人[美国最大的印第安部落]) and Apache (阿帕契族).

★ The Eastern Woodland Indians inhabited a wide area in the eastern part of the United States that extended eastward from the Mississippi River, through the Great Lakes region, to the Atlantic Ocean. The inhabitants in this region were forest dwellers. Living and learning from the land, they learned to use wood and wood products as the basic raw materials in their lives. The Woodland Indians tended to live near water in the forested areas. Many of the Eastern Woodland tribes were not nomadic and relied on agriculture to provide food for the tribe. Being expert farmers, farming was the main focus of their lives.

It was not until 1924 that the Indians, more often called Native Americans in urban areas, become United States citizens, with the right to vote.

Navajo Indian Reservation, Arizona, USA

Indian Reservation

In the United States there are about 300 reservations today, which were areas that the United States government set up for native tribes that had lost their lands to European settlers. Some reservations are larger than American states. The largest is the Navajo Reservation of some 16 million acres of land in Arizona, New Mexico, and Utah. Many of the smaller reservations are less than 1,000 acres with the smallest less than 100 acres. The United States Interior Department's Bureau of Indian Affairs supervises these territories. Tribes on reservations have limited self-rule. On reservations, much of their way of life is like that of other people in the US. But the cultures are still alive. They are being passed on to new generations with pride. Children are learning their people's customs and beliefs. They learn traditional tribal songs and dances. They study ancient arts and crafts. And they, in turn, will pass this culture on to their children.

Some tribes have managed to profit from the natural resources on their lands and the inhabitants have become rather wealthy. On other reservations, the residents exploit thriving tourist businesses. Unfortunately, many tribes own few resources and the inhabitants of their reservations live in poverty. Because of isolation, unemployment and lack of business development, third world living conditions are typical of many reservations:

Economic Conditions

Generally, American Indians do not enjoy the same economic and educational success as other Americans. Indian communities lag far behind mainstream American communities in many important social indicators. A continuing study by Harvard University says American Indians generally earn less money and have more unemployment than other Americans. In Gallup, the unemployment rate for Indians was 12.0%; for all Gallup residents, it was 5.8%. One fourth of the Native American families live below the poverty level. The median income of households where the householder reported they were American Indian and Alaska Native is $33,627. (The median income is based on a three-year average from 2003 to 2005.)

75% of the population earn less than $7,000 per year.
45% live below the poverty level.
The average unemployment rate is 45%.
Unemployment on some reservations is 90%.

The study says they also have higher rates of disease and die younger than other American groups. The average life expectancy is around 50 years—about 20 years below that for the country as a whole.

Alcohol mortality is 627% greater for Indian people than all other races combined.
Tuberculosis (肺结核) is 533% greater than all other Americans.
Diabetes (糖尿病) is 6.8 times greater than all other Americans.
Fetal (胎儿的) Alcohol Syndrome is 33 times higher than for other Americans
One in six adolescents has attempted suicide-four times that of all other teenagers
Homicide (杀人行为) is 63% greater than all other Americans

The Bureau of Indian Affairs provides education services to almost 50,000 Indian children in 184 schools. Experts from Harvard say college attendance rates among the Indian population is half that of the general population. But, they also say the situation is improving; the number of Native American Indians seeking higher education has more than doubled in the last twenty years.

In the past, education was a tool used by the US government to suppress Indian identity. Native children were forcibly separated from their families and forced to attend boarding schools where they were not allowed to speak their native language, were forced to wear European clothing and eat European food. Many children were subjected to harsh physical punishment and emotional abuse. Partly as a result of this legacy (传统), Native American educational achievement lags far behind the nation as a whole.

> Only 52% of Native American youth finish high school.
> Only 17% attend college and only 4% graduate.

Harvard researchers also say that the American Indian economy has grown at three times the national rate since the 1980s. Some of the improvement has come from expansion of the American Indian gambling industry. More than two hundred Indian tribes have legalized gambling on their reservations. Native American casinos and other gambling businesses earn more than twenty billion dollars each year.

Family and Traditional Native American Values

Various Native American families shared certain characteristics. For example, infants were born in special birth huts. During the years of breastfeeding, mothers refrained from sex. Physical punishment was rarely used to discipline children, who were taught instead by example. Children learned adult roles at an early age, so that most girls were married between ages 12 and 15, and boys between ages 15 and 20. Most tribes were monogamous (一夫一妻的). Only a few allowed men to have two wives or engage in extramarital (婚外的) sex when their wives were pregnant or breastfeeding. Extended family networks predominated, and kinshipties and obligations to relatives flourished.

Today this traditional family life has disappeared among many Native Americans. Between 1870 and 1930 the US government embarked (发动) on a program of destroying the Native Americans to the white culture by, among other things, sending their children to white-run boarding schools. Today only a small minority of Native Americans have successfully resisted assimilation (同化) and kept alive their traditional values, particularly the importance of kinship ties and obligations. The rest have either adopted white values completely or adopted a mixture of white and Indian values. Compared with other ethnic groups, Native Americans suffer from higher rates of poverty, alcoholism, suicide, and other problems, all of which create severe difficulties for many Native Americans.

Native Americans' Contributions

★ Food

Nearly half the world's leading food crops can be traced to plants first domesticated by Indians. Native farmers introduced Europeans to a cornucopia (丰富) of nutritious plants, including potatoes, peanuts, manioc (木薯), beans, tomatoes, sunflowers, and yams (sweet potatoes). Maize, or corn, was by far the most significant contribution, now grown on every continent except Antarctica (南极洲).

★ Medicine

Native Americans have also made contributions to medicine. For hundred of years, they have used plant roots and herbs as medicines. Many of these were used by European settlers. What we know today as aspirin is made from an ingredient the Native Americans got from willow bark. At least 59 drugs, including quinine (奎宁, 用来治疗疟疾) have come from wild plants that Native Americans used as medicines. They developed pain medicines, birth-control drugs, and treatment for scurvy (坏血病). Many Indian medicines became part of what we call "folk medicine" and almost 200 plants used by Indians are now listed in the official *United States Pharmacopeias Dictionary of Drug Names* (药典).

★ Outdoor Gear (装备)

Parkas (毛皮风雪大衣)

[Today's ski jackets owe their origins in part to hooded coats Eskimo women fashioned from

layers of skins.]
    Snow Goggles (防雪盲的墨镜)
    Moccasins (鹿皮鞋)
★ Government
    While the US was still a colony of England, the Iroquois (易洛魁族) tribes had an advanced form of government. It was called the League (联盟) of the Iroquois, or the Six Nations. There were representatives from all the tribes. They took part in decisions that affected more than one tribe. The United States government has representatives from each state as the League had representatives from each tribe.
★ Sports
    The rubber ball came from native South Americans. Native North Americans invented lacrosse (长曲棍球), a popular sport.
★ Other things

We now use many other things the Native Americans invented, and we often use the native names for them:
    Canoe, hammock (吊床), toboggan (平底雪橇) are few examples. We also use rubber, pipes, and cigars—all from the Native Americans.

English Language
    The English language is full of Native American words. Many animals are called by their native names. *Chipmunks* (花栗鼠), *skunks* (臭鼬), *moose* (驼鹿), and *raccoons* (浣熊) are just a few such animals. Many tree names, such as *hickory*, *catalpa* (梓树), and *pecan* (美洲山核桃树), are also Native American. Words as different as *powwow* (巫师), *hurricane* (飓风), and *totem* (图腾) have their roots in Native American languages.
    States, towns, lakes and rivers all over America have Native American names. *Ohio*, *Chicago*, *Kansas*, *Miami*, *Milwaukee* (密尔沃基), *Mississippi*, *Omaha* (奥马哈, 美国内布拉斯加州东部一城市), *Peoria*, *Seattle* (西雅图), *Tallahassee* (塔拉哈西, 佛罗里达州首府), *Tucson* (图森), *Tulsa* (塔尔萨), and *Wichita* are Native American names. So are *Canada* and *Mexico*.
    We can see Native Americans' contributions in almost every part of American life. These contributions have not stopped. There are still things we can learn from Native Americans. Today, some traditional Native American values, such as respect for the land, may be especially important to all people.

Native American Proverbs and Wisdom

With a long history, rich culture, and more than 300 spoken languages, the wisdom of Native American tribes has been passed down through the centuries.

＊Don't be afraid to cry. It will free your mind of sorrowful thoughts.

＊Day and night cannot dwell together.

＊It is better to have less thunder in the mouth and more lightning in the hand.

＊They are not dead who live in the hearts they leave behind.

＊All plants are our brothers and sisters. They talk to us and if we listen, we can hear them.

＊Tell me and I'll forget. Show me, and I may not remember. Involve me, and I'll understand.

＊When we show our respect for other living things, they respond with respect for us.

＊If we wonder often, the gift of knowledge will come.

＊Most of us do not look as handsome to others as we do to ourselves.

* What is life? It is the flash of a firefly (萤火虫) in the night. It is the breath of a buffalo in the wintertime. It is the little shadow which runs across the grass and loses itself in the sunset.

* When you were born, you cried and the world rejoiced. Live your life so that when you die, the world cries and you rejoice.

* Those who have one foot in the canoe, and one foot in the boat, are going to fall into the river.

* The weakness of the enemy makes our strength.

* A good soldier is a poor scout (侦探).

* We will be known forever by the tracks we leave.

* Do not judge your neighbor until you walk two moons in his moccasins.

* There is nothing as eloquent as a rattlesnake's tail.

* Our first teacher is our own heart.

* Everyone who is successful must have dreamed of something.

* All who have died are equal.

* What the people believe is true.

* You can't wake a person who is pretending to be asleep.

* Beware of the man who does not talk, and the dog that does not bark.

* He who would do great things should not attempt them all alone.

* If a man is as wise as a serpent (像蛇一样地灵巧), he can afford to be as harmless as a dove.

* A brave man dies but once, a coward many times.

* When a man moves away from nature his heart becomes hard.

4. The Amish People (德裔宾州人,指17、18世纪移居美国宾夕法尼亚州的德国和瑞士人的后裔)

Quick Facts about Amish people

Amish	
Total population	198,000 (2000 est.)
Regions with significant populations	United States, especially Pennsylvania, Ohio, Indiana, Maryland, Kalona and Iowa; Ontario, Canada
Language	Pennsylvania Dutch, English, Swiss German
Religion	Anabaptist Christianity
Related ethnic groups	Swiss German

The Amish are found primarily in the United States and Ontario, Canada that are known for restrictions on the use of modern devices such as automobiles and telephones. Most Amish today descend primarily from 18th century immigrants. The Amish are united by a common Swiss-German ancestry, language, and culture, and marry within the Amish community.

The Amish separate themselves from civil society for religious reasons: They do not join the military, draw (nor are forced into) Social Security, or accept any form of assistance from the government, and many avoid insurance. Most speak a German dialect known as Pennsylvania Dutch (or Pennsylvanian German, 宾州德语,德裔宾州人使用的一种混有英语的德语方言), which the Amish call Deitsch.

In 2000, Raber's Almanac estimated there were 198,000 Old Order Amish in the United States. Ohio has the largest population (55,000), followed by Pennsylvania (47,000) and Indiana (37,000). Significant populations are also seen in Michigan, Iowa and Wisconsin. With an average of seven children per family, the Amish population is growing rapidly, and new settlements are constantly being formed to obtain sufficient farmland.

History

The Amish were a small religious group in Europe. Most were German-speaking farmers. The Amish had strong religious beliefs. These beliefs were often different from the teachings of the main churches in Europe. Thus, the Amish were forced to move many times. There were few places in Europe where they were safe. Some of them were drowned, burned, or tortured. So the Amish came to the New World. They came for the freedom to practice their religious beliefs. They wanted to lead a hardworking farming life. They would not dress in fancy clothes or live in fancy homes. They felt they were different from other groups. Over the years, Amish culture has changed very, very slowly. Today, many things the Amish do and believe have not changed since these people first came to North America.

The Amish are an important people to study. By studying the Amish, we can examine some values that may have an important meaning for the people of the United States today.

Some Important Amish Values

1) Amish people lead a simple farming life and are self-sufficient. They grow much of the food they eat. They build their own buildings. They sew their own clothes. For transportation, they use mostly horses. They could keep going even if all the machines stopped. Their way of life depends on skills many people in the United States have now lost.

2) Amish people waste very little and their way of living does not harm the environment. It does not foul the air and rivers.

3) The Amish help one another often and believe in a close family and community life. They look out for one another in times of need.

The Amish have kept all these old ways. They have chosen to do so even though most of the world is changing around them.

The Front Room—The Old Order Amish of Lancaster County hold church services in their homes. In this room, the wooden benches are arranged in preparation for an Amish service. Grandfather clock, wood stove, oil lamp, hand-woven rag rugs indicate a 19th-century home

Life Style

The Amish keep pretty much to themselves. They don't want too many ideas from the outside to change their way of life.

★ Amish House

The Amish are friendly people. But unless you are Amish, you probably won't get to see the inside of their houses.

Amish homes are large with several rooms opening into one large room where they hold church. The houses are furnished very simply with benches on which the families sit to eat their meals. The floors are bare and the windows are covered with plain colored cloth. You won't see pictures of the family, as the Amish don't like their pictures taken.

★ Appearance and Attire (服饰)

Symbolic of their faith, Amish clothing styles encourage humility and separation from the world. The Amish choose to wear simple homemade clothes. For some groups buttons are prohibited, allowing only hooks and eyes (钩眼) to keep clothing closed. The restriction on buttons is attributed in part to their former association with military uniforms, and also to their potential for serving as opportunities for vain display. Straight-pins are often used to hold articles of clothing together. In all things, the aesthetic value is "plainness": Clothing should not call attention to the wearer by cut, color or any other feature. Prints such as florals, stripes, polka-dots (圆点花纹图案), etc. are not encouraged in Amish dress.

Amish women usually wear modest long dresses in a solid, plain color such as blue. Aprons are often worn, usually in white or black, at home and always worn when attending church. A cape (披肩) which consists of a triangular shape of cloth is usually worn beginning around the teenage years and pinned into the apron. They wear black stockings and flat shoes. In the cold months, they wear black wool shawls.

They never cut their hair, and wear it in a braid (发辫) or bun (圆髻) on the back of the head concealed with a small white cap or black bonnet. Clothing is fastened with straight pins or snaps (摁扣). Amish women are not permitted to wear make-up or jewelry.

An Amish girl (left) and a married Amish woman in Lancaster County, Pennsylvania

Amish men in general wear straight-cut dark suits and coats without collars, lapels (翻领), or pockets. Trousers never have creases (折缝) or cuffs (翻边) and are worn with suspenders. Belts are forbidden, as are sweaters, neckties and gloves. The Amish call such things "modern" or sometimes "English". They wear solid-colored (纯色) shirts, black socks and shoes, and black or straw broad-brimmed (宽边的) hats in the warmer months and black felt (毡) hats in the colder months. Men's shirts fasten with conventional buttons, but their suit coats and vests fasten with hooks and eyes.

Typically, single Amish men are clean-shaven and married men grow a beard; a long beard is the mark of an adult Amish man. Mustaches are generally not allowed, because they are seen as symbols of both pride and the military.

From left to right—1) Amish Suspenders; 2) Amish Haircut; 3) Clean shaven; 4) When a man is married he grows a beard by tradition. Different ages are judged by the grayness of the beard.

The Amish & Modern Technology

Many Amish are renowned for their avoidance of modern technologies. Electricity, for instance, is viewed as a connection to the "World," the "English," or "Yankees" (the outside world). There are no electrical wires going into the large, neat Amish farms. (Today some Amish have built new homes with electrical wiring. But the wiring is not connected.) The Amish don't believe in using electricity or machines that run by electrical power. They think it would complicate the Amish tradition of a simple life, and introduce individualist competition for worldly goods that would be destructive of community.

They know what television is. They shop in stores that are brightly lit and air-conditioned. But they don't want such things as electric lights, TV sets, radios, computers etc for themselves. Nor do they want other Amish to buy TV sets. If an Amish person does buy a TV. Other Amish people stop talking to the person. This is a very big cost to an Amish.

Twelve-volt batteries are acceptable. Most twelve-volt power sources cannot generate enough current to power what are viewed as worldly, modern appliances such as televisions or hair dryers. Many communities will allow gas powered farm equipment, but only if they are pushed by a human or pulled by a horse. Electric generators can only be used for welding (焊接), recharging batteries, and powering milk stirrers. Many Amish families have non-electric versions of vital

From left to right right—1) They use kerosene for their stoves and refrigerators; 2) Some Amish families have this type washing machines run by generators ; 3) Covered Bridge and Amish Buggy

appliances, such as kerosene-powered refrigerators.

The telephone is despised (厌恶) because it eliminates face-to-face communication. Most Amish use telephones with the restriction that the phone booth must be far enough from the house, as not to make its use too convenient. Almost all of these Amish phones have voice mail service from the phone companies. The Amish will also use trusted English neighbors as contact points for passing on family emergency messages.

It is not proper for an Amish person to own a car, truck, or tractor. They think if you own something, it is usually because you want it. The Amish don't want motor vehicles. They drive in horse-drawn buggies (小型轻便的一匹马拉的四轮马车), which are usually painted black. The Amish will hire drivers for visiting family, monthly grocery shopping, commuting to the workplace off the farm, though this too is subject to local regulation and variation. Hiring a taxi is forbidden on Sundays.

Farming

An average Amish farm consists of approximately 80 acres. Until a few years ago, farming was their only way of life. In the Amish country, everybody goes to bed early and gets up early. Work on the farm starts at sunrise or before. Main crops raised by Amish in Lancaster County, Pennsylvania in order of acreage, are corn, hay, wheat, tobacco, soybeans, barley, potatoes, and other vegetables. Farmers also grow various grasses for grazing. Farming is done with horse-drawn equipment with metal wheels (no rubber tires).

Amish Family Life

The family is the most important social unit in the Amish culture. The immediate family (直系亲属), the extended family (大家庭), and the church district form the building blocks of Amish society. Amish parents typically raise about seven children, but ten or more children are not uncommon. About 50 percent of the population is under 18 years of age. A person will often have more than 75 first cousins and a typical grandmother will count more than 35 grandchildren. Members of the extended family often live nearby, across the field, down the lane, or beyond the hill. Youth grow up in this thick network of family relations where one is rarely alone, always embedded in a caring community in time of need and disaster. The elderly retire at home, usually in a small apartment built onto the main house of a homestead. Because the Amish reject government aid, there are virtually no families that receive public assistance. The community provides a supportive social hammock from cradle to grave.

Amish marry Amish—no intermarriage is allowed. When the young people are married they are often given a parcel of land by one of the fathers from which they are to make their living. Divorce is not permitted and separation is very rare. In some settlements, Amish babies are born in hospitals, but they are also born at home or in local birthing centers. Weddings and funerals occur at home. There are frequent trips to other settlements or even out of state to visit relatives and friends. But for the most part the Amish world pivots (以……为轴心而转动) on local turf (活

动范围). When someone dies, the body is sent from the undertaker (殡仪事业经营人) to the home with 3 hours. The body is viewed in an upstairs room in a home made casket (棺材).

These Amish families are gathered together to eat a traditional meal

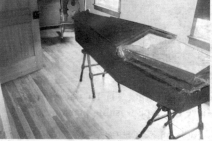

A home made casket

Amish society is patriarchal (父权制的). Although school teachers are generally women, men assume the helm (支配地位) of most leadership roles. Chores are clearly divided by sexual role in the Amish home—the man usually works on the farm, while the wife does the washing, cleaning, cooking, and other household chores. The Amish women are good cooks, but only cook plain foods raised on their farms, such as pork, beef, chicken, turkey, and garden vegetables. Although husband and wife preside over distinct spheres of domestic life, many tasks are shared. The isolated housewife is rarely found in Amish society. The husband holds spiritual authority in the home but spouses have considerable freedom within their distinctive spheres.

The wedding season is a festive time in Amish life. Coming on the heels of the harvest, weddings are typically held on Tuesdays and Thursdays from late October through early December. The larger communities may have as many as 150 weddings in one season. Fifteen weddings may be scattered across the settlement on the same day. Typically staged (举行) in the home of the bride, these joyous events may involve upwards of 350 guests, two meals, singing, snacks, festivities, and a three-hour service. The specific practices vary from settlement to settlement.

Young persons typically marry in their early twenties. A couple may date for one to two years before announcing their engagement. The wedding day is an enormous undertaking (任务) for the bride's family and for the relatives and friends who assist with preparations. According to custom, the day before the wedding the groom decapitates (将……斩首) several dozen chickens. The noontime wedding menu includes chicken roast—chicken mixed with bread filling, mashed potatoes, gravy (肉汁), creamed celery, pepper cabbage, and other items. Desserts include pears, peaches, puddings, dozens of pies, and hundreds of cookies and doughnuts.

The three-hour service—without flowers, rings, solos, or instrumental music—is similar to an Amish worship service. The wedding includes congregational (教堂会众的) singing, prayers, wedding vows, and two sermons (布道). Four single friends serve the bride and groom as attendants: no one is designated maid of honor (女傧相) or best man. Amish brides typically make their own wedding dresses from blue or purple material crafted (手工制作) in traditional styles. In addition to the groom's new but customary black coat and vest, he and his attendants often wear small black bow ties (领结). Several games, snacks, and singing follow the noon meal. Young people are paired off somewhat randomly for the singing. Following the evening meal another more lively singing takes place in which couples who are dating pair off—arousing considerable interest because this may be their first public appearance. Festivities may continue until nearly midnight as guests gradually leave. Some guests, invited to several weddings on the same day, may rotate between them.

Newly married couples usually set up housekeeping in the spring after their wedding. Until then the groom may live at the bride's home or continue to live with his parents. Couples do not take a traditional honeymoon, but visit relatives on weekends during the winter months. Several newlywed couples may visit together, sometimes staying overnight at the home of close relatives. During these visits, family and friends present gifts to the newlyweds to add to the bride's dowry (嫁妆), which often consists of furniture. Young men begin growing a beard, the functional equivalent of a wedding ring, soon after their marriage.

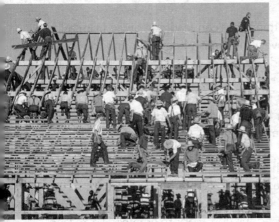

Mutual Assistance

The practice of mutual aid distinguishes Amish society. Although the Amish own private property, they have long emphasized mutual aid as a Christian duty in the face of disaster and special need. There is much neighboring in the Amish community, and helping each other is the most common way of socializing. The Amish carry no life or property insurance; the church assists in cases of major loss. Large families generally give assurance of care for the elderly. Retired Amish farmers do not receive Social Security.

In an Amish community, people often do things together. Amish people help one another to build barns (called barn raisings 帮助邻居建造谷仓的聚会), butch animal for food. For weddings, worship services, and other large get-togethers, relatives and neighbors help the host family prepare the food. When a family member has an accident or is sick, neighbors come to help at the farm. They may also help care for the children. Amish adults often lend money to young farming couples. When Amish men and women grow old, they stay on the farm and do whatever work they can.

Language

Most Amish are trilingual. They speak a dialect of German called Pennsylvania Dutch at home; they use High German at their worship services; and they learn English at school. They speak English when they deal with anyone who is not Amish.

The dialect is the Amish native tongue and should not be confused with the Dutch language of the Netherlands. Originally a German dialect, Pennsylvania Dutch was spoken by Germanic settlers in southeastern Pennsylvania. The folk pronunciation of the word German, Deutsche, gradually became Dutch in English, and eventually the dialect became known as Pennsylvania Dutch. Even the Amish who live outside of Pennsylvania speak the Pennsylvania German dialect.

Amish Schools & Education

The Amish do not value formal education. Although they pay school taxes, the Amish have fought to keep their children out of public schools. In 1972, the Supreme Court handed down a landmark unanimous (一致同意的) decision that exempted (免除) the Old Order Amish and related groups from state compulsory attendance laws beyond the eighth grade.

Amish children generally attend school through the eighth grade, often in their own church-funded one-room schoolhouses. Usually there is one teacher and two

Amish children play in the schoolyard

teacher's helpers. They are usually Amish. They take turns teaching the various age groups in the class. About 30 children, from 6 to 16 years of age, share one classroom. The one-room schoolhouse teaches Amish children that they are all one group. Even though there is a big difference in sizes and ages, they are all Amish.

The subjects most Amish children study are:

Bible (in German)   Reading (English)   Spelling (English)   Penmanship (English)
Arithmetic   Geography   Amish history

The schoolbooks they use are written especially for Amish children. Some states have let the Amish set up vocational schools to follow the eighth grade. In the vocational schools, they learn more about farming and caring for the home.

Higher education is considered unnecessary and something that can lead one away from a life of simplicity and humility as well as the community. However, the Amish know the importance of informal education. The Amish society is, in itself, a trade-school of sorts. It trains their young people in the fine art of craftsmanship in fine cabinetry (细木家具), furniture, carpentry, farming, and last but not least homemakers. An Amish girl that is twelve years old knows how to cook a meal for a whole crew of workers, and the young Amish boy knows a farming operation by the time he is a teenager. The Amish have no unemployment among them.

● *Asian-Americans*

Asian Americans are Americans of Asian descent. They or their ancestors came from Asian countries, particularly Cambodia, China, India, Indonesia, Japan, Korea, Laos, Pakistan, the Philippines, Thailand, and Vietnam. According to the 2000 US Census, those who identify only as Asian-American comprise 3.6 percent of the American population, approximately 10 million individuals. Asian-American populations are generally concentrated in the western states, the Northeast, and parts of the South. The states with the greatest concentration of Asian Americans are Hawaii, California, Washington, New Jersey, and New York.

Many Asian-Americans are successful partly because they already had good skills when they came to the US. They had completed university studies in science, medicine, law or engineering. And they had been successful in their jobs in their homelands. A number of Asians who became very successful arrived in the 1940s and 1950s. Experts say three Asian traditions best explain the success of Asian-Americans: education, hard work, and family. Education is considered the key to success. Asian-American parents expect their children to be the best students. Asian-American young people spend more time studying than other American students. They are supposed to show gratitude toward parents by bringing parents reflected glory by achieving success in educational and occupational activities.

Compared with other US families, Asian American families—particularly Chinese, Japanese, Korean, and Vietnamese—generally are more stable, having lower divorce rate, fewer female-headed households, fewer problems with child-rearing), greater family solidarity, and stronger kinship associations.

The influence of this traditional culture declines with succeeding generations of Asian Americans. Thus, among the third or fourth generations, the family has fewer children, and divorce is more common. But the Confucian culture still has a residual (残留的) effect on many Asian American families, making them more stable than other US families.

● *Chinese-Americans*

The largest group of Asian-Americans is the Chinese-Americans, comprising of 22.4% of the Asian American population. They constitute 1.2% of the United States as a whole. In 2006, the Chinese American population numbered approximately 3.6 million. As a whole, Chinese American populations continue to grow at a rapid rate due to immigration. However, they also on average have birth rates lower than those of White Americans, and as such their population is aging relatively quickly.

The first Chinese immigrants arrived in 1820 according to US government records. Most Chinese immigration to the US took place between 1850 and 1880 during the California Gold Rush, but they were banned from emigrating between 1885 and 1965 when the ban on Asian immigrants was lifted by the *Immigration Reform and Control Act.*

Chinese Americans retain many aspects of their ancient culture, even after having lived here for several generations. For example, their family ties continue to be remarkably strong. Members of the family lend each other more support and also practical help when necessary. From a very young age, children are imbued (灌输) with the old values and attitudes, including respect for their elders and a feeling of responsibility to the family. This helps to explain why there is so little juvenile delinquency among them. The high regard for education which is deeply imbedded (植根于) in Chinese culture, and willingness to work very hard to gain advancement, are other noteworthy characteristics of theirs. This explains why so many descendants of uneducated laborers have succeeded in becoming doctors, lawyers, and other professionals.

Next to the Chinese-Americans, the Japanese-Americans form the second largest group. There are also Filipinos, South Koreans, Vietnamese, Laotians, and Cambodians.

Basic American Values

Historically, the United States has been viewed as "the land of opportunity," attracting immigrants from all over the world. The opportunities they believed they would find in America and the experiences they actually had when they arrived nurtured this set of values. Six basic values have become "traditional" American values.

Three represent traditional reasons why immigrants have been drawn to America: the chance for individual freedom, equality of opportunity (机会均等), and material wealth (物质财富). In order to achieve these benefits, however, there were prices to be paid: self-reliance, competition, and hard work. In time, these prices themselves became a part of the traditional values system.

● *1. Individual Freedom and Self-Reliance*
Individual Freedom

The earliest settlers came to the North American continent to establish colonies that were free from the controls that existed in European societies. They wanted to escape the controls placed on their lives by kings and governments, priests and churches, noblemen and aristocrats. To a great extent, they succeeded. In 1776, the British colonial settlers declared their independence from England and established a new nation, the United States of America. In doing so, they overthrew the king of England and declared that the power to govern would lie in hands of the people. In 1789, when they wrote the Constitution for their new nation, they separated church and state so that there would never be a government-supported church. This greatly limited the power of the church. Also, in writing the Constitution, they expressly (明白地) forbade titles of nobility to ensure that an aristocratic society would not develop.

The historic decisions made by those first settlers have had a profound effect on the shaping of the American character. By limiting the power of the government and the churches and eliminating a formal aristocracy, they created a climate of freedom where the emphasis was on the individual. The United States came to be associated in their minds with the concept of individual freedom. This is probably the most basic of all the American values.

Self-reliance

There is, however, a price to be paid for the individual freedom: self-reliance (自力更生).

Individuals must learn to rely on themselves or risk losing freedom. This means achieving both financial and emotional independence from their parents as early as possible, usually by age 18 or 21. It means that Americans believe they "stand on their own two feet."

This strong belief in self-reliance continues today as a traditional basic American value. It is perhaps one of the most difficult aspects of the American character to understand, but it is profoundly important. Most Americans believe that they must be self-reliant in order to keep their freedom. If people are dependent, they risk losing freedom as well as the respect of their peers (同龄人). In order to be in the mainstream of American life—to have power and /or respect—individuals must be seen as self-reliant. Although receiving financial support from charity, family, or the government is allowed, it is never admired.

● **2. Equality of Opportunity and Competition**
Equality of Opportunity

The second important reason why immigrants have traditionally been drawn to the United States is the belief that everyone has a chance to succeed here. They have felt that because individuals are free from excessive political, religious, and social controls, they have a better chance for personal success. Of particular importance is the lack of a hereditary aristocracy (世袭的贵族统治).

Because titles of nobility were forbidden in the Constitution, no formal class system developed in the United States. In the early years of American history, many immigrants chose to leave the older European societies, because they believed that they had a better chance to succeed in America. The hopes and dreams of many of these early immigrants were fulfilled in their new country. The lower social class into which many were born did not prevent them from trying to rise to a higher social position. Many found that they did indeed have a better chance to succeed in the United States than in the old country. Because millions of these immigrants succeeded, Americans came to believe in equality of opportunity.

When the Americans say they believe in equality of opportunity, they mean that each individual should have an equal chance for success. Americans see much of life as a race for success. For them, equality means that everyone should have an equal chance to enter the race and win. It helps ensure that the race for success is a fair one and that a person does not win just because he or she was born into a wealthy family, or lose because of race or religion. This American concept of "fair play" is an important aspect of the belief in equality of opportunity.

Competition

There is, however, a price to be paid for this equality of opportunity: competition. If much of life is seen as a race, then a person must run the race in order to succeed; a person must compete with others. Americans match their energy and intelligence against that of others in a competitive contest for success. People who like to compete and are more successful than others are honored by being called winners. On the other hand, those who do not like to compete and are not successful when they try are often dishonored by being called losers.

The pressures of competition in the life of an American begin in childhood and continue until retirement from work. Learning to compete successfully is part of growing up in the United States. The pressure to compete causes Americans to be energetic, but it also places a constant emotional strain on them. When they retire (traditionally at the age of 65), they are at last free from the pressures of competition. But then a new problem arises. They may feel useless and unwanted in a society that gives so much prestige to those who compete well. This is one reason why older people in the United States do not have as much honor and respect as they have in other, less competitive societies. In fact, any groups of people who do not compete successfully—for whatever reason—do not fit into the mainstream of American life as well as those who do compete.

● 3. *Material Wealth and Hard Work*
Material Wealth

The third reason why immigrants have traditionally come to the United States is to have a better life. Because of its incredibly abundant natural resources, the United States appeared to be a "land of plenty" where millions could come to seek their fortunes. Of course, most immigrants did not "get rich overnight", and many of them suffered terribly, but the majority of them were eventually able to achieve the economic success they wanted. The phrase "going from rags to riches (从赤贫一跃而成巨富)" became a slogan for the great American Dream (the belief that everyone in the US has the chance to be successful, rich and happy if they work hard). Because of the vast riches of the North American continent, the dream came true for many of the immigrants. They achieved material success and they became very attached to material things. Material wealth became a value to the American people.

Placing a high value on material possessions is called materialism, but this is a word that most Americans find offensive. To say that a person is materialistic is an insult because they feel that this unfairly accuses them of loving only material things and of having no religious values. In fact, most Americans do have other values and ideals. Nevertheless, acquiring and maintaining a large number of material possessions is of great importance to most Americans. Why is this so?

Probably the main reason is that material wealth has traditionally been a widely accepted measure of social status in the United States. Because Americans rejected the European system of hereditary (世袭的) aristocracy and titles of nobility, they had to find a substitute for judging social status. The quality and quantity of an individual's material possessions became an accepted measure of success and social status. Moreover, the Puritan work ethic associated material success with godliness (信仰).

Hard Work

Americans have paid a price, however, for their material wealth: hard work. The North American continent was rich in natural resources when the first settlers arrived, but all these resources were undeveloped. Only by hard work could these natural resources be converted into material possessions, allowing a more comfortable standard of living. Hard work has been both necessary and rewarding for most Americans throughout their history. Because of this, they came to see material possessions as the natural reward for their hard work.

Each one of these values has a rich and complex heritage. Despite the transformations (变化) in America's life-styles, these core values have endured. Virtually all Americans share them; compositely, they make American culture distinctive. The United States is a nation of immense diversity geographically, ethnically, economically, politically. And yet, this tiny cluster (组) of values holds Americans together as a single people and nation.

● *Ways of Life*
The Impact of Consumerism

Consumption drives the American economy. The American lifestyle is often associated with buying things, such as clothing, houses, electronic gadgets (小器具), and other products, as well as with leisure time. As advertising stimulates the desire for updated or improved products, people increasingly equate (等同) their well-being with owning certain things and acquiring the latest model.

Living Patterns

A fundamental element in the life of the American people was the enormous expanse of land

This sweet little house looks to be in remarkably good condition considering it was built 106 years ago and is one of the first homes to be built in the area.

available. The idea of possessing land was deeply etched into American cultural patterns and national consciousness. The desire for residential privacy has remained a significant feature of American culture. Americans are committed to living in private dwellings set apart from neighbors. Despite the rapid urbanization that began in the late 19th century, Americans insisted that each nuclear family be privately housed and that as many families as possible own their own homes.

Shopping Malls

As cities became more densely populated, Americans moved to the suburbs. As a result of Americans choosing to live in the suburbs, a distinctly American phenomenon developed in the form of the shopping mall. Modern malls emphasize consumption as an exclusive activity. The shopping mall, filled with department stores, specialty shops (专卖店), fast-food franchises (特许加盟店), and movie multiplexes (复合式建筑), has come to dominate retailing (零售业), making suburban areas across America more and more alike. In malls, Americans purchase food, clothing, and entertainment in an isolated environment surrounded by parking lots.

Food and Cuisine

The United States has rich and productive land that has provided Americans with plentiful resources for a healthy diet. American food also grew more similar around the country as American malls and fast-food outlets tended to standardize eating patterns throughout the nation, especially among young people. Nevertheless, American food has become more complex as it draws from the diverse cuisines that immigrants have brought with them.

★ Food originated in America

Traditional American cuisine has included conventional European foodstuffs such as wheat, dairy products, pork, beef, and poultry. It has also incorporated products that were either known only in the New World or that were grown there first and then introduced to Europe. Such foods include potatoes, corn, tomatoes, peppers, pumpkin and other squashes, codfish (鳕鱼), molasses (糖蜜), and peanuts. The first pumpkin pie was baked in New Haven with English techniques in 1796. Apple pie is considered such a quintessential (精粹的) American dessert that it inspired the saying, "as American as apple pie." Chili in the form of meat hash (大杂烩) or stew with peppers started in the southwest in the 1800s. In 1977 Chili was declared the state food of Texas. George Crum invented potato chips in 1853 in Saratoga Springs, New York.

Other things include:
1. Coca-Cola, 1886
2. Fig Newton, 1891
3. Cream of Wheat, 1893
4. Juicy Fruit gum, 1893
5. Chili powder, 1894
6. Shredded (细条) coconut, 1895
7. Heinz started marketing pickles (腌渍品) and preserves, 1896
8. Grape Nuts cereal, 1897

Pumpkin pie with orange marmalade and Apple Pie

9. The hot dog and the cone for ice cream debuted (初次登场) at the St. Louis World's Fair in 1904. Also in the same year, we got Dr Pepper (中文名称常译作:樂倍、澎泉、胡椒博士、派珀博士等,是美国 Dr Pepper/Seven Up (七喜) 公司生产的一种焦糖碳酸饮料), and banana split (香蕉船).

10. Hamburger buns and Life Savers (candy), 1912
11. French dip sandwich, 1918
12. Egg cream and Wonder Bread in the 1920s (Despite its name, the egg cream contains neither eggs nor cream. The basic ingredients are milk, seltzer 苏打水, and chocolate syrup).
13. A&W Root Beer, 1922
14. Lenders bagels (百吉饼;硬面包圈), 1927
15. Kool-Aid, 1927
16. Po' Boy sandwich, 1929
17. Bisquick, 1930
18. Toll House cookies, 1930
19. Twinkies, 1930
20. Miracle Whip introduced by Kraft in 1933
21. Sunsweet prune juice, 1933
22. V8 Juice, 1933
23. Waldorf salad, 1933 (沃尔多夫色拉:用生苹果丁、芹菜丝、碎核桃肉、蛋黄酱拌成的色拉)

From left—Fig Newton/Grape Nuts cereal/Dr Peppe /banana split/ Life Savers

From left—French dip sandwich; Egg cream; Lenders bagels; Kool-Aid; Po' Boy sandwich; Bisquick; Toll House cookies; Twinkies; Waldorf salad

★ Food introduced by immigrants

By the late 19th century, immigrants from Europe and Asia were introducing more variations into the American diet. American cuisine began to reflect these foreign cuisines, not only in their original forms but in Americanized versions as well.

Immigrants from Japan and Italy introduced a range of fresh vegetables that added important nutrients as well as variety to the protein-heavy American diet. Germans and Italians contributed new skills and refinements to the production of alcoholic beverages, especially beer and wine. Some imports became distinctly American products, such as hot dogs, which are descended from German wurst, or sausage. Spaghetti and pizza from Italy, especially, grew increasingly more American and developed many regional spin-offs. Americans even adapted chow mein from China into a simple American dish.

America's foods began to affect the rest of the world—not only raw staples such as wheat and corn, but a new American cuisine that spread throughout the world. American emphasis on convenience and rapid consumption is best represented in fast foods such as hamburgers, French fries, and soft drinks. By the 1960s and 1970s fast foods became one of America's strongest exports as franchises for McDonald's and Burger King spread through Europe and other parts of the world, including China. By the late 20th century, Americans had become more conscious of their diets, eating more poultry, fish, and fresh fruits and vegetables and fewer eggs and less beef.

Dress

In many regions of the world, people wear traditional costumes at festivals or holidays. Americans, however, do not have distinctive folk attire (服装) with a long tradition. American dress is derived from the fabrics and fashions of the Europeans who began colonizing the country in the 17th century. Early settlers incorporated some of the forms worn by native peoples,

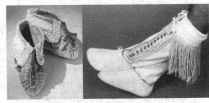

Moccasin

USA 1971—Levi's jeans

such as moccasins (鹿皮鞋) and garments made from animal skins, but in general, fashion in the United States adapted and modified European styles.

Despite the number and variety of immigrants in the United States, American clothing has tended to be homogeneous (相似的), and attire from an immigrant's homeland was often rapidly exchanged for American apparel (装饰).

American dress is distinctive because of its casualness. American style in the 20th century is recognizably more informal than in Europe. American informality in dress is such a strong part of American culture that many workplaces have adopted the idea of "casual Friday," a day when workers are encouraged to dress down from their usual professional attire. For many high-tech industries located along the West Coast, as well as among faculty at colleges and universities, this emphasis on casual attire is a daily occurrence, not just reserved for Fridays.

Although European designs remain a significant influence on American tastes, American fashions more often come from popular sources, such as the school and the street, as well as television and movies. In the last quarter of the 20th century, American designers often found inspiration in the imaginative attire worn by young people in cities and ballparks, and that worn by workers in factories and fields. Blue jeans are probably the single most representative article of American clothing. They were originally invented by tailor Jacob Davis, who together with dry-goods salesman Levi Strauss patented the idea in 1873 as durable clothing for miners. By the late 1970s, almost everyone in the United States wore blue jeans, and youths around the world sought them.

II American Education

A Brief Introduction

Education has always been a great concern for Americans. When the Puritan settlers in Massachusetts came to the New World, they brought with them a belief that education was fundamental to religion and to service for the commonwealth (国民整体). Even before the American Revolution, several famous colleges were set up. The Boston Latin School was found in 1635 and Harvard College in 1636.

Following the lead of the settlers in New England, the American colonies set up schools, academies, and colleges by the hundreds all through the colonial period. By the time of the American Revolution, public schools, charity schools (慈善学校), church schools, and academies were teaching children, and nine colleges scattered through the American wilderness, among these colleges were College of William and Mary in Williamsburg, Virginia in 1639 and Yale in New Haven, Connecticut in 1701.

Since the US Constitution mentions nothing on education, all educational matters are left to individual states, the Federal government has no power to make laws in the field of education; it can give financial help but not order. In America, there is

Christopher Wren Building (1695—99) of College of William & Mary, was the oldest academic building in use in America.

not one but 50 educational systems. Each state has an educational administration, not subject (隶属于) to federal control, and the state authorities lay down general principles concerning the organization of schools and such matters as the ages of compulsory (义务的) education. Schools are managed by local community boards of education, whose members are elected. Most schools are run on taxes levied (征收) by local districts and states.

As early as 1853, the state of Massachusetts passed the first compulsory school attendance law. By 1918, all states had laws requiring children to receive at least primary education. Today, most states have passed laws extending compulsory education to the age of 16.

In America, education is carried out at various levels, which are mainly divided into elementary education, secondary education, and higher education.

Elementary and Secondary Education

Elementary and secondary education covers 12 years from age 6 through 18. The most popular pattern is 8-4 (8 years for elementary school and 4 years for high school). Other common patterns include 6-2-4 (2 years for junior high and 4 years for senior high school), 6-3-3 ,4-4-4, and 6-6. All the states have laws that require children to go to school, generally until the age of 16, unless they are seriously handicapped. In addition, the elementary school offers five-year-olds a year of kindergarten, usually half-day sessions (授课时间), before they have formal instruction in reading and writing in the first grade.

Third Grade Elementary School Class Recites the Pledge of Allegiance to the American Flag Every Morning

At elementary stage, nearly all the teachers are women, mostly married. The atmosphere is usually very friendly, and the teachers have accepted the idea that the important thing is to make the children happy and interested. Courses for children include reading, arithmetic, and language arts such as creative writing, spelling, and handwriting, and there are also social courses (such as history, geography, and civics〔公民学〕of government), science, art and music. They can also learn cooking and manual skills such as carpentry and sewing. Children can do physical exercises on the playground or in gymnasiums.

Currently, there are nearly 58,000 public elementary schools and 21,000 public secondary schools in the US, with a student body of 40.3 million. Another 5.7 million attend private schools. Elementary and secondary education is free and compulsory. The total financial support for public schools is approximately 185 billion dollars a year.

A pupil goes to high school automatically after finishing his elementary school education. There is no entrance exam. High schools are made up of comprehensive, academic, vocational (职业的) and technical schools with somewhat different tasks. Comprehensive high schools provide both academic and vocational education; academic high schools only aim to prepare students for college; vocational and technical ones generally provide for a variety of occupations and vocations though some are specialized in a single vocational or technical area.

A typical high school curriculum includes almost all the subjects for elementary schools, but is more specialized. Many high schools offer dozens and sometimes hundreds of electives.

Higher Education

Higher education in the United States began with the founding of Harvard College in 1636. In the past years, it has developed into a big enterprise with a very complex system of undergraduate study and graduate study.

According to a survey in 1994, there are all together 3,595 institutions of higher education in the US. Slightly more than half of all institutions of higher education are privately supported, many of them by religious groups. The total funding for higher education was about 100 billion

Harvard Campus, 1828

dollars a year.

There are 12.5 million students in higher education, 78% of whom attend public institutions, although there are more private institutions than public ones. Many of the top universities in the US are private universities. The top 10 universities are all private ones. They are:

Harvard University, Princeton University, Yale University, Massachusetts Institute of Technology (MIT), California Institute of Technology, Duke University, Stanford University, University of Pennsylvania, Dartmouth University and Washington University in St. Louis.

There are different types of institutions. Two-year College was originally called "junior college," but now it is called "community college." Most community colleges are public institutions supported by both state and local taxes; so tuition for these schools is much lower than that at the state universities. It serves as a bridge which connects secondary schools and universities.

Four-year College is another type of institution, which is called a "Liberal arts college" or "college of arts and science." Its curriculum is confined to humanities, social and behavioral sciences and the natural sciences.

An American university is an institution which is more comprehensive and complex than any other kind of US higher educational establishment. A university may have several colleges within it and its curriculum is broader and deeper. Compared with four-year colleges, universities are generally larger in enrollment, with better libraries, more research work, and the teachers with higher doctorates. Significant differences can be seen in their quality. Famous universities such as Harvard (below), Yale, Princeton, Columbia, and MIT in the east, as well as Stanford and Berkeley in the west coast, are usually among the best research universities.

The cost of a college education has doubled within the last 15 years and tripled within the last thirty. A typical college now charges about 3,000 dollars a year for room, board (膳食费用), and tuition. The student attending a private Eastern college spends at least 3,500 dollars and probably closer to 5,000 a year, including tuition, housing, food, books and personal expenses. In the west, a student attending a state college in rural area may get by on 1,500 dollars a year. State colleges

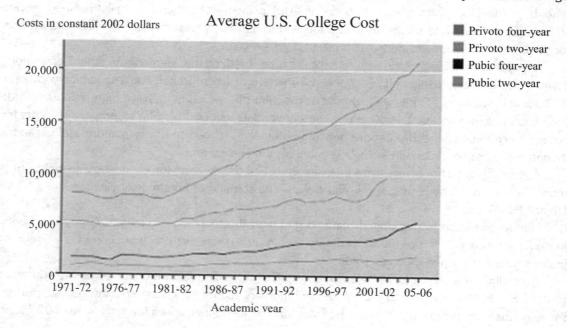

and universities have rather low tuition fees (ranging from about 60 to 450 dollars) for state residents. Financial help is available from many sources. Each year college students receive more than 300 million dollars in monetary assistance, including scholarships, loans, and part-jobs.

American colleges and universities offer three main categories of degrees: bachelor, master, and doctorate or Ph. D. After earning a bachelor's degree, students can go to graduated schools to study for a master or doctor degree. There are two ways for students to get the master's degree.

Oldest College Graduate Age 95

One requires a thesis paper, which counts for a certain number of credits that usually constitute part of the degree program. Another one requires no thesis paper, but more credits in the process of study. And an oral or written examination may also be asked for the degree. A master's degree requires from one to three academic years of study beyond the bachelor's degree. A doctorate degree normally takes at least three years beyond the master's. To earn a Ph. D in almost every field, a student has to accumulate enough class credits: pass comprehensive written and oral examinations in his specialty, known as the preliminary or qualifying exams; produce a long research paper called thesis or dissertation that makes an original contribution to his or her field of study; and pass examinations in one or two foreign languages.

Introduction to Some Famous Universities

● *Harvard University*

Harvard College was established in 1636 and was named for its first benefactor, John Harvard of Charlestown. Harvard was a young minister who, on his death in 1638, left his library and half his estate to the newly established institution.

Harvard is the oldest institution of higher learning in the United States. Eight presidents of the United States (John Adams, John Quincy Adams, Theodore and Franklin Delano Roosevelt, Rutherford B Hayes, John F. Kennedy, George W. Bush and Barack Obama) were graduates of Harvard. Its faculty has produced 40 Nobel laureates. The US News & World Report ranks Harvard at No 1 in its rating for America's best universities for the year 2005.

● *Yale University*

Yale's roots can be traced back to the 1640s, when colonial clergymen led an effort to establish a college in New Haven to preserve the tradition of European liberal education in the New World. This vision was fulfilled in 1701 when the charter was granted. In 1718 the school was renamed "Yale College" in gratitude to the Welsh merchant Elihu Yale, who had donated the proceeds (收益) from the sale of nine bales (大包) of goods together with 417 books and a portrait of King George I.

Yale University comprises three major academic components: Yale College (the undergraduate program), the Graduate School of Arts and Sciences, and the professional schools.

International students have made their way to Yale since the 1830s, when the first Latin American student enrolled. The first Chinese citizen to earn a degree at a Western college or university came to Yale in 1850. Today, international students make up nearly 9 percent of the undergraduate student body, and 16 percent of all students at the university. The university began admitting women students at the graduate level in 1869 and as undergraduates in 1969.

Yale College was transformed, beginning in the early 1930s, by the establishment of residential colleges ([美] 住宿学院). Taking medieval English universities such as Oxford and Cambridge as its model, this distinctive system divides the undergraduate population into twelve separate colleges of approximately 450 members each, thereby enabling Yale to offer its students

Branford Court, typical of Yale's enclose courtyards, provides space for planned and spontaneous residential college activities.

both the intimacy of a small college environment and the vast resources of a major research university. Each college surrounds a courtyard and occupies up to a full city block, providing a congenial (适意的) community where residents live, eat, socialize, and pursue a variety of academic and extracurricular (课外的) activities. Each college has a master and dean, as well as a number of resident faculty members known as fellows (校务委员会委员), and each has its own dining hall, library, seminar rooms, recreation lounges, and other facilities.

Today, Yale has matured into one of the world's great universities. Its 11,000 students come from all 50 American states and from 108 countries. The 3,200-member faculty is a richly diverse group of men and women who are leaders in their respective fields.

Yale's 260 buildings include contributions from distinguished architects of every period in its history. Styles range from New England Colonial to High Victorian Gothic, from Moorish (摩尔人风格的) Revival to contemporary. Yale's buildings, towers, lawns, courtyards, walkways, gates, and arches comprise what one architecture critic has called "the most beautiful urban campus in America."

● *Massachusetts Institute of Technology (MIT)*

MIT is probably one of the most famous universities in the world. But did you know its founder, William Barton Rogers, apparently never received a degree? In 1853, he moved to Boston, where he enlisted (获得) the support of the scientific community to create an institution for technical and scientific education. It was largely through his efforts that the Massachusetts Institute of Technology was born in 1861.

Today, the Institute has more than 900 faculty and 10,000 undergraduate and graduate students. It is organized into five Schools—Architecture and Planning, Engineering, Humanities, Arts, and Social Sciences, Management, and Science—and the Whitaker College of Health Sciences and Technology. Fifty-nine current or former members of the MIT community have won the Nobel Prize. The *US News & World Report* ranks MIT—along with Stanford University and Duke University—at No. 5 in its rating for America's best universities for the year 2005.

● *Princeton University*

Princeton University is a private research university located in Princeton, New Jersey. The school is one of the eight universities of the Ivy League and is considered one of the Colonial Colleges.

Princeton provides undergraduate and graduate instruction in the humanities, social sciences, natural sciences, and engineering, though it has traditionally focused on undergraduate education. Founded in 1746 at Elizabeth, New Jersey, as the College of New Jersey, it was moved to Newark in 1747, then to Princeton in 1756 and renamed Princeton University in 1896. Princeton was the fourth institution of higher education in the US to conduct classes. The university, unlike most American universities that were founded at the same time, did not have an official religious affiliation. At one time, it had close ties to the

Presbyterian Church, but today it is nonsectarian and makes no religious demands of its students.

Princeton University has been and is home to a renowned group of scholars, scientists, writers, chief justices, and statesmen who include four United States presidents, two of whom, James Madison and Woodrow Wilson, graduated from the university. Grover Cleveland was not an alumnus but served as a trustee, and John F. Kennedy spent his freshman fall at the university before leaving due to illness and later transferring to Harvard College. Additionally, First Lady Michelle Obama graduated from Princeton.

From 2001 to 2008, Princeton University was ranked first among national universities by *US News & World Report* (USNWR). After one year at second place in 2009, Princeton returned to the number one spot in 2010, sharing that honor with Harvard University. It has been ranked fifth among top 50 for Natural Sciences by THES, and 8th among world universities by *THES—QS World University Rankings*. This last source also ranked the university third in North America, behind Harvard and Yale.

● *University of California, Berkeley*

The roots of the University of California went back to the gold rush days of 1849, when the drafters of the states constitution required the legislature to encourage by all suitable means the promotion of intellectual, scientific, moral and agricultural improvement of the people of California. The university that was born nearly 20 years later—on March 23, 1868—was the product of a merger (合并) between the College of California (a private institution) and the Agricultural, Mining, and Mechanical Arts College.

Among other things, the university is credited with the isolation of the human polio (脊髓灰质炎) virus and the discovery of all artificial elements heavier than uranium (铀). Eighteen members of the Berkeley faculty have been awarded Nobel Prizes for these and subsequent discoveries, as well as in literature and economics.

● *Stanford University*

Leland Stanford Junior University, commonly known as Stanford University (or simply Stanford), is a private university. Located between San Francisco and San Jose (圣何塞,美国加利福尼亚西部一城市) in the heart of Silicon Valley, Stanford University is recognized as one of the world's leading research and teaching institutions. Stanford was founded by railroad magnate (巨头) and California Governor Leland Stanford and his wife, Jane Stanford. It is named in honor of their only child, Leland Stanford Jr. The University officially opened on October 1, 1891, to 559 students, with free tuition and 15 faculty members. Stanford University is governed by a board of trustees (董事会), in conjunction with (与……协力) the university president, provosts (教务长), faculty senate, and the deans of the various schools.

Stanford has been coeducational since its founding. However, between approximately 1899 and 1933, there was a policy in place limiting female enrollment to 500 students and maintaining a ratio of three males for every one female student. By the late 1960s the "ratio" was about 2:1 for undergraduates and much more skewed (倾斜) at the graduate level, except in the humanities. As of 2005, undergraduate enrollment is split nearly evenly

Main Quad
As the architectural center of campus, Stanford's Main Quad (方庭)contains the university's first buildings, constructed between 1887 and 1891.

between the sexes, but male enrollees outnumber female enrollees about 2:1 at the graduate level.

The schools of stanford include the School of Humanities and Sciences, School of Engineering, School of Earth Sciences, School of Education, Graduate School of Business, Stanford Law School and the Stanford University School of Medicine. stanford enrolls approximately 6,700 undergraduates and 8,000 graduate students. The university has approximately 1,700 faculty members. The largest part of the faculty (40 percent) is affiliated (与……有关系) with the medical school, while a third serve in the School of Humanities and Sciences. Stanford built its international reputation as the pioneering Silicon Valley institution through top programs in business, engineering and the sciences.

- *California Institute of Technology*

The California Institute of Technology (commonly referred to as Caltech) is a private research university located in Pasadena, California. The Institute maintains a strong emphasis on the natural sciences and engineering, and operates and manages NASA's neighboring Jet Propulsion(喷气推进) Laboratory. Caltech is a small school, with only about 2100 students (about 900 undergraduates and 1200 graduate students), but it is ranked number 2 in the world according to Global University Ranking and in the top ten universities worldwide by metrics (测量) such as Science Watch, Nobel Prizes, and general university rankings.

For the core curriculum, students are required to take five terms of math, two terms of chemistry, and a term of biology, as well as two terms of laboratory classes.

Caltech has a relatively low four-year graduation rate, compared to most leading US universities. This rate is currently about 80 percent, despite the fact that entering students have consistently higher average test scores than any other university or college, as indicated by the major college rankings. On the other hand, almost all students major in science or engineering, fields that traditionally suffer low graduation rates. In any case, the situation has improved

recently; approximately 90 percent of entering students graduate in six years or less, compared to a substantially smaller fraction in the 1960s and 70s.

You may have run into the work of past Caltech scientists without even knowing it. For example, if you take Vitamin C to prevent a cold, you can thank Linus Pauling, the Caltech chemist who discovered the nature of the chemical bond in 1930 (his ideas about vitamins came later). Pauling won the Nobel Prize for chemistry in 1954 and the Nobel Peace Prize in 1962.

III American Literature

Americans started writing soon after the first European settlers arrived in the 1600s. After that, American literature had been greatly influenced by the European culture for a long period. It was not until America's independence, did Americans realize that they need national literature strongly, and American literature began to develop. The Civil War was a watershed in the history, after which American literature entered a period of full blooming. Like the flowers of spring, there were suddenly many different kinds of writing at the same time. Romantics, which emphasized individualism and intuition (直觉) and Transcendentalism (超验主义：一种文

学和哲学运动) represented by Emerson came out into being. They have given depth and strength to American literature, and accelerated the forming of High Romantics. But due to the influence of Civil War, the American society was in a turbulent situation. The writings about local life, critical realism and unveiling the dark side of the society were increased. After The First World War, Americans were at a loss postwar, and the Modern American literature began.

The process of American literature can be briefly divided into following five periods:

Colonial and early American literature;
American literature in the 18th century;
The flourishing of American literature in 19th century;
American Literature during the Realistic Period;
Modern American Literature.

Colonial and Early American Literature

The American Continent had been inhabited by the Asian immigrants, later known as American Indians or Native Americans for more than two thousand years before Christopher Columbus discovered it in 1492. These inhabitants, though they did not have written literature, did develop a rich heritage of cultures and have colorful oral literature.

Captain John Smith

Then came the European settlers with different backgrounds and cultures. On the one hand, they were eager to tell people living in "the old world" what they saw and what they experienced in this "new world". So they wrote a lot of diaries, letters, and travel accounts to describe the new land. No wonder some critics say that the earliest American literature was the travel accounts written by European adventurers. On the other hand, in order to prepare the new immigrants physically and spiritually for bearing the hardships of building up the new land into the Second Eden, they developed American Puritanism and spread it over the New England areas, which besides stressing predestination, original sin, hard work, thrift, piety and sobriety, advocated that earthly success was a sign of election, wealth and status being sought not only for themselves, but as welcome reassurances of spiritual health and promises of eternal life. So American writings of this period were dominated by the Puritan values. The most important figures of the period were John Smith, William Bradford and Anne Bradstreet.

American Literature in the 18th Century

With the development of colonial economy and society, colonial people in general began to seek their national identity politically and literarily. Some intellectuals considered Puritan values, of original sin in particular, had become obstacles to achieving these goals. So they energetically advocated to study "man" instead of "God," believing that the "evils" in human civilization stemmed from social injustice, not from "original sin," that man could "perfect himself" and decide his own destiny. They also put great stress on reason, on education and scientific research. They called on people to pay attention to the social reality. This movement was referred to as American Enlightenment, which introduced ideas of justice, liberty and equality as the natural rights of man to American thoughts and, above all, prepared the colonial people ideologically for their independence and enhanced their determination to obtain their independence realistically.

Due to the particular situation in America, among all categories of the literary works, political essays occupied an outstanding position and most of the writers were active supporters or participants of the American Revolution. For all the Americans, the most important document from this period was a single sheet of paper called *The Declaration of Independence* (1776), mainly written by Thomas Jefferson and Benjamin Franklin. Benjamin Franklin, Thomas Paine and Philip Freneau were the most brilliant literary figures of the time.

The Flourishing of American Literature in the 19th Century

After Americans gained their independence politically, they immediately got down to seeking for their cultural identity internationally through developing national literature as they developed their economy and society. The country was prosperous and the people were optimistic about their own future and the future of their nation. In the tens of the 19th century, the territory of the country had been expanded as far as the Appalachians, and its population also doubled. Under such circumstances, when the Romantic Movement came to America, Americans tinted (给……着色) it with American color and came into being the American Transcendentalism (超验主义), which was, in essence, a romantic idealism on Puritan soil and an intellectual movement, exerting a tremendous impact on intellectual thinking in America. The transcendental movement was based on a fundamental belief in the unity of the world and God. The soul of each individual was thought to be identical with the world— a microcosm (缩影) of the world itself. The doctrine of self-reliance and individualism developed through the belief in the identification of the individual soul with God. It was the most significant development of American literature in the mid-19th century and regarded as the first Renaissance in the American literary history.

The Romantic Movement or Romanticism (浪漫主义) reached America around the year 1820. It placed emphasis on imagination, emotion, and individuality instead of formality, order and authority. The romantics showed a profound admiration and love for nature and for the wild and mysterious. Though influenced by their European counterparts, romantics in America expressed themselves in a distinctive American voice: they wrote about the exotic landscape, the frontier life, the westward expansion, the Puritan heritage and they tended to moralize, to edify rather than to entertain.

Early romanticism was best represented by Washington Irving, James Fenimore Cooper, and New England poets William Cullen Bryant and Henry Wadsworth Longfellow. Among the representatives of post-romanticism are novelists Nathaniel Hawthorne and Herman Melville; poets Edgar Allan Poe and Walt Whitman; essayists Ralph Waldo Emerson and Henry David Thoreau, etc.

Another thing worth mentioning is that during this period America produced its two great women writers for the first time: Harriet Beecher Stowe (1811—1896), the woman writer called by President Lincoln "the little lady who wrote the book that made this great war" with her anti-slavery novel *Uncle Tom's Cabin*, and Emily Dickinson (1830—1886), the poetess of about 1700 poems and one of the finest poets in the English language, who was a keen observer of nature and a wise interpreter of human passion and developed her own forms of poetry and pursued her own visions, not paying attention to the fashions of literature of her day.

American Literature during the Realistic Period (1875—1914)

After the Civil War (1861—1865), America was set on the ever-increasingly rapid path of all-round development. Westward expansion and the gold rush added freshness and new vision to the established eastern New Englanders' life and thus enlarged subject matter of literature. On the other hand, the American society was in a turbulent (动荡的) situation through several economical crises. Problems of urbanization and industrialization appeared. This was what Mark Twain called "The Gilded Age," an age of extremes: of decline and progress, of poverty and dazzling wealth, of gloom and buoyant (高涨的) hope. The writings of critical realism unveiling the dark side of the society were increased. They were mainly focus on bankrupt in countries, difficult life or struggle of low-position people and so on. Thus Romanticism was on the wane (处于正在衰退的时期) with passing days, while Realism rose and became more and more popular. William Dean Howells (1837—1920), the most influential American literary realist in the last quarter of the 19th century, precisely defined it as "nothing more and nothing less than the truthful treatment of material and moral problems of society."

Local Color Fiction was one trend deserving our special attention. It first appeared in the early 19th century, and it had further developing after the Civil War. This kind of literature mainly describes the local life. Its keynote was optimistic, and the language was narrative and humorous. Mark Twain was also famous for his strong local colors.

Novels made unprecedented progress in this period in terms of technique and subject matter as well as the great amount. Sparkling novelists came one after another producing enduring works of their own. Besides Mark Twain, there were Henry James and Frank Norris, short story writer O. Henry (1862—1910) (penname for William Sidney Porter) with more than 300 short stories, all his characters being common people and always having an ironical and surprised ending, Jack London with his *The Call of the Wild*, an all-time best seller, and two towering pessimistic realists (also referred to as writers of naturalism) Stephen Crane and Theodore Dreiser.

Modern American Literature

The 20th century witnessed more historically and culturally influential events than previous ones. Catastrophic (悲惨的) and reform-oriented (导向的) events succeeded one after another. Firstly, the First World War not only brought misfortune on humanity and damaged the people's life, but also led to a turbulent situation of the American society. People of this time were named "The Lost Generation" (The Lost Generation refers to a group of young disappointed American writers, such as Ernest Hemingway and F. Scott Fitzgerald, chose Paris as their place of exile and used their wartime experience as the basis for their works. Generally they rebelled against former ideals and values, unable to come to terms with the new era when civilization had gone mad, and showed a sense of loss and took up the despairing tone of *The Waste Land*). On the other hand, it was an important factor in stimulating American economic expansion, which led America to the decade-long "thriving" stage, also frequently called "the Jazz Age." Then, the unexpected Great Depression shattered (严重破坏) the exciting acceleration in the tempo (发展速度) of American life, bringing all contradictions of the society to the front.

Even before Americans found solutions to this problem the Second World War took place, in which, the United States was heavily involved and suffered great loss. After the war, Americans were brought to face a completely new world which old rules and guidelines turned out to be helpless.

The Cold War, the Korean War and the Vietnam War, etc., made disillusionment spread throughout the United States and anti-war movement grew in size. Meanwhile, social reforms aiming to better and perfect the American society were under way. The civil rights and women's rights movements accelerated the process of American democracy, resulting in "Renaissance of American blacks" and prosperity of American women literature.

In short, such complex social background posed great challenge as well as opportunity to American literalists. To mirror the reality or express their feelings about it, American poets and writers of the century resorted to a variety of unmodeled literary techniques and forms. Their bold and creative experiments endorsed American literature of the time a term "modernism," used to show the literary art possessing outstanding characteristics in conception, feeling, form and style after the First World War. American literature uncontroversially won a place in the world literature and American writing was translated into other languages. American writers began to influence writers in other countries.

Ezra Pound, T. S. Eliot and E. E. Cummings are three poets who opened the way to modern poetry. New England poet Robert Frost also deserves some space to mention. After World War II, there appeared a tendency that most of the poets are grouped under such poetical schools as

Black Mountain, the Beat Generation, New York poets, Black poets, Confessional poets, and West Coast School. Robert Lowell (1917—1977) and Allen Ginsberg (1926—) are most brilliant poets after the war. Ginsberg identified as a representative of the Beat Generation, got his acclaim for the masterpiece *Howl* (1956), in which he shows his anger at the society and the government.

In terms of fiction, the 20th century was a stage on which all kinds of literary schools and movements competed interrelatedly to present themselves along with the traditional realism, such as the Lost Generation, the Beat Generation, psychological fiction, the Southern fiction, Jewish fiction, African-American fiction, science fiction, feminist fiction, etc., all of which produced brilliant novelists and displayed a prosperous panorama of literature. Among the greatest were Ernest Hemingway, William Faulkner, Saul Bellow and Toni Morrison.

The development of 20-century American drama owed a lot to Eugene O'Neill (1888—1953), who was the first American playwright awarded the Nobel Prize for Literature. His poetically autobiographical masterpiece *Long Day's Journey Into Night* (1956) laid down a new criterion for American dramatists. Tennessee Williams (1911—1983) and Arthur Miller (1915—2005) are another two great figures of American theater, the former famous for his *A Streetcar Named Desire* (1949) while the latter produced a landmark work *Death of a Salesman* in 1949, a study of man's search for merit and worth in his life and the realization that failure invariably looms (逼近).

Epilogue (结语)

American literature is well on the way after about 300 years of development. The living American literature has been providing potent thinking headsprings (源泉) for the writers past and nowadays, and it will continue reanimating (激发) the talents to bequeath (把……传下去) and enrich the tradition of American literature, of which deserved to be proud. It has been not only a genuine reflection of American history, society and culture but also an indispensable part of world civilization.

IV Sports

Baseball

From Little League to the World Series, baseball is the game that most Americans know best. Most Americans have played some form of baseball and the game has been called America's national pastime. There are many phrases in English that are related to baseball. We say of a strange idea that it comes "out of left field." "Hitting a home run" signals success. "Throwing a curve ball" means giving somebody a surprise.

Basketball

Basketball is one of the world's most popular sports. It's played in more than 200 countries, in playgrounds, school gyms, and sports arenas. All you need is a ball and a hoop. In the United States, most high schools and colleges have basketball programs. At the end of the season, the best teams compete in local, state, or national tournaments. The highest level of play for men is in the National Basketball Association (NBA) and for women is in the Women's National Basketball Association (WNBA).

Basketball Greats

Michael Jordan is generally regarded as the greatest basketball player ever. He led the

Chicago Bulls to six NBA championships during the 1990s. Kareem Abdul Jabbar is the NBA's all-time scoring leader with 38,387 points. Other leading NBA stars of the past include Magic Johnson, Larry Bird, Julius "Dr. J" Erving, Bill Russell, Wilt Chamberlain and Oscar Robertson.

Today's NBA stars include Tracy McGrady, Allen Iverson, Kobe Bryant, Kevin Garnett, Shaquille O'Neal, Tim Duncan, Carmelo Anthony and LeBron James. Leading players in the WNBA include Sheryl Swoopes, Lisa Leslie and Lauren Jackson.

Left—Michael Jordan of Chicago Bulls
Right—Kobe Bryant of the Los Angeles Lakers

Football

What's the most watched single sports event on television most years? It's the Super Bowl! More than 100 million people worldwide typically watch the championship game of the National Football League (NFL). It is the most important professional league in the United States. Football is a popular sport that uses an oval-shaped ball. Two opposing teams try to pass, kick, or carry the ball across each other's goal line to score points. Football players use moves such as blocking and tackling to prevent their opponents from advancing the ball.

Football is played at hundreds of colleges and universities across the United States and Canada. College football dates back to 1869. Each year, the top player in college football receives an award called the Heisman Trophy. Sportswriters vote to decide the winner. Some schools have become celebrated for their outstanding football teams. Three such schools are the University of Alabama (nicknamed the Crimson Tide), the University of Nebraska (Cornhuskers), and the University of Notre Dame (Fighting Irish).

Football season in the United States is in the fall. College teams usually play 11 or 12 games during the regular football season—before the bowl games. Professional teams play 16 games. College teams with the best winning records are invited to play in bowl games at the end of the football season. The bowl games help decide the national champion. The oldest of these is the Rose Bowl. The important bowl games include the Sugar Bowl, Cotton Bowl, Rose Bowl, Orange Bowl, and Fiesta Bowl. Colorful festivities go along with the games. For example, floats decorated with flowers take part in the Rose Parade before the Rose Bowl.

Many of the best college players go on to play football for a professional team. The most important professional league in the United States is the National Football League (NFL). College athletes can also play on professional football teams in Europe.

Ice Hockey

It's been called the fastest game in the world. It's certainly one of the roughest. Players on ice skates collide at great speeds. Shots streak toward the goal at more than 161 kilometers per hour! The game is ice hockey, a sport invented in Canada. Today, ice hockey is played in many other countries, including the United States. But it's still especially popular in Canada, earning it the nickname "Canada's game."

Ice hockey is played by two teams of six players. It can be played indoors or outdoors. Most games are played indoors on an ice hockey rink. Near each end of the rink, a goal with a meshed net is attached to the ice. Players try to score by using long, curved sticks to hit a hard rubber disk, called a puck (冰球), into the other team's goal. The team that scores the most goals wins.

Today, ice hockey is played in many countries, including the United States. Teams from

about 30 countries around the world compete in the Olympic Winter Games and other international hockey tournaments. Men's ice hockey has been a part of Olympic competition since 1920. Women's ice hockey became an Olympic sport in 1998. Teams from Europe and Russia are among the best in the world, along with those from Canada and the United States. One of the most dramatic upsets in the history of international hockey competition came in 1980. An inexperienced American team beat the heavily favored Soviet Union team in the Olympics. The American team went on to win its first gold medal in ice hockey. This is sometimes called "the miracle on ice."

The highest level of ice hockey competition occurs in the National Hockey League (NHL), which is considered the world's top professional league. The 30 NHL teams represent cities in Canada and the United States. Teams in the NHL play an 82-game schedule. The NHL season usually lasts from October to April. The top teams then compete in playoffs for the Stanley Cup, the NHL championship trophy.

V Holidays and Special Days

A holiday is a day that is set apart for religious observance or for the commemoration of some extraordinary event or significant person, or for some other public events. Originally, in ancient times, holidays were mainly religious. The word holiday is actually derived from "holy day." Afterwards, non-religious holidays commemorating historical occasions or distinguished people outnumbered holy days, despite the fact that many ancient religious rituals and customs have been carried over into modern times. Holidays and festivals connect the present with the past. They give new generations of people the chance to learn about people or events that shaped their culture. For religious and ethnic groups, holidays and festivals are a way to remember their roots.

Legal Holidays

US Legal Holidays	
New Year's Day	January 1
Birthday of Martin Luther King Jr.	Third Monday in January
Washington's Birthday (Presidents' Day)	Third Monday in February
Memorial Day	Last Monday in May
Independence Day	July 4
Labor Day	First Monday in September
Columbus Day	Second Monday in October
Veterans Day	November 11
Thanksgiving Day	Fourth Thursday in November
Christmas Day	December 25

In the following part, we will give a brief introduction to the major legal holidays observed in the United States.

Chapter 5 Society and Culture

● *New Year*

New Years Day is the first day of the year, January 1st. It is a celebration of the old year and the new one to come. New Year festivals are among the oldest and most universally observed. In some countries, parties are thrown on New Year's Eve which last until the early hours of New Year's Day. It is traditional to greet the New Year at midnight and then celebrate at least the first few minutes in the company of friends and family. Many people make New Year resolutions—a list of decisions about how they will live during the coming year, which may or may not be kept.

Each year huge crowds of people celebrate New Year's Eve in Times Square in New York City. At midnight, confetti (五彩纸屑) is thrown from the tall buildings surrounding the square. This tradition started as early as 1904 when the New York Times inaugurated its new headquarters in Times Square and celebrated the renaming of Longacre Square to Times Square. The first Ball Lowering celebration was held on December 31, 1907 and is now a worldwide symbol of the turn of the New Year, seen via satellite by more than one billion people each year. At 11:59 p.m., the Ball begins its descent as millions of voices unite to count down the final seconds of the year, and celebrate the beginning of a new year full of hopes, challenges, changes and dreams. *Auld Lang Syne* is sung at the stroke (报时的钟声) of midnight in almost every English-speaking country in the world to bring in the new year. It wouldn't be New Year without it. Some of the New Year's traditions include: the making of New Year's resolution; the use of a baby to signify the New Year and the Tournament of Roses Parade.

Traditional New Year foods are thought to bring luck. Many cultures believe that anything in the shape of a ring is good luck, because it symbolizes "coming full circle," completing a year's cycle. For that reason, eating donuts on New Year's Day is thought to bring good fortune. Many parts of the US celebrate the New Year by consuming black-eyed peas. These peas are typically accompanied by either hog jowls (面颊) or ham. Black-eyed peas and other legumes(豆类) have been considered good luck in many cultures. The hog, and thus its meat, is considered lucky because it symbolizes prosperity. Cabbage is another "good luck" vegetable that is consumed on New Year's Day by many. Cabbage leaves are also considered a sign of prosperity, being representative of paper currency. In some regions, rice is a lucky food eaten on New Year's Day.

● *Birthday of Martin Luther King, Jr.*

Each year on the third Monday of January, a day that falls on or near King's birthday of January 15, schools, federal offices, post office and banks across America close as people celebrate the newest American national holiday—Martin Luther King Day, the only federal holiday commemorating an African-American.

Dr. Martin Luther King Jr. was the most important voice of the American civil rights movement, which worked for equal rights for all. King spent his life protesting the unfair treatment of African Americans in the United States. He used peaceful marches and powerful speeches to make Americans realize that treating people differently because of their skin color was wrong.

On August 28, 1963, Martin Luther King led the "March on Washington." On the steps of the Lincoln Memorial that day, Dr. King delivered a speech that was later entitled "I Have a Dream" to the 250,000 people presented. The march was one of the largest gatherings of black and white people that the nation's capital had ever seen and one of the first to have extensive television coverage (报导).

The protests in Birmingham (美国阿拉巴马州中部一城市) and in Washington helped convince the US Congress to pass the Civil Rights Act of 1964. This act made it illegal in America to treat blacks or other ethnic groups unfairly. That same year King's peaceful efforts to win civil rights earned him the Nobel Peace Prize. He was the youngest man to have received the Nobel Peace Prize.

On the evening of April 4, 1968, King was shot and died in hospital. King is remembered for the great changes he made to American society and for the peaceful means that he used to make them. The third Monday of every January is a national holiday that honors King's birthday.

● *President's Day*

Presidents' Day is an official holiday commemorating the birthdays of George Washington and Abraham Lincoln. It is celebrated on the third Monday in February.

● *Memorial Day*

Memorial Day is a legal holiday that takes place every year on the last Monday in May. Memorial Day is in honor of the nation's armed forces that were killed defending their country in wars. Memorial Day was originally called Decoration Day. Americans observe Memorial Day with parades, speeches, musical concerts, and other events in memory of the nation's war dead. People still decorate graves with flowers, wreaths, and flags on Memorial Day. Memorial Day is also a popular time to begin summer activities. People gather for picnics, sports, and other outdoor fun. It is also the traditional day for people to open up their swimming pools!

● *Independence Day*

Independence Day, also known as 4th of July, is the birthday of the United States of America commemorating the formal adoption of *the Declaration of Independence* by the Continental Congress on July 4, 1776 in Philadelphia, Pennsylvania. This document declared that the American colonies no longer belonged to Great Britain. They were free and independent states. Although the signing of *the Declaration* was not completed until August, the Fourth of July has been accepted as the official anniversary of US independence and is celebrated in all states and territories of the US.

The Fourth of July is the main patriotic holiday of the entire country. Veterans of the Revolutionary War made a tradition of gathering on the Fourth to remember their victory. Americans celebrate the holiday with parades, sporting events, patriotic speeches, and picnics. Shops display red, white, and blue decorations; Communities all over the country light up the night sky with fireworks to honor the nation's birthday. Family picnics and outings are a feature of private Fourth of July celebrations. In 1941, the US Congress proclaimed the Fourth of July a national holiday.

● *Labor Day*

Labor Day is a legal holiday celebrated on the first Monday in September. The celebration of Labor Day is in honor of the working class. Parades are held throughout the cities and towns of the United States. Generally, Labor Day is the last day of summer celebrations. It is a signal to students across the country that school is ready to begin again!

Today, many Americans have forgotten the holiday's roots in unionism. Relaxing at the beach or barbeque, it's easy to forget those who marched in the streets in huge parades celebrating the working man's efforts with a show of solidarity. Without union intervention, overtime pay (加班费), vacations and sick leave policies might not exist, nor workplace safety rules protect us.

The father of labor day is Peter McGuire, an Irish-American cabinet (橱柜) maker and pioneer unionist (工会主义者) who proposed a day dedicated to all who labor. He introduced the idea for the holiday formally at a meeting of the Central Labor Union on May 18, 1882.

● *Columbus Day*

Columbus Day, the second Monday in October, is celebrated in the United States to honor Christopher Columbus's first voyage to America in 1492. On that voyage Columbus encountered the islands that became known as the West Indies, in the Caribbean Sea.

Italian-Americans first began observing Columbus Day in New York City on Oct. 12, 1866, but the first official Columbus Day was declared by Colorado governor. Jesse F. McDonald in 1905. In April 1934, at the request of the Knights of Columbus, Congress and President Franklin D. Roosevelt set aside Columbus Day as a federal holiday.

When Columbus crossed the Atlantic, he changed the world forever. His voyage to the Americas opened an exciting period in history. Animals, plants, and new ideas were exchanged between continents. However, the land Columbus discovered never bore his name. It was named for Amerigo Vespucci, another Italian who explored the eastern coast of South America for Portugal after Columbus sailed for Spain. Vespucci proved that the land was not India, but a new continent. His claim led a German mapmaker to suggest in 1507 that the newly discovered world be called the "land of Americus, for Americus its discoverer."

● *Veterans Day*

Veterans Day is celebrated on November 11 in honor of those who have served in the armed forces of the United States. It is a legal federal holiday. The observation was originally designated in 1919 by President Woodrow Wilson as Armistice Day (第一次世界大战停战纪念日). Wilson selected November 11 because the Armistice ending World War I had been signed on this date in 1918. Wilson wanted to make sure that Americans did not forget the tragedies of the war. In 1938, Congress passed legislation which designated Armistice Day as a federal holiday. In 1954, President Dwight D. Eisenhower signed a law changing the name of the holiday to Veterans Day. The reason was so that veterans of other wars could also be honored, not just soldiers from World War I.

Veterans Day ceremonies involve gatherings of old soldiers with grateful citizens. In many cities and towns, there are parades and speeches to remind people of the sacrifices soldiers have made. Often, flowers are laid at the gravesides of dead soldiers. Special services take place at the Tomb of the Unknown Soldier in Arlington National Cemetery on Veterans Day.

● *Thanksgiving Day*

Thanksgiving Day is a typical American holiday and not celebrated in continental Europe. It is a legal holiday marking the feast given in thanks for the harvest by the Pilgrim colonists in 1621. People in the United States celebrate Thanksgiving Day on the fourth Thursday in November. In Canada, Thanksgiving is celebrated on the second Monday in October.

People gather around a table with family and friends to share a holiday feast with a traditional turkey dinner, usually in the mid-afternoon. They give thanks for the blessings of the past year. For Americans and Canadians alike, these activities are an important part of Thanksgiving Day celebrations. Thanksgiving is a time for each person to think of what and who they are thankful for. As Americans celebrate Thanksgiving, they also pay tribute to the Pilgrims and Native Americans who shared the first Thanksgiving feast nearly 400 years ago.

Traditional Thanksgiving foods include turkey with bread stuffing, mashed potatoes, sweet potatoes, corn and cranberry sauce. Pumpkin pie is a classic dessert. A favorite side-dish of many families is cranberry sauce and cranberry relish. Most of these basic foods are native to North America. They help Americans recall the simple way of life of the Pilgrims. But these traditional dishes are not the only foods of modern Thanksgiving celebrations. As people have immigrated to America from other lands, they have added their own traditions.

Every Thanksgiving Day since 1924, Macy's department store has hosted a parade in New York City. The parade is known for its huge balloons.

● *Christmas*

Christmas is a holiday celebrated every year on December 25. It commemorates the birth of Jesus Christ more than 2,000 years ago. In many countries of the world, the celebration of Christmas on December 25th is a high point of the year. Colored lights decorate many town centers and shops, along with shiny decorations, and artificial snow painted on shop windows. Christmas trees are decorated with lights and Christmas ornaments. Shopping centers become busier as December approaches and often stay open till late. Groups of people often sing carols on the streets to raise money for charity. Most places of work will hold a short Christmas party about a week before Christmas. People give gifts and post Christmas greeting cards to their friends and family, and Children wait excitedly for Santa Claus to arrive on Christmas Eve and leave presents under the Christmas tree. At midnight on Christmas Eve, most churches hold special candlelight services that feature decorations, candles, and singing. Christmas has become known as a time for family gathering, friendship, giving, and cheers. It a festival of goodwill, which many Americans wish could continue throughout the entire year.

The official Christmas season is popularly known as the Twelve Days of Christmas. It extends from the anniversary of Christ's birth on December 25 to the feast of Epiphany (主显节) on January 6, which honors Jesus' baptism (洗礼) and the arrival of the Three Wise Men in Bethlehem. No one knows exactly when Jesus Christ was born. For many years, local Christian churches celebrated Christ's birth at different times. Then, in the AD 300s, the Roman Catholic Church set the birth date at December 25.

There are many traditions associated with Christmas that individual families brought with them when they came to the United States.

★ **The custom of sending Christmas cards** started in Britain in 1840 when the first "Penny Post" public postal deliveries began.

★ **The custom of exchanging gifts** at Christmas came from the ancient Romans. The Biblical (圣经的) story of the Three Wise Men who presented gifts to baby Jesus also shaped this Christmas custom.

★ **The custom of Christmas trees** was brought to the United States by German immigrants in the 1800s.

★ **The custom of decorating with mistletoe and holly** at Christmastime dates to the Romans. They thought of mistletoe as a symbol of peace. The Christmas custom of kissing under the mistletoe is thought to come from this ancient belief. Holly is also a popular Christmas decoration. Its sharp, pointed leaves are considered a symbol of Christ's crown of thorns. Christ wore the crown when he was nailed to the cross.

★ **Santa Claus** (or Father Christmas) is based on a real person, St. Nicholas, a Christian leader from Myra (in modern-day Turkey) in the 4th century AD. It is said that Santa Claus lives near the North Pole, and arrives through the sky on a sledge pulled by reindeer. He comes into houses down the chimney at midnight and places presents in socks or bags of in front of the family Christmas tree for every child who's tried to do their best.

★ **Sharing Christmas cookies** is also an American tradition.

★ **Ornaments of Stars and Lights.** The Star of Bethlehem is one of the oldest symbols of Christmas. A star traditionally sits atop Christmas trees and is said to have guided the three Wise Men to Bethlehem on the holy night when Christ was born. Lighted candles have always been a part of Christmas celebrations. The candles represent Jesus Christ, who the Bible calls "the light of the world."

★ **Candy canes are a traditional Christmas candy.** They are curved on top to represent the walking sticks used by the shepherds who were the first visitors to the baby Jesus.

★ **The singing of Christmas Carols.** Throughout the world, singing Christmas carols plays an important part in Christmas festivities, which symbolizes the Angels' Announcement of Christ's Birth.

Other Holidays

● *Valentine's Day*

Valentine's Day or Saint Valentine's Day is a day that is set aside to promote the idea of "love." It is celebrated on February 14th by many people throughout the world. In the English-speaking countries, it is the traditional day on which lovers express their love for each other by sending Valentine's cards, presenting flowers, or offering candy, all in the name of St. Valentine. The day is most closely associated with the mutual exchange of love notes in the form of "valentines." Modern Valentine symbols include the heart-shaped outline, doves, and the figure of the winged Cupid.

The sending of Valentines was a fashion in nineteenth-century Great Britain. In 1847, Esther Howland developed a successful business in her Worcester, Massachusetts home with hand-made Valentine cards based on British models. Since the 19th century, handwritten notes have largely given way to mass-produced greeting cards. In the second half of the twentieth century, the practice of exchanging cards was extended to all manner of gifts in the United States, usually from a man to a woman. Such gifts typically include roses and chocolates packed in a red satin, heart-shaped box. In the 1980s, the diamond industry began to promote Valentine's Day as an occasion for giving jewelry. The rise of Internet popularity at the turn of the millennium is creating new traditions. Millions of people use, every year, digital means of creating and sending Valentine's Day greeting messages such as e-cards, love coupons or the printable greeting cards.

The US Greeting Card Association estimates that approximately one billion valentines are sent each year worldwide, making the day the second largest card-sending holiday of the year, behind Christmas. The association estimates that, in the US, men spend on average twice as much money as women.

There are varying opinions as to the origin of Valentine's Day. Some experts state that it originated from St. Valentine, a Roman who was martyred (殉难) for refusing to give up Christianity. He died on February 14, 269 AD. Legend also says that St. Valentine left a farewell note for the jailer's daughter, who had become his friend, and signed it "From Your Valentine." Other aspects of the story say that Saint Valentine served as a priest at the temple during the reign of Emperor Claudius. Claudius then had Valentine jailed for defying (违抗) him. In 496 AD, Pope Gelasius set aside February 14 to honor St. Valentine. Gradually, February 14 became the date for exchanging love messages and St. Valentine became the patron saint of lovers.

● *Easter*

For Christians, Easter is a joyous holiday which commemorates the day of Jesus Christ's

Children roll Easter eggs during the annual White House Easter Egg Roll on the South Lawn

resurrection or rebirth. It is always celebrated on a Sunday. But the exact date changes from year to year. Today, most Christians celebrate Easter on the first Sunday after the first full moon following the first day of spring. So Easter became a "movable" feast which can occur as early as March 22 or as late as April 25. The word "Easter" is named after Eastre, the Anglo-Saxon goddess of spring.

Many Easter traditions began long before Christianity. The Easter holiday is rooted in older festivals that celebrated the arrival of spring. The Easter bunny and Easter eggs are very old traditions that symbolize spring and new life. Easter eggs are specially decorated eggs given out to celebrate the Easter holiday or springtime. The oldest tradition is to use dyed and painted chicken eggs, but a modern custom is to substitute chocolate eggs, or plastic eggs filled with candy such as jellybeans. The Romans believed that "All life comes from an egg." Christians consider eggs to be "the seed of life" and so they are symbolic of the resurrection of Jesus Christ. Over time, people added Easter baskets, Easter Egg Hunts, Easter Egg Roll and candies to the festivities.

Rolling eggs on the Monday after Easter was a tradition observed by many Washington families, including those of the President. In 1880, the First Lady invited children to the White House for the Egg Roll and it has been held there ever since then, only canceled during times of war. The wife of the President sponsors it for the children of the entire country. The egg rolling event is open to children twelve years old and under. Adults are allowed only when accompanied by children! That day hundreds of children come with baskets filled with brightly decorated eggs and roll them down the famous lawn, hoping the President of the US is watching the fun.

The Easter Bunny is a rabbit-spirit. Long ago, he was called the "Easter Hare." Hare and rabbit were the most fertile animals known and they served as symbols of the new life during the spring season. The bunny as an Easter symbol seems to have its origins in Germany and was introduced to American folklore by the German settlers who arrived in the Pennsylvania Dutch (17 或 18 世纪移居美国宾夕法尼亚州的德国人和瑞士人的后裔) country during the 1700s. Today on Easter Sunday children wake up to find that the Easter Bunny has left them baskets of candy.

Traditionally, many celebrants bought new clothes for Easter which they wore to church. After church services, everyone went for a walk around the town. This led to the American custom of Easter parades all over the country. Perhaps the most famous is that along Fifth Avenue in New York City. The New York City Easter Parade has been an annual tradition since Civil War days and features marchers in elaborate Easter finery (华丽的服饰), including some of the fanciest Easter bonnets imaginable.

● *April Fools' Day*

April Fools' Day is a day to play jokes on others. It is a "for-fun-only" observance. Nobody is expected to buy gifts or to take their "significant other" out to eat in a fancy restaurant. Nobody gets off work or school. It's simply a fun little holiday, but a holiday on which one must remain forever vigilant, for he may be the next April Fool!

Unlike most of the other non-foolish holidays, the origin of April Fools' Day, sometimes called All Fools' Day, is rather uncertain. However, the common belief holds that the closest point in time that can be identified as the beginning of this tradition was in 1582 in France. During the reformation of the calendar the date for the New Year was moved from April 1st to January 1st.

During that time in history there was no television and no radio so word spread slowly. There were also those who chose to simply ignore the change all together and those who merely forgot. These people were considered "fools" and invitations to non-existent parties and other practical jokes were played on them.

Some suggest that the origin began with the celebrations of the Spring Equinox (春分). While some believe it has to do with a Roman festival known as Hilaria, the end of the Celtic New Year. The tradition eventually spread to England and Scotland in the eighteenth century. It was later introduced to the American colonies of both the English and French.

Each country celebrates April Fools' Day differently. In England, people play jokes only in the morning. You are a "noodle" (笨人) if someone fools you. In the United States, pranks are played on just about everybody. Pranks range from the standard "Your shoe is untied," to some very creative and elaborate ideas. The only "rule" is that no one should be harmed. Corporations, newspapers, and television stations will also play practical jokes on April Fools' Day.

● *Halloween*

October 31st was the eve of the Celtic (凯尔特的) New Year but sometime in the 800's, November 1st became the Christian All Saints' Day (万圣节), also known as Allhallows or Hallowmas, a holy day in the Roman Catholic and Anglican churches. The evening before was All Hallows Eve, or Halloween. Halloween is a holiday celebrated in most areas of North America and in some areas of Western Europe. It is symbolically associated with death and the supernatural.

By tradition, Halloween begins after sunset. Long ago, people believed that witches gathered together and ghosts roamed (漫游) the world on Halloween. Today, most people no longer believe in ghosts and witches. But these supernatural beings are still a part of Halloween.

Dressing in masks and costumes is a popular Halloween activity. Costumes can be traditional and scary, such as a witch's pointy hat and black gown. Costumes may also have a modern flavor. Many children dress up as movie characters or a favorite superhero. But Halloween is not just for children. Many adults enjoy showing off their costumes at Halloween parties! On Halloween, children dress in costumes and go from house to house asking for candy by saying "Trick or Treat!" As neighbors give each child a treat they try to guess who is under the mask. This practice is called trick-or-treat, because children used to play tricks on neighbors who didn't give treats.

The pumpkin is one of the symbols of Halloween. Carving vegetables into jack-o'-lanterns is a Halloween custom dating back to Ireland. A jack-o'-lantern is a hollowed-out pumpkin with a face carved on one side. Candles are usually placed inside, giving the face a spooky (幽灵般的) glow and grins from a porch as the children pass. According to legend, jack-o'-lanterns protect people in their homes from ghostly spirits.

● *Arbor Day*

In the Unites States, Arbor Day is a nationally-celebrated observance that encourages tree planting and care to beautify towns or to forest empty areas of land. In Latin arbor means "tree." Founded by J. Sterling Morton in Nebraska in 1872, National Arbor Day is celebrated each year on the last Friday in April in the United States. Most public schools celebrate Arbor Day in order to teach students about protecting the forests, and in some states it is a legal holiday.

It's Arbor Day — Plant a tree!

Understanding Canada

A General Survey of Canada

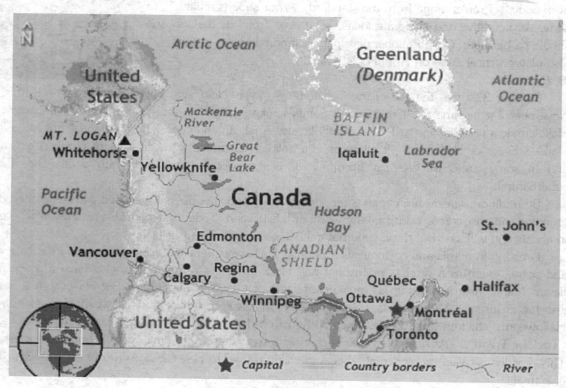

Map of Canada

With an area of 9,984,670 square kilometers, Canada is a huge country, second in size only to Russia and slightly larger than China. Yet it has only 33 million people, which is less than half the population of the United Kingdom.

Situated in northern half of the North America, it extends from the Great Lakes in the south to the majestic Rocky Mountains in the west, and the bleak Arctic Islands in the far north. With 10 provinces and 3 territories, Canada became a self-governing dominion (英联邦的自治领) in 1867 while retaining ties to the British crown. Economically and technologically the nation has developed in parallel with the U.S., its neighbor to the south across an unfortified (不设防的) border.

Country Name

The simple official country name of Canada has many explanations. The most popular one is as follows:

A General Survey of Canada

Jacques Cartier, the first European navigator who discovered what is now Canada, went ashore on July 24, 1534, at a spot later to be known as Québec City. There he asked some local Indians what that place was called. The Indians, thinking that he meant their little town, replied Kanada, which means "a settlement" in the Huron-Iroquois Indian language (休伦—易洛魁印第安语). On returning to Europe, Cartier announced that he had discovered a new land named Kanada. Thus in misunderstanding, the place later became known as Canada.

The name "Canada" later referred to a large area north of the St. Lawrence River. As more land was explored "Canada" grew. The first time "Canada" was used as an official name was in 1791 for the colonies of Upper and Lower Canada. In 1867, at the time of Confederation, the new country became known as Canada.

Capital

The capital of Canada is the city of Ottawa, which is in the province of Ontario, located above the Great Lakes. Ever since it was named Canada's capital by Queen Victoria in 1857, Ottawa has grown into a city for all seasons, alive with vitality and rich in historic traditions.

Parliament Hill on Ottawa River

Language

Canada is a multilingual society with English and French as its official languages. About 59.3% of Canadians speak English while 23.2% speak French. Most French speakers (francophone 讲法语的人) live in Québec where they form a majority.

As more Chinese immigrants settle in Canada, Chinese is reaffirmed as Canada's third most common mother tongue. Cree (克里语), as one of the Indian languages, has the largest language group in Canada.

Currency

The official currency of Canada is the Canadian dollar. It is normally abbreviated with the dollar sign $, or C$ to distinguish it from other dollar-denominated currencies. It is divided into 100 cents. As of 2007, the Canadian dollar was the 7th most traded currency in the world.

Canadian Coins

Religion

Like Americans, most Canadians are Christians. According to 2001 census, 42.6% of the population is Roman Catholic, 23.3% Protestant and other Christian 4.4%. For others, 1.9% is Muslim, other and unspecified 11.8%, and none 16%.

The National Flag

The National Flag of Canada, popularly known as the Maple Leaf and l'Unifolié (French for "the one-leaved"), is a base red flag with a white square in its centre featuring a stylized, 11-pointed, red maple leaf. Adopted in 1964, the flag made its first appearance on February 15, 1965, which is now celebrated annually as Flag Day.

The National Anthem

The title of the National Anthem of Canada is "Canada O Canada." Originally, it was written in French. Not long after it was set to music and was first performed on June 24, 1880. Seven years later, the Montreal judge and poet R. Stanly Weir wrote its English version.

The National Emblems

Actually, there are two national emblems of Canada. The first one is the Canadian beaver, a clever and hardworking semi-aquatic (半水栖的) animal. Its use dated back to the early 17th century. Now it is officially regarded as the symbol of the sovereignty of Canada.

The second national emblem of Canada is the Canadian maple leaf. However, its use as the national symbol has shorter history, dating back only to the middle 19th century. With the proclamation of the national flag of Canada, it was confirmed as an official symbol. A maple leaf is always found on Canadian officials' business cards.

The National Shield

The national shield of Canada came into being in 1921 after many designs and redesigns. It is a combination of British, French and Canadian symbols that make it a reflection of Canada's historic and cultural traditions.

A Collection of Fast Facts of Canada

Official name	Canada
Capital	Ottawa
Population	33 million people
Rank among countries in population	36th
Major cities	Toronto, Montréal, Vancouver
Area	9,984,670 km^2
Rank in area worldwide	2nd
Highest point	Mt. Logan, 5,959 meters
Lowest point	Atlantic Ocean, 0 meter
Currency	Canadian dollar
Principal Languages	English and French
Major Religion	Christianity
Literacy Rate	99%
Administrative divisions	10 provinces, 3 territories
National Day	Canada Day, 1 July (1867)

Chapter 6 Geography and History

A. Geography

I Geographic Features

"From Sea to Sea"
   Occupying most of the northern portion of the continent of North America, Canada spans an immense territory between the Pacific Ocean to the west and the Atlantic Ocean to the east, with the United States to the south and northwest (Alaska), and the Arctic Ocean to the north; Greenland is to the northeast. It has the world's longest coastline of 202,080 kilometers.

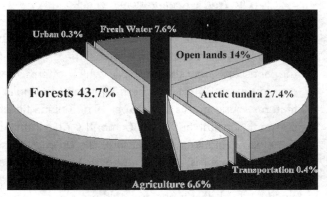

Canada's Physical Makeup

Canada's Physical Regions
   Canada has clearly defined political and physical regions. It is divided into 13 political regions: ten provinces and three territories. There are 6 physical regions, each with a very different landscape and climate. They are the Atlantic Region, the Great Lakes & St. Lawrence Region, the Canadian Shield, the Great Plains, the Cordillera and the North.

   1. *Atlantic Region* is the most eastern region of Canada located between the Atlantic Ocean and the heavily forested Appalachian Mountain. It was the first physical region that was re-discovered and inhabited by the early European settlers. This region of low hills, plains, islands, and peninsulas includes the Atlantic Provinces of Newfoundland, Nova Scotia, Prince Edward Island and New Brunswick. The sea has long shaped the life of the Appalachian region.

   2. *Great Lakes-St. Lawrence Region* is an area of fertile lowlands that stretches along the St. Lawrence River and the Great Lakes. The St. Lawrence Seaway, a system of locks and highways connect the Canadian interior to the Atlantic Ocean. Good transportation, fertile soil and a mild climate have helped to make this region the agricultural and industrial center of Canada, containing Canada's two largest cities, Montreal and Toronto. In this small region, 50 percent of Canadians live and 70 percent of Canada's manufactured goods are produced.

   3. *The Canadian Shield* covers almost half of Canada, stretching west and north from the Atlantic Ocean to the Arctic Ocean. It consists of low hills, swamps, lakes and streams. Because the soil is poor and the climate is cold, few people live in this region. Canadian Shield cuts the country in half and contributes to divisions between the easterners and westerners. The shield is rich in mineral resources. Its forest once supported huge numbers of fur bearing animals.

   4. *Great Plains* lie farther west. It is a physiographic (地形学的) region in central Canada and the United States. The region has a vast, generally high plateau, called the plains, which feature productive grain and livestock farms (畜牧场) and extensive petroleum and coal deposits.

   5. *The Cordillera (Western Mountain Group)* is a mountainous strip of land about 805 km wide, stretching from the towering Rocky Mountains to the Coastal Ranges along the Pacific. Between the mountains lie rugged plateaus. The word Cordillera is a Spanish word meaning mountain ranges.

The natural resources of the Cordillera are forestry (this is the biggest industry in the region), agriculture, mining and fisheries. The Western Mountains form an imposing barrier. Until the late 1800's, the people in the province of British Columbia was isolated from the rest of Canada. Even today, people in the far west have an intense regional pride and sense of independence. Distance also affects trade patterns. Vancouver (温哥华), British Columbia is closer to Tokyo, Japan than to Halifax, Nova Scotia. As a result British Columbia has developed trade ties with the countries of the Pacific Rim.

6. *The North Region* includes Yukon, Northwest Territories, Nunavut, Northern Québec and the most extreme tip of Labrador and Newfoundland. This area is very unique compared to the rest of Canada: the Northern Landscape, a combination of the Cordillera, Plains and Canadian Shield, is the only landscape where the ground is frozen all year. In the summer the top layer of the landscape may thaw (解冻), which often forms lakes or swamps. Icecaps (冰冠) or glaciers, barren tundra (苔原), northern lights and the polar ice pack (浮冰群) are just a few of the unique features found in this landscape. The unique tilt of our Earth's axis gives this region 6 months of constant sunlight and then 6 months of continual darkness. In summer the sun would still be shinning at midnight. Because of the unique landscape and climate conditions (extremely cold in the winter months) this area has the lowest human population in Canada. The majority of the people will live where the land is level and/or where there is a water source nearby. In the north, zinc (锌), lead, diamonds and gold are some of the minerals that can be found.

Polar Bear Resting on Iceberg

Northern Lights

II Mountains, Rivers and Lakes

Mountains

Canada's vast area means it has many varying types of terrain (地形), much of which is mountainous. The principal mountainous region is the Western Cordillera, or Cordilleran, which is a mountain system located in western Canada in British Columbia, Alberta, Yukon Territory and Northwest Territories. This region comprises a series of mountain belts some 800 kilometers wide along Canada's Pacific coast.

East ridge of Mount Logan in the Yukon

Chapter 6　Geography and History　||111

A second major mountain system in Canada is located along the north-eastern seaboard(沿海地方) from Ellesmere Island in Nunavut down through to the Torngat Mountains of Québec and Newfoundland and Labrador.

A third system of significance is the Appalachians which cross much of eastern Canada.

The highest peak in Canada is Mount Logan (5,951 meters) in the Yukon Territory of northwest Canada.

Rivers and Lakes

The two principal river systems in Canada are the Mackenzie and St Lawrence. The St. Lawrence, with its tributaries, is navigable for over 3058 kilometers and empties into the Gulf of St. Lawrence. It is the largest river in Canada in volume of water discharged at its mouth. Flowing between the Canadian Shield and the Rocky mountains in west Canada, the Mackenzie is the second largest river system of North America. It empties into the Arctic Ocean and drains a large part of northwestern Canada. Through its tributary, the Peace River, and tracing to its source in the Finlay River of British Columbia, the Mackenzie is 4,241 km long and is the longest river in Canada and one of the longest rivers in the world. Other large and important rivers are the Yukon River, the Columbia River (partly in the USA), the Nelson River, the Churchill River, and the Fraser River.

Canada contains more lakes and inland waters than any other country in the world. In addition to the Great Lakes on the American border (all partly within Canada except Lake Michigan), the country has 31 lakes or reservoirs of about 1,300 sq km in area.

Canada's two largest lakes are Superior and Huron, at 82,100 sq km and 59,600 sq km respectively. About one-third of Lake Superior and about three-fifths of Lake Huron are in Canada. The deepest lake in Canada is Great Slave Lake in Northwest Territories, which has a depth of 614 meters. The largest fresh water lake entirely within Canada is Great Bear Lake in the Western Canadian Arctic, with an area of 31,326 square kilometers. The highest lake in Canada is Chilko Lake, BC at 1,171 meters. Other very large bodies of freshwater are Lake Athabasca and Reindeer Lake in Saskatchewan and the Smallwood Reservoir in Newfoundland and Labrador.

In general, all rivers and lakes in Canada have value as sources of water for agricultural, industrial, urban, and recreational uses; but some have more specific commercial uses. The Great Lakes and the St. Lawrence Seaway, which is a deep waterway extending 3,700 km from the

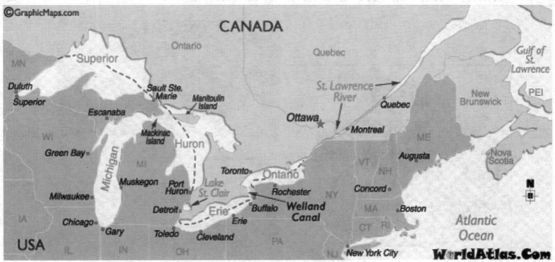

Saint Laurence River & Great Lakes

Understanding Canada

Atlantic Ocean to the head of the Great Lakes, form an important transportation network for eastern Canada, and have been important for the industrial development of the St. Lawrence—Great Lakes region.

Falls

People often say if you haven't been to Niagara Falls (尼亚加拉大瀑布), you cannot be said to have been to Canada. Is Niagara Falls the highest waterfall in the world? No. It is by no means the world's highest waterfall. Actually, it is not even the highest waterfall in Canada. Della Falls is the highest waterfall in Canada and tenth highest in the world.

The greatest waterfall by volume is Niagara Falls. The Niagara Falls is one of the most powerful waterfalls in the world with about six million cubic meters of water flowing per minute. It is present in the Canada-America border and consists of a set of waterfalls namely the American Falls, Bridal Veil Falls, both are on the American side, and the Horseshoe Falls, which is on the Canadian side and is considered to be the most impressive of the three falls. Approximately 90% of the water of the Niagara River flows over Horseshoe Falls, while the other 10% flows over the American Falls.

The name is derived from its curving, horseshoe-shaped crest that is 671 meters in width. At the center of the Horseshoe Falls the water is about 3 meters deep. It passes over the crest at a speed of about 32 km/h. The fall is 53 meters high, has an average crest elevation of 152 meters. It dumps 5,365 sq meters per second into the Niagara River.

Horseshoe Falls of Niagara Falls

There are six bridges that cross the International Border between Canada and the U.S.A. along the Niagara River. All are International Border Crossings. In the middle of one of the bridges, the Rainbow Bridge, there are two flags, the American star and stripe flag and the Canadian maple leaf flag, marking the demarcation (边界) line between the U.S and Canada.

III Administrative Areas and Major Cities

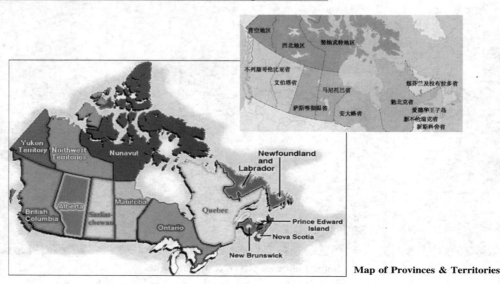
Map of Provinces & Territories

Chapter 6 Geography and History

Just as the United States is a federation of states, Canada is a federation of provinces. It is now made up of ten provinces—Newfoundland and Labrador, Nova Scotia, New Brunswick, Prince Edward Island, Québec, Ontario, Manitoba, Saskatchewan, Alberta, and British Columbia—and three territories—Nunavut, the Northwest Territories, and the Yukon Territory. Each area has its own provincial flag.

Canada's capital is Ottawa (渥太华) and its largest city is Toronto (多伦多). Other important cities include Vancouver (温哥华), Montreal (蒙特利尔), Québec (魁北克), Edmonton (埃德蒙顿), Calgary (卡尔加里), Winnipeg (温尼伯), Victoria (维多利亚), etc.

A Western Province: British Columbia (不列颠哥伦比亚省) 西海岸地区

Popularly known by its initials, BC, British Columbia, the westernmost province of Canada is bounded on the west by the Pacific Ocean. Along its deeply indented(犬牙交错的) Pacific coast lie many islands, notably Vancouver Island (450 km long) and the sparsely inhabited Queen Charlotte Islands.

The province is almost wholly mountainous, with three major mountain ranges: the Rocky Mts. in the southeast, the Coast Mts. along the Pacific, and the Stikine Mts. in the northwest.

Chief of the many rivers is the Fraser, which flows to the Pacific. Hydroelectric resources in British Columbia are highly developed. The station at Kemano on the Nechako River serves one of the biggest aluminum plants in the world. Long, narrow lakes are found throughout the interior; Williston Lake, on the Peace River, is the largest of these. Lake Louise, located in the

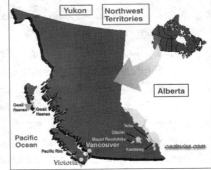

Map of British Columbia

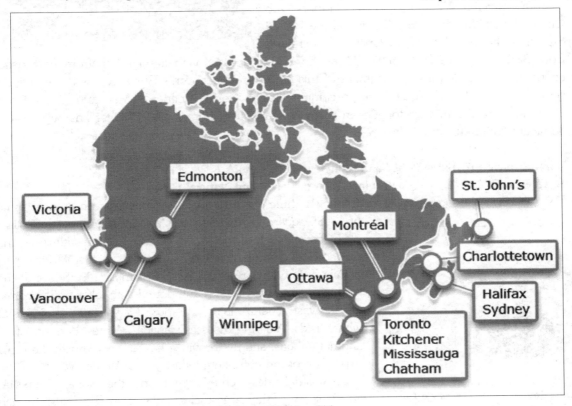

Map of Major Cities

Rockies, is the most famous image of the Canadian landscape. British Columbia attracts millions of visitors annually.

Victoria is the capital. The largest city and chief port is Vancouver. Other population centers include Richmond, Kelowna, New Westminster, North Vancouver, Nanaimo, Kamloops, and Prince George.

Victoria, a Garden City

● *Victoria* (维多利亚), *Capital of British Columbia*

Victoria is located on Vancouver Island and Juan de Fuca Strait. It is the largest city on the island and its major port and business center. In addition to its importance as the seat of provincial government, Victoria is noted as a garden city, a residential city because of its mild climate, beautiful scenery, many parks and drives. It is also a popular center for American and Canadian tourists. It is the seat of the Dominion Astrophysical Observatory (加拿大自治领天体物理台) and the University of Victoria.

● *Vancouver* (温哥华), *Largest City and Chief Port of B.C.*

Situated on a peninsula opposite Vancouver Island, Vancouver is the third largest city in Canada (after Toronto and Montréal) and the most livable city in the world. It is a leading Pacific Coast seaport and the main commercial, manufacturing, financial, tourist, and cultural center of British Columbia.

Vancouver's leading trading partners are China, Japan, South Korea, Brazil and the United States. The population of Vancouver increased from 384,500 in 1961 to 545,671 at the 2001 census, with immigration from East Asian countries contributing a large segment of this growth. Vancouver's Chinatown is the traditional center of one of the largest Chinese communities in North America. Mandarin Chinese and Cantonese are the mother tongues in so many Vancouver homes that Chinese has become the dominant "minority" ethnic group.

Three Prairie Provinces: Alberta, Saskatchewan, Manitoba (草原区)

1. Alberta (阿尔伯塔省) —**A Province Rich in Petrol and Natural Gases**

Alberta is the westernmost of Canada's three Prairie Provinces, covering an area of some 661,185 square kilometers. It is a land of contrasts. Rolling plains cover much of the province, but in the southwest, the rugged Rocky Mountains and its foothills (丘陵地带) form part of Alberta's boundary with British Columbia. In the north the land is covered with forests and dotted with lakes and streams. On the vast Alberta plains, oil rigs (钻塔) rise above great wheat fields. Alberta possesses Canada's largest deposits of oil and natural gas, and the province has prospered with the rapid expansion of the petroleum industry after World War II.

Location Map of Three Prairie Province

Industrial cities such as Edmonton, the capital of Alberta, and Calgary, the largest city, thrive in the midst of rich agricultural lands.

- **Edmonton, Capital City of Alberta**

Edmonton is situated in central Alberta, occupying a land area of 670 sq km. It has long, cold and relatively dry winters and cool summers. The metropolitan area is largely taken up with parks, golf courses, and such attractions as the Muttart Conservatory, Fort Edmonton Park, and the Valley Zoo. Other important public buildings include the Alberta Legislature, the Provincial Museum, and the University of Alberta (founded in 1906). North of the valley is the downtown district, marked by a dense cluster of office towers. Edmonton, which describes itself as "The Gateway to the North", is the transportation and distribution center for an area reaching to the Arctic Ocean. In recent years, Edmonton has become an advanced research center specializing in oil sands technology and medicine.

- **Calgary (卡尔加里), Largest City of Alberta & Energy City of Canada**

Calgary has the most striking setting of all of Canada's prairie cities. It lies at the very edge of the high plains, where they rise into the foothills of the Rocky Mountains, on a site deeply carved by the Bow and Elbow rivers.

The river valleys are natural corridors for roads and railways and have had a strong influence on Calgary's layout. In the eastern sector of the city the valleys are largely used for industry, but elsewhere they provide attractive sites for homes, parks, and recreation facilities. The downtown district sits on the widest part of the valley floor. It stands out as a dense clump of tall, modern office buildings. Olympic Plaza is the main downtown square. Petro Canada Tower, the city's tallest structure at 55 stories, is one of several tall buildings that dominate downtown.

Calgary is known as the Energy Capital of Canada as a number of oil companies have headquarters in the city. It is one of the country's most important business centers.

2. **Saskatchewan (萨斯喀彻温省)—A Prairie Province Rich in Wheat and Oil**

Saskatchewan borders Manitoba province on the east, Alberta province on the west. Its name is derived from the Cree term for "swiftly flowing," which was first applied to the Saskatchewan River. Saskatchewan became a province of Canada on September 1, 1905. It is one of the only two Canadian provinces with no saltwater coast (the other one being Alberta). This province was once famous for its "wheat economy," with wheat farming as its main industry. Now this area is also rich in farming, fur producing, mining, etc. Regina is the capital of Saskatchewan, and Saskatoon is the largest city.

- **Regina (里贾纳), Capital of Saskatchewan**

Regina is the capital and the second largest city of Saskatchewan next to Saskatoon (萨斯卡通). The Latin word Regina means "queen," and the city is sometimes called the Queen City of the Plains because of its location in the heart of Canada's prairie region. Regina has a severe, dry climate, with cold winters and short summers, but is very well suited to growing wheat.

Regina is now considered a cultural and commercial center for southern Saskatchewan. It attracts numerous visitors due to the vivacity of its commerce, theatre, concerts, restaurants and the summer agricultural fair. Regina is also home to many museums, which depict the diverse history that surrounds Regina.

However Regina's main claim to fame is Canada's Royal Canadian Mounted Police (RCMP 加拿大皇家骑警) training centre. The RCMP have called Regina home since the late 1800's. One evening each week during July to mid August, this prestige police force performs a

RCMP Sunset Ceremonies

special 'Sunset Ceremony'—renowned as one of Canada's top 20 attractions.

Regina is home to more trees than citizens. It has a large percentage of its overall area devoted to parks and green-space. The city has many biking paths and recreational facilities.

3. Manitoba (马尼托巴省)—Keystone Province of Canada

As the easternmost of Canada's three Prairie provinces, Manitoba has been known as the keystone (拱心石) of the continent from the Atlantic to the Pacific. Winnipeg (温尼伯) is its capital.

Comparatively level, Manitoba generally ranges from 150 meters to 300 meters above sea level. Baldy Mountain is Manitoba's highest point, at 2831 meters.

Agricultural land lies in a triangle, bordering Saskatchewan and the US, cutting diagonally across Lake Winnipeg. In northernmost Manitoba lies tundra (苔原) and permafrost (永久冻结带). All waters in Manitoba flow to Hudson Bay.

Major cities in Manitoba include Winnipeg (the largest), Brandon (second largest), Saint Boniface (a French settlement), etc.

● *Winnipeg (温尼伯), Capital of Manitoba & Gateway to the West*

Winnipeg is the oldest city in the Prairie Provinces. In addition to being the capital of Manitoba, Winnipeg is also a leading trading center for the grain originating in all three Prairie Provinces and the site of one of the world's leading commodity exchanges, the Winnipeg Commodity Exchange. It is also a major railway junction, and railways and rivers together played a major role in the city's early development, making it "the gateway to the west."

Central Canada (中部区)

1. Ontario (安大略省), the Heartland Province

Southernmost Province of Canada, Ontario is the second largest of Canada's ten provinces in area and the largest in terms of population. Commonly called the Heartland Province, Ontario is the center of Canada's industry, population, and agriculture.

Ontario has access to excellent transportation facilities, especially the St. Lawrence Seaway, which connects Lake Superior in the west to the Atlantic Ocean and is a vital trade link. The varied landscape includes the vast, rocky and mineral-rich Canadian Shield, which separates the fertile farmland in the south and the grassy lowlands of the north. There are over 250,000 lakes in Ontario—they make up about one-third of the world's fresh water. In summer, temperatures can soar above 30°C, while in winter they can drop to below −40°C

Map of Ontario

Ontario's industries range from cultivating crops, to mining minerals, manufacturing automobiles, to designing software and leading-edge technology.

Ottawa, the capital city of Canada, and Toronto, the province's capital and Canada's most populous city, are both situated in Ontario.

● *Toronto (多伦多), Largest City of Canada*

Located on the northwestern shore of Lake Ontario, Toronto is Canada's largest city and the provincial capital of Ontario, with a population of 2,518,772. Residents of Toronto are called Torontonians. Toronto has the largest metropolitan area in Canada and is the financial center of the country. The city is part of the Golden Horseshoe, a highly urbanized and industrialized region extending around the west end of Lake Ontario.

The City of Toronto covers 97 sq km. It is composed of six communities: Toronto, North York, Scarborough, Etobicoke, York, and East York. The city and its surrounding area is called Toronto's census metropolitan area (CMA). Toronto is one of the top green cities across Canada. Low daily water consumption, an insecticide (杀虫剂) ban and solar-powered parking meters are just a few of Toronto's green features.

Toronto Skyline

Government buildings are prominent in the city. Queen's Park, the site of the Ontario Parliament buildings, stands at the head of Toronto's wide ceremonial street, University Avenue. Conspicuous in the downtown are the new Metro Hall and the more spectacular City Hall with two curved towers that stands in Nathan Phillips Square. Commanding the whole region, the CN Tower near the central waterfront rises high over the city at 553 m. It is the tallest freestanding(独立式的)structure in the world.

● *Ottawa, Capital of Canada*

Ottawa, the capital of Canada, is situated in the southeastern part of the province of Ontario. It is the administrative center of Canada. The city and surrounding municipalities form Canada's National Capital Region, which includes government agencies, parks, and tourist sites. Ottawa is one of the coldest national capitals in the world and is a city of great natural beauty.

Located on the southern bank of the Ottawa River opposite the city of Hull, Ottawa covers a land area of 110 sq km and is surrounded by a 42,000-acre protected greenbelt to the south and west, both the Rideau River and the Rideau Canal flow through the city. The Canadian Parliament buildings are located on Parliament Hill, overlooking the Ottawa Rive. Sussex Drive, leading away from Parliament toward the municipality of Rockcliffe Park, is also lined with public buildings. To its east lies the Byward Market, a thriving commercial area that features a farmers' market and is the center of Ottawa's nightlife.

2. Québec (魁北克省), the Largest Province of Canada

Québec is located in the eastern part of Canada and extends north from the United States border to Hudson Strait and east from the shores of Hudson Bay to the region of Labrador. Québec is nicknamed La Belle Province (the Beautiful Province) because of the splendor and diversity of its landscape and architecture. The site of the first permanent French settlement in North America, Québec is unique among the Canadian provinces in that the vast majority of its population is of French descent and speaks French as a first language. To many French Canadians, Québec is far more than a province; it is a cultural homeland.

Québec is the oldest province in Canada, settled by the French in the 1600s. It was one of the four original provinces that united in 1867 to form the Dominion of Canada. Its capital, Québec City, is the oldest city in Canada, and its largest city, Montréal, is the second largest metropolitan area in the country after Toronto, Ontario.

Québec's most important river is the St. Lawrence River, which is 1,300 km long and traverses the entire province, connecting the Atlantic Ocean with the Great Lakes. From Montréal to Québec City, the river is seldom less than 1 km wide.

● *Québec City (魁北克市), Capital City of Québec*

Québec City is the capital of the province of Québec. It is the second most populous city in

118　Understanding Canada

the province—after Montreal, about 233 kilometers to the southwest. As of the 2006 Canadian Census, the city has a population of 491,142.

Located at the confluence of the St. Lawrence and Saint Charles rivers in the southern part of the province, Québec is dominated by a dramatic promontory(岬或海角), Cap Diamant (Cape Diamond), situated 98 m above a narrowing of the St. Lawrence River. The city's name is from an Algonquian(阿尔贡金语,北美印第安语的一种) word meaning "where the river narrows."

Québec City is internationally known for its Summer Festival, Winter Carnival and the Château Frontenac (芬堤娜城堡饭店), a historic hotel built in 1892, which overlooks the St. Lawrence River, 100 meters below and dominates the Québec City skyline. It has a historic elegance possibly unmatched in North America. The National Assembly of Québec (provincial parliament), the National Museum of Fine Arts and the Museum of Civilization are found within or near Vieux-Québec. Among the tourist attractions near the city are Montmorency Falls which, at 84 meters high, are the highest in the province of Québec and 30 m higher than Niagara Falls; and the Basilica of Sainte-Anne-de-Beaupré (圣安妮大教堂) in the town of Beaupré.

Founded in 1608 by Samuel de Champlain, Québec City is one of the oldest cities in North America. The ramparts (城墙) surrounding Old Québec are the only remaining fortified city walls that still exist in the Americas north of Mexico, and were declared a World Heritage Site by UNESCO in 1985 as the "Historic District of Old Québec".

● *Montréal*(蒙特利尔市), *the largest city in Quebec & second-largest in Canada*

Montréal is the second-largest city in Canada and the largest city in the province of Québec. Originally called Ville-Marie ("City-Mary"), the city had come to be known as Montréal by the end of the 17th century, a name derived from the French Mont Royal ("Mount Royal"), the name of the three-head hill at the heart of the city.

Formerly the largest metropolis of Canada (a distinction acquired by Toronto in the mid-1970s), it is the second-largest French-speaking city in the Western world after Paris. As of the 2006 Canadian Census, 1,620,693 people resided in the city of Montréal proper. In 2007, Montréal was ranked as the 10th cleanest city in the world.

Montréal is the second most visited city in Canada, after Toronto, and is a hugely popular destination for tourists from around the world. American tourists usually label the city as "unparallel" in North America and a "world class destination" to visit.

The Atlantic Provinces (东部大西洋区)

Atlantic Provinces refer to the three Maritime (沿海的) Provinces of New Brunswick, Nova Scotia, and Prince Edward Island, plus Newfoundland and Labrador. The Atlantic Provinces are on the far east coast of the country. Rugged and sparsely populated, the provinces have traditionally made much of their income from the area's large fisheries. This is changing in the region, as oil production, information technology, biomedical research, post secondary education and tourism become more important for local economies.

1. New Brunswick (新布伦兹维克省)

New Brunswick is the largest of Canada's three Maritime Provinces. It is bordered by the Canadian provinces of Québec and Nova Scotia, and the American state of Maine. It is blessed with two distinct shorelines; one with rocky cliffs, and the other fringed with long stretches of sand and dunes (海边被风吹积成的沙丘). Fishing wharves, charming villages, and cityscapes (都市风景) that provide blocks of Victorian architecture, are available as well as vast forests, fabled salmon rivers, islands and rolling farmland hills. Forests cover about 85 percent of the land and the manufacture of lumber, paper, and other forest products is important to the province's economy. New Brunswick also has rich farmland in the St. John River Valley. Mineral deposits have been discovered in the northeastern part of the province and the province's rivers have been harnessed to provide electricity.

Fredericton is the provincial capital, and Saint John is the largest city.

The Bay of Fundy New Brunswick/Nova Scotia has the highest tides(16.2 meters) in the world and is renown for its coastal rock formations.

The Swallowtail Lighthouse, New Brunswick

2. Nova Scotia

Nova Scotia (Latin for New Scotland) is located on Canada's southeastern coast. It is the most populous province in the Maritimes, and its capital, Halifax, is a major economic centre of the region. Nova Scotia is the second smallest province in Canada, with an area of 55,284 km². Its population of 934,405 makes it the fourth least populous province of the country, though second most densely populated.

Nova Scotia's economy is traditionally largely resource-based, but has in recent decades become more diverse. Industries such as fishing, mining, forestry and agriculture remain very important, and have been joined by tourism, technology, film production, music and the financial service industries.

● *Halifax* (哈利法克斯), ***Capital of Nova Scotia***

Located in the south-central part of the province on the Atlantic Ocean, Halifax is the capital city of Nova Scotia and the largest city in the Atlantic Provinces of Canada. The city's origins and rich maritime history derive from a strategic location and one of the world's great natural harbors. Founded in 1749, it served as an important naval base in the American Revolution, the War of 1812, and both World Wars. In the 19th and early 20th century,

Star-shaped Citadel

Halifax was the entry point for European immigration to Canada. Today, Halifax is a busy Atlantic seaport and the economic and cultural hub of Eastern Canada.

An old fort on a hill overlooking the city and the harbor, Halifax Citadel (要塞) is a national historic site and home to a museum and a small ceremonial garrison. The waterfront offers a great variety of restaurants, tours, and other entertainment. Brewery Market is considered the oldest running Farmer's Market in North America. It is always bustling with people buying ethnic and local foods, plants, artwork, and clothing.

3. Maritimes Province, Prince Edward Island (爱德华王子岛省)

Prince Edward Island (PEI) is located in the southern Gulf of St. Lawrence. This maritime province is the smallest in the nation in both land area and population (excluding the territories). The island has a few other names: "Garden of the Gulf" referring to the pastoral scenery and lush agricultural lands throughout the province; and "Birthplace of Confederation," referring to the Charlottetown Conference in 1864.

The island was discovered by Jacques Cartier in 1534 and named île St. Jean by Samuel de Champlain in 1603. It was renamed in 1798 after Prince Edward, Duke of Kent and Strathearn (1767—1820), the fourth son of King George III and the father of Queen Victoria. It joined the confederacy in 1873.

Confederation Bridge between PEI and New Brunswick

According to the 2009 estimates, Prince Edward Island has 140,402 residents. It is the 104th largest island in the world, and Canada's 23rd largest island. The island has two urban areas. The largest surrounds Charlottetown Harbor, situated centrally on the island's southern shore, and consists of the capital city Charlottetown, and its suburban towns. A much smaller urban area surrounds Summerside Harbor, situated on the southern shore 40 km west of Charlottetown Harbor, and consists primarily of the city of Summerside.

The 12.9-kilometre long Confederation Bridge links Prince Edward Island with mainland New Brunswick, Canada.

4. Newfoundland and Labrador

Newfoundland and Labrador is a province on the country's Atlantic coast in northeastern North America. This easternmost Canadian province comprises two main parts: the island of Newfoundland off the country's eastern coast, and Labrador on the mainland to the northwest of the island. St. John's is the capital and the largest city.

A former colony and dominion of the United Kingdom, it became the tenth province to enter the Canadian Confederation on 31 March 1949, named simply as Newfoundland. On 6 December 2001, an amendment was made to the Constitution of Canada to change the province's official name to Newfoundland and Labrador. In day-to-day conversation, however, Canadians generally still refer to the province itself as Newfoundland and to the region on the Canadian mainland as Labrador.

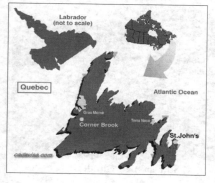

As of January 2009, the province's population is estimated to be 508,990. Approximately 94% of the province's population resides on the Island of Newfoundland (including its associated smaller islands).

St. John's is the provincial capital,. It is the most easterly city in North America, as well as the second largest city in Atlantic Provinces after Halifax, Nova Scotia and 20th largest metropolitan area in Canada with a population of 183,493.

The North Region of Canada (北部区)
　　Canada extends up north into the Arctic Circle to the North Pole. The north is a scarcely populated area of ice and oceans, which is sometimes called "the Land of the Midnight Sun." This region is currently divided into three administrative territories—the Yukon (育空地区), the Northwest Territories and Nunavat (努纳武特地区), a territory carved from eastern part of the original Northwest Territories in 1999.
　　As of 2006, only about 101,310 people were living in this vast area larger than the size of Western Europe. About 51% of the population of the three territories is Aboriginal, and the Inuit are the largest group of Aboriginal peoples in Northern Canada. There are also many more recent immigrants from around the world; Yukon has the largest percentage of non-Aboriginal inhabitants of the territories.

The Northern Lights most often occur from Sept. to Oct. and from March to April. The scientific name for the phenomenon is "Aurora Borealis."

　　The north region is heavily endowed with natural resources, but in most cases they are too expensive to extract. Though GDP per person is higher than elsewhere in Canada, the region remains relatively poor, mostly because of the extremely high cost of most consumer goods. The region is heavily subsidized (资助) by the Government of Canada. The traditional economy in this region was based on hunting and trapping animals for food and pelts, but now oil and gas deposits are also being developed.
　　Whitehorse (怀特霍斯), Yellowknife (耶洛奈夫) and Iqualui (伊凯鲁特) are major cities and towns of this sparsely-populated region.

1. Yukon (育空地区)
　　Yukon is the westernmost and smallest of Canada's three federal territories. It was named after the Yukon River (3,700 km), which means "Great River" and empties into the Bering Sea. Created in 1898 as the Yukon Territory, the federal government's most recent update of the Yukon Act in 2003 confirmed "Yukon," rather than "Yukon Territory," as the current usage standard.
　　Yukon is a sparsely populated territory with a population of about 33,442 (2009). Most of the territory is in the watershed (流域) of the Yukon River. Yukon abounds with snow-melt lakes and perennial snow-capped mountains. Mount Logan (5,959 m), in the territory's southwest, is the highest mountain in Canada and the second highest of North America (after Mount McKinley in the U.S. state of Alaska). Although the climate is Arctic and sub-arctic (亚北极的) and very dry, with long, cold winters, the long sunshine hours in short summer allow hardy (耐寒的) crops and vegetables, along with a profusion of flowers and fruit to blossom.
　　The Yukon's historical major industry has been mining. The territory's historical sites as well as the scenic wonders and outdoor recreation make tourism the second most important industry. Manufacturing follows in importance. The traditional industries of trapping and fishing have declined. Today, the government sector is by far the biggest employer in the territory, directly employing approximately 5,000 out of a labor force of 12,500.
　　Whitehorse is the capital and largest city of Yukon, which accounts for almost 3/4 of the territory's population and is the largest city in the three Canadian territories. The city gets its name from the White Horse rapids, which were said to look like the mane (鬃毛) of a white horse. Whitehorse is also famous for natural parks and landscapes, receiving the National Civic Lead

award for its natural beauty. The second largest is Dawson City, (pop. 1,250) which was the capital until 1952.

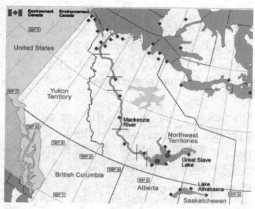

2. The Northwest Territories(西北地区)

Northwest Territories (N.W.T.) is the second largest of the three territories in Canada with a land area of 1,140,835 square kilometres. It extends from the 60th parallel to the North Pole and includes several large islands located in the Arctic Ocean.

The population is about 42,514 (2008 estimate Statistics Canada) and more than half of the people are aboriginal. The largest community is Yellowknife, which has been the capital city since 1967 and is known as the Diamond Capital of North America. Most people are living in the Mackenzie River Valley or around Great Slave Lake.

The first people were the Dene (达尼人,居住在加拿大西北及阿拉斯加内陆) and the Inuit. In 1870 the area became Canada's first territory. Yukon, Nunavut, Alberta, Saskatchewan, parts of Manitoba, Ontario, and Quebec were once part of the N.W.T. In 1999 the former Northwest Territories was divided, creating the new territory of Nunavut.

Mackenzie and Franklin Mountain Ranges are in the western part of the N.W.T. Great Bear Lake, located on the Arctic Circle, is the largest lake entirely within Canada, the third largest in North America, and the seventh largest in the world. Great Slave Lake is the deepest lake in Canada and tenth largest lake in the world. Mackenzie River (1,738 km), which originates in Great Slave Lake and flows north into the Arctic Ocean, is the longest river in Canada and the second longest in North America. The NWT's geological resources include gold, diamonds, natural gas and petroleum.

The vast natural resources and relatively low population give the Northwest Territories the highest per capita GDP of all provinces or territories in Canada. In fact, its per capita GDP of C$97,923 would rank it first in the world if it were considered as its own country.

The Northwest Territories' Official Languages Act recognizes eleven official languages with English and French included, which are more than in any other political division in the Americas.

Yellowknife (pop.about 20,000) has been the capital of the Northwest Territories (NWT) since 1967 and is the hub for mining, industry, transportation, communications, education, health, tourism, commerce, and government activity. It is located on the north shore of beautiful Great Slave Lake, only about 400 km south of the Arctic Circle. Yellowknife and its surrounding water bodies were named after the local Yellowknives, one of the five main groups of the Dene (达尼人) indigenous people that live in the Northwest Territories. The name derives from the color of the tools made from local copper deposits.

As the largest city in the Northwest Territories, Yellowknife is built on gold, nurtured by government and growing with diamonds. It was first settled in 1935, after gold had been found in the area, and soon became the centre of economic activity in the NWT. As gold production began to wane, Yellowknife shifted from being a mining town to being a centre of government services in the 1980s. However, with the recent discovery of diamonds north of Yellowknife, this shift has begun to reverse.

3. Nunavut (努纳武特地区)

The establishment of Nunavut, which means "our land" in Inuktitut, represents a landmark event in the history of Inuit and Canada. On April 1, 1999, Nunavut became the newest federal territory of Canada, encompassing the central and eastern Arctic regions, covering 1,932,255 km² of land and 160,935 km² of water. This makes it the largest of all Canada's provinces and Territories and the fifth largest administrative division in the world. Originally part of the Northwest Territories, Nunavut was separated officially from the Northwest Territories on April 1, 1999 though the actual boundaries had been established in 1993.

Nunavut is both the geographically largest and the least populated of the provinces and territories of Canada. It has a population of 29,474 spread over an area of the size of Western Europe, of whom 85 per cent are Inuit and 60 per cent are under the age of 25. The population density is 0.015 persons per square kilometer, one of the lowest in the world.

Winter is close to nine months long in this region, with snow covering the ground for most of the year. Mining, shrimp and scallop (扇贝) fishing, hunting and trapping, arts and crafts production are the key industries. Tourism is also a growing industry.

Iqaluit is the territorial capital and the largest community of Nunavut, with a population of 6, 184 (2006). It has the distinction of being the smallest Canadian capital in terms of population. Most of the people of Iqaluit are Inuit, and the town's name means "the place where the fish are" in the Inuit language. Before 1987 Iqaluit was known by the European name of Frobisher Bay. Located on an island remote from the Canadian highway system, Iqaluit is the only capital that is not connected to other settlements by a highway and is the only city for thousands of miles in any direction. There are no roads in or out of Iqaluit and the city is generally only accessible by aircraft and by boat. It is about 3.5 flying hours north of Ottawa, the country's capital.

Iqaluit has a typically Arctic climate with very cold winters and short summers that are too cool to permit the growth of trees. Average monthly temperatures are below freezing for eight months of the year. In late January, the average daytime high was -22 C. Since Iqaluit is well below the Arctic Circle, it never gets 24 hours of darkness. In late January it gets light about 8 am and dark about 3 pm.

Inuit Hunters Killing a Polar Bear

IV Climate

People tend to think that as Canada is a northern country, its winters must be harsh and long. But contrary to popular belief, on the whole Canada is a very sunny land with a distinctive change of seasons. Climatic conditions range from the extreme cold of the Arctic regions to the moderate temperatures of more southerly latitudes.

In winter, temperatures fall below freezing point throughout most of Canada, the air is generally very dry. Therefore, when no wind is present, the coldest climate of Canada is surprisingly bearable. Along the Arctic Circle, mean temperatures are below freezing for seven months a year.

The south-western coast has a relatively mild climate. During the summer months the southern provinces often experience high levels of humidity and temperatures that can surpass 30 degrees Celsius regularly. In the summer, a temperature of 30°C, can feel like 45°C when it's very humid.

Precipitation (降水量) is not equally distributed over the Canadian territory. The Pacific region, and the Atlantic provinces receive the most, while the southern Prairie region are dry with

250 mm to 500 mm of rain every year. Average summer temperatures range from 8°C in the far north to more than 22°C in some parts of the far south. Average January temperatures range from −35°C in the far north to 3°C in southwestern British Columbia.

Six Climate Regions

Since Canada is such a vast country, its climate varies greatly from region to region. When talking about Canada's climate, people usually divide it into seven climatic regions:

● *The Arctic Region* (北极地区)—*northeastern Nunavut*

The Arctic Region is truly cold. During winter, the whole area is normally covered by ice and temperature easily reaches −60° C. During summer, the tundra is the main vegetation and, in the warmest parts of the Arctic, shrubs, willow, and birch can be found. Animal life is poor in the number of species. There are polar bears, arctic foxes and musk oxen.

Map of seven general climatic regions.

A musk ox

● *The Northern Region* (sub-Arctic, 北方地区)

The Northern Regions comprise lands that lie south of the Arctic Circle including southwestern Nunavut, northern portions of Alberta, Saskatchewan, and Manitoba, most of Ontario and Québec (including Labrador, QC). The region display arctic weather conditions during some or all of the year. Typically, most of these areas have a climate where the temperature is above 10 degrees Celsius for at least one month, but no more than three months. There is usually between 40 and 100 centimeters of precipitation a year, much of which is in the form of snow. Ontario and Québec, which has great variations in heat and cold, is the snowiest region in Canada.

● *The Pacific Region* (West, 西部沿岸地区)

This region is made up of coastal portion of British Columbia. Here is where one finds the wettest weather, tallest trees, and deepest fjords (海湾) in the country. The beautiful coast of British Columbia is well known for its temperate climate. Summer temperatures average 13℃, while winters average −1.5℃; there is less difference between winter and summer temperatures here than elsewhere in the country. The precipitation can exceed 4000 mm a year in the north, although some areas get far less than that. Victoria, the capital of British Columbia claims the mildest climate in Canada because the Pacific Ocean in this region maintains a constant temperature of 10°C. Victoria enjoys an average of 2,183 hours of sunshine each year, with flowers is in bloom year-round.

● *Cordillera Region* (山脉地区)

Yukon and British Columbia interior compose the Cordillera Region. The word "cordillera" means mountain ranges. The mountains, the nearby Pacific Ocean, and differences in latitude cause the climate of the Cordillera region to vary widely. Winters are long and cold, with January mean(平均的) temperatures between –15℃ and –27℃. Summers are warm but short, with July mean temperatures between 12℃ and 15℃. In the Canadian Cordillera, the higher western slopes, particularly the Rockies, receive sizable amounts of rain and snow. The eastern slopes and the central plateau receive little precipitation (降水量). In the eastern Canadian Cordillera, the Chinook (奇努克风,从落基山脉东坡吹下的干燥暖风), a warm, dry westerly wind, makes winters substantially less severe in the Rocky Mountain foothills and adjoining plains. While the higher elevations and more northern latitudes have a very cold and dry climate, not unlike the arctic climate.

● *The Prairies* (草原地区)

The Prairies cover the southern portions of Alberta, Saskatchewan and Manitoba. The climate is marked by the most extreme ranges of summer heat and winter cold due to the lack of access to the ocean's buffering (缓冲作用). Winter temperatures average –10℃ and summers average 15℃. Spring showers and temperate autumn weather makes the Prairies one of the top grain-growing areas of the world.

● *The Southeastern Region* (东南部地区)

The densely-populated Southern Ontario, southwestern Québec, and New-Brunswick interior form the Southeastern Region. Smallest as it is, the Southeastern Region is nonetheless home to half of Canada's population. Its cool winters (average temperature –5℃) and warm summers (average temperature 17℃) are prone to highly changeable weather, as the region is in one of the major storm tracks of North America. In the Atlantic Provinces, the ocean lessens the extremes of winter cold and summer heat but also causes considerable fog and precipitation (降水).

● *Atlantic Region (East,* 东部沿岸地区)

The Atlantic Region comprises New Brunswick coast, Nova Scotia, Prince Edward Island, Newfoundland. Climate here is strongly influenced by the Atlantic Ocean, which produces cooler summers and warmer winters. Winter temperatures average –5℃ and summers average 14°C, with coastal areas having slightly warmer winters and cooler summers than inland. The Atlantic also provides moisture to the region, producing mean precipitation of 900 mm a year inland and over 1500 mm a year on the coast; this high precipitation also means that the region has more storms than anywhere else in the country. The coasts are also often shrouded in a thick fog, especially along the Bay of Fundy and on the island of Newfoundland. The Bay of Fundy features the largest tides in the world, the difference between high and low tide topping 15 meters.

Significant Climatic Changes in Canada

Similar to the extreme temperature change, Canada's precipitation (降水量) ranges from near-desert conditions of less than 300 mm per year in the far north to very wet conditions of more than 2,400 mm in parts of the west coast.

Generally speaking, spring begins in mid-March and ends in mid-May. It is regarded as a transitional time in Canada. In many parts of Canada, the first sign of spring is the trickling (流淌) of sap (树液) from thousands of maple-trees. It is in spring that farmers reap their special harvest —maple-syrup (枫树汁)to make delicious sugar products.

Summer is longer than spring, lasting for about four months in places near the U.S.- Canadian border, from mid-May to mid-Sept.

Sugar maple tree in spring

126 Understanding Canada

Skating on Rideau Canal, Ottawa

Warm and sunny, it's the golden time for vacationers.

Autumn is brief but spectacular, beginning from mid-Sept to mid-Nov. Leaves turned into millions of shades of gold and scarlet against the background of blue sky.

Winter is the longest season in most of Canada, prolonging from mid-Nov to mid-March. Canadians will never deny that they have more than their share of ice and snow. It is a golden time for skiing, skating, ice-fishing and tobogganing (滑雪橇).

Designated by UNESCO as a World Heritage Site, the Rideau Canal becomes the world's largest skating rink every winter.

Climate and Canadian Life

Climate has been a factor in the development of Canada because people have settled where temperatures are warmest and agricultural growing seasons longest. Climate also influences vegetation, producing, for example, the rain forest of coastal British Columbia. Southern Ontario and southwestern British Columbia have the mildest climates and greatest population densities in Canada. In contrast, the central and northern regions are sparsely populated.

The permafrost (永久冻结带) region in the north poses great challenges for settlement and development. Yukon, the Northwest Territories, the Nunavut Territory, northern Québec and Labrador, and the far northern areas of Ontario and Manitoba are all affected by this condition.

Scientist collecting soil samples in the permafrost in the Yukon, Canada

IV Natural Resources

Canada is rich in valuable natural resources that are commercially indispensable to the economy. Most are specific to one region or another; for this reason separate resource-based economies have tended to develop across Canada.

Forestry

Canadian forests cover 34% of the country's land area and abound in commercially valuable stands of timber, especially in British Columbia, Québec, northern Ontario, the northern Prairie Provinces, and the Maritimes.

Mineral resources

Canada's extensive mineral resources provide valuable exports and also supply domestic industries. Five of the country's six major regions contribute to these resources. The Québec portion of the Appalachian Region has the world's largest reserves of asbestos (石棉), along with deposits of copper and zinc.

The Canadian Shield is a rich source of metals such as nickel, copper, gold, uranium (铀), silver, aluminum, and zinc. Minerals from the shield helped fuel the manufacturing development of southern Ontario and Québec.

The Great Plains region is rich in reserves of crude petroleum and natural gas; these are concentrated in the Prairie Provinces, particularly in Alberta. These fuel deposits are responsible for the dynamic energy-producing economy of these provinces.

The western Canadian Cordillera provides copper, lead, zinc, molybdenum (钼), and asbestos; the Canadian Arctic Archipelago (多岛海区) provides zinc and lead. Increasingly important to the mining industry, the Canadian Arctic Archipelago features the world's northernmost base metal mine, the Polaris mine, on Little Cornwallis Island.

Hydroelectric Energy

The river and lake systems of the country combine with topography to make hydroelectric energy one of the permanent natural assets of Canada. Here British Columbia and the shield provinces are particularly well endowed. As with other natural resources, much of the energy is exported.

Wild life

The wildlife of the country is extensive and varied and attracts tourists from around the world. But it is the fish stocks that have the greatest economic value. Saltwater fish in the Pacific and the Atlantic Oceans, as well as freshwater fish in Canada's numerous lakes and rivers, are economically significant and also provide a source of food and revenue for many local communities.

Cougar (美洲狮)   **Polar bear** (北极熊)   **Raccoon** (浣熊)   **Moose** (驼鹿)

B. History

First inhabited for thousands of years by aboriginal peoples, Canada has evolved from a group of European colonies into an officially bilingual, multicultural federation. France sent the first large group of settlers in the 17th century, but Canada came to be dominated by the British until the country peacefully attained full independence in the 20th century. Its history has been affected by its inhabitants, its geography, and its relations with the outside world.

First Peoples

Many indigenous peoples have inhabited the region that is now Canada for thousands of years and have their own diverse histories. Indigenous peoples include First Nations people (Canadian Indians), Inuit (因纽特人,加拿大北冰洋地区的爱斯基摩人) and Métis (美地人,土著与白人的混血种). Indigenous peoples contributed significantly to the culture and economy of the early European colonies and have played an important role in fostering a unique Canadian cultural identity.

European Contact (985—1600)

There are a number of reports of contact made before Columbus between the first peoples and those from other continents. It is said that British, Portuguese and Spanish explorers had visited Canada, but it was the French who first began to explore further inland and set up colonies, beginning in 1534 with French navigator Jacques Cartier, who in 1534 first explored and described the Gulf of St-Lawrence and the shores of the Saint Lawrence River, which he named Canada and claimed its shores for the French crown.

Jacques Cartier
(1491—1557)

Understanding Canada

Samuel de Champlain (1567?—1635)

Under Samuel de Champlain, who was regarded "father of New France" and "founder of Québec City," the first French settlement was made in 1605 at Port-Royal (today's Annapolis Royal), and in 1608 the heart of New-France was established, which later grew to be Québec City. The French claimed Canada as their own and 6,000 settlers arrived, settling along the St. Lawrence and in the Maritimes.

Britain also had a presence in Newfoundland and with the advent of settlements, claimed the south of Nova Scotia as well as the areas around the Hudson Bay.

The first agricultural settlements in what was to become Canada were located around the French settlement of Port Royal in what is now Nova Scotia. The population of Acadians, as this group became known, reached 5,000 by 1713.

New France (1604—1763)

Québec City became the capital of New France after Champlain's founding in 1608. The coastal communities were based upon the cod fishery; the economy along the St. Lawrence River was based on farming. Encouraging settlement was always difficult, and while some immigration did occur, by 1759 New France only had a population of some 60,000. The economy was primitive and much of the population was involved in little more than simple agriculture. The colonists also engaged in a long running series of wars with the Iroquois.

Britain and France repeatedly went to war in the 17th and 18th centuries, and made their colonial empires into battlefields. Numerous naval battles were fought in the West Indies; the main land battles were fought in and around Canada.

The first areas won by the British were the Maritime Provinces. After Queen Anne's War (1701—1714), Nova Scotia was ceded to the British. This gave Britain control over thousands of French-speaking Acadians. Not trusting these new subjects, the British brought in Protestants settlers from Europe and a new migration of Yankees from New England who transformed Nova Scotia.

Canada was also an important battlefield in the Seven Years' War, during which Great Britain gained control of Québec City after the Battle of the Plains of Abraham in 1759, and Montreal in 1760.

Canada under British Imperial Control (1764—1867)

With the end of the Seven Years' War and the signing of the Treaty of Paris on February 10, 1763, France ceded almost all of its territory in North America. Violent conflict continued during the next century, leading Canada into the War of 1812 and a pair of Rebellions in 1837.

In 1838 a new Whig government sent Lord Durham to examine the situation and his Durham Report strongly recommended responsible government. A less well received recommendation, however, was the amalgamation (合并) of Upper and Lower Canada in order to

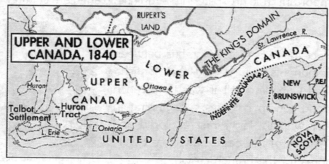

Map of Upper and Lower Canada in 1840 Upper Canada was a British province officially existed from 1791 to 1841 and covered generally present-day Southern Ontario. Lower Canada was on the lower Saint Lawrence River and the shores of the Gulf of Saint Lawrence (1791—1841) covering the southern portion of the modern-day province of Québec.

forcibly assimilate the French speaking population. The Canadas were merged into a single, quasi (准的)-federal colony, the United Province of Canada, with the Act of Union (1840).

Once the United States agreed to the 49th parallel north as the border separating it from western British North America, the British government created the Pacific coast colonies of British Columbia in 1848 and Vancouver Island in 1849. They were eventually united in 1866.

A set of proposals called the Seventy-Two Resolutions were drafted at the 1864 Québec Conference. They laid out the framework for an independent Canada. They were adopted by the majority of the provinces of Canada, and became the basis for the London Conference of 1866.

Dominion of Canada (1867—1914)

On July 1, 1867, with the passing of the British North America Act by the British Parliament, the Province of Canada (divided into Québec and Ontario), New Brunswick, and Nova Scotia became a federation. The term dominion was chosen to indicate Canada's status as a self-governing colony of the British Empire, the first time it was used in reference to a country.

With the construction of the Canadian Pacific Railway, the new country expanded East, West and North, to assert its authority over a greater territory. Manitoba joined the Dominion in 1870 and British Columbia in 1871. In 1905, Saskatchewan and Alberta were admitted as provinces.

Canada in World Wars and Interwar Years (1914—1945)

Canada's participation in the First World War (1914—1917) helped to foster a sense of Canadian nationhood. As a result of the war, the Canadian government became more assertive and less obedient to British authority.

Canada is sometimes considered to be the country hardest hit by the interwar Great Depression. The economy fell further than that of any nation other than the United States. The financial crisis of the Great Depression, soured (恶化) by rampant corruption, had led Newfoundlanders to relinquish (放弃) responsible government in 1934 and become a crown colony ruled by a British governor.

Canada's involvement in the Second World War began when Canada declared war on Germany on September 10, 1939, one week after Britain. Canadian forces were involved in the failed defense of Hong Kong, the Dieppe Raid (迪耶普突袭) in August 1942, the Allied invasion of Italy, and the Battle of Normandy.

Post-war Canada (1945—present)

Prosperity returned to Canada during Second World War. With continued Liberal governments, national policies increasingly turned to social welfare, including hospital insurance, old-age pensions, and veterans' pensions.

In 1949 Newfoundland and Labrador, until then a British dominion separate from Canada, chose in a hotly contested referendum to become Canada's tenth province.

Industrial growth was matched by population growth. Immigration, mostly from Europe, and the postwar baby boom (a great increase in the birthrate) raised Canada's population by 50 percent, from 12 million to 18 million, between 1946 and 1961.

Canada's foreign policy during the Cold War was closely tied to that of the U.S., demonstrated by membership in NATO, sending combat troops into the Korean War, and establishing a joint air defense system (NORAD) with the U.S.

In the 1960s, a Quiet Revolution took place in Québec. Québécois nationalists demanded independence and ten-

A Canadian boy displays a newspaper headline declaring "Victory," May 7, 1945.

sions rose until violence erupted during the 1970 October Crisis, when Québec nationalists and FLQ (Québec Liberation Front, 魁北克解放前线,激进的魁北克独立组织) members kidnapped British diplomat James Cross and Québec provincial cabinet minister Pierre Laporte, who was later murdered. The October Crisis raised fears in Canada of a militant terrorist faction rising up against the government.

In the past decade and a half, Canada experienced a second Québec referendum on sovereignty, and the creation of a new territory, Nunavut (in 1999). While long standing issues like immigration continued to demand attention, new debates over same-sex marriage (made legal in Canada in July, 2005) and international peacekeeping would increasingly take the forefront.

As of 2007, Stephen Harper (斯蒂芬·哈珀) is the Prime Minister of Canada, leading the Conservative Party in a minority government.

A Brief History of French Canada

1608	French begin to colonize Canada.
1760	Great Britain conquers Canada. Nearly all of the French colonists remain.
1763	Royal Proclamation of King George III applies British law in Canada.
1774	The Québec Act adopts French civil law and grants civil rights to Catholics.
1791	Lower Canada (French) and Upper Canada (English) are separated, each with its own legislative assembly.
1834	Lower Canada's assembly drafts its 92 Resolutions requesting responsible government.
1837—1838	Great Britain rejects the 92 Resolutions, and rebellion breaks out. British troops put down the insurgents.
1841—1848	Act of Union merges Upper and Lower Canada, which share a single Legislature. French— and English-speaking politicians form alliances and work to achieve responsible government.
1867	The Dominion of Canada is formed. Québec becomes a province and gains greater local autonomy.
1885	Execution of Métis leader Louis Riel inflames public opinion in Québec.
1890	Manitoba abolishes separate school system for French speakers.
1905	Separate school systems for French speakers are abolished in Alberta and Saskatchewan when they become provinces.
1912	Ontario abolishes schools for French speakers.
1917	French Canadians in Québec stage massive protests against conscription to fight what they call "England's war."
1960	The Quiet Revolution, a modernization of Québec society, begins under the administration of Premier Jean Lesage.
1969—1977	Provincial legislation enhances the status of the French language in Québec.
1970	In the October Crisis, terrorists seeking independence for Québec kidnap two government officials and murder one of them.

1976	Québec elects a government run by Parti Québecois, which seeks to establish "sovereignty-association"—independence for Québec with economic links to Canada.
1980	In a referendum, Québec voters reject sovereignty-association by a 20 percent margin.
1982	Canada adopts a new constitution over the objections of Québec.
1990	Meech Lake Accord, an attempt to make the constitution agreeable to Québec, fails.
1992	A second attempt, the Charlottetown Accord, also fails.
1995	In a second referendum, Québec voters reject sovereignty-association by the barest of margins—less than 1 percent.

Chapter 7 Political System and National Economy

I Political System

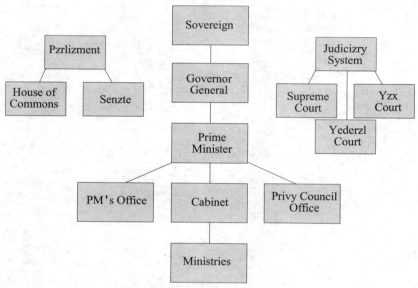

Construction of the Canadian Government

Political System

Canada is an independent federation governed under a parliamentary democracy and constitutional monarchy (君主立宪制). It is a member of Commonwealth (英联邦). The Canadian political system as it is known today was first drafted by the "Fathers of Confederation" at the Québec Conference of 1864. This then became law when the Constitution Act was passed in 1867. This act gave the formal executive authority to Queen Victoria (Queen of Great Britain) which made Canada a sovereign democracy. The Canadian political system is therefore loosely based on the British system.

Now, Canada is a Federal state with the Queen still the head of state. Her powers are extremely limited however, as the Parliament passes the laws which the Queen gives the "Royal Assent" as the final step.

The opening of the Twenty-Third Parliament of Canada on October 14, 1957, was an occasion of unprecedented significance for Canadians. Her Majesty Queen Elizabeth II, accompanied by His Royal Highness the Prince Philip, read the Speech from the Throne and thus became the first Sovereign to inaugurate in person a session of Parliament as Head of State of Canada.

Governor General of Canada

The Governor General is appointed by The Queen (on the advice of the Canadian Prime Minister) and carries out all the Royal obligations when the Queen is not in Canada. The length of office is normally five years.

Head of Government

Canada's Head of Government is the Prime Minister who is an elected representative of the people of Canada and head of his political party and has the mandate to govern through policies and programs.

The Houses of Parliament

Located in Canada's capital city, Ottawa, there are 3 main sections to the Canadian Parliament: the Queen as the Head of State; the Senate (appointed on the Prime Minister's recommendations) and the elected House of Commons. The Federal Government has the power to "make laws for the peace, order and good government of Canada" which includes international policies, defense, immigration, criminal law, customs and border control.

Canadian Governor General's Residence (Canada's "White House"). The ceremonial guards remind you of the close ties between Canada and Great Britain.

● *The Senate*

The Senate is made up of 105 Senators who are appointed by the Governor General on the recommendation of the Prime Minister. These

Senators are men and women from all of the Provinces and from a wide variety of backgrounds. Each Province or Territory has a set number of Senators—24 each from the Maritimes, Quebec and Ontario; 6 each from Alberta, BC, Manitoba and Saskatchewan; 6 from Newfoundland and Labrador; and a further 1 each from the three Territories.

The main role of the Senate is to read over and examine the "Bills" sent from the House of Commons though they can also initiate Bills. This process ensures that no rogue bills will become law, though only rarely do the Senate reject a Bill - sending it back to the House for amendment. The Bills are subjected to the full legislative process by the Senate and if passed will be given to the Governor General for Royal Assent and thus become Law.

● *The House of Commons*

The real power is held by the House of Commons. Here, the members of Parliament (MP's) are elected by the general public during a Federal election - normally every 5 years. The country is split up into 308 constituencies (选区) by population size and whichever candidate has the most votes wins the right to represent that constituency and take their "seat" in the Parliament.

Most candidates represent a particular political party and the party with the most "seats" takes over as the Government. The main parties in Canada are Conservatives Liberals, New Democratic Party, Bloc Québecois and The Green Party to name the largest.

The leader of the political party that wins the election becomes the Prime Minister of Canada. The Prime Minister effectively runs the country with the support and advice of his Cabinet. The Cabinet is made up of "Ministers" chosen by the Prime Minister to be responsible for certain areas of the Government.

The MP's main duties are debating the laws to be made and, depending on their Party, either supporting or opposing the Government. The opposition is the political party with the second most seats in the House and their main job is to hold the government accountable (负责任的) for their decisions.

The Supreme Court of Canada

The Supreme Court Building of Canada, Ottawa // Judges of the Supreme Court of Canada, 2009

The Supreme Court of Canada is the highest court in Canada. Courts administer justice. They decide who is right and who is wrong in cases or disputes brought to them. The Supreme Court makes the final decision over disputes in Canada. Nine justices (judges) are on the Supreme Court of Canada.

Provincial Governments

Governmental powers in Canada are divided between the central or federal government and the provincial and territorial governments. Territories have less autonomy(自治权) from the federal government than provinces have.

The head of the provincial government is the premier (加拿大省份的主要行政官员), who is appointed by the lieutenant governor (副总督) after his or her party wins a general election. The premier's role is similar to that of the prime minister in Ottawa.

The three territories are administered by Ottawa through the Department of Indian Affairs and Northern Development. The chief executives are commissioners, appointed by the federal government and assisted by local councils.

Foreign Affairs

Foreign policy is coordinated by Canada's Department of Foreign Affairs and International Trade. Canada belongs to a variety of major international organizations. One is the Commonwealth of Nations, which developed gradually after World War I as former British colonies gained their independence.

Canada was a charter member (发起人) of the United Nations (UN). Other international groups that Canada has joined are the International Monetary Fund (国际货币基金会); World Bank; World Trade Organization; Organization for Economic Cooperation and Development (1961); Group of Eight; and Asia-Pacific Economic Cooperation organization (1994).

II National Economy

Canada is one of the world's wealthiest nations, and a member of the Organization for Economic Co-operation and Development (OECD, 经合组织) and Group of Eight (G8, 八国集团). Historically, much of its wealth has been generated through the extraction and processing of natural resources, especially fish, furs, timber, minerals, and farm produce. Now manufacturing and service activities have been added, and Canada now has one of the most complex economies in the world. Canada is also highly integrated into the global economy through trade, with more than a third of its GDP dedicated to exports.

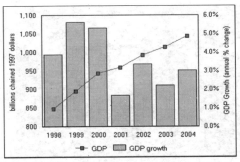
Canadian GDP Growth 1997—2004

Agriculture

Agriculture is not as important to the Canadian economy as it was in the 19th century, but it continues to be the mainstay (支柱) of several regions and is a significant source of export income. In early 2006 there were 229, 400 farms in Canada, averaging 295 hectares in size. Some 340,000 men and women worked in agricultural jobs in 2005, representing 2.1 percent of the total labor force.

Farms in Canada are about equally divided between crop raising and livestock production. Wheat is the most important single crop, and the Prairie Provinces of Alberta, Manitoba, and Saskatchewan form one of the greatest wheat—growing areas of the world.

Farmer in mature wheat field in Manitoba, Canada

In 2003 the Canadian cattle industry was damaged when a cow in Alberta tested positive for bovine spongiform encephalopathy (BSE; 牛海绵状脑病), also known as mad cow disease. A feature of such disease is the inability of the infected animal to stand. The discovery caused several nations to ban the importing of Canadian cattle. The ban was finally lifted in mid-2005, but not before costing the industry an estimated C$7 billion in lost sales.

Forestry

Forest products contribute significantly to regional and rural economies in Canada. It is estimated that the full range of forestry activities generates roughly 1 in 15 Canadian jobs, with activities concentrated in British Columbia, Québec, and Ontario. Despite heavy harvesting by early settlers, forests, mainly coniferous (松柏科的), still cover 34 percent of the country's land area. Most of the forestland is owned and managed by the provincial and federal governments.

A cow with BSE

Canadian wood products are among the finest in the world. The famous ones include Canadian softwood lumber and Canadian pulp (纸浆), which is known for strong, light-colored paper products. Canada is the world's largest producer of newsprint (新闻用纸) and exports the vast majority of it. It is also the world's second largest producer of pulp, the third largest producer of sawn lumber, and the world's largest exporter of softwood lumber.

Pacific halibut are the largest flatfish (比目鱼) in the ocean

Fisheries

Fisheries and Oceans Canada (DFO) has six administrative regions: Pacific, Central and Arctic, Quebec, Maritimes, Gulf, and Newfoundland and Labrador. Canada is one of the world's

Fur traders in Canada, 1777

largest exporters of fish and seafood. Cod (鳕), herring (鲱), crab, lobster, and scallops (扇贝) have been the most important exports from the Atlantic coast, and halibut (大比目鱼) and salmon (鲑) from the Pacific coast. There is also a commercial freshwater fishery in Ontario, focused on Lake Erie. Commercial sport fishing industries have been developed throughout Canada.

Furs

In many ways, the fur industry created Canada in the pre-Confederation period. But by the late 20th century demand for fur had declined, and the income of indigenous (本土的) trappers had suffered severely. Canada's remaining fur farms are mainly concentrated in Ontario, Nova Scotia, Québec, and British Columbia. Trapping is carried on primarily in northern Canada; Ontario, Québec, Alberta, Saskatchewan, and Manitoba are the main producers of wildlife pelts.

Mining

Mining in Canada has a long history of exploration and development. The country is one of the world's leading producers and exporters of minerals such as uranium (铀), zinc, potash (碳酸钾), nickel, elemental sulfur, asbestos, cadmium (镉), platinum, gypsum (石膏), copper, lead, cobalt (钴), titanium (钛), and molybdenum (钼). Much exploration and development activity in Canada is now devoted to diamond mining, especially in the Northwest Territories, the Prairie Provinces, and the Canadian Shield. Oil and natural gas are also important to Canada's mining industry. Oil and gas production is centered mainly in Alberta, where crude oil and natural gas are transported throughout Canada and to the United States.

Manufacturing

Manufacturing is a key component of the Canadian economy, employing about 15 percent of the country's workforce and accounting for 17 percent of the GDP and around 75 percent of goods exported. Canada's chief manufacturing industry is transportation equipment, especially automobiles and auto parts. This sector makes up almost one-quarter of the total value of the country's manufacturing output. In recent decades, the transportation equipment industry has evolved toward a single continental market in North America. Other significant manufacturing sectors include food processing, paper products, chemical products, primary metal processing, petroleum refining (石油加工), electrical and electronic products, metal fabricating, and wood processing. Many of these manufactures rely on Canada's vigorous resource industries.

Energy

As a large country rich in natural resources, Canada's energy industry is one of the biggest in the world. Each year the country produces much more energy than it consumes, making it a significant exporter of this resource, especially to the United States. In 2003 Canada's annual output of electricity was 566 billion kilowatt hours, of which 59 percent was provided by hydroelectric plants, 12 percent by nuclear power plants, and 27.28 percent by conventional thermal plants using fossil fuels. Wind-generated energy is the fastest-growing sector of the industry.

Foreign Trade

Canada has just 0.6 percent of the world's population, but accounts for 4 percent of total exports in world trade. Exports have always been important to Canada's economy. In the early colonial period, the leading Canadian items of export were fish and furs. During the 19th century, timber became the staple export item. With the improvement of railway lines early in the 20th century and settlement of the prairies, wheat became the chief item of export. Gradually, manufacturing industries emerged and now produce more than three-quarters of Canada's exports.

Most of Canada's foreign trade is with the United States. A large portion of this trade is made up of motor vehicles and motor vehicle parts. Canada also has significant export trade with other countries, including the United Kingdom, Germany, South Korea, the Netherlands, and China. Canada's leading imports include machinery, transportation equipment, communications and office equipment (especially computers), and other consumer goods.

Currency and Banking

The unit of currency in Canada is the Canadian dollar, which consists of 100 cents (C$1.20 equals US$1, 2005 average). The Bank of Canada, which was founded in 1935 and is owned by the federal government, has the sole right to issue paper money for circulation.

In everyday commerce, the banks in Canada are generally referred to in two categories: 1) the five large national banks and 2) smaller second tier (等级) banks. The five largest banks in Canada are the Royal Bank of Canada, the Toronto Dominion Bank, the Bank of Montreal, the Bank of Nova Scotia, and the Canadian Imperial Bank of Commerce. The Big Five are not just Canadian banks, but are instead better described as international financial conglomerates (金融机构), each with a large Canadian banking division.

Gold Covered Building of Royal Bank of Canada, Toronto

Notable second tier banks include the National Bank of Canada, the Mouvement Desjardins (technically not a bank but an alliance of credit unions), HSBC Bank Canada, and ING Bank of Canada. These second tier organizations are largely Canadian domestic banking organizations. Insurance companies in Canada have also created deposit-taking bank subsidiaries.

Most foreign-owned and major domestic banks in Canada have their head offices in Toronto, and a few are based in Montréal. Trust and mortgage loan companies, provincial savings banks, and credit unions also provide banking services. Securities exchanges operate in Toronto, Montréal, Winnipeg, Calgary, and Vancouver.

Transportation

Since the earliest explorations, water travel has been important to Canada. The St. Lawrence—Great Lakes navigation system extends 3,769 km from the Gulf of St. Lawrence into the center of the continent. The opening of the St. Lawrence Seaway in 1959 contributed greatly to industrial expansion, but the seaway is declining in significance with the growth of inter-modal transport (联运).

Canada does not have a large merchant marine and the great majority of Canadian overseas trade is carried in ships of other countries. Most ships of Canadian registry operate along the coast, on the St. Lawrence Seaway, or on the Great Lakes. Ships called lake carriers, or "lakers," are built in eastern Canada specifically for the Seaway—Great Lakes traffic.

Via Rail of Canada

Rail transportation has been crucial to the formation of Canada but has declined in recent decades, due chiefly to the popularity of motor vehicles. The two major railways are the Canadian National (CN), formerly a federally owned corporation, and the Canadian Pacific Railway (CPR). Their declining revenues led Ottawa to create a combined passenger network, VIA Rail, in 1977. However, revenue from passenger service was not sufficient to cover the costs of the service, and in 1990 half the routes were closed.

Canada has one of the world's best highway systems; good roads are essential to a country of such wide spaces, scattered people, and geographic barriers. The national highway system in Canada carries about a third of all road traffic in the country. The Trans—Canada Highway, completed in 1962, stretches from St. John's, Newfoundland and Labrador, to Victoria, British Columbia.

Canada's largest airline, Air Canada, maintains a broad network of domestic and international routes. Air travel is particularly important in the far north because the widely scattered communities of the region are not connected by road or rail and water transport is limited to the brief summer periods. The busiest airports in Canada are Lester B. Pearson International in Toronto, Vancouver International, Trudeau and Mirabel in Montréal, and Calgary International.

Tourism

Canada boasts a large domestic and foreign tourist industry. The second largest country in the world, Canada's incredible geographical variety is a significant tourist attracter. Canada's three largest cities, Toronto, Vancouver, and Montreal are major metropolitan areas, well-known for their culture and diversity. Canadian historic sites across the nation are also important to the tourist industry.

Canada's variety of seasons and scenic attractions draws large numbers of tourists from around the world. There are many festivals, including spring blossom festivals in the Annapolis Valley of Nova Scotia and the Okanagan Valley in British Columbia, the Ottawa Festival of Spring, and the Calgary Exhibition and Stampede. The Niagara Grape and Wine Festival and color tours in central Ontario and the Laurentian Mountains of Québec are autumn attractions. Cosmopolitan cities such as Vancouver, Montréal, and Toronto draw millions of visitors annually to their many cultural attractions. Visitors are also drawn to Canadian wilderness areas. In the winter the abundant snowfall supports a number of world-class skiing centers, especially in the Canadian Cordillera region. Many terrestrial and marine areas have been preserved in their natural state as national parks, and each of the provinces and territories also has set aside land as provincial or territorial parks.

Canada Place in Vancouver
Rebuilt for Expo '86, a gala World's Fair that was held in Vancouver, Canada Place was originally the site of an old cargo pier. This multi-use commercial facility is Western Canada's largest convention facility and home to offices, shops, and a variety of attractions and special events that can be enjoyed by visitors of all ages.

Chapter 8　Society and Culture

I　Canadian Society

Canadian People

As a nation of immigrants, Canada is usually described as being a "mosaic", where no particular concept of an overarching Canadian identity would be promoted. Some of the ethnic groups in Canada are: English, French, Irish, Scottish, German, Italian, Ukrainian (乌克兰人), Dutch, Polish, Chinese, South Asian, Jewish, West Indian, Portuguese and Scandinavian. About 45% of all Canadians are of British descent (血统), and about 29% are of French ancestry. French Canadians, most of whom live in Quebec, have kept the language and many customs of their ancestors.

Way of Life

The complex regional and cultural composition of Canadian society means that there is no single Canadian way of life, but certain generalizations can be made. Canada enjoys a high standard of living. Most Canadians are well housed, fed, and clothed. Canadians also enjoy an advanced, efficient health care system that is universally available to all citizens and landed immigrants (immigrants who are allowed permanent residence in the country) regardless of their location, income, or social standing. Canadians see this system of socialized medicine as a defining characteristic of their national identity.

The nature of Canadian households has changed considerably over the past quarter-century. With the liberalization of divorce legislation in the late 1960s and changing social attitudes about marriage, the number of single-parent households and common-law unions (事实婚姻) has increased. On July 20, 2005, Canada became the fourth country in the world to legalize same-sex marriage nationwide with the approval of the Civil Marriage Act.

Holidays and Important Dates

Such holidays as Christmas, Good Friday (耶稣受难节), and Easter are among the most widely celebrated holidays in Canada.

The country's Scottish element is reflected in its enthusiastic celebration on New Year's Day and Halloween, and its American links in the observation of Thanksgiving, Labor Day, Mother's Day, and Father's Day.

● **Canada Day (Canada's National Day)**

National holidays particular to Canada are Canada Day (July.1), commemorating

Two same-sex couples pledged their love at a dual wedding ceremony in Windsor, Ontario to commemorate the two year anniversary of the Bill C38, the Canadian law that legalized same-sex marriages.

Prime Minister Stephen Harper greets the crowd during Canada Day celebrations on Parliament Hill in Ottawa on July 1, 2009.

the creation of the Dominion of Canada, (July 1st, 1867 加拿大自治领联邦); and Victoria Day in May, commemorating the British monarch who played the greatest role in Canadian history.

Canada Day celebrates the events that occurred on July 1, 1867, when the British North America Act created the Canadian federal government. On that day, Canada was united as a single country with four provinces: Nova Scotia, New Brunswick and the Province of Canada (which was later divided into Ontario and Québec). Before 1982 Canada Day had been known as Dominion Day, which was officially renamed "Canada Day" by an Act of Parliament on October 27, 1982.

Canada's national celebration is always observed on July 1, unless that date falls on a Sunday, in which case it is observed the following day. Communities all across Canada celebrate with outdoor public events, such as parades, carnivals, festivals, barbeques, air and maritime shows, fireworks and free musical concerts!! Parliament Hill in Canada's Capital city of Ottawa, Ontario, holds the largest free outdoor celebration concert in Canada.

Canada Day is also considered a Family Day with outings, picnics and celebrations of the birth of the nation. All Canadians are entitled to Canada Day off work—although some people have to work, like Police, Fire and emergency service workers.

- **Winterlude—Canada's Winter Celebration!**

Winterlude is an annual festival held over the first three weekends of February in Ottawa, Ontario and Gatineau, Québec (加蒂诺，加拿大魁北克西南部一镇) that celebrates winter. Winterlude is run by Canada's National Capital Commission and was started in 1979. The event is one of Ottawa's most important tourist draws, attracting hundreds of thousands of visitors each year. It is more than a festival; it's a celebration of Canada's distinctive northern identity.

Winterlude is a very large festival of outdoor activities including public skating along the canal and skating displays, snow carving and ice sculpture competitions, musical concerts at the Winterlude Snowbowl, children's play areas, an "ice lounge," bed race and waiter race, and numerous off-site events. Winterlude is most famous for the Rideau Canal Skateway which is cleared for ice skating displays and musical concerts. The Canal is claimed to be the world's largest skating rink winding 7.8 kilometers through the heart of the Capital from Dows Lake to the National Arts Centre.

Michaélle Jean, Governor General of Canada and her daughter Marie-Éden meet with the Ice Hogs, Winterlude's loveable mascots(吉祥物)

The Bed Race

Other primary sites include Jacques Cartier Park in Gatineau which is turned into a massive snow park with slides and structures, events and activities for children and the snow sculpture competition. Confederation Park is the site for the ice sculpture competition, the ice lounge and musical concerts. Dow's Lake has a large skating area and hosts the various bed and waiter races.

The Holidays All of Canada Celebrates	
Jan. 1st	New Year's Day
April (date is not fixed)	Good Friday
April (date is not fixed)	Easter Monday
May (date is not fixed)	Victoria Day
July 1st	Canada Day
Sept. (first Monday)	Labor Day
Oct. (date is not fixed)	Thanksgiving Day
Nov. 11th	Remembrance Day
Dec. 25th	Christmas
Dec. 26th	Boxing Day

II Education

General Introduction

Education in Canada is provided, funded and overseen by federal, provincial, and local governments. There is no national or federal department of education and no integrated (统一的) national system of education. Education is a provincial responsibility and the curriculum is overseen by the province. Each province has a Department/Ministry of Education headed by a minister who is an elected member of the provincial cabinet or, in the case of the Yukon and Northwest Territories, a counselor. Within the provinces under the ministry of education, there are district school boards administering the educational programs.

The federal Government is responsible for education in the Yukon and Northwest Territories, Native Indian schools, military stations and military colleges. In addition, it finances vocational training for adults, and provides financial support to the provinces for the operating cost of post-secondary education.

Canada spends about 7% of its GDP on education and offers a multiplicity of top quality education programs for students home and abroad. Since the adoption of section 23 of the Constitution Act, 1982, education in both English and French has been available in most places across Canada.

Education in Canada is generally divided into **Elementary** (Primary School, Public School), followed by **Secondary** (High School) and **Post Secondary** (University, College). According to Statistics Canada data, there are approximately 15,500 schools, 163 recognized public and private universities and 183 recognized public colleges and institutes in Canada:

The Canadian education system is a system with much diversity. Most Canadian education systems continue up to grade twelve (age seventeen to eighteen). In Québec, the typical high school term ends after Secondary V/Grade eleven (age sixteen to seventeen); following this, students who wish to pursue their studies to the university level have to attend

CEGEP, which is a two or three year college program taken after high school and before university. (CEGEP is a French acronym[首字母缩拼词], meaning "College of General and Vocational Education").

The ages for compulsory schooling also vary, but most require attendance in school from age 6 to age 16. In some cases, compulsory schooling starts at 5, and in others it extends to age 18 or graduation from secondary school.

Kindergarten to Grade 12 education is publicly funded and free to all Canadian citizens and permanent residents until the end of secondary school—normally, age 18. In Québec, college level education is also free to Québec residents, but tuition is charged for university education. All other Canadian students pay tuition fees to attend colleges and universities. Canada generally has 190 school days in the year, officially starting from September (after Labor Day, the first Monday in September) to the end of June (usually the last Friday of the month).

Public Education

Public education in Canada has an excellent reputation worldwide. Canada's primary and secondary public school system is co-educational (男女合校的) and paid for by the Canadian government.

● *Elementary Education (K-12)*

Elementary education in most provinces and territories covers the first 6 or 8 years of compulsory schooling. It refers to grades 1 through 6, but may also include grades 7 and 8. Almost 98 per cent of elementary students go on to the secondary level. The elementary school curriculum emphasizes the basic subjects of language, mathematics, social studies, science, health and physical education, and introductory arts; some jurisdictions include second-language learning.

Interactive Learning in the Classroom

Preschool programs or kindergartens, operated by local school authorities, provide pre-elementary education for 4—5 year-olds. Kindergarten programs are offered in elementary schools in all provinces and territories.

● *Secondary Education*

Following elementary or middle school, children proceed to secondary school (also called high school or senior high school) where they continue to grade 12 (grade 11 in Québec). Curriculum programs at the secondary level include both academic and vocational programs. In China we have 2 streams in high school, sciences and liberal arts. Canada also has 2 streams in high school: academic and commercial. But university entrance may be gained only from the academic stream.

In the first years, students take mostly compulsory courses, with some options (选修科目). The proportion of options increases in the later years so that students may take specialized courses to prepare for the job market or to meet the differing entrance requirements of postsecondary institutions. Secondary school diplomas are awarded to students who complete the requisite number of compulsory and optional courses. In most cases, vocational and academic programs are offered within the same secondary schools; in others, technical and vocational programs are offered in separate, dedicated (专门的) vocational training centers. For students with an interest in a specific trade, programs varying in length from less than one year to three years are offered, many of them leading to diplomas and certificates. About one-half of all Canadians have a high school graduation certificate.

Rosemount High School, Montreal, Québec

Postsecondary Education (Colleges & Universities)

The Association of Universities and Colleges of Canada (AUCC) defines two distinct types of post-secondary institutions in Canada: universities and colleges. Universities grant university degrees, which include bachelor's degrees, master's degrees, and doctoral degrees; and colleges, also known as community colleges, provide diplomas. Postsecondary education, sometimes called "tertiary" (第三级的) education, is available in both government-supported and private institutions.

There are 83 universities in Canada with degree-granting authority. The oldest university in Canada is Université Laval, established in 1663. The Quest University is the smallest university in the country, with 80 students, and the largest one is the University of Québec, which is a system of ten provincially-run public universities in Québec, with its headquarters in Québec City. The university has more than 87,000 students, making it the largest university in Canada.

Provincial and territorial governments provide the majority of funding to their public universities, with the remainder of funding coming from the federal government, tuition fees, and research grants. The primary variation between universities in the provinces is the amount of funding they receive. Universities in Québec receive the most funding and have the lowest tuition fees, while universities in Atlantic Canada generally receive the least funding.

Tuition costs at universities averaged $4,524 in 2007—2008, with international student fees for an undergraduate program averaging about $14,000 annually. At colleges and institutes (in the nine provinces outside Québec), the average tuition was about $2,400 (Québec residents do not pay college tuition). Education is also funded through the money that governments transfer to individual students through loans, grants, and education tax credits (课税扣除). Under the Constitution Act of 1982, the federal government is largely responsible for funding higher education opportunities for Aboriginal learners.

According to the Association of Universities and Colleges of Canada in 2005, there were 806,000 full-time university students (an increase of nearly 150,000 in the previous four years), as well as 273,000 part-time students. Universities employed close to 40,000 full-time faculty members. Among G7 countries (The G7 is the meeting of the finance ministers from a group of seven industrialized nations. It was formed in 1976), Canada has the highest proportion of post-secondary education graduates and one of the highest percentages of university graduates in the workforce, with 22%. Among Canada's adult population aged 25 to 64, 46% had completed post-secondary education in 2005, the highest percentage among OECD member countries, and well above the OECD average of 26%.

University degrees are offered at three consecutive (连续的) levels:
- Students enter at the bachelor's level after having successfully completed secondary school or the two-year cégep program in Québec. Most universities also have special entrance requirements and paths for mature students. Bachelor's degrees normally require three or four years of full-time study, depending on the province and whether the program is general or specialized.
- A master's degree typically requires two years of study after the bachelor's degree.
- For a doctoral degree, three to five years of additional study and research plus a dissertation are the normal requirements.

Besides universities there are thousands of public and private colleges and institutes in Canada. Of these, over 150 are recognized public colleges and institutes. These educational institutions may be called public colleges, specialized institutes, community colleges, institutes of technology, colleges of applied arts and technology, or cégeps. The private colleges are most often called career colleges. Colleges and institutes offer a range of vocation-oriented programs in a wide variety of professional and technical fields, including business, health, applied arts, technology, and social services. Some of the institutions are specialized and provide training in a single field such as fisheries, arts, paramedical technology, and agriculture. Colleges also provide literacy and academic upgrading (精选的) programs, pre-employment and pre-apprenticeship programs, and the in-class portions of registered apprenticeship programs. As well, many different workshops, short programs, and upgrades for skilled workers and professionals are made available.

Diplomas (文凭，毕业证书) are generally awarded for successful completion of two-and three-year college and institute programs, while certificate (结业证书) programs usually take up to one year. University degrees and applied degrees are offered in some colleges and institutes, and others provide university transfer programs.

Canada's Top 10 Research Universities 2008				
2007	2006	Rank 2008	University	Province
1	1	1	University of Toronto	Ontario
2	5	2	University of Alberta	Alberta
3	2	3	Université de Montréal	Québec
4	3	4	The University of British Columbia	British Columbia
5	4	5	McGill University	Québec
6	6	6	McMaster University	Ontario
7	8	7	Université Laval	Québec

8	7	8	University of Calgary	Alberta
9	10	9	The University of Western Ontario	Ontario
10	9	10	University of Ottawa	Ontario

University of Toronto, Ontario

University of Alberta

University of Montréal, Québec

University of British Columbia, B.C.

McGill University, Québec

University of McMaster, Ontario

University of Laval, Québec

University of Calgary, Albert

University of Western Ontario

University of Ottawa

Private Schools & Career Colleges

Canada has a large number of private or independent schools (some of which are religious in orientation) and private career colleges. They function independently of the public school system and charge fees.

Career Colleges in Canada are privately owned and operated postsecondary institutions which focus exclusively on preparing students for employment in a specific trade or occupation such as secretarial skills; massage therapy; paralegal (律师助手); business; cosmetology (美容术); information technology; graphic (电脑绘图) design; truck driving and many other fields. Scheduling is often flexible so that students can attend courses and work at the same time. Correspondence courses are common at these schools.

Private career colleges do not receive funding support from provincial or territorial governments unless they are affiliated with a public institution. Although privately owned, these schools are provincially approved and regulated, ensuring that program standards and quality are maintained.

Home Schooling

Homeschooling is becoming more and more popular as an alternative choice for education and is allowed in all provinces and territories of Canada under similar restrictions as those for independent schools. Home schooling Parents who wish to educate their own children throughout, or for part of, their compulsory school years, must meet the

general standards, curriculum, and diploma requirements prescribed by the relevant provincial or territorial authority.

Special Needs Students

Special needs students, such as the physically or mentally disabled, the gifted, etc., are accommodated in the public schools in various ways. In some cases, separate programs are available to meet their needs; in others, these students are integrated into the regular classroom and, to the extent possible, follow the regular program of instruction.

Bilingual Instruction

As Canada is a bilingual country, there are both universities giving instruction in English and universities giving instruction in French. The French language universities are mainly found in the Province of Québec. There are two such bilingual universities. One of them is the University of Ottawa. It is located in the capital Ottawa; the other is Laurentian University, established in Sudbury, Ontario in 1962.

Those who wish to be enrolled in a French language university must pass the language test set by the university. Those wishing to enter an English language university must be able to pass any of the internationally accepted English tests. The most common one is TOEFl, Test of English as a Foreign Language prepared by the Princeton Educational Testing Service.

III Arts and Sports

Literature and Important Writers

The field of Canadian literature is large and complex, and includes voices from the various regions and many cultural groups of the country.

Notable Canadian poets, among others, include Irving Layton (1912–2006) with his *Waiting for the Messiah* and Dorothy Livesay (1909–1996) with her *Archive for Our Times*. Hugh MacLennan, Robertson Davies, Sinclair Ross and Margaret Laurence set new standards for Canadian fiction in the mid-20th century. Children around the world have enjoyed *Anne of Green Gables*, by L. M. Montgomery, a 1908 novel set in rural Prince Edward Island. Other important writers have followed, such as Margaret Atwood, Gabrielle Roy, and Alice Munro. Many have drawn on their experiences as immigrants or members of minority groups in their fiction: Mordecai Richler (Jewish), Michael Ondaatje (Sri Lankan), and Neil Bissoondath (Caribbean) are just a few examples.

Visual Art

The earliest works of visual art in North America were produced by indigenous groups. European colonists introduced their artistic traditions almost as soon as they settled in the land that became Canada.

However, the defining moment for post-Confederation Canadian art, is generally acknowledged to have been the formation of the Group of Seven in Toronto during the 1910s and 1920s. The post-Impressionist images of elemental nature created by these painters have inspired generations of Canadian artists. Other distinctly Canadian schools were the Canadian Group, the Contemporary Art Society, Les Automatistes, and Painters Eleven. The Canadian Group, formed in Toronto in 1933, practiced regionalist painting, which took daily life as its subject matter. The Contemporary Art Society was formed in Montreal in 1940 to produce experimental work based on Parisian models.

Céline Dion

There are thousands of artists now at work in Canada, producing paintings, sculptures, and other media of great variety. Among the best-known are Michael Snow, Joyce Wieland, Greg Curnoe, and Bill Reid.

Musicians

Pianist Glenn Gould is probably Canada's most widely recognized classical musician, particularly for his innovative interpretations of Bach. In the 1990s, guitarist Liona Boyd and opera tenor Ben Heppner were among the more visible Canadians on the international stage.

In the past, Canadian popular-music artists looked to the United States as the primary market for their music. However, a thriving Canadian popular-music industry emerged in the 1980s and 1990s; a few particularly well-known Canadian performers are Bryan Adams, Céline Dion, k.d. lang, Shania Twain, and Alanis Morissette.

Sports

Although lacrosse (长曲棍球), a sport with Aboriginal origins, is Canada's oldest sport and official summer sport, ice hockey (冰球)is its most popular sport. At the professional level, there are six National Hockey League (NHL) teams in Canada, including two of its most venerable, the *Montréal Canadiens* and the *Toronto Maple Leafs*.

Lacrosse players

In Canada, the term football is used to refer to Canadian football and American football collectively, or either sport specifically, depending on the context.

Canadian football is played almost exclusively in Canada. It was originally more closely related to rugby until the Burnside rules brought the game closer to its American counterpart. The Burnside rules were a set of rules that transformed North American football from a rugby-style game to the gridiron-style game played in both Canada (Canadian football) and the United States (American football). The rules introduced sweeping changes to the way football was played.

Both the Canadian Football League (CFL), the sport's top professional league, and Football Canada, the governing body for amateur play, trace their roots to 1884 and the founding of the Canadian Rugby Football Union. Currently active teams such as the Toronto Argonauts and Hamilton Tiger-Cats have similar longevity. The CFL is the most popular and only major professional Canadian football league. Its eight teams, which are located in eight cities, are divided into two divisions of four teams each (East and West). The league's nineteen-week regular season runs from mid-June to early November. Its championship game, the Grey Cup, is the country's single largest sporting event and is watched by nearly one third of Canadian television households. Canadian football is also played at the high school, junior, collegiate, and semi-professional levels.

Calgary Stampeders quarterback and game MVP Henry Burris holds Grey Cup after defeating the Alouettes at the 96th CFL Grey Cup Nov. 23, 2008 in Montreal.

Baseball has been played in Canada since at least 1838, and a Canadian professional league was established in 1876. The *Montréal* Expos became Canada's first major league baseball team in 1969. The

Toronto Blue Jays began play eight years later and became one of the sport's most successful teams, attracting more than 4 million fans in a single season and winning the World Series twice: 1992, which was the first World Championship won by a Canadian team in the history of Major League Baseball, and 1993.

Basketball is the fastest growing sport in Canada, and attracts many young Canadians from all backgrounds. Canada Basketball is a non-profit organization and the governing body for basketball in Canada. This national federation was founded in 1928. The organization is responsible for the selection and training of players who represent the Men's and Women's national teams and then represent Canada in international competition.

Toronto Blue Jays v. Detroit Tigers during their MLB game at the Rogers Centre April 6, 2009 in Toronto, Ontario

Since there is no professional basketball league within Canada, many Canadian men and women playing basketball after university and college choose to play professionally overseas. Canadians who are currently playing in the NBA (National Basketball Association of the US) include: Steve Nash, Jamaal Magloire, Samuel Dalembert, and Joel Anthony. Two Canadian teams joined NBA in the 1990s: the *Toronto Raptors* (猛禽) and the *Vancouver Grizzlies* (灰熊).

Another sport form worth mentioning is **curling** (冰壶运动), which is a team sport with similarities to bowls and shuffleboard, played by two teams of four players each on a rectangular sheet (冰壶场地) of carefully prepared ice. Teams take turns sliding heavy, polished granite stones down the ice towards the target. The complex nature of stone placement and shot selection has led some to refer to curling as "chess on ice" (冰上博弈).

The game of curling is thought to have been invented in late medieval Scotland and outdoor curling was very popular there between the 16th and 19th centuries. Scotland is home to the international governing body for curling. Today, the game is most firmly established in Canada, having been taken there by Scottish emigrants. The Royal Montreal Curling Club, the oldest established sports club still active in North America, was established in 1807. Today, curling is played all over Europe and has spread to Asia.

Canada consistently produces Olympic medal winners in a variety of sports, including ice hockey, rowing, track and field, and, most notably, ice skating. A large and growing number of ordinary Canadians regularly participate in sporting leagues, fitness classes, and individual exercise.

Understanding U.K. & Ireland

A General Survey of UK

United Kingdom is the third most populous state in the European Union and is a founding member of the North Atlantic Treaty Organization (NATO) and the United Nations (UN), where it holds a permanent seat on the Security Council (安理会). The UK is also one of the world's major nuclear powers.

Country Name

The full and official name of the country is the United Kingdom of Great Britain and Northern Island. It's usually shortened or abbreviated to the United Kingdom or U.K., Great Britain, Britain, or sometimes informally England.

Many foreigners say *England* and *English* when they mean *Britain*, or the *UK*, and *British*. This is very annoying for the 5 million people who live in Scotland, the 2.8 million in Wales and 1.6 million in Northern Ireland who are certainly not English. (46 million people live in England.) However, the people from Scotland, Wales, Northern Ireland and England are all British. So what is the difference between the names *Great Britain* and *the United Kingdom*, and what about "*the British Isles*"?

Map of the United Kingdom

The United Kingdom is an abbreviation of *the United Kingdom of Great Britain and Northern Ireland*. It is often further abbreviated to *UK*, and is the political name of the country which is made up of England, Scotland, Wales and Northern Ireland. Several islands off the British coast are also part of the United Kingdom; all these islands do recognize the Queen.

Great Britain is the name of the island which is made up of England, Scotland and Wales and so, strictly speaking, it does not include Northern Ireland.

The British Isles is the geographical name that refers to all the islands off the north west coast of the European continent: Great Britain, the whole of Ireland, the Channel Islands and the Isle of Man (马恩岛).

The nickname of the country is John Bull (约翰牛). In the 18th century, a Scottish writer John Arbuthnot wrote a book called "The History of John Bull" in which he described the frankness and funniness of a gentleman called John Bull, in order to exemplify the Englishmen. So the nickname spread wide and has become a synonym for Britain. It is a personification of England or the English people as stolidity (不易激动的) and determination. It marks the national character.

Location and Size

The United Kingdom lies off the northwest coast of Europe and is separated from the European continent by the North Sea, the Strait of Dover (多佛尔海峡, 在英国东南部和法国北部之间) and the English Channels.

There are two main islands—Great Britain and Ireland. There are hundreds of smaller ones, too, especially off the coast of Scotland in the north. Northern Ireland is on the same island with the country of Ireland, but it is part of the United Kingdom. The total area is 244,820 square kilometers. However, there are only nine other countries with more people. The population is 60,600,000.

Component Parts

The United Kingdom is a country made up of four parts: England, Scotland, Wales, and Northern Ireland. Each part was once ruled separately. Each has its own culture and its own native language.

England is the largest of the four with an area of 130,000 square kilometers, which takes up nearly 60% of the British Isles. It is the most populous and richest section of the country.

Scotland, with an area of 78,760 square kilometers, occupies the northern part of the British Isles. About two thirds of Scotland is covered by the Highlands. The highest mountain on the island, Ben Nevis, is in the highlands.

Most of ***Wales*** is mountainous. The area is about 20,700 square kilometers, which takes up less than 9% of the whole island.

Northern Ireland, with an area of 14,147 square kilometers, occupies the northern sixth of Ireland. Before the early 20th century, it was part of Ireland as a whole. In 1920 Northern Ireland became part of the United Kingdom, with a separated parliament and self-government.

Capital

London, the capital of the United Kingdom is located in England. It is the biggest city in Europe and the world's seventh biggest city. More than 7 million people live there.

Greater London was created in 1965. It includes the City of London and 32 boroughs. London has great churches like Saint Paul's Cathedral and Westminster Abbey (威斯敏斯特教堂, 英国名人墓地). It has a castle called the Tower of London and a large public square called Trafalgar Square (特拉法尔加广场). There's Big Ben (大本钟), the famous clock tower at the Houses of Parliament. There's also a famous shopping and entertainment center called Piccadilly Circus (皮卡迪利广场, 位于伦敦西部, 是戏院及娱乐中心, 交通交叉口和大众集会的地方). Now London has become the great center of commerce, administration, culture and transportation of Britain, and of the largest international ports in the world.

Language

English is the official language of the United Kingdom and spoken by most of the population. The major languages are English, Gaelic (盖尔语) and Welsh. Now Less than a quarter of all Welsh people (600,000 out of 2,800,000) speak Welsh and only 1% speaks only Welsh. Scottish Gaelic and Irish Gaelic are still spoken, although they have suffered more than Welsh from the spread of

152 | Understanding U.K. & Ireland

English. However, all three languages are now officially encouraged and taught in schools.

The United Kingdom is the birthplace of the English language. Today, English is spoken in more parts of the world than any other language. English developed from Anglo-Saxon and is a Germanic language (日尔曼语). However, all the invading peoples, particularly the Norman French, influenced the English language and many words in English are French in origin. Nowadays all Welsh, Scottish and Irish people speak English (even if they speak their own language as well), but all the countries have their own special accents and dialects, and their people are easily recognizable as soon as they speak. A southern English accent is generally accepted to be the most easily understood, and is the accent usually taught to foreigners.

Currency

The official currency in the UK is the British Pound Sterling. Under this system 100 pence is equal to one pound. The symbol used for pounds is **£** or is sometimes shown as GBP (Great Britain Pounds) and the symbol used for pence is **p.** So two pound forty pence would be written **£2.40** or **GBP 2.40**. Twenty pence would be written **20p**.

Currently the currency in use is as follows:

Coins: 1 pence, 2 pence, 5 pence, 10 pence, 50 pence, one pound, 2 pounds. The 1 and 2 pence piece are bronze, the 5, 10, 20 and 50 pence pieces are silver and the 1 and 2 pound coins are gold. All coins carry the Queens head on the front.

The notes start at £5, £10, £20, £50, and £100 pounds. You won't often see the larger notes any more to combat loss to counterfeits (伪造品). There are other currencies as well. In Scotland, some of the Channel Islands and elsewhere, they have their own printed / minted coins and notes, they are exchanged at the equivalent of the Pound Sterling. Scottish notes are legal tender (法定货币) in the rest of the UK, but Channel Islands notes and coins are not. At the beginning of the 21st century there were four denominations of pound note in circulation: £5, £10, £20, and £50.

The Europe Union established the euro as its unit of currency, and other EU members made the transition to the euro between 1999 and 2002. However, the British government elected not to do so and instead retained the pound as its currency.

Religion

The main religion in Britain is Christianity as practiced by the Anglican (英国国教的) Church. Followers of this branch of Christianity are known as Protestants (新教徒) and make up the majority of the population. There are also many Roman Catholics. The Queen is head of the Church of England.

A Christian who belongs to The Church of England worships in the Established Church (英国国教,圣公会). The Anglican Church is based on the parochial (教区的) system. The country is divided into parishes, and every parish is in a diocese (主教教区). There are forty-three dioceses in total in England and Wales. The Bishop (主教) is the chief pastor (本堂牧师) or shepherd of the diocese. Priests lead parish churches under the Bishop's jurisdiction or license.

The national flag

Union Flag

The Union Flag, or Union Jack, is the national flag of the United Kingdom. It is so called because it combines the crosses of the three countries united under one Sovereign— the kingdoms of England and Wales, of Scotland and of Northern Ireland.

England—The cross of St George, patron saint of England since the 1270's, is a red cross on a white ground dates from the time of Crusades. After James I succeeded to the throne, it was combined with the cross of St Andrew in 1606. St George (ca. 275/281—23 April 303) was a brave Roman soldier who protested against the Romans' torture of Christians and died for his beliefs. He is the patron saint of England and among the most famous of Christian figures.

Crucifixion of St Andrew

Scotland—The cross saltier (X形十字，圣安得鲁十字) of St Andrew, patron saint of Scotland, is a diagonal white cross on a dark blue ground. (This color was adopted for the general background of the Union Flag)—origin is obscure, and probably nothing to do with the apostle (门徒)Andrew. The reason for the white surround the red Cross of St George is that it is an heraldic (纹章学的) taboo to place red directly on blue.

Ireland—The cross saltier of St Patrick, patron saint of Ireland, is a diagonal (斜的) red cross on a white background. This was combined with the previous Union Flag of St George and St Andrew, after the Act of Union of Ireland with England (and Wales) and Scotland on 1 January 1801, to create the Union Flag that has been flown ever since. Saint Patrick was the patron saint and national apostle (传道者) of Ireland who is credited with bringing Christianity to Ireland. The stories of Saint Patrick's driving the snakes from Ireland are likely a metaphor for his bringing Christianity to Ireland and driving out the pagan (异教的) religions.

the Cross Saltier of St Patrick

The Queen

The queen has very little power when compared with earlier English kings and queens. Today, an elected prime minister and Parliament hold most government power. But Elizabeth II is popular with her people. You'll find her image on every British stamp, banknote, and coin!

The National Anthem

The National Anthem is **God Save the Queen**, which was a patriotic song first publicly performed in London in 1745 and came to be known as the National Anthem at the beginning of the 19th century. The words and tune are anonymous, and may date back to the 17th century. There is no authorized version of the National Anthem as the words are a matter of tradition. The words used today are those sung in 1745, substituting "Queen" for "King" where appropriate. On official occasions, only the first verse is usually sung, as follows:

God Save the Queen	天佑我王
God save our gracious Queen,	上帝保佑我们慈祥的女王，
Long live our noble Queen,	我们高贵的女王万寿无疆，
God save the Queen:	上帝保佑我们的女王：
Send her victorious,	赋予她胜利，
Happy and glorious,	快乐与显赫，
Long to reign over us:	长久君临臣民：
God save the Queen	上帝保佑我王

The National Emblem of UK

The Sovereign's coat of arms has evolved over many years and reflects the history of the Monarchy and of the country. In the design the shield shows the various Royal emblems of different parts of the United Kingdom: the three lions of England in the first and fourth quarters, the lion of Scotland in the second and the harp of Ireland in the third. The shield is supported by the English lion and Scottish unicorn and is surmounted (在……顶上覆盖着) by the Royal crown. Below it appears the motto of the Sovereign, *Dieu et mon droit* (*God and my right*). The mottoes read *In defense* and *No one will attack me with impunity* (不受惩罚).

The National Flower

What are the Symbols of England, Scotland and Wales? Each country in Britain has its own patron saint and floral emblem:

England—St George and the Rose
The national flower of England is the rose. The flower has been adopted as England's emblem since the time of the Wars of the Roses-civil wars (1455—1485) between the royal house of Lancaster (whose emblem was a red rose) and the royal house of York (whose emblem was a white rose).

Scotland—St Andrew—the Thistle (蓟) and Scottish Bluebell
The national flower of Scotland is the thistle, a prickly-leaved purple flower which was first used in the 15th century as a symbol of defense. The Scottish Bluebell is also seen as the flower of Scotland.

Wales—St David and the Daffodil (水仙花)
The national flower of Wales is the daffodil, which is traditionally worn on St. David's Day. The vegetable called leek is also considered to be a traditional emblem of Wales.

Northern Ireland—St Patrick and the Shamrock (三叶草)
The national flower of Northern Ireland is the shamrock, a three-leaved plant similar to clover. An Irish tale tells of how Patrick used the three-leafed shamrock to explain the Trinity. He used it in his sermons to represent how the Father, the Son, and the Holy Spirit could all exist as separate elements of the same entity. His followers adopted the custom of wearing a shamrock on his feast day.

A Collection of Fast Facts of UK

	The UK is a country in north-western Europe. It is bordered to the south by the English Channel; to the east by the North Sea; to the west by the Irish Sea and the Atlantic Ocean.
Countries in the UK	England, Scotland, Wales, and Northern Ireland
Full Name	United Kingdom of Great Britain and Northern Ireland
Flag: The Union Flag	The Union Flag
Type of Government	Constitutional monarchy
Capital City	London

Highest mountain	Ben Nevis in Scotland, at 1,343m
Longest river	River Severn, 354 km long. It rises in Wales and flows to the Bristol Channel.
Largest lake	Lough Neagh 396 sq km Northern Ireland
Deepest Lake	Loch Morar in the Highlands of Scotland, 310 m deep
Climate	
Annual mean temperature	London 9.7C
Annual mean rainfall	London 753mm
People	
Major languages	English, Welsh, Irish Gaelic, Scottish Gaelic.
Main Religion	Christianity
Major ethnic groups	British, Irish, West Indian, South Asian.
Total population	60,600,000
Annual population growth rate	0.29% (2004 est.)
Population density per sq.km	245
Population by region	Scotland 5,119,000; England 49,753,000 Wales 2,937,000; N. Ireland 1,692,000
Top 5 populous cities	London 7,285,000; Birmingham 1,018,000; Leeds 725,000; Glasgow 611,000; Sheffield 529,000
Land	
Total land area (sq.km)	244,110 sq km
Coast Line	12,429 km
Length	Just under 1,000 km from North to South
Width	About 480 km from east to west
Natural Resources	coal, petroleum, natural gas, tin, limestone, iron ore, salt, clay, chalk, gypsum, lead, silica, arable land

Chapter 9　Geography and History of UK

A. Geography

I Geographic Features

The island of Great Britain can be divided into two major natural regions—lowland zone (平原区) and the highland zone (山地区). The lowland zone in the south and east consists mostly of rolling plains. The highland zone is an area of high hills and mountains in the north and west. The zones are divided by an imaginary line running through England from the River Exe on the southwest coast to the mouth of the River Tees on the northeast coast. The lowland zone has a milder climate and better soils for farming. Historically, most people in Britain have lived in the lowland zone rather than in the harsher highland zone.

The lowland zone comprises Midland, southern and eastern England. The Midlands is the area lies between Southern England, Northern England, East Anglia and Wales, and its largest city is Birmingham. In general the lowland zone is a great plain with extensive areas of almost-level ground. It receives less rain and more sunshine than the highland zone and much of the soil is fertile. Most of the lowland region is less than 150m above sea level, and the hills rarely reach more than 300m above sea level. It has been extensively inhabited, farmed, and grazed for thousands of years. Most of Britain's population lives densely into the lowland zone, which covers most of England. The metropolis of London and most of Britain's large cities are located in the lowland zone.

The highland zone consists of 1) the broad central upland (高地) known as the Pennines (奔宁山脉); 2) the Lake District; 3) most of Wales and Scotland. Often said to be the "backbone of England, the Pennines are a low-rising mountain range in northern England and southern Scotland. They separate the North West of England from Yorkshire and the North East. The highland zone contains what is often called rough country (丘陵地带), with a large extent of rugged hills, mountains, and eroded areas frequently broken by valleys and plains. The highest elevations in the British Isles are in the highland zone; The highland zone is cooler than the lowland zone, and receives more rainfall and less sunlight. In many places farming is impossible. Even where it is feasible, the soil is often thin and stony, with a hard rock formation (岩层) below. Rainwater often cannot escape readily; so many areas tend to be waterlogged (涝的). Ben Nevis, in western Scotland's Grampian Mountains, is the tallest mountain in the British Isles.

England, with a total area of more than 130,000 square kilometers, may be divided into three landforms: the east and the southeast are made up of rolling downs and low-paying plains; middle England is a region of mountains formed by the Pennines, which, with the average altitude between 200 and 500 meters, extending south from the Scottish border to Derbyshire (德贝郡). Cross Fell, 893 meters high, is the highest peak of the Pennines. The north and west of England are hilly, partly formed by the Cumbrian Mountain Range, the highest mountain peak of which is Scafell (977m), the highest in England but the third highest mountain throughout the country.

Scotland has an area of 78,760 square kilometers. About two thirds of Scotland is covered by the Highlands. The chief range in the Highlands is the Grampian Mountains, which contain Ben Nevis (1334m), the highest mountain on the island of Great Britain. The central lowlands of Scotland include the valleys of the Clyde, Tay and Forth rivers. This is the most important area in Scotland, which contains most of the industry and population. Edinburgh, the capital of Scotland, and Glasgow, the largest city in Scotland, are both located in this area. The southeastern Uplands are a region of rolling moorlands (高原的沼地) cut by some small fertile river valleys. The Southern Uplands reach their highest point in Merrick.

Wales covers an area of about 20,700 square kilometers. It is geographically divided into the industrial south, the central plateaus and lakes, and the mountainous north of the farmers and tourists. Most of Wales is mountainous, mainly formed by the Cambrian Mountain Range. Its highest peak Snowdon (1085m) is the second highest mountain in Britain. In Wales, only 12% of the land is arable (可耕作的), 6% is covered with forest, and much of the land is pastureland for sheep and cattle. The most fertile land in Wales is found near the coast and in the interior valleys.

The central part of **Northern Ireland** is composed of plains surrounded by such highlands and mountains. On the central plain lies Lough (〈爱尔兰〉湖) Neagh, the largest lake in the whole country. Northern Ireland is mainly agricultural, with industry concentrated in the two parts of Belfast and Londonderry.

II Rivers, Lakes and Mountains

Rivers and lakes

> *Quick Facts about the Rivers and Lakes*
> ＊Lough Neagh is the largest lake in Britain which is located in Northern Ireland (396 km).
> ＊The most important river in Britain is the Thames River (338km), which rises in southwest England, flows through the capital city London and empties into the English Channel. The river is the second longest and navigable for large ships to London. Oxford is also on the Thames.
> ＊The longest river is the Severn River (354km), which rises in northeast Wales and flows through central England to the Bristol Channel.
> ＊River Clyde is the most important river in Scotland which flows through Glasgow
> Being short and swift, few rivers in Britain are navigable.

Since Britain has a moist climate with much rainfall, rivers and lakes are numerous. Rivers in central and eastern Britain tend to flow slowly and steadily all year long because they are fed by the frequent rain. Rivers and streams moving westward down from the Highlands tend to be swift and turbulent; rivers flowing eastward tend to be long, graceful, and gentle, with slowly moving waters. The Thames River is the most important river in England and the main source of London's water supply. Other important rivers in England are the River Humber on the east coast, into which the Trent River and several other rivers flow; and the Tyne River in northern England, which flows past Newcastle upon Tyne to the North Sea.

Lakes in Britain are chiefly found in the English Lake District, the Scottish Highlands, the Welsh mountains and Northern Ireland. The largest lake in England is Lake Windermere. It is located in the Lake District, which is an area of mountains and lakes in northwestern England. Lake District is one of the popular touring spots in England. It is commonly accounted the most beautiful part of England, where William Wordsworth and the other Lake Poets were inspired by the perfection of water, trees and heather-covered slopes.

Coastline

For a small country of islands Britain has a great length of coastline (about 11,450 kilometers). The coast is very varied, with perhaps the best parts in the southwest of England and in the west of Scotland. Britain's coastline is highly irregular, with many bays and inlets that provide harbors and shelters for ships and boats. Coastal trade involving ships sailing along the coast has been carried on since ancient times. The western coast is characterized by cliffs and rocky headlands (向水中突出的陆地). On the more gentle southern and eastern coasts there are many sand or pebble beaches as well as tall limestone(石灰岩) or chalk (白垩) cliffs, the most famous of which are the White Cliffs of Dover in the southeast.

Mountains

Ben Nevis, in western Scotland, is the tallest mountain in the United Kingdom (1,343 meters). England has an area of mountains and lakes called the Lake District. Wales is almost entirely covered by craggy (多峭壁的) mountains and deep, green valleys. The highest peak is the huge mountain called Snowdon (1,085 meters). Northern Ireland consists of hilly highlands similar to those of Scotland. The highest part of Northern Ireland is the Mourne Mountains in the southeast, which reach a maximum elevation of 852 meters above sea level.

III Climate and Natural Resources

Climate

Britain has a temperate, maritime climate, which is damp and warm all year round. The air temperature is about 10 degree centigrade, varying from around 5℃ in the coldest month (January) to 17℃ in the warmest month (July) on average. Rain or overcast (多云的，阴的) skies can be expected for up to 300 days each year. That's why so much of the countryside is lush and green! Britain has a steady rainfall throughout the whole year. The average annual rainfall in Britain is over 1,000mm. There is a water surplus in the north and west, and a water deficit (缺乏) in the south and east.

● *Three Features of the Climate*

1) There are more fogs and smog in winter, for which London is famous.

2) There are more rainy days but less sunny days. The rainfall is not very heavy. In some places there are over 260 rainy days a year.

3) Instability or changeability of the weather.

In no country other than England, can one experience four seasons in the course of a single day. "Other country have a climate; in England we have weather". This statement is made by Englishmen to describe the peculiar meteorological conditions (气象条件) of the country.

● *Major Factors That Affect the Weather*

1) The surrounding waters tend to balance the seasonal differences by heating up the land in winter and cooling it off in summer;

2) The prevailing south-west winds blow over the country all the year round bringing warm and wet air in winter and keeping the temperatures moderate;

3) The North Atlantic Drift passes the western coast of the British Isles and warms them.

Natural Resources

Britain is rich in coal, petroleum, natural gas deposits. The other main natural resources in Britain are iron ore, limestone (石灰石), clay, shale (页岩), chalk and tin. Coal and petroleum are the most important. For many years coal was mined extensively, providing the primary source of energy in Britain. It was also exported. Only small quantities of oil had been found in Britain before big oil fields were discovered under the North Sea, east of the British Isles in 1965. By 1980 the annual output of oil had reached 100 million tons. Britain has become the fifth largest oil exporter in the world.

Forest

With its mild climate, varied soils and long growing season, Britain has a diverse pattern of natural vegetation. Trees grow well and quickly. Originally, most of the country was covered with thick, deciduous forests (落叶林) in which oak trees predominated. For a long time prehistoric settlers did not have tools strong enough to cut down the heavy oak forests. Over the centuries the expanding human population cut back the forests, so that today only 11.8 percent of the United Kingdom is forested, roughly 3 million hectares. Efforts have been made in Britain to grow more trees and expand the managed forest areas. Local authorities have the power to protect trees and woodlands. It is an offense to cut down trees without permission, and when trees protected by the government die they must be replaced.

Animals

An estimated 30,000 animal species live in Britain, although many have limited distribution and are on the endangered list. Britain has many smaller mammals. The only surviving large mammals are red deer, which live in the Scottish Highlands and in Exmoor in southwestern England, and roe deer (狍), found in the woodlands of Scotland and southern England. Semi wild ponies also inhabit Exmoor and the Shetland Islands (苏格兰东北的设得兰群岛). Many smaller mammals inhabit Britain, including badgers (獾), foxes, red squirrels, and wildcats. The red squirrel is now limited mainly to the Isle of Wight and Scotland.

Britain is home to a large variety of birds. About 200 species are regularly seen in Britain. Bird watching is a popular national pastime. The most common are birds that remain year-round, such as blackbirds, chaffinches (花鸡，一种欧洲鸣禽), sparrows, and starlings (八哥). Other well-known resident birds include crows, kingfishers (鱼狗), robins, wrens (鹪鹩), woodpeckers, and various tits (山雀). Cuckoos, swallows, and swifts (褐雨燕) are the best-known summer visitors.

IV Major Cities

As the first industrialized country in the world, The United Kingdom boasts many cities that have long been known to the world, such as London, Birmingham, Manchester, Edinburgh, Glasgow etc.

London

London is the capital of the United Kingdom. It's located in England and is the biggest city in Europe. More than 7 million people live there. Greater London was created in 1965. It includes the City of London and 32 boroughs. The City of London is located at the center of the metropolitan area and serves as the financial center, where there is a concentration of banks, including the Bank of England, insurance companies and stock exchanges. The City of London and 12 surrounding boroughs are referred to as Inner London, the remaining 20 boroughs are the Outer London. London is nearly 2,000 years old. It was founded by the ancient Romans soon after they invaded Britain in AD 43. The city has been destroyed several times by invaders and it has also been destroyed by fire. In 1666, the Great Fire of London burned down a large part of the city.

During the 18th and 19th centuries, London was the world's largest city. It sat at the center of a vast and powerful British empire that circled the globe. The city was heavily damaged by

160 | Understanding U.K. & Ireland

German bombing during World War II (1939—1945). The damaged areas were rebuilt after the war.

The residents of this sprawling city today are a mix of many races and nationalities. Many Londoners come from former British colonies, such as India, Pakistan, Jamaica, South Africa, and Hong Kong. This makes London one of the world's most international cities. Now London has become the great center of commerce, politics, administration, culture and transportation of the United Kingdom, and of the largest international ports in the world. As the biggest manufacturing center, London has such industries as printing, publishing, food processing, chemicals, clothing and electric and mechanical engineering.

To the east of the City of London is the large area called the East End, which is the industrial area and the port of London, With houses for workers, this used to be poorest quarter of London, but nowadays luxuries houses have been built on the waterfront (滨水地区) and some of the richest people live there. To the west are the shops and theatres of the area vaguely known as the West End. The southern part of this area is the City of Westminster (威斯敏斯特市,伦敦市的一个行政区,英国议会所在地), the political center of the country, where are located the Buckingham Palace, the Palace of Westminster, White Hall, No.10 Downing Street and Hyde Park. London boasts many historical buildings. It has great churches like Saint Paul's Cathedral and Westminster Abbey; a castle called the Tower of London and a large public square called Trafalgar Square. There's Big Ben, the famous clock tower at the Houses of Parliament. There's also a famous shopping and entertainment center called Piccadilly Circus.

Other Cities

The United Kingdom has other capital cities such as Edinburgh in Scotland, Belfast in Northern Ireland, and Cardiff in Wales.

Edinburgh (爱丁堡)

Edinburgh, the capital of Scotland, is a fine old city. It is now one of the important financial and transportation center in Britain. Its main industries are shipbuilding, chemicals, distilling (蒸馏) and brewing (酿造). It also serves as the hub of communications of Scotland and a center of art and culture. Every year from mid-August to mid-September Edinburgh welcomes thousands of visitors to its world famous festival. The festival includes several different arts festivals. It was founded in 1947.

Cardiff (加的夫)

Cardiff, the capital of Wales, is Europe's youngest Capital with a population of 284,000. It is one of the largest coal shipping ports in the world, and a center of iron and steel industry in Britain.

Belfast (贝尔法斯特)

Belfast, the capital of Northern Ireland, has a population of 400,000. It is an important industrial, commercial and cultural center in Northern Ireland. Its industries include ship building, linen, man-made fibers and aircraft manufacture. The majestic City Hall building, shown here, is a landmark located in Donegall Square in central Belfast. The name Belfast translates as "Mouth of the (River) Farset." This term refers to the sand bar that formed where the River Farset met the River Lagan at Donegall Quay and flowed into Belfast Lough (湖), which became the hub around which the city developed. It is the largest urban area in Northern Ireland and the province of Ulster and the second-largest city in Ireland. Belfast has been the capital of Northern Ireland since its creation in 1920 by the Government of Ireland Act.

Birmingham

Birmingham in central England is the second-most populous British city, with a population of 1,006,500 (2006 estimate). The city was a powerhouse of the Industrial

Revolution in England, a fact which led to Birmingham being known as "the workshop of the world" or the "city of a thousand trades". Its heavy industry, particularly in such fields as metallurgy, machinery-building, automobile manufacture and chemicals is important to the nation's economy.

Today although Birmingham's industrial importance has declined, it has developed into a national commercial centre, being named as the second-best place in the United Kingdom to locate a business, and the 14th best in Europe by Cushman & Wakefield in 2009. It is also the fourth most visited city by foreign visitors in the UK. In 2007, Birmingham was ranked as the 55th most livable city in the world and the second most livable in the UK. Birmingham was also one of the founding cities for the Eurocities group and is also sitting as chair. Birmingham has the second-largest city economy in the UK, and was ranked 72nd in the world in 2008. Birmingham is often thought of only as an industrial center, yet it has a greater length of canals than Venice in Italy. Originally built to support the city's trade, they are today used primarily by pleasure craft.

People from Birmingham are known as "Brummies," a term derived from the city's nickname of "Brum."

Manchester

Situated in the south-central part of North West England and forming part of the English Core Cities Group, Manchester today is a centre of the arts, the media, higher education and commerce with a population of 458,100 in 2007. In a poll of British business leaders published in 2006, Manchester was regarded as the best place in the UK to locate a business. It is the "fastest-growing city" economically and the third-most visited city in the

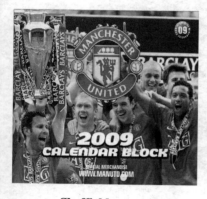

United Kingdom by foreign visitors. Manchester is the place where the industrial Revolution started and has long been the center of Britain's textile industry. Its other industrial products, such as machinery, aircraft, clothing, paper, and chemicals are also important. The city is connected with the Sea by a 57-kilometer-long Manchester Ship Canal that was built in 1894. The city's best known newspaper, the Guardian, is read all over the world. The University of Manchester, established in 1880, is a pride of the city. Manchester is well-known for being a city of sport. Two Premiership football clubs bear the city's name, Manchester United and Manchester City.

Sheffield

Sheffield is located in South Yorkshire of England. It is an important center of Great Britain for the production of cast iron, high-grade steel and steel manufactures.

Plymouth

Plymouth is the main city if Southwest Devon. It is a port city with a fine harbor where the British Royal Navy has its base. Its pillar industries include shipbuilding and fishing.

Glasgow

Glasgow is the largest city in Scotland and third most populous in the United Kingdom with a population of 734,000. The city is situated on the River Clyde in the country's west central lowlands. From the 18th century it became one of Europe's main hubs of transatlantic trade with the Americas. With the Industrial Revolution, the city and surrounding region grew to become one of the world's pre-eminent centers of engineering and shipbuilding, constructing many innovative and famous vessels. Glasgow was known as the "Second City of the British

Empire" for much of the Victorian era and Edwardian period. In the late 19th and early 20th centuries Glasgow grew to a population of over one million, and was the fourth-largest city in Europe, after London, Paris and Berlin.

Today it is one of Europe's top twenty financial centers and is home to many of Scotland's leading businesses. The city has particular strengths in shipbuilding, engineering, food and drink, printing, publishing, chemicals and textiles as well as new growth sectors such as optoelectronics （光电子学）, software development and biotechnology. Glasgow forms the western part of the Silicon Glen, which is a nickname for the high tech sector of Scotland. A growing number of Blue chip （蓝筹股：由于公众对其长期稳定收入的信心而售价很高的股票） financial sector companies have significant operations or headquarters in the city. The city is also famous for the University of Glasgow, which was established in 1451 and is the fourth oldest university in the English-speaking world. A person from Glasgow is known as a Glaswegian, which is also the name of the local dialect.

Newcastle

Many towns throughout Britain became manufacturing centers during the Industrial Revolution in the 18th and 19th centuries. Newcastle upon Tyne, in northeastern England, became important for steel production and shipbuilding. In the 1990s it was still a transportation hub.

Liverpool

During the 19th century Liverpool was a major British port, second only to London. The broad estuary of the Mersey River was the main scene of activity. Today this stretch of the river is used mostly by ferries and recreational craft. Liverpool is one of the large ports in Britain. It has a population of 491,000. Now the city is a district of Merseyside metropolitan area.

Bristol

Bristol, located on the Lower Avon River in England, has been a thriving port city since the 10th century. It is transformed into arts and recreation centers. The most important port in the United Kingdom is London; other important commercial ports are at Forth in Scotland, Grimsby and Birmingham in eastern England, Liverpool in western England, and Southampton and Dover in southern England.

B. History

British History Timeline

Celts	Romans	Saxons	Vikings	Normans	Tudors	Victorians	WW II
500 BC	AD 43	450	793	1066	1485	1837	1939+

Thousands of years ago, Great Britain was joined to Europe and was covered with ice. About 15,000 years ago, the weather became warmer. The ice melted and the sea level rose. Great Britain became an island about 8000 years ago. Little is known about people inhabiting the British Isles in the pre-Celtic period (before 800 BC). Some monuments built by them have been preserved such as Stonehenge, erected some time before 1000 BC or Newgrange monument—it is a tomb.

The Celts

The first Celtic tribes, the Goidels or Gales (盖尔人) are believed to have come to the British Isles between 800 & 700 BC. Two centuries later they were followed by the Brythons or ancient Britons after whom the country was called Britain. The word Celt comes from the Greek word, Keltoi, meaning barbarians. No one called the people living in Britain during the Iron Age *Celts* until the eighteenth century. In fact the Romans called these people Britons, not Celts.

The Celts were a warlike people who tended to have battles that frequently devolved into individual combats; where the victor would cut off the head of the loser and display it on a pole outside his hut. From around 750 BC to 12 BC, the Celts were the most powerful people in central and northern Europe and Northwest Europe was dominated by three main Celtic groups:

- the Gauls (高卢人,高卢是西欧一古老地区,基本相当于现代的法国和比利时)
- the Britons (二千年前罗马人入侵时不列颠南部的凯尔特人)
- the Gaels (盖尔人,苏格兰、爱尔兰或马恩岛的说盖尔语的凯尔特人)

The Celts were ancestors of the Scots, the Irish and the Welsh, and their languages are the basis of Welsh and Gaelic. Celtic civilization in Britain was most advanced in the south and southeast. The Celts lived both in villages and in OPPIDA (towns); their townspeople knew the concept of division of labor. Some Celtic peoples had a coinage. Celtic society was divided into three main classes: the warrior aristocracy, the Druids (古代盖尔人或不列颠人中的牧师) who were the religious leaders and at the same time teachers. Women were also regarded highly amongst the Celts, which was unusual during ancient times, some even becoming tribal leaders. Celtic Britain was far from united. There was no union among the tribes, and wars were frequent. By the time of Julius Caesar, Celtic peoples have dominated the British islands.

Roman Britain (55BC—410AD)

British recorded history begins with the Roman invasion. The first Roman invasion was led by Julius Caesar in 55 BC. But Britain was not conquered until some 90 years later, under Emperor Claudius, in 43 AD. For nearly 400 years, Britain was under the Roman occupation.

The Romans brought the Britons into great contact with Roman civilization. One of the greatest achievements of the Roman Empire was its system of roads. They constructed a network of roads between the large towns. Many of them are still in use now because of their remarkable solidity. They also allowed the movement of agricultural products from farm to market. The Roman built many towns, roads, baths, temples, amphitheaters(古罗马的圆形剧场,竞技场) and beautiful villas and buildings. They also brought to Britain the new religion, Christianity, which had thoroughly replaced the old Celtic gods by the close of the 4th Century, but Romanization was not successful in other areas. Apart from the villas and fortified settlements, the great mass of the British people did not seem to have become Romanized and people did not adopt the Latin language, so Latin did not displace Celtic.

The Angle-Saxon Conquest (446—871)

Germanic tribes from northwestern Europe began to raid Roman-occupied Britain in the third century, carrying away grain, cattle, and other valuables. In the mid-5th century, not long after Roman troops were withdrawn from Britain, a new wave of invaders, the three Teutonic tribes (日耳曼人的,条顿人的)—Jutes(朱特人), Saxons, and Angles, collectively known as the

Chapter 9 Geography and History of UK

Anglo-Saxons—came to Britain across the North Sea in search of land for settlement.

According to tradition, the first important settlement was made about 449 on Britain's eastern coast by the Jutes, who had fished and farmed in Jutland(日德兰半岛, 由丹麦的大陆部分和德国北部组成). Then came the Saxons, users of the short-sword from northern Germany, from the end of the 5th century to the beginning of the 6th century. In the second half of the 6th century, the Angles, also from northern Germany, arrived. Unlike the Romans who only took 35 years to conquer all of Britain except the (Scottish) Highlands, the Angles, Saxons, and Jutes fought for more than two centuries before they controlled even half of the island. It was a bitter struggle, but the Germanic tribes were thorough. For nearly two centuries, the invaders penetrated the island by way of its inland rivers, ravaging as they advanced. Roman civilization was destroyed; its language, religion, and customs disappeared. Most of the native Britons were killed, enslaved, or driven into Wales and to Brittany (in France).

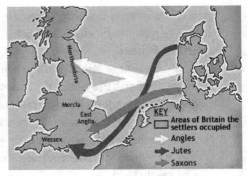

A map showing the various migration routes taken by Germanic tribes from the 5th and 11th centuries

About 613 the Anglo-Saxon conquest of central Britain was completed. Anglo-Saxon England was divided into a number of small kingdoms. The Jutes occupied the region called Kent, between the Thames River and the Strait of Dover. The Saxons settled to the south and west of London. Their major kingdoms were Sussex, Essex, and Wessex. The Angles, who gave their name to the country, settled in the eastern coast from the territory of the Saxons northward into the Scottish lowlands. They formed the kingdoms of East Anglia(英吉利,英格兰的中世纪和晚期拉丁语名称), Mercia(麦西亚,英格兰中部的一个盎格鲁—撒克逊王国), and Northumbria(诺森伯兰,北英格兰—盎格鲁—撒克逊王国).

Constant conflict followed during the four centuries after the conquest of Britain. The Anglo-Saxons warred among themselves, against the Welsh (Britons in Wales), and later against Danish and Norwegian invaders (the Vikings). The more powerful Anglo-Saxon kingdoms absorbed their weaker neighbors. From the seven major kingdoms that developed during the invasions, three dominant states emerged—Northumbria, Mercia, and Wessex.

Anglo-Saxon domination lasted for four centuries, though it did not include Scotland, where the Picts(皮克特人,英国北部的古代民族之一)and the Scots established a separate kingdom. The Anglo Saxon period can be characterised as a period of transition from a tribal to feudal organisation of society. Although barbarians, the Anglo-Saxons were more advanced than the Britons had been before the Roman occupation. The Anglo-Saxons laid the foundations of the English state. They divided the country into shires(郡), with shire courts and shire reeves(地方行政官), or sheriffs, responsible for administering law. They devised an effective farming system which was in use to the 18th century. Finally, they created the Witan(盎格鲁—撒克逊时代的议会,council or meeting of the wise-men) to advise the king, the basis of the Council which still exists today.

They brought to Britain their own Teutonic religion, which was dominant over Christianity until the end of the 6th century, when in 597 Saint Augustine, sent by Pope Gregory I, arrived in Kent to convert the people of the British Isles to Christianity. By the end of the seventh century, missionaries had converted all of England and monasteries(修道院) were established and became centers of learning. Christianity played an important role in civilizing the Anglo-Saxons.

Viking and Danish invasions (793—1066)

From the 8th century the Anglo-Saxons had to face Scandinavian invaders—the Danes and the Norsemen (meaning "people from the North"), sometimes referred to as Vikings—who came across the North Sea, just as the Anglo-Saxons had done 400 years earlier, and occupied parts of Britain.

Vikings were great travelers and sailed in their long boats all over Europe and the Atlantic Ocean, where they traded, raided, and often settled. They were also farmers, fishermen, trappers and traders. Viking craftsmen made beautiful objects out of wood, metal and bone; Viking women were skilful weavers, produced fine, warm textiles. The reason for most Vikings to sail overseas was simply searching for better land for their farms. At home their land was not very good for farming. Norway was very hilly, Sweden was covered in forests, and Denmark had a lot of sandy land.

The Scandinavian invasions continued till the 11th century, when they were defeated at sea by Alfred the Great (849—899), king of Wessex and the founder of the British navy. The Vikings settled peacefully in an area of Britain which became known as Danelaw (施行丹麦法的英国地区) and eventually the Vikings were assimilated.

Alfred the Great was noted for resisting the Danes and uniting the various English kingdoms under one rule. "The father of the British navy and a promoter of learning and legal system as well as a skillful military leader and administrator, Alfred is the only English king to be labeled "the Great."

The Norman Conquest (1066)

The Norman conquest of England began in 1066. In January 1066, King Edward, the last Saxon king, died childless. He had promised to leave the English throne to his cousin William, but he chose Harold, his wife's brother as king. So William led his army to invade the Kingdom of England. In October 1066, during the important battle of Hastings, William of Normandy's army of some 12,000 horse and 20,000 foot defeated King Harold Godwinson's 25,000 Saxons on Senlac Hill near Hastings. King Harold was killed. He is one of only two Kings of England to have died in battle (the other being Richard III). On Christmas Day, William was crowned king of England. This resulted in Norman control of England, which was firmly established during the next few years.

The Norman Conquest of 1066 was important event in English history. It brought about many consequences. William confiscated (没收) almost all the land and gave it to his Norman followers. He replaced the weak Saxon rule with a strong Norman government. So the feudal system was completely established in England. Relations with the Continent were opened, and civilization and commerce were extended. Norman-French culture, language, manners, and architecture were introduced. The church was brought into closer connection with Rome, and the church courts were separated from the civil courts. The Norman Conquest also had important consequences for the rest of the British Isles, paving the way for further Norman invasions in Wales and Ireland, and the extensive penetration of the aristocracy of Scotland by Norman and other French-speaking families.

The Plantagenet's (金雀花王朝, 1154—1485) and Tudors (1485—1603)

From 1154 to 1547 much of English history was shaped by the shifting alliances of the Plantagenet and Tudor kings. Royal succession was by no means assured during this period of conflict and disease—nearly half the population was killed by the Black Death in 1348—49. International relations were dominated by struggle with France, including the Hundred Years War (1337—1453). In domestic politics, Wales was subjugated (被征服)by 1288, and Scottish independence was recognized in 1314, when English forces were defeated by Robert Bruce at the Battle of Bannockburn.

The Wars of the Roses (battles between the House of Lancaster, symbolized by the red rose, and that of York, symbolized by the white) in the period from 1455 to 1485 illustrated that those who could obtain the greatest military power from a majority of rival barons were able to claim the throne. Henry Tudor, descendant of Duke of Lancaster won victory of the Wars of the Roses in 1485 and put the country under the rule of the Tudors. It weakened the great medieval nobility and promoted the development of English society. It also allowed the Tudor monarch to establish a powerful central government. The Tudor Period (1485—1603) was a turning point in English history. England became one of the leading powers. The two famous rulers of the House of Tudor were **Henry VIII** (28 June 1491—28 January 1547) and **Elisabeth I** (7 September 1533—24 March 1603).

Britain's most famous king was **Henry VIII** (1509—1547), remembered not only for his six wives (two of whom he had beheaded), but also for bringing about the Reformation. He established the Church of England as the national church of the country, and made himself the supreme head of the Church of England. As a result of the Reformation, England became a Protestant country, rather than a Catholic one.

Henry VIII's reform stressed the power of the monarch and certainly strengthened Henry's position; Parliament had never done such a long and important piece of work before, its importance grew as a result. Henry also took advantage of a growing resentment for the excessive wealth and privilege of the Church; thus he was able to seize enough monastic lands and property to finance his rule. He created the Royal Navy, which became the basis of future British sea power.

Henry's quarrel with the Church was centered on the Pope's refusal to annul(废除)his marriage with Catherine of Aragon(阿拉贡,西班牙东北部的前王国), who could not give him a male heir to the throne.

Portrait of Henry VIII, Britain's most famous king was Henry VIII (1509—1547)

The Elizabethan Age (1558—1603)

Under **Elizabeth I**, daughter of Henry VIII and Anne Boleyn, England entered a Golden Age. Among the events of the Elizabethan Age were the defeat of the Spanish Armada in 1588, Sir Walter Raleigh's discovery of tobacco in Virginia, and Sir Francis Drake's circumnavigation of the world. The Elizabethan age saw the flourishing of English poetry, music and literature and produced the world's greatest playwright William Shakespeare. It was also the end of the period when England was a separate realm before its royal union with Scotland.

The Elizabethan Age is viewed so highly because of the contrasts with the periods before and after. It was a brief period of largely internal peace between the English Reformation and the battles between Protestants and Catholics and the battles between parliament and the monarchy that engulfed the seventeenth century. The Protestant/Catholic divide was settled, for a time, by the Elizabethan Religious Settlement, and parliament was not yet strong enough to challenge royal absolutism. England was also well-off compared to the other nations of Europe and the century's long conflict between France and England was largely suspended for most of Elizabeth's reign.

Queen Elizabeth I

The Stuarts (斯图亚特王朝, 1603—1714)

The **Stuart period** of British history usually refers to the period between 1603 and 1714. After the death of Elizabeth, the "Virgin Queen" who left no male heir, the throne was occupied by James VI of Scotland, James inaugurated the Stuart dynasty and ruled the kingdom of England, Scotland, and Ireland for 22 years, from 1603 to 1625, often using the title *King of Great Britain*, until his death at the age of 58. The period ended with Queen Anne and the accession of George I from the House of Hanover.

Conflict between the Crown and Parliament characterized the Stuart period. James I would have preferred to have no Parliament at all, since he was a firm believer in the Divine Right of Kings, which was the belief that kings received their power from God and thus could not be deposed (废黜).

His Successor Charles I dissolved Parliament and introduced a period of absolute rule which lasted eleven years. The result of the conflict was **Civil War** (1642—1649), also called the Puritan Revolution. The Civil War ended with the Parliamentary victory. Charles I was condemned to death and his son, Charles II was exiled. The English Civil War overthrew feudal system in England and led to the replacement of English monarchy first with the Commonwealth of England (1649—53), and then with a Protectorate (1653—59,护国公政体), under **Oliver Cromwell**'s personal rule. It also shook the foundation of the feudal rule in Europe. Under the rule of Oliver Cromwell, a period of republicanism followed, but after Cromwell's death in 1658, the monarchy was restored and prospered under Charles II, the late King's son who was asked to return from his exile in France as the king. This was called **the Restoration**.

The Glorious Revolution of 1688

In 1685 Charles II died and was succeeded by his brother James II, who was a Catholic king in a country that was thoroughly Protestant and wanted nothing to do with the Pope in Rome. James wanted to change the State religion of England back to Catholicism. He is best known for his belief in absolute monarchy and his attempts to create religious liberty for his subjects. Both of these went against the wishes of the English Parliament and of most of his subjects. So the English politicians rejected James II, and appealed to a Protestant king, the Dutch Stadtholder William of Orange (荷兰执政奥兰治亲王威廉), to invade and take the English throne.

William landed in England in 1688 and takeover was relatively smooth, with no bloodshed, nor any execution of the king. This was known as the "Glorious Revolution." It was indeed a revolution and paved the way for Parliament's dominance over the Crown. James was then replaced not by his Catholic son, James Francis Edward, but by his Protestant daughter Mary II and his son-in-aw William III, who became joint rulers in 1689. Authority was simplified when Mary's death in 1694 left William the sole monarch.

The overthrow of James II in 1688 was the second time in the 17th century that a Stuart king had lost his crown. However, unlike Charles I, his father, James II did not lose his head as well.

James II made one serious attempt to recover his crowns when he landed in Ireland in 1689, but, after the defeat of the Jacobite (英王詹姆斯二世的拥护者,1688年后斯图尔特王朝的拥护者) forces by the Williamite forces at the Battle of the Boyne in the summer of 1690, James returned to France. He lived out the rest of his life under the protection of his cousin and ally, King Louis XIV.

The Glorious Revolution of 1688 is the greatest landmark in the history of England. This revolution is so called because it achieved its objective without any bloodshed. The struggle between the King and the Parliament ended in victory for the people (i.e. the representative of the people—the parliament). It marks the end of absolutism, never since has the monarch held absolute power, and the beginning of modern English parliamentary democracy. The Bill of Rights has become one of the most important documents in the political history of Britain.

The deposition of the Roman Catholic James II ended any chance of Catholicism becoming re-established in England, and also led to limited toleration for nonconformist Protestants—it would be some time before they had full political rights. For Catholics, however, it was disastrous both socially and politically. Catholics were denied the right to vote and sit in the Westminster Parliament for over 100 years afterwards. They were also denied commissions in the army and the monarch was forbidden to be Catholic or marry a Catholic, thus ensuring the Protestant succession.

Georgian Era (1714 to 1830) and Victorian Age (1837—1901)

England and Scotland were united in 1707 by the Act of Union. The **House of Hanover** succeeded the House of Stuart as monarchs of Great Britain and Ireland in 1714 and held that office until the death of Victoria in 1901. George I of Hanover was the first British monarch of the House of Hanover and Queen Victoria was the last. The dynasty provided six British monarchs:

- George I   (r.1714—1727)
- George II   (r.1727—1760)
- George III (r.1760—1820)
- George IV   (r.1820—1830)
- William IV (r.1830—1837)
- Victoria   (r.1837—1901).

The **Georgian era** is normally defined as including the reigns of the kings George I, George II, George III and George IV, i.e. covering the period from 1714 to 1830, (with the sub-period of the Regency, defined by the Regency of George IV as Prince of Wales during the illness of his father George III). Sometimes the reign of William IV (1830 to 1837) is also included.

During George I's reign the powers of the monarchy diminished and Britain began a transition to the modern system of cabinet government led by a prime minister. Towards the end of his reign, actual power was held by Sir Robert Walpole, Great Britain's first actual prime minister. George died in 1727 on a trip to his native Hanover, where he was buried.

The Victorian Age comprised the second half of the 19th century and is generally agreed to stretch through the reign of Queen Victoria from June 1837 until her death on the 22nd of January 1901. It was preceded by the Georgian era and succeeded by the Edwardian period.

Queen Victoria was the only child of Edward Duke of Kent, the granddaughter of George III and was a descendant of most major European royal houses. At age eighteen Victoria ascended the English throne in June of 1837 following the death of her uncle King William IV. In 1840 she married her first cousin Albert. She arranged marriages for her children and grandchildren across the continent, tying Europe together; this earned her the nickname "the grandmother of Europe."

The Victorian Age was a period in which Britain became the strongest world power: besides being the greatest financial and commercial power, the greatest sea power and the greatest colonial power and is often characterized as a long period of peace and prosperity for the British people, as profits gained from the overseas British Empire, as well as from industrial improvements at home allowed an educated middle class to develop. It was a tremendously exciting era when many artistic styles, literary schools, as well as, social, political and religious movements flourished. It was a time of prosperity, broad imperial expansion, and great political reform.

The Victorian Age was also a time of tremendous scientific progress and ideas. The Industrial Revolution had already occurred, but it was during this period that the full effects of industrialization made themselves felt, leading to the mass consumer society of the 20th century. This is also the period when the railway network developed all over the country.

During the early part of the era, the House of Commons was headed by the two parties, the

Understanding U.K. & Ireland

An 1883 painting of Queen Victoria (1819—1901). Behind the queen is a portrait of her deceased(已故的) consort, Prince Albert. The box beside her is labeled "First Lord of the Treasury."

Whigs and the Tories. From the late 1850s onwards, the Whigs became the Liberals; the Tories became the Conservatives. These parties were led by many prominent statesmen.

Without a doubt, The Victorian Age was an extraordinarily complex age, which has sometimes been called the Second English Renaissance. It is, however, also the beginning of Modern Times. Queen Victoria's nearly 64-year reign (1837—1901) was the longest in British history, and is foreseeably likely to be exceeded only if the present monarch (Queen Elizabeth II) remains on the throne to 2017. Queen Victoria was succeeded by her eldest son, the Prince of Wales, who reigned as King Edward VII. Today it is her great-great granddaughter that rules the United Kingdom, and Elizabeth's consort, Philip, is Victoria's great-great grandson.

The Industrial Revolution (1760—1850)

The **Industrial Revolution** refers to the mechanization of industry and the consequent changes in social and economic organization in Britain in the late 18th and early 19th centuries. It started with the mechanization of the textile industries, the development of iron-making techniques and the increased use of refined coal. The onset of the Industrial Revolution marked a major turning point in human history; it forever transformed the way people live and work in most parts of the world.

Before the Industrial Revolution, most people lived by farming. There was little industry. Any manufacturing was done in homes or in small workshops close to home. People used craft skills, such as weaving or woodworking, to produce goods for their families or to sell in towns. The Industrial Revolution took production out of homes and workshops and into big factories, People moved from the countryside into industrial cities. New roads, canals, railroads, and steamships were built to carry factory-made goods and the raw materials to make them. The British government was eager to increase the country's income from trade, and it encouraged industry. Business people also hoped to make more money. They saw opportunities to profit from new inventions and new ways of making goods.

The invention of the steam engine was an important step in the Industrial Revolution. Steam engines powered factories and drove the trains that carried goods over long distances. The first big factories in Britain grew up around the textile industry. For centuries, spinning yarn and weaving cloth was done mostly by hand. British business owners realized they could profit more by increasing production. They developed new machines that could weave cloth, and they built large, new factories to hold them. Before long, Britain was supplying cloth to countries throughout the world.

Huge factories were also built near sources of iron, coal, and water. Three regions of Britain—northern England, central England, and central Scotland—became industrial zones and workers moved to big new industrial cities such as Birmingham, Manchester, Newcastle on Tyne, and Glasgow as more and more factories opened there.

From the 18th century, new agricultural machines began to replace more and more of the traditional farming implements that had been used for centuries. By about 1800, the new inventions and work techniques in Britain spread to Europe and North America. A second phase of the Industrial Revolution began about 1850. Inventors discovered new processes, such as better ways to make steel.

Chapter 9 Geography and History of UK

There were several reasons for Britain became the first country to industrialize: First, Britain had a favorable geographical location to participate in European and world trade; it was a country in which the main towns were never too far from seaports, or from rivers, which could distribute their products. Secondly, Britain had political stability and a peaceful society. After the 17th century, it was increasingly interested in overseas trade and colonies. Thirdly, Britain had a good foundation in economy. The limited monarchy which resulted from the Glorious Revolution of 1688 ensured that the powerful economic interests in the community could exert their influence over Government policy. Fourthly, Britain had many rivers, which were useful for transport but also for water and steam power. Britain also had useful mineral resources. The last reason was that British engineers had skilled craftsmen.

Typical inventions during the Industrial Revolution included:
- John Kay's flying shuttle in 1733;

John Kay's flying shuttle

James Hargreaves' Spinning Jenny

James Watt's steam engine

- James Hargreaves' Spinning Jenny in 1766;
- Richard Arkwright's water frame in 1769;
- Edmund Cartwright's power looms in 1784;
- James Watt's steam engine in 1765.

Britain in the Twentieth Century

The 20th century is a period of the decline of Britain as a world power, a period of crises of the two world wars, from which Britain emerged as a victor, but greatly weakened. It is characterised by the disintegration (瓦解) of Britain's colonial empire and the effort to adjust Britain to the new situation by joining the other developed capitalist countries of Western Europe in EEC (European Economic Community 欧洲经济共同体).

In 1952 Princess Elizabeth was crowned Queen Elizabeth II. As Britain entered the 1960s, new universities were built and a reinvigorated culture emerged. While its heavy industry struggled, Britain led the world in fashion and pop music. Inflation and unemployment soared in the 1970s and endless strikes resulted from labor unrest.

In 1973 Britain joined the European Community, but there seemed to be few obvious economic benefits. Margaret Thatcher came to power in 1979 and went on to win two more elections. By 1990 her popularity was so diminished that her party replaced her with John Major, who won the 1992 election. But a reinvigorated Labor Party under Tony Blair won in 1997. The economy remained weak, and Britain continued to distrust the European Community. Nationalism continued to simmer(酝酿; 骚动) in Scotland and Wales, and conflict continued in Northern Ireland. James Gordon Brown became Prime Minister in June 2007, after the resignation of Tony Blair and three days after becoming leader of the governing Labor Party.

Queen Elizabeth II

Chapter 10 Political System and Economy of UK

A. Political System

Government of United Kingdom

Form of government	Constitutional monarchy
Head of state	Monarch
Head of government	Prime minister
Legislature	Bicameral legislature: House of Commons, 646 members House of Lords, 713 members (595 life peers and 118 hereditary members)
Voting qualifications	Universal at age 18
Constitution	Unwritten; partly statutes, partly common law and practice
Highest court	House of Lords High Court of Justiciary (the supreme criminal court of Scotland)

Parliamentary Democracy

Great Britain (UK) is a parliamentary democracy with a constitutional Monarch as Head of State with limited powers. The principle behind British democracy is that the people elect Members of Parliament (MPs) to the House of Commons in London at a general election, held no more than five years apart. Most MPs belong to a political party, and the party with the largest number of MPs in the House of Commons forms the government. Britain's democratic government is based on a constitution composed of various historical documents, laws, and formal customs adopted over the years.

Constitution

King John of England set his seal to Magna Carta on June 15, 1215

The British constitution regulates how the country is governed and ensures that the government acts at all times within the rule of law and that the government serves the people, and not that the people serve the government.

In Britain, monarch was gradually replaced by a limited, representative government based on **unwritten constitution**. The constitution is said to be "unwritten" because it is taken partly from various written documents and partly from unwritten customs and laws. These legal rules and laws are contained in documents such as Magna Carta 1215 (自由大宪章), The Petition of Rights 1628 (权利请愿书), Habeus Corpus Act 1679, the Bill of Rights 1689 (权利法案), the Act of Settlement 1701 (王位继承法), the Act of Union 1707 (联合法案) and the Act of Union 1800. The two main features of the British Constitution are the Rule of Law and the Supremacy of Parliament.

The most important part of the English constitution is the **Magna Charta**, or **Great Charter**, sealed by King John in 1215. This document limited the king's power in several ways. Chiefly, it took away his right to collect taxes without the noble's consent. A few years later John's successor, Edward I, called the first meeting of Parliament, England's legislative body.

The Glorious Revolution of 1688 (光荣革命，英国 1688—1689年间发生的一场革命，废黜了詹姆士二世，确立了威廉和玛丽的联合统治,亦称"不流血革命") put power solidly into the hands of Parliament. No law could be passed, no tax collected, no army maintained without Parliament's consents. By this time, Parliament was made up of two houses. Members of the House of Lords were nobles who held their seats by right of inheritance. Members of the House of Commons were elected. Following the Glorious Revolution, the House of Commons began to assume more power than either the king or the House of Lords.

King William III and Queen Mary II

The democratically elected House of Commons can alter these laws with a majority vote. The constitution continually evolves as new laws are passed and judicial decisions are handed down. All laws passed by Parliament are regarded as constitutional, and amendments to the constitution occur whenever new legislation overrides existing law. Although the Crown gives its royal assent to legislation, this is a mere formality.

The Constitutional Monarchy

The politics of the United Kingdom of Great Britain and Northern Ireland takes place in the framework of a constitutional monarchy, in which the Monarch is head of state and the Prime Minister of the United Kingdom is the head of government.

Constitutional monarchy (君主立宪制) means that the power of the monarch is limited by the country's constitution, the legal authority is given to Parliament and the executive authority to the government. The Sovereign reigns, but does not rule ("临朝而不理政","统而不治"). The country is governed in the name of the Sovereign by His or Her Majesty's Government who is responsible to the Parliament.

Queen Elizabeth II and Prince Philip at the official coronation (加冕礼, 2 June 1953)

Executive power is exercised by the UK government, the devolved governments of Scotland and Wales, and the Executive of Northern Ireland. Legislative power is vested in both the government and the two chambers of Parliament, the House of Commons and the House of Lords, as well as in the Scottish parliament and Welsh and Northern Ireland assemblies. The judiciary is independent of the executive and the legislature, though several senior judges are still members of the House of Lords.

The British monarchy has been a hereditary position since the 9th century. Primogeniture (长子继承权), the passing of the throne to the eldest son when a monarch dies, has been the rule of succession, and when there are no sons, the eldest daughter ascends the throne. This was the case when Elizabeth II succeeded to the throne in February 1952 upon the death of her father, George VI. Her husband, Prince Philip, has the title of Prince Consort, but no rank or privileges. The current heir to the throne is Elizabeth II's eldest son, Charles, Prince of Wales. According to the Act of Settlement of 1701, only Protestants are eligible to succeed to the throne. A regent (摄政王) may be appointed to rule for the sovereign if he or she is underage (未成年的).

Left: Queen Elizabeth II, wearing the English crown during her coronation in 1953
Right: Queen Elizabeth II, wearing the English crown for her eightieth birthday

As the official head of state, the monarch formally summons and dismisses Parliament and the ministers of the Cabinet. The monarch also serves as head of the judiciary, commander in chief of the armed forces, and Supreme Governor of the Church of England and the Church of Scotland. In reality, the government carries out the duties associated with these functions. Theoretically, the monarch appoints all judges, military officers, diplomats, and archbishops, as well as other church officers. The monarch also bestows honors and awards, such as knighthoods and peerages. In reality, all of these appointments are made upon the advice of the prime minister. The prime minister declares war and peace and concludes treaties with foreign states in the name of the crown. The monarch serves as the ceremonial head of the Commonwealth of Nations and is the ceremonial head of state for 16 Commonwealth countries.

The real work of the monarchy consists largely of signing papers. The monarch has the right to be consulted on all aspects of national life and review all important government documents. The monarch may also meet with the Privy Council, a now largely ceremonial body made up of Cabinet members that serves in an advisory capacity to the monarch. Since Britain is a

Left: Buckingham Palace is the official London residence of the British sovereign

Right: Guards at Buckingham Palace

Left: Houses of Parliament, London. Built between 1840 and 1850, the neo-Gothic complex of buildings is officially called the New Palace of Westminster.

Right: Queen Elizabeth II speaks from the throne, as Prince Philip listens, in the House of Lords, during the State Opening of Parliament in London, Dec. 3.

democracy, the monarchy could potentially be abolished if a majority of the population decides to do so. In the early 21st century the monarchy generally remained popular. Tourism related to the royal family brings a substantial amount of money into the country.

The Parliament

The Parliament of the United Kingdom of Great Britain and Northern Ireland is the supreme legislative body in the United Kingdom and British overseas territories. At its head is the Sovereign, Queen Elizabeth II. Government is drawn from and answerable to it.

The parliament is bicameral (两院制的), with an upper house, the House of Lords, and a lower house, the House of Commons. The Queen is the third component of the legislature. The House of Commons is far more influential than the House of Lords.

The House of Lords includes two different types of members: the Lords Spiritual (the senior bishops of the Church of England) and the Lords Temporal (members of the Peerage) whose members are not elected by the population at large, but are appointed by the Sovereign on advice of the Prime Minister. Prior to the opening of the Supreme Court in October 2009 the House of Lords also performed a judicial role through the Law Lords. The House of Commons is a democratically elected chamber with elections to it held at least every 5 years.

Parliamentary sessions are held each year and begin in October or November. The two Houses of Parliament meet in separate chambers at the Houses of Parliament in London, officially called the *New Palace of Westminster*. The Parliament of the United Kingdom legislates for the entire nation and includes representatives from England, Scotland, Wales, and Northern Ireland. By constitutional convention, all government ministers, including the Prime Minister, are members of the House of Commons or, less often, the House of Lords, and are thereby technically accountable to the respective branches of the legislature.

History

The Parliament of Great Britain was formed in 1707 following the ratification of the Treaty of Union by both the Parliament of England and Parliament of Scotland passing Acts of Union. However, in practice the parliament was a continuation of the English parliament with the addition of Scottish MPs and peers. Parliament was further enlarged by the ratification by the Parliament of Great Britain and the Parliament of Ireland of the Act of Union (1800), which abolished the Irish Parliament; this added 100 Irish members to the Commons and 32 to the Lords to create the Parliament of the United Kingdom of Great Britain and Ireland.

England has been called "the mother of parliaments", its democratic institutions having set the standards for many democracies throughout the world.

The Parliament of England had itself originated from the early medieval councils that advised the sovereigns of England. Later, Parliament served to supplement royal revenues by making grants of taxation—that is, by granting the monarch's request for extra subsidies to pay for wars. The crown invited all great nobles and church leaders to attend these councils. By the end of the 13th century representatives from the counties, called *knights of the shire*, and representatives of the towns, called *burgesses*, were also being summoned to attend regularly. The knights and the burgesses eventually came to sit separately from the nobles and church leaders, in what eventually became the *House of Commons*. The nobles and church leaders sat in what came to be called the *House of Lords*. By the end of the Middle Ages Parliament had taken on a form that would be recognized today. It legislated and approved taxes and passed laws.

In theory, supreme legislative power is vested in the Queen-in-Parliament; in practice, real power has passed from the crown to the Lords to its final resting place in the House of Commons over the course of centuries. For the past 280 years the monarch's royal assent to legislation has been given automatically and the Sovereign generally acts on the advice of the Prime Minister.

The powers of the House of Lords are limited. Today the House of Lords can only delay legislation.

Parliament is elected roughly every five years and is dissolved by the crown on the advice of the prime minister, who then calls a general election.

> Interesting Fact
> No King or Queen has entered the House of Commons since 1642, when Charles I stormed in with his soldiers and tried to arrest five members of Parliament who were there.

The House of Lords

The House of Lords was previously a largely hereditary aristocratic chamber, with 574 life peers(爵位不能世袭的终身贵族), 92 hereditary peers, and 26 bishops;

The House of Lords today is more a place of discussion and debate than one of power, and it normally passes legislation already approved by the House of Commons. Its members are not elected. The House of Lords comprises the lords temporal, the lords spiritual, and the law lords. **The lords temporal** are either hereditary peers or life peers. Life peers are appointed by the monarch for the duration of the person's lifetime. These appointments are usually made in recognition of outstanding careers or contributions to society. Famous people who have been made peers are former British Prime ministers Winston Churchill and Harold Wilson. **The lords spiritual** include the archbishops of Canterbury and York; the bishops of London, Durham, and Winchester; and the 21 next most senior bishops. Prior to the opening of the Supreme Court in October 2009 the House of Lords also performed a judicial role through the **Law Lords.**

The House of Lords was stripped of most of its power in 1911, and now its main function is to revise legislation. The powers of the House of Lords are limited because most Britons believe that in a modern democracy a nonelected house should only act as a forum for opinion, one that is comparatively free from party politics and pressures.

The House of Commons

The Countries of the United Kingdom are divided into parliamentary constituencies of broadly equal population. Each constituency elects a Member of Parliament (MP) to the House of Commons at General Elections and, if required, at by-elections (an election held to fill a political office that has become vacant between regularly scheduled elections, known in the United States as a special election). MPs in the House of Commons may remain MPs until Parliament is dissolved, which must occur within 5 years of the last general election, as stated in the Parliament Act 1911.

Over the history of the House of Commons, the number of Members of Parliament (MPs) has varied for different reasons, with increases in recent years due to increases in the population of the United Kingdom. There are currently 646 MPs, corresponding to approximately one for every 92,000 people, or one for every 68,000 parliamentary electors.

In modern times, all Prime Ministers and Leaders of the Opposition have been drawn from the Commons, not the Lords. The House of Commons is the source of real political power in the United Kingdom. Its members are democratically elected by citizens over the age of 18. Certain groups that are denied the right to vote, including members of the House of Lords, and those convicted of corrupt or illegal election practices in the previous five years.

General Elections

A session of Parliament lasts for five years unless the Prime minister dissolves Parliament. Although the monarch officially dissolves Parliament, this happens only after the Prime Minister calls for it. At the end of the five years or before, a general election has to take place so new members of parliament can be elected by the people. The election is called by the Prime Minister.

General Election in the US is like voting for a Congressman or Senator. However, unlike the

US, the voters can only vote for a MP to represent them in the House of Commons, they do not choose the Prime Minister (PM). He/she is voted for within their party. The Lords are appointed or inherited. The last General Election was in 2005, when Labor won 356 seats and became the leading party and therefore the Government.

Who can become an MP?

People are nominated as candidates to become MPs. Any one over the age of 21 can be a candidate. When an MP gets the most votes for his constituency he gains a seat. This means he has a place in Parliament.

No individual may be a member of both Houses, and members of the House of Lords are legally barred from voting in elections for members of the House of Commons.

The Government

Her Majesty's Government is the government of the United Kingdom. It is answerable to the House of Commons. However, neither the Prime Minister nor members of the Government are elected by the House of Commons. Instead, the Queen requests the person most likely to command the support of a majority in the House, normally the leader of the largest party in the House of Commons, to form a government. So that they may be accountable (有责任的) to the Lower House, the Prime Minister and most members of the Cabinet are, by convention, members of the House of Commons.

Her Majesty's Government Coat of Arms

Under the Constitution of the United Kingdom, executive authority notionally lies with the monarch but is exercised in practice by her ministers. Her Majesty's Government is the collective name for these ministers, and it is effectively an executive authority for the U.K.

The Prime Minister

The Prime Minister of the United Kingdom of Great Britain and Northern Ireland is the Head of Her Majesty's Government. He or she is the leader of the party that holds the most seats in the House of Commons. The Prime Minister and Cabinet (consisting of all the most senior government department heads) are collectively accountable for their policies and actions to the Sovereign, to Parliament, to their political party, and ultimately to the electorate.

The monarch goes through the ceremony of selecting as prime minister the person from the House of Commons who is head of the majority party. The prime minister presides over the Cabinet and selects the other Cabinet members, who join him or her to form the government. Acting through the Cabinet and in the name of the monarch, the prime minister exercises all of the theoretical powers of the crown including making appointments. Every week the Prime Minister appears before the House of Commons and must answer questions put to him or her by the members of Parliament.

James Gordon Brown (born 20 February 1951) is the Prime Minister of the United Kingdom and Leader of the Labor Party. Brown became Prime Minister in June 2007, after the resignation of Tony Blair and three days after becoming leader of the governing Labor Party.

In the past, prime ministers also came from the House of Lords. Today, in the unlikely circumstance that a peer (a member of the House of Lords) is sought as a prime minister by one of the parties, he

Number 10 Downing Street in London has been the official residence of the British prime minister since Sir Robert Walpole in 1732.

or she must first resign from the House of Lords and gain election to the House of Commons.

The Prime Minister is based at 10 Downing Street, which along with most government departments, is located in Westminster. The current Prime Minister is Gordon Brown, leader of the Labor Party. He was appointed by Queen Elizabeth II on 27 June 2007. He leads a government composed of 127 ministers; mostly Labor Party MPs.

The Prime Minister also has a house in the country called Chequers (英国首相乡间别墅) near Ellesborough in Buckinghamshire, England, which was given to the nation as a country retreat for the serving Prime Minister by the Chequers Estate Act 1917. It is used as the Prime Minister's non-London residence. If the PM needs to hold a private conference of some of his Ministers or receive foreign visitors over a weekend, Chequers is usually where it is done. It is also used by Prime Ministers to entertain guests as a special privilege.

The Cabinet

The **Cabinet** is the collective decision-making body of Her Majesty's Government, composed of the Prime Minister and some 22 Cabinet Ministers, the most senior of government ministers. H.M. Ministers, and especially Cabinet Ministers, are selected primarily from the elected members of House of Commons, but also from the House of Lords, by the Prime Minister.

The most important ministers are called Secretaries of State and they form the Cabinet. The Secretaries of State are in charge of a Government Department (a ministry). Each minister is responsible for his department, and makes sure that his department applies the policy of the government. The prime minister serves as the first lord of the treasury and as minister for the civil service.

In addition to the various secretaries of state, the Cabinet includes ministers who hold traditional offices—such as the Lord President of the Council (枢密院大臣, presides over the Privy Council), the Paymaster General (主计大臣), and the Lord Privy Seal (掌玺大臣)—and Ministers without Portfolio (政务委员), who do not have specific responsibilities but are assigned to specific tasks as needed. The Lord Chancellor (上议院的大法官) holds a unique position. The Lord Chancellor's executive duties as a Cabinet member include being responsible for legal affairs in the United Kingdom, but he or she is also head of the judiciary, which is a separate part of the British government.

The Prime Minister has the power to move members of the Cabinet from post to post, or to drop individuals from the Cabinet entirely. Former Cabinet ministers may retain their positions as members of Parliament.

The Cabinet meets on a regular basis, usually weekly on a Tuesday morning notionally to discuss the most important issues of government policy, and to make decisions. For a long period of time, Cabinet met on a Thursday, and it was only after the appointment of Gordon Brown as Prime Minister that the meeting day was switched to Tuesday. The length of meetings varies according to the style of the Prime Minister and political conditions, but today meetings can be as little as 30 minutes in length. The Prime Minister normally has a weekly audience with The Queen thereafter.

Currently, following Gordon Brown's reshuffle in June 2009, there are 31 ministers who are members of the Cabinet or attend its meetings, compared with only nine in Winston Churchill's Cabinet which co-ordinated Britain's wartime defenses in 1940.

Chapter 10 Political System and Economy of UK

The Cabinet developed during the 18th century out of informal meetings of key government ministers during the reigns of the Hanoverian monarchs, who took relatively little interest in politics. During the 19th century this committee of key ministers evolved into an effective body that wielded (行使) the monarch's executive power.

Two key doctrines of Cabinet government are collective responsibility and ministerial responsibility. Collective responsibility means that the Cabinet acts unanimously, even when Cabinet ministers do not all agree upon a subject. If an important decision is unacceptable to a particular Cabinet member, it is expected that he or she will resign to signify dissent. Ministerial responsibility means that ministers are responsible for the work of their departments and answer to Parliament for the activities of their departments. The policy of departmental ministers must be consistent with that of the government as a whole. The ministers bear the responsibility for any failure of their department in terms of administration or policy.

Shadow Cabinet

The Shadow Cabinet is a senior group of opposition spokespeople in the Westminster system of government (a democratic parliamentary system of government) who together under the leadership of the Leader of the Opposition form an alternative cabinet to the government's, whose members *shadow* or mark each individual member of the government. Members of a shadow cabinet are often but not always appointed to a Cabinet post if and when their party gets into government. It is the Shadow Cabinet's responsibility to pass criticism on the current government and its respective legislation, as well as offering alternative policies.

In the United Kingdom, Canada and Australia the major opposition party and specifically its shadow cabinet is often called *His* or *Her Majesty's Loyal Opposition*. The adjective "loyal" is used because, while the role of the opposition is to oppose Her Majesty's Government, it does not dispute the sovereign's right to the throne and therefore the legitimacy of the government.

In most countries, a member of the shadow cabinet is referred to as a Shadow Minister. In Canada, however, the term Opposition Critic is more usual.

The Privy Council (枢密院)

The Cabinet is technically the executive committee of Her Majesty's Privy Council. The Privy Council is a large, and generally ceremonial, body of more than 450 members that developed out of the royal council that existed in the Middle Ages. By the 18th century the Privy Council had taken over all the powers of the royal council. The Privy Council comprises all current and former Cabinet members, as well as important public figures in Britain and the Commonwealth. The council advises the monarch and arranges for the formal handling of documents. It has a large number of committees, each with a specific task, such as dealing with outlying islands, universities, or legal matters. The most important committee is the Judicial Committee of the Privy Council, which is the highest court of appeal for certain nations in the Commonwealth, some church-related appeals, and for disciplinary committees of some professions.

The Royal Courts of Justice is the building in London which houses the Court of Appeal of England and Wales and the High Court of Justice of England and Wales. The building is a large grey stone edifice in the Victorian Gothic style and was built in the 1870s. The Royal Courts of Justice were opened by Queen Victoria in December 1882. It is on The Strand, in the City of Westminster.

The Judiciary

Britain has a long judicial history. Its legal system has been emulated (仿效) throughout the world and many of its key principles and rights are part of U.S law. The principles derived from British law include the right to trial by jury; the right to due process of law; freedom from unlawful imprisonment, called the writ of habeas corpus(人身保护权令状); the trial system of prosecution and defense; and the presumption that a person is innocent until proven guilty.

The judicial system has its roots in the Anglo-Saxon period, when the monarch established local courts to provide justice for all subjects. Monarchs delegated(授权) the power to hear cases to royal justices, who presided over courts in the monarch's name.

The British legal system relies on common law (习惯法), which is based on custom and on decisions in previous legal cases, called precedents. Common law originated in the 12th century, growing out of the rules and traditions that ordinary people had worked out over time. Through the centuries common law evolved as it incorporated legal decisions made in specific cases, and it remains the basis of British law except when superseded (代替) by legislation. Unlike the United States, Britain does not have a Supreme Court that reviews legislation to determine its constitutionality; that responsibility falls to Parliament.

Britain has several layers of courts and two kinds of legal proceedings, criminal and civil. Criminal law is concerned with acts punishable by the state, such as murder. Civil law involves disputes between private parties, either individuals, organizations or companies. The final court of appeal for both civil and criminal cases is the House of Lords, where appeals are heard by the law lords.

Criminal cases are handled in one of two ways. Petty offenses, such as simple theft or vandalism, are brought before a local magistrate, or justice of the peace (JP). These unpaid magistrates are appointed by the Lord Chancellor and members of the community who are assisted by legal experts. The vast majority of criminal cases in Britain are minor enough to be handled by JPs. More serious criminal offenses, such as murder, rape, and robbery, are sent to a Crown Court, where they are tried before a High Court or a circuit judge and a jury of local citizens.

Civil cases are heard in county courts before a single judge. County courts hear cases dealing with families, property, contracts, and torts (民事侵权行为). Above the county courts is the High Court, which hears more complicated civil cases. High Court cases are sent to one of three divisions: the Family Division, which handles complex divorce cases, adoptions, and matters relating to children; the Chancery Division (大法官法庭,英国最高法院部门之一,由大法官主持), which handles business matters and estate cases; or the Queen's Bench Division, which handles property matters and torts, as well as maritime and commercial cases. Appeals are heard by the Court of Appeals for the Civil Division, and ultimately by the House of Lords.

Different types of courts have different styles of judges. They also form a strict hierarchy of importance. Judges of the Court of Appeal of England and Wales are generally given more weight than district judges sitting in County Courts and Magistrates. By statute, judges are guaranteed continuing judicial independence.

Lord Chief Justice and Lord Chancellor

On 3rd April 2006, when the Constitutional Reform Act 2005 came into force, the Lord Chief Justice became head of the judiciary of England and Wales, a role previously held by the Lord Chancellor. The Lord Chief Justice is also the presiding judge of the Criminal Division of the Court of Appeal. The first Lord Chief Justice to act as head of the judiciary after the Lord Chancellor relinquished that role was Lord Phillips of Worth Matravers.

Under the Constitutional Reform Act 2005, the Lord Chief Justice has some 400 statutory duties (法定责任). His key responsibilities include:

- Representing the views of the judiciary of England and Wales to Parliament and

Government.

- The welfare, training and guidance of the judiciary in England and Wales within resources made available by the Lord Chancellor. The Lord Chief Justice discusses with Government the provision of resources for the judiciary.
- The deployment of judges and allocation of work in courts in England and Wales.

He and the senior judiciary are supported by a team of civil servants who form the Directorate of Judicial Offices.

Although the **Lord Chancellor** is no longer a judge, he still exercises disciplinary authority over the judges, jointly with the Lord Chief Justice. He also has a role in appointing judges. In law reports, the Lord Chief Justice is referred to as (for example) "Smith LCJ", and the Lord Chancellor as "Smith LC."

The Supreme Court

The **Supreme Court of the United Kingdom** is the supreme court in all matters under English law, Welsh law, Northern Irish law and Scottish civil law (the court has no authority over criminal cases in Scotland, where the High Court of Justiciary remains the supreme criminal court). It sits in the Middlesex Guildhall in Westminster, London, which it shares with the Judicial Committee of the Privy Council.

President of the new British Supreme Court, Lord Phillips (middle) stands with the fellow Justices, wearing their ceremonial robes, outside the new Supreme Court building in Parliament Square, London, after being sworn in, Oct 1, 2009

The Supreme Court was established by Part 3 of the Constitutional Reform Act 2005 and started work on 1 October 2009. It assumed the judicial functions of the House of Lords, which were exercised by the Lords of Appeal in Ordinary (Law Lords). Its jurisdiction over devolution matters had previously been held by the Judicial Committee of the Privy Council. Its title, "The Supreme Court," has led some British lawyers to be concerned that it might eventually take on powers like the American Supreme Court, which can strike down laws. Its proponents say the court is a healthy separation of the judiciary from the legislature.

The judges of the Supreme Court of the United Kingdom are known as Justices of the Supreme Court, and they are also Privy Counselors.

The Court of Appeal

Judges of the Court of Appeal are known as Lord Justices, and they too are Privy Counselors. Before swearing in they may be addressed as *The Honorable Lord Justice Smith*, and after swearing in as *the Right Honorable Lord Justice Smith*. Female Lord Justices are only known as Lady Justices informally, addressed as "My Lord" or "My Lady". In law reports, referred to as "Smith LJ," and, for more than one judge, "Smith and Jones LJJ."

Formerly, Lord Justices of Appeal could only be drawn from barristers of at least 10 years' standing. In practice, much greater experience was necessary and as of 21 July 2008, a potential Lord Justice of Appeal must satisfy the judicial-appointment eligibility condition on a 7-year basis.

High Court

High Court judges are not normally Privy Counselors and are referred to as the (Right) Honorable Mr/Mrs Justice Smith, dressed as "My Lord" or "My Lady." In law reports, referred to as "Smith J," and, for more than one judge, "Smith and Jones JJ."

Solicitors and Barristers

Those who practice law in Britain are divided into solicitors (不是律师界成员，只能在低级法庭出庭的初级律师) and barristers (在英国有资格出席高等法庭并辩护的律师). Solicitors perform the everyday work of the law, particularly legal matters that can be handled solely with paperwork. Barristers plead (为……辩护) cases in court. In Scotland barristers are called advocates. Solicitors engage barristers when they believe a client needs to go to court. Eminent barristers and, since 1996, some solicitors, may become Queen's Counselors, or QCs. When they do it is said that they "take silk,' because they switch from wearing cotton gowns to silk gowns in court. Barristers with long and distinguished careers may be chosen to become crown judges by the Lord Chancellor, the head of the judicial system in England and Wales. Scotland and Northern Ireland have their own legal systems.

The main Political Parties

The UK is a multi-party system and since the 1920s, the two largest political parties have been the *Conservative Party* and the *Labor Party*. Though coalition and minority governments have been an occasional feature of parliamentary politics, the first-past-the-post electoral system used for general elections tends to maintain the dominance of these two parties, though each has in the past century relied upon a third party to deliver a working majority (使执政党得以继续执政所需的议会中的多数) in Parliament.

The *Liberal Democrats*, a party formed by the merger of the former Liberal Party and Social Democratic Party in 1988, is the third largest party in the British parliament. It seeks a reform of the electoral system to address the disproportionate dominance of the two main parties that results from the current system. As well as the three major political parties the UK also has various minor ones, some of whom have seats in parliament.

The leader of the political party with the most MPs in the House of Commons is asked by the Queen to become Prime Minister and to form a government that will manage the country.

The party in power today is the Labor Party which won 356 seats (for their Ministers of Parliament) in the 2005 General Election, while Conservatives 198 seats and Liberal Democrats 62. As the Labor Party won the most seats, its leader at the time, Tony Blair, was asked to form the government. The current voting system is called "first past the post." This means that the party and candidates receiving the most votes win the election and become the party in power even if they do not receive more than 50 percent of the vote.

B. National Economy

An Overview

The United Kingdom is a highly developed country and one of the seven major Western economic powers, whose economy is the fifthlargest in the world (2006), the second largest in Europe after Germany, and the sixthlargest overall by purchasing power parity (PPP) exchange rates. British economy is based on the Anglo-Saxon model, focusing on the principles of liberalization, the free market, and low taxation and regulation.

Economic Sectors

The British were the first in the world to enter the Industrial Revolution, and, like most industrializing countries at the time, initially concentrated on heavy industries such as ship-building, coal mining, steel production, and textiles. The empire created an overseas market for British products, allowing the United Kingdom to dominate international trade in the 19th century. However, as other nations industrialized and surplus labor from agriculture began to dry up, the United Kingdom started to lose its economic advantage. As a result, heavy industry declined throughout the 20th century. The British service sector, however, has grown substantially, and now makes up about 73% of GDP and employed almost four-fifths of the workforce. The service industries include finance, retailing, wholesaling, tourism, business services, transport, insurance, investment, advertising, public relations, market research, education, administration, and government and professional service.

New Industries

New industries include microprocessors and computers, biotechnology, new materials and other high-tech industries. There are three areas in Britain which have seen some high-tech industrial growth: (1) the area between London and South Wales, (2) the Cambridge area of East Anglia and (3) the area between Glasgow and Edinburgh in Scotland. The third area is the most spectacular of the three and is now often referred to as the "Silicon Glen" (硅谷).

The Government's Role in the Economy

Like many modern developed countries, the United Kingdom has a mixed economy. This means that some sectors of the economy are operated by the government and some are operated by private businesses. Since World War II (1939—1945), Britain has worked to balance the mix of private and public enterprises in order to maximize the country's economy and ensure the economic well-being of its citizens. Historically, Britain's Conservative Party has sought a stronger private component in the mix while the Labor Party has sought to strengthen the public component. Both parties are committed to a healthy mix of both elements, however.

The public component consists of the welfare system, which includes socialized medicine, known as the National Health Service, plus government controls over business, banking, and the money supply. The welfare system provides support from before birth to the grave.

After World War II the government nationalized a number of large and troubled industries. These included coal, electricity, transport, gas, oil, steel, certain car and truck manufacturing, shipbuilding, and aircraft building. Since the 1950s, the government has privatized a number of these industries, such as the steel and road transportation industries. The Conservative governments between 1979 and 1996 denationalized oil companies, telecommunications, car and truck production, gas, airlines and aircraft building, electricity, water, railways, and nuclear power. The government also seeks to encourage competition in the economy and increase productivity by sponsoring and subsidizing (补助) training and educational programs.

In the early 2000s Britain's levels of inflation and unemployment remained among the lowest in the European Union.

Economy of United Kingdom

Currency	British Pound (GBP)
Trade organizations	EU, BCN, OECD and WTO
GDP (PPP)	$2.772 trillion (2007 est.) (5th)
GDP growth	3.1% (2007 est.)
GDP per capita	$45,575 (2007 est. nom.) (12th)
GDP by sector	Agriculture (1%), industry (26%), services (73%)
Inflation (CPI)	2.3% (2006 est.)
Labor force	31 million (includes unemployed) (2007 est.)
Labor force by occupation	Services (81%), industry (18%) and agriculture (1%) (excludes unemployed) (2007)
Main industries	machine tools, industrial equipment, scientific equipment, shipbuilding, aircraft, motor vehicles and parts, electronic machinery, computers, processed metals, chemical products, coal mining, oil production, paper, food processing, textiles, clothing and other consumer goods.

Exports	$470 billion (2007 est.)
Main export partners	USA 15%, Germany 11%, France 10%, Ireland 7%, Netherlands 6%, Belgium 6%, Spain 5%, Italy 4% (2007)
Imports	$600 billion (2007 est.)
Main import partners	Germany 14%, USA 9%, France 8%, Netherlands 7%, Belgium 6%, Italy 5%, The People's Republic of China 4%, Ireland 4%

Agriculture

Britain's land surface is minimal compared to many other nations and by European standards its agriculture sector is small in terms of employment and contribution to the GDP. In the early 2000s agriculture employed approximately 1.4% of the workforce and contributed 1.0% of the GDP. But British agriculture is very intensive and highly productive. Only a few farmers employ full-time farm workers. In Northern Ireland, all are self-reliant rural farmers without land rental. The British government has adopted policies on subsidies for agriculture.

Livestock Farming

Many of Britain's full-time farms are devoted to livestock farming—raising cattle for dairy products or beef, or raising sheep for wool and meat. The treatment of farm animals became a growing concern in Britain in the late 20th century. Factory farming of chickens produced protests, as did the practice of raising calves in confined spaces. Concerns over animal welfare have led some British citizens to become vegetarians.

Grave concern arose in the 1980s over cattle infected with bovine spongiform encephalopathy (BSE), popularly known as mad cow disease. Human beings who eat infected beef may develop Creutzfeldt-Jakob disease (CJD). BSE was first discovered in Britain in 1986, and consumer confidence in British beef declined, and in 1996 the European Union banned Britain from exporting any beef or beef by-products. After considerable action by the government to halt the spread of the disease, the EU lifted the ban in 1999.

Livestock farmers in Britain faced another crisis in 2001, when several cases of foot-and-mouth disease were detected in a British slaughterhouse. The highly infectious viral disease, which rarely infects humans, can quickly cripple cattle, sheep, pigs, and other animals with cloven hooves. The dangers of foot-and-mouth disease are largely economic, since infected animals often lose weight or stop producing milk. As the outbreak spread across the British countryside, the British government ordered the slaughter of more than 1 million animals to contain the virus.

Crop Farming

Most crop farming in Britain takes place in eastern and south central England and in eastern Scotland. The leading crops in the early 2000s were wheat, sugar beets, potatoes, barley, and rapeseed (油菜籽). As concern has grown about the use of fertilizers, pesticides, and biologically engineered seeds and their effect on the environment, some farmers have turned to organic farming, with support from the government.

Forestry

Britain was once covered with thick forests. The kind of forests in the U.K is called temperate forests. Temperate forests usually comprised of deciduous (落叶的)forests and coniferous (松柏科的)forests. But in some places, there is another type of forest called broad-leaved (阔叶的) evergreen forest. Over the centuries the expanding human population steadily deforested nearly the entire country, felling trees for fuel and building materials. Despite the fact that trees grow quickly in the cool, moist climate of the United Kingdom, only remnants of the great oak forests remained at the end of the 20th century.

Fishing

At one time the fishing industry not only provided a cheap source of protein for Britons, but it was also the training ground for the Royal Navy. Today fishing is a far less vital economic activity. Fish and fish products are both imported into and exported from Britain. In recent decades over-fishing and conservation restrictions imposed by the European Union have caused a decline in the deep-sea industry.

Mining and Manufacturing
Mining

Mining has been enormously important in British economic history, for example, in ancient times traders from the Mediterranean shipped tin from the mines of Cornwall; salt mining dates from prehistoric times. But today these tin mines are exhausted, and the last tin mine in Britain closed in 1998. Britain's abundant coal resources were very important during the Industrial Revolution, when it was mined, used, and exported in large quantities, the entire populations moved to work at coal and iron sites in the north and Midlands of England. Peak production occurred in 1913, when more than 300 million tons were mined. Today coal has become less important to the British economy and supplies an ever-smaller proportion of Britain's total energy need, production in 2003 was only 28 million tons.

Raw materials for construction form the bulk of mineral production, including limestone (石灰石), dolomite (白云石), sand, gravel (沙砾), sandstone, common clay, and shale (页岩). Some coal is still mined, but petroleum and natural gas are far more important. Mining and quarrying (采石, 挖沙), including oil and gas extraction, accounted for 2.6 percent of the GDP in the early 2000s and employed less than 1 percent of the labor force.

Manufacturing

Manufacturing accounted for about 16 percent of the gross domestic product (GDP) and about 12 percent of the workforce was engaged in manufacturing in the early 2000s.

The history of manufacturing in Britain is unique because Britain was the birthplace of the Industrial Revolution. During the Middle Ages the production of woolen textiles was a key industry in Britain. In the 16th and 17th centuries, new industries developed. These included silk weaving, garment making, and the manufacturing of hats, pottery (陶器), and cutlery (刀具). All of these operations were generally conducted in small craft shops and were labor-intensive. In the 18th century a number of changes in British society prepared the way for the Industrial Revolution. Coal and iron mining developed as Britain's forests decreased, which created the need for another energy source, and new smelting techniques made iron implements cheaper to produce. An agricultural revolution in the 18th century introduced new crops and crop rotation (轮作) techniques, better breeding methods, and mechanical devices for cultivation. During the Industrial Revolution new methods of manufacturing products were developed. Instead of being made by hand, many products were made by machine. Production moved from small craft shops to factories. Textiles, shipbuilding, iron, and steel emerged as important industries, and coal remained the most important industrial fuel. The Industrial Revolution dramatically raised the overall standard of living.

In the last half of the 20th century, the structure of British industry changed substantially. The coal mining and cotton textile industries declined sharply. As coal production declined, oil production replaced it as a major industry. Motor vehicle production became a significant part of the industrial base but was subject to severe foreign competition. As incomes increased, consumer demand rose for durable goods such as cars and kitchen appliances.

British industrial production also expanded into communications equipment, including fiber optics (光学), computers, computer-controlled machine tools, and robots. Growing industries in recent decades include paper products and publishing; chemicals, such as pharmaceuticals (制药的); rubber and plastics; and electronic and optical equipment.

Banking and Financial Services

Britain is one of the world's leading financial centers. Banking, finance, insurance, and other business services accounted for about more than a quarter percent of Britain's output in the early 2000s and more than 5 million people were employed in this sector. Historically, the financial services industry has been based in the City of London in an area called the Square Mile. The City is a small part of the Greater London metropolitan area that surrounds it. The City concentrates on more than 800 banks and financial institutions. The London Stock Exchange, the London International Financial Futures and Options Exchange, and the Lloyd's of London insurance market all based in the City. It also has the largest concentration of foreign bank branches in the world.

Leeds, Manchester, Cardiff, Liverpool, Edinburgh, and Glasgow have developed as financial centers in recent decades.

Banking System

Financial system is formed of the central bank, commercial banks and other financial institutions. In the banking system also includes insurance companies, trust and investment banks, savings banks, the Stock Exchange. There are three types of banks: High Street Banks, Building Societies and Direct Bank.

High Street Banks are the main banks, such as Royal Bank of Scotland, HSBC, NatWest, Citibank, and Barclays.

Building Societies such as Woolich, Abbey National, and Halifax were created for those who wanted to save in order to buy a house and offer pretty much the same services as the other banks.

Direct Banks such as Co-op (Smile.co.uk) and First Direct don't have branches, but you can bank at First Direct at the Post Office and Co-op bank at their grocery outlets. There are telephone banks which have grown in popularity over the last few years.

The Bank of England, chartered in 1694, and nationalized in 1946, is the only bank that issues banknotes in England and Wales. Several banks in Scotland and Northern Ireland issue currencies in limited amounts. After the Labor government was elected in 1997 the Bank of England was given operational independence in monetary policy. This means it can set interest rates independent of the government in power, much as the Federal Reserve does in the United States.

There are more than a dozen major commercial banks in Britain, including Lloyds TSB, Barclays, National Westminster, and HSBC. The postal system, savings banks, and cooperative and building societies also provide some banking services.

You cannot open a bank account without having the original copy of your signed lease (租借) of the property in which you wish to reside. This law is very strict and has quite an impact because it is difficult to rent an apartment or house without a bank account to which you can be traced!

Currency

The British pound sterling has been a major currency of foreign exchange for centuries. At the beginning of the 21st century there were four denominations (面值) of pound note in circulation: £5, £10, £20 (shown above), and £50. The £1 note was last issued in 1984, the year after the introduction of its replacement, the £1 coin.

The European Union established the euro as its unit of currency, and other EU members made the transition to the euro between 1999 and 2002. However, the British government elected not to do so and instead retained the pound as its currency.

Transportation and Tourism
Transportation

Britain has historically been an innovator and world leader in many forms of transportation, from shipping, rail systems to aviation.

Shipping

Britain is an island, so shipping has always been important in its history. The irregular coastlines provide many natural harbors. 3,200 km of canals and navigable rivers have been conductive to shipping. As early as the 16th century Britain defeated Spain, its greatest rival at sea. In the 17th and 18th centuries France was defeated, then Germany in the early 20th century. Prior to World War II, Britain had the largest merchant fleet in the world and continued to be the world leader in shipping until World War II, when submarine attacks by Germany sank many British vessels and the tremendous output of the American shipbuilding industry made the United States the world leader. Today most British passenger shipping involves ferry trips to the continent of Europe or to Ireland. Tankers carrying oil and dry bulk (散装) cargo make up the majority of oceanic shipping.

British ports were nationalized in the late 1940s, and in recent years most have moved into the private sector or are governed by independent trusts (托拉斯). The most important port in the United Kingdom is London; other important commercial ports are at Forth in Scotland, Grimsby and Birmingham in eastern England, Liverpool in western England, and Southampton and Dover in southern England.

Railways

The Victorian era was known as the Railway Age. The world's first public railway was the Stockton and Darlington, which opened in 1825. A period of hectic railway building followed for the next quarter century as different companies competed to lay track. Over the next century smaller railway companies were absorbed or merged into a few large companies. In 1948 the government nationalized the four remaining companies, and in the 1960s they became the British Railways Board. In 1955 a modernization program began to replace steam trains with diesel and electric ones. The last steam locomotive was withdrawn in 1968.

The Eurostar, a high-speed passenger train that connects England with continental Europe, leaves from Waterloo Station in London.

Railroads were part of the wave of privatization that took place in the early 1990s. The moves to fully privatize BR were highly contentious (有争议的) and generated considerable criticism within Britain.

A railway tunnel beneath the English Channel was completed in 1993, connecting England and the European continent. Trains carry both passengers and freight through the tunnel. Motorists can drive their cars on and off the train. The trip through the tunnel takes about 35 minutes.

The London Underground

The London Underground operated 408 km of railway in the early 2000s, of which about 42 percent is under the ground. Known as the tube, the system serves 275 stations, with more than 500 trains running during peak periods. Despite its problems, the Underground provides reliable public transportation for an impressive number of commuters across a large metropolitan area. There are also urban rail systems in Glasgow, Liverpool, Tyne and Wear, Manchester, and Sheffield.

Air Travel

British Airways is one of the world's leading airlines and has one of the largest fleets in Europe. The number of passengers and volume are the first in world airways.

Along with other industries, Britain's airlines were nationalized after World War II and then were privatized in the late 1980s. It was formed in 1974 by combining the two state-run airlines. Together with Air France, British Airways in 1976 introduced the first supersonic passenger service, using the Concorde aircraft. Concorde service was discontinued in 2003. Britain has numerous independent airlines, as well.

London's main airports, Heathrow and Gatwick, are among the world's busiest centers for international travel. Heathrow handles more than 67 million passengers a year, and is the world's busiest airport for international travel. There are nearly 150 other licensed civil airfields in Britain.

Roads

About 90 percent of all passenger travel in Britain is by road, and primarily by private car rather than public transportation. The growth in cars during the 20th century was paralleled by rising public concern about the environmental effects of increased traffic and especially concern about air pollution. The Transport Act of 2000 gave local authorities the power to charge drivers for use of the roads in an effort to reduce congestion. In 2003 London motorists began to pay for the privilege of driving into the center of the city.

Tourism

Tourism is an essential part of Britain's income. It employed about 1.4 million people and contributed about 3.5 percent to the GDP in the early 2000s. Visitors to Britain come from all over the world, with the largest number from the United States, followed by France, Germany Ireland, and Netherlands. They were attracted by Britain's heritage and arts, historic buildings, monuments, museums, and galleries. With over 27 million tourists a year, the United Kingdom is ranked as the sixth major tourist destination in the world.

The British Tourist Authority, which is supported by the government, promotes tourism in Britain and maintains hundreds of Tourist Information Centers to assist visitors. England, Scotland, Wales, and Northern Ireland have their own government-supported tourist boards as well.

London, the most popular tourist destination, is crowded with tourists throughout the year. Among the sites regularly visited by millions are the Tower of London, the Houses of Parliament, Buckingham Palace, and Westminster Abbey. At night visitors enjoy the hundreds of theaters and pubs in London. Liverpool is a city in the metropolitan county of Merseyside in north west England The second largest export port of Britain, it still possesses some manufacturing base. Liverpool is world famous as the city where the Beatles came from. Northwest Wales has many excellent castles, among them Conwy, Caernarfon, and Harlech. In Scotland, historic Edinburgh Castle looms over the capital. Great cathedrals from the Middle Ages still dominate the skylines of many English cities. In Wales the remains of Tintern Abbey and the small but beautiful Saint David's Cathedral are outstanding. There are a lot of stately (堂皇的) homes in Britain. Among the more famous is Blenheim Palace, the home of the Churchill family. Hampton Court Palace, just outside of London, was one of the homes of Henry VIII. The Palace of the Holyrood House in Scotland was once the home of Mary, Queen of Scots.

Among other worthwhile places to visit are Oxford and Cambridge, both are university towns with many ancient buildings, and the Tudor home in which William Shakespeare was born.

Chapter 11 Society and Culture of UK

1 British People and Their Ways of Life

General Characters & Manners of the People

It is very difficult to generalize about the British. The characteristics of the people living in different regions and of different social classes vary enormously. However, the following are regards as general qualities of the British, especially the upper and upper-middle classes in the south of England.

Exclusiveness

"I am English, you stay away from me. I am exclusive. I am quite happy to be myself. I do not need you. Leave me alone." This is the best-known quality of the British people, particularly of the English people. That is because of the special geographical location and the distinct development of its history. King James Bible, Shakespeare's plays, the British parliament as early as 1215 and the Industrial Revolution account for the shaping of their general character.

Conservativeness

Generally speaking, the British tend to be reserved. They have to wait a long time before they are prepared to try something new; they do not accept change although they are told to, for example, the use of fireplaces in the large cities such as London, Liverpool, Manchester and Birmingham.

Politeness

Language—Most British people use the words "please" and "thank you" all the time, particularly when asking for or after receiving help from someone.

Punctuality—British people expect punctuality especially in the work place or place of study. This means that if a lecture begins at 2pm, you must be present in the lecture room at or before 2pm.

Day to day etiquette—British people will normally queue in shops or whilst waiting for buses, buying tickets and so on. You should expect to do the same.

—Most people in the UK have a mobile telephone. It is considered impolite to use a mobile telephone in certain formal situations such as in lectures and meetings.

—When you are invited to dinner, ten minutes late is excellent. When at table, it is polite to sit straight, to keep your elbows off the table and never to talk with your mouth full of food; you have to copy everyone else, ask what to do if you are not sure and keep the conversation going.

—It is customary to leave a 10% tip when eating in restaurants for good service (but not in fast food restaurants such as McDonalds.)

Love of privacy

The following words best describe British people's attitude towards privacy.

"My home is my castle. The wind can come in, but the Kings and Queens and human beings can never come in without my permission."

Stiff upper lip

The British do not show their feelings very much. They do not show their emotion if they are very happy and nor if they are sad. They always keep a stiff upper lip

Sense of humor

The humor is self-deprecating (谦虚的), that is, laughing at oneself. The British enjoys making fun of their own customs, class system and even their government.

Ways of Life

Knowing the customs of a country is, in effect, a guide to understanding the soul of that country and its people. Britain is the birthplace of Newton, Darwin, Shakespeare and the Beatles, home of the world's largest foreign exchange market and the world's richest football club—Manchester United, the inventor of the hovercraft (气垫船) and the JK Rowling, the author of the Harry Potter books. From Scotland to Cornwall, Britain is full of customs and traditions. A lot of them have very long histories. Some are funny and some are strange. But they're all interesting and are all part of the British way of life. Throughout this section you will have the chance to discover the customs and traditions of Great Britain.

Marriage and Family Life

The family in Britain is changing. The once typical British family headed by two parents has undergone substantial changes during the twentieth century. In particular there has been a rise in the number of single-person households. By the year 2020, it is estimated that there will be more single people than married people. Fifty years ago this would have been socially unacceptable in Britain. In the past, people got married and stayed married. Divorce was very difficult, expensive and took a long time. Today, people's views on marriage are changing. Many couples, mostly in their twenties or thirties, live together without getting married. Only about 60% of these couples will eventually get married. In the past, people married before they had children, but now about 40% of children in Britain are born to unmarried parents. In 2000, around a quarter of unmarried people between the ages of 16 and 59 were cohabiting (同居) in Great Britain. Before 1960 this was very unusual, but in 2001 around 23 percent of births in the UK were to cohabiting couples.

Marriage is legal at age 16 but usually takes place when people are in their mid to late 20s and many women do not want to have children immediately. They prefer to concentrate on their jobs and put off having a baby until late thirties. The number of single-parent families is increasing. This is mainly due to more marriages ending in divorce, but some women are also choosing to have children as lone parents without being married.

Housing

Most people in England live in urban areas. In England, an average of 7,000 hectares of farmland, countryside and green space were converted to urban use every year between 1985 and 1998.

More people are buying their own homes than in the past. About two thirds of the people in England and the rest of Britain either own, or are in the process of buying, their own home. Most others live in houses or flats that they rent from a private landlord, the local council, or housing association. People buying their property almost always pay for it with a special loan called a mortgage (抵押贷款), which they must repay, with interest, over a long period of time, usually 25 years.

Cottages in England

Most houses in England are made of stone or brick from the local area where the houses are built. The colors of the stones and bricks vary across the country. England has many types of homes. In the large cities, people often live in apartments, which are called flats. In most towns, there are streets of houses joined together in

long rows. They are called *terraced houses*. The main types of houses in England are:
- Detached (a house not joined to another house)
- Semi-detached (two houses joined together)
- Terrace (several houses joined together)
- Flats (apartments)

The most popular type of home in England is semi-detached (more than 27% of all homes), closely followed by detached and then terraced. Almost half of London's households are flats, maisonettes (出租房间) or apartments.

Eating

Britain has a very diverse population due to the large number of immigrants, this provoked (促使) that the food was diversified. British food has traditionally been based on beef, lamb, pork, chicken and fish and generally served with potatoes and one other vegetable. The most common and typical foods eaten in Britain include sandwich, fish and chips, pies like the Cornish pasty, trifle and roasts dinners. Some of the main dishes have strange names like Bubble & Squeak and Toad-in-the-Hole(面拖烤香肠,裹面粉、牛奶、鸡蛋糊后油煎的肉或肠).

The staple foods of Britain are meat, fish, potatoes, flour, butter and eggs. Many of the dishes are based on these foods. Some of the most traditional foods are described below:

Fish and chips are a classic, traditional national food of England, made up with French fried potatoes and the fish deep fried in flour batter (牛奶鸡蛋面糊).

Yorkshire pudding is a traditional and popular British dish, originating from the North-east of England, made from flour, eggs and milk, is a sort of batter baked in the oven and usually moistened with gravy (肉汁).

Toad-in-the-Hole is similar to Yorkshire pudding but with sausages placed in the batter before cooking.

Lancashire Hotpot consists essentially of meat, onion and potatoes baked in the oven all day in a heavy pot and on a low heat.

Bubble & Squeak (土豆卷心菜炒肉)

Bubble and squeak (sometimes just called bubble) is a traditional English dish made with the shallow-fried leftover vegetables from a roast dinner. The chief ingredients are potato and cabbage, but carrots, peas, brussels sprouts, and other vegetables can be added. It is traditionally served with cold meat from the Sunday roast, and pickles. Traditionally, the meat was added to the bubble and squeak itself, although nowadays it is more commonly made without meat. The cold chopped vegetables (and cold chopped meat if used) are fried in a pan together with mashed potato until the mixture is well-cooked and brown on the sides.

Nowadays many traditional foods such as beef and potatoes have given way to poultry and pasta dishes. Fast food has also become more available, and hamburger restaurants now rival the traditional fish-and-chip shops in popularity. Numerous Chinese and Indian restaurants and pizza houses provide take-away service, and many pubs (public houses) serve anything from snacks to full meals as well as alcoholic beverages.

The English people generally eat three meals a day. A traditional English breakfast consists of

Yorkshire pudding

Toad-in-the-Hole

Lancashire Hotpot

Bubble & Squeak

any or all of the following: bacon, sausages, grilled or fried tomatoes, mushrooms, eggs, or toast. Kippers (smoked herring) or black pudding (blood pudding) may also appear on the menu. However, fewer people now eat a cooked breakfast on a regular basis, preferring various combinations of cereal, toast, juice or fruit, and tea or coffee.

The midday meal is usually referred to as lunch and the evening meal as dinner or, when it is less formal, as supper. Working-class people tend to call the midday meal dinner and the meal they have in the early evening "tea." The tradition of afternoon tea, when tea, biscuits, and cakes are enjoyed at about 4 PM, has declined. Similarly, many people no longer have more than a light lunch or snack in the middle of the day.

Socializing

The English often say "How do you do?" or "Pleased to meet you" when meeting for the first time. People usually shake hands when first introduced or when greeting and parting in business and other formal situations. Otherwise many English people will simply say "Hello" when they see each other. Among friends, women are often kissed (by men and women) lightly on one cheek. The use of first names is widespread; titles such as "Mr." and "Mrs." are being used less frequently, even when children address adults.

It is customary to respect people's privacy by telephoning before visiting. When invited to a meal by friends, guests often bring a bottle of wine or another small gift.

Pubs continue to be one of the main places for people to get together in the evenings. Older people often meet their friends in the morning, to chat over coffee or tea and a scone (烤饼). Relaxing in the home, however, is still more popular.

Sports and Recreation

Sports play an important part in the life of the Englishmen and are a popular leisure activity. A great number of major sports originated in the United Kingdom, including: Football (soccer), squash (壁球), golf, boxing, rugby (rugby union and rugby league), cricket, snooker (桌球), billiards (台球), badminton and curling (冰壶).

The England Football Team

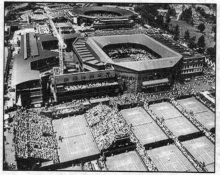
Wimbledon Lawn Tennis Court

Cricket—The traditional summer sport is cricket. It is England's national sport and often is played on village greens on Sundays from April to August.

Football (soccer)—Wintertime national sports are football (soccer) and Rugby Union. Football is undoubtedly the most popular sport in England and has been played for hundreds of years. Some of England's football teams are world famous, the most famous being Manchester United, Arsenal and Liverpool. In the English Football League there are 92 professional clubs. These are semi-professional, so most players have other full-time jobs. Hundreds of thousands of people also play football in parks and playgrounds just for fun. The highlight of the English football year is the FA (Football Association) Cup Final each May.

Rugby—Rugby originated from Rugby school in Warwickshire (沃里克郡). It is similar to football, but played with an oval ball. Players can carry the ball and tackle each other. The best rugby teams compete in the Super League final each September. For many years Rugby was only played by the rich upper classes, but now it is popular all over the country.

Tennis—Modern lawn tennis was first played in England.

The world's most famous tennis tournament is Wimbledon (温布尔登). It started at a small club in south London in the nineteenth century. It begins on the nearest Monday to June 22, at a time when English often have the finest weather. Millions of people watch the Championships on TV live. It is traditional for visitors to eat strawberries and cream whilst they watch the tennis.

Number one

Horseracing—One of the most popular spectator sports is horseracing (over jumps in the winter and on a flat track in the summer). People can place bets on the races at legal off-track betting shops. Some of the best-known horse races are held at Ascot, Newmarket, Goodwood and Epsom. Ascot, a small town in the south of England, becomes the centre of horse-racing world for one week in June. It's called Royal Ascot because the Queen always goes to Ascot. She has a lot of racehorses and likes to watch racing.

Foxhunting—Traditionally Boxing Day is a day for fox hunting. The huntsmen and huntswomen ride horses. They use dogs too. The dogs (fox hounds) follow the smell of the fox. Then the huntsmen and huntswomen follow the hounds. Before a Boxing Day hunt, the huntsmen and huntswomen drink hot wine. But the tradition of the December 26th is changing. Now, some people want to stop Boxing Day hunts (and other hunts too). They don't like fox hunting. For them it is not a sport-it is cruel.

Rowing—In the nineteenth century, students at Oxford and Cambridge, Britain's two oldest universities were huge fans of rowing. In 1829, the two schools agreed to hold a race against each other for the first time on the Thames River. The Oxford boat won and a tradition was born. Today, the University Boat Race is held every spring in either late March or early April.

With the exception of U.S. citizens, the British watch more television than anyone else in the world and claim that one reason for this is the high quality of British programming. Videos are also popular, but many people equally enjoy seeing films at the cinema. All types of music and theater are well supported. The country is also rich in art galleries and museums.

Ⅱ Holidays and Special Days

Britain has relatively few public holidays compared with other European countries. They are usually described as Bank Holidays because they are days when banks are officially closed. Many holidays and festivals in Britain are centuries old, some involving months of careful planning and preparations, others requiring simply a worrying desire to make a complete and utter fool of oneself.

What are public holidays?

Generally, public holidays include bank holidays, holidays by Royal Proclamation and "common law holidays." Banks are not allowed to operate on bank holidays. When public holidays in the Christmas and New Year period fall on Saturdays and Sundays, alternative week days are declared public holidays.

What are "bank" holidays?

British bank holidays are public holidays and have been recognized since 1871. The name Bank Holiday comes from the time when banks were shut and so no trading could take place.

Traditionally many businesses close on Bank Holidays to enable the workers to have a holiday. This time is often spent with the family on mini breaks and outings. Because of this, anyone who works on Bank Holidays usually gets paid extra —"time-and-a-half" or even "double time," negotiated for them by the Trades Unions.

Today even though banks are still closed on these days many shops now remain open. Shops, museums and other public attractions, such as historic houses and sports centers, may close on certain public holidays, particularly Christmas Day.

Does the U.K. have a National Day?

National Days are not celebrated in the same extent as National Days are in a number of other countries. Only St Patrick's Day in Northern Ireland (and the republic of Ireland) and St Andrew's Day in Scotland (from 2007) are taken as an official holiday. All the other national days are normal working days. Each part of the United Kingdom has its own Saint's Day:

Brief Introduction to National Days

● **St. David's Day (1 March)**

St. David's Day is the national day of Wales celebrated in Wales on 1 March, in honor of St David, the patron saint of Wales. He was a Celtic monk, abbot (修道士) and bishop, who lived in the sixth century. He spread the word of Christianity across Wales. The most famous story about Saint David tells how he was preaching to a huge crowd and the ground is said to have risen up, so that he was standing on a hill and everyone had a better chance of hearing him.

St David's Day is commemorated by the wearing of daffodils or leeks. Both plants are traditionally regarded as national emblems. On St David's Day, some children in Wales dress in their national costume, which consists of a tall black hat, white frilled cap and long dress. The national flag of Wales, depicting a fiery red dragon against a green and white background, is also flown.

● **St. Patrick's Day (17 March)**

St. Patrick's Day is the national day of Northern Ireland and Republic of Ireland. Saint Patrick is the patron saint of Ireland. He is credited with bringing Christianity to Ireland. Born in Britain, he was carried off by pirates and spent six years in slavery before escaping and training as a missionary. The most famous story about Saint Patrick is his driving the snakes from Ireland. The stories of Saint Patrick and the snakes are likely a metaphor for his bringing Christianity to Ireland and driving out the pagan (异教的) religions (serpents were a common symbol in many of these religions).

The day is marked by the wearing of shamrocks (三叶草), the national emblem of both Northern Ireland and the Republic of Ireland. According to legend, Saint Patrick used a shamrock to explain about God. The shamrock has three leaves on each stem. Saint Patrick told the people that the shamrock was like the idea of the Trinity—that in the one God there are three divine beings: the Father, the Son and the Holy Spirit. The shamrock was sacred to the Druids, so Saint Patrick's use of it in explaining the trinity was very wise.

● **St. George's Day (23 April)**

St. George's Day is the national day of England. A story dating back to the 6th century tells that St. George rescued a maiden by slaying a fearsome fire-breathing dragon. The Saint's name was shouted as a battle cry by English knights who fought beneath the red-cross banner of St George during the Hundred Years War (1338—1453). Some people wear a red rose on St Georges Day.

● **St. Andrew's Day (30 November)**

St. Andrew's Day is the national day of Scotland. He was one of Christ's twelve apostles (门徒). Some of his bones are said to

St. George and the Dragon

have been brought to what is now St. Andrews in Fife during the 4th century. Since medieval times the X-shaped saltire (X 形十字) cross upon which St. Andrew was supposedly crucified (十字架上钉死) has been the Scottish national symbol.

Brief Introduction to Some Holidays and Celebrations

● **April Fools' Day (1 April)**

April Fools' Day or All Fools' Day is the first day of April. On this day it is customary to play practical jokes on people, causing them to believe something that isn't true or to go on a fruitless errand. Although the origin of the custom is unknown, a common theory is that it developed as part of ancient spring festivals.

April Fools' Day jokes are generally amusing but harmless. For example, someone may give a friend the telephone number of the zoo, telling her to return a call from "Mr. Fox." April 1 is recognized as a day for pranks in Germany, France, Great Britain, the United States, Canada, and elsewhere. In India, the last day of the feast of Huli, March 31, is regarded as a day for mischief. In France, an April fool's prank is called a poisson d'Avril (April fish), and in Scotland it is an April gowk or cuckoo.

● **Guy Fawkes or Bonfire Night (5 Nov.)**

On Guy Fawkes or Bonfire Night, fireworks and bonfires on which effigies of Guy Fawkes are burned celebrate Fawkes's failure in his attempt to blow up the Houses of Parliament on 4 November 1605.

● **Remembrance Day (11 Nov. or the preceding Sunday)**

Remembrance Day honors veterans. Red paper poppies (罂粟) are sold by the British Legion (英国退伍军人协会,创立于 1921 年) to raise money for veterans.

● **Christmas (25 Dec.)**

During Christmas dinner, the traditional "cracker" is supposed to be laid beside each plate. Those seated next to each other pull the ends of each other's crackers, which make a loud bang! Inside there is a crepe-paper (皱纹纸)hat and a trinket (小饰物).

● **Boxing Day (26 Dec.)**

In England, Wales, parts of Canada, and in some other countries of the Commonwealth of Nations, Boxing Day is a popular term applied to December 26, the day following Christmas Day. This word comes from the custom which started in the Middle Ages around 800 years ago: churches would open their "alms boxe" (boxes in which people had placed gifts of money) and distribute the contents to poor people in the neighborhood on the day after Christmas. Traditionally, on that day the gentry would give presents, generally of money, to servants, trades-people, and others of humble life. These presents came to be known as Christmas boxes. The tradition continues today—small gifts are often given to delivery workers such as postal staff and children who deliver newspapers. Boxing Day is now simply a leisure day and a very busy day in the sporting calendar. It is a legal bank holiday, many offices, but not shops, close for all of the Christmas-to-New Year period.

Brief Introduction to Some Christian Festivals

Lent, Easter and Christmas are the main religious festivals of the Christian Year. Most people in England celebrate Christmas and Easter. School children have two weeks off school during Christmas and Easter.

● **Lent**

Lent is the 40 day period before Easter beginning with Ash Wednesday, the weekdays of this period being devoted to fasting and penitence (四旬斋,复活节前四十日,在此期内非星期日时需斋戒和忏悔).

- **Easter**

Easter is the season in which Christians remember the death and resurrection (复活) of Jesus. It is the most important festival in the Christian year. Jesus' resurrection is at the centre of the Christian faith. Jesus died for the sins of humanity and by coming back to life promises eternal life for all those who believe in him.

Easter is the story of Jesus' last days in Jerusalem before the death of Jesus.

- **Christmas**

Christmas commemorates Jesus' birth.

- **Quarter-days**

A quarter-day (四季结账日) is the first legal day of a quarter (季度) of the year, on which rents and other monthly accounts are paid. In England the four quarter-days are Lady Day, Midsummer Day, Michaelmas and Christmas.

Lady Day (25 March, 天使报喜节, 为英国四大结账日之一)

Lady Day (festival), British name for the Christian festival of the Annunciation (天使报喜, 天使加百列向圣母玛利亚奉告她将生耶稣) of the Virgin Mary. Until 1752 it was the beginning of the legal year in England, and it is still a quarter day (date for the payment of quarterly rates or dues).

Michaelmas (29 September 米迦勒节, 天使长米迦勒之祭日, 为英国四大结账日之一)

Michaelmas is old English name for the feast day of Saint Michael and All Angels, The date is believed to have been selected because it is the anniversary of the dedication of the Church of Saint Michael and All Angels on the Salarian Way in Rome in the 6th century. In England, Michaelmas is one of the quarter days, traditionally marked by the election of magistrates, the beginning of the legal and university terms, and the collection of quarterly rents.

List of Holidays

New Year's Day	January 01
Good Friday	March 25
Easter Monday	March 25
May Day Bank Holiday	May 02
Spring Bank Holiday	May 30
Summer Bank Holiday	August 29
Christmas Day	December 25
Boxing Day	December 26
Christmas(forwarded to Monday)	December 27
Boxing Day (forwarded to Tuesday)	December 28

III Education

Education is an important part of British life, because a highly developed nation depends upon educated professionals and a skilled workforce. The literacy rate in Britain is one of the highest in the world at over 99 percent. Children are required by law to have an education until they are 16 years old. Education is compulsory, but school is not, children are not required to attend school. They could be educated at home.

Chapter 11　Society and Culture of UK

> Section 7 of the 1996 Education Act U.K. states:
> *"The parent of every child of compulsory school age shall cause him to receive efficient full-time education suitable (a) to his age, ability and aptitude, and (b) to any special educational needs he may have, either by regular attendance at school or otherwise."*

Primary & Secondary Education

Education is free for all children from 5 to 18. Children's education in England is normally divided into two separate stages. They begin with primary education at the age of 5 (at age 4 in Northern Ireland) and this usually lasts until they are 11. They study English, arithmetic, science, religious education, history, geography, music, art and crafts, physical education, and information technology. At the age of 11, they move on to regular high schools, known as secondary schools, where they stay until they reach 16, 17 or 18 years of age.

Types of Schools in Britain

For primary and secondary education, there are two main categories of school: **local authority maintained schools** (State Schools) and **independent schools** (Private/Public Schools).

● State schools are maintained by local government and offer pupils free education up to the age of 18. State schools are funded from taxes and most are organized by Local Authorities (LA).

● Independent schools or private schools are called *public schools*, a term that means just the opposite in the United States. What are called *public schools* in the United States is called *state schools* in Britain. Public schools are private institutions that charge attendance fees, parents pay for their children's education.

Private schools that take pupils from the age of 7 to the age of 11, 12, or 13 are called preparatory schools and Private schools that take older pupils from the age of 11, 12, or 13 to 18 or 19 are often referred to as public schools. Only 7 percent of British students attend private school. Independent schools are free from government control. Now, there are about 2500 independent schools in the whole country.

The most famous schools in Britain are private boarding schools, such as Eton College (which is a private secondary school in Berkshire County in southern England. The preparatory school was founded by King Henry VI in 1440. A statue of Henry VI stands in the courtyard of the college), Harrow School, Rugby School, and Winchester School. These famous private schools, founded during the Middle Ages, are theoretically open to the public, but in reality are attended by those who can afford the fees. Many of Britain's leaders have attended these private schools, which cater to the wealthy and influential but also offer some scholarships to gifted poorer children. Local authorities and the central authority also provide assistance to some families who are unable to pay the fees. Only a small percentage of the population can attend these ancient and highly prestigious schools. A variety of other schools are also private, including kindergartens, day schools, and newer boarding schools.

Curriculum and the School Year

England and Wales have a national curriculum of core courses for students 5 to 16 years old, and all government-run schools, state schools follow the same National Curriculum. The schools are inspected by the Office for Standards in Education. National tests at the ages of 7, 11, and 14 assess students' progress. Schools must provide religious education and daily collective worship for all pupils, although parents can withdraw their children from these.

The school year is 39 weeks long and is divided into six terms and the term form is used to designate grade:

● September to October

- October to December
- January to February
- February to March
- April to May
- June to July

The main school holidays are:
Christmas—2 weeks; Spring—2 weeks; Summer—6 weeks

Tests

An examination, known as the "Eleven-plus" test, is given to all children after they have finished primary education at age 11 to test the children's knowledge in English and arithmetic. Those who do well will go on to grammar schools.

Grammar schools are selective, which offer academically oriented general education. Grammar schools are university preparatory schools. In 1960s and 1970s, Comprehensive schools were established; almost all of the former grammar schools have been absorbed into the comprehensive schools. Comprehensive schools, on the other hand, are non-selective, and they do not select pupils on grounds of ability. They take children of all abilities and provide a wide range of secondary education. Secondary modern schools provide vocational education rather than preparation for university entrance.

At the age of 16, prior to leaving secondary school, students take an examination called the GCSE (General Certificate of Secondary Education). All students are tested in mathematics, English literature, English composition, chemistry, biology, physics, history or the Classics, one modern language, and one other subject, such as art or computer studies.

After completing the GCSE, some students (about a third) leave school usually taking lower-level jobs in the work-force, others go onto technical college, whilst others continue at high school for two more years and take a further set of standardized exams, known as A levels, in three or four subjects. These exams determine whether a student is eligible for university.

Higher Education
Introduction

Higher education refers to a level of education that is provided by universities, vocational universities, community colleges, liberal arts colleges, institutes of technology and other collegiate level institutions, such as vocational schools, trade schools and career colleges that award academic degrees or professional certifications.

British higher education sector, over the last few decades, has been growing at an unprecedented pace. Now, there are a total number of 170 higher education institutions, including universities, university sector colleges and teacher-training colleges.

The percentage of young people entering universities in Britain is far lower than in the United States, where more than half attend. In Britain there is more emphasis on segregating pupils at the lower levels on the basis of ability. There has been an even greater increase in students benefiting from higher education, from 621,000 in the 1970s to almost 2.6 million in 2007.

Types of Universities

Britain has about 90 universities, which may be classified into 6 main categories:
- Ancient universities—the seven universities founded between the 12th and 16th centuries.
- The University of London, The University of Wales and Durham University—which were chartered in the 19th century.
- Red Brick universities—the six large civic universities chartered at the turn of the 20th century before World War I.

● Plate Glass (平板玻璃) universities — the universities chartered in the 1960s (formerly described as the 'new universities').

● The Open University—Britain's "open to all" distance learning University (established 1968).

● New Universities—the Post-1992 universities formed from polytechnics or colleges of Higher Education.

The foremost ancient universities are the University of Oxford and the University of Cambridge, both founded in the Middle Ages. The University of Oxford, located in the city of Oxford, is the oldest surviving university in the English-speaking world and is regarded as one of the world's leading academic institutions. It is a federation of 35 colleges, each with its own structure and activities. Although the exact date of foundation remains unclear, there is evidence of teaching there as far back as the 11th century. The University grew rapidly from 1167 when Henry II banned English students from attending the University of Paris and consistently ranks in the world's top 10. Buildings in Oxford demonstrate an example of every British architectural period since the arrival of the Saxons, including the iconic, mid-18th century Radcliffe Camera.

Some of the college and university buildings in central Oxford

Oxford Graduation

The University of Cambridge, located in the City of Cambridge is the second oldest university in the English-speaking world and the fourth oldest in Europe. The university grew out of an association of scholars in the city of Cambridge that was formed in 1209 by scholars leaving Oxford after a dispute with townsfolk there. Academically, Cambridge is consistently ranked in the world's top five universities and as a premier leading university in Europe by numerous media and academic rankings. The University's alumni include 85 Nobel Laureates as of 2009.

The term *Oxbridge* is used to refer to both universities as a single entity (实体), much as Americans would use the term Ivy League in reference to the group of prestigious East Coast universities. In addition to cultural and practical associations as a historic part of British society, the two universities also have a long history of rivalry with each other.

Scotland has equivalent ancient institutions at Edinburgh, Glasgow, and St. Andrews.

King's College, Cambridge founded by King Henry VI in 1441

"Red Brick" refer to six particular British universities founded in the major industrial cities of England, all of which achieved university status before World War I and were initially established as civic science and/or engineering colleges. Officially, the six institutions are members of the Russell Group (which receives two-thirds of all research grants funding in the United Kingdom).

The term "red brick" was first coined by a professor of Spanish at the University of Liverpool to describe these civic universities. His reference was inspired by the fact that The Victoria Building at the University of Liverpool is built from a distinctive red

The Victoria Building, University of Liverpool

Aston Webb Building, University of Birmingham

The University of York's Central Hall is an example of plateglass architectural design.

pressed brick (压制砖), with terracotta decorative dressings. On this basis the University of Liverpool considers itself to be the original Red Brick institution. The University of Birmingham states, however, that it was the first to gain official university status, and that the popularity of the term owes to its own domed Aston Webb brick buildings.

The large number of ultramodern (超现代化的) universities that sprouted up in the last half of the 20th century are often called cement block and plateglass universities (P-universities). The term "plateglass" The large number of ultramodern (超现代化的) universities that sprouted up in the last half of the 20th century are often called cement block and plateglass universities (P-universities). The term "plateglass" reflects their modern architectural design, which often contains wide expanses of plate glass in steel or concrete frames. This contrasts with the "red brick universities" and the older "ancient universities." "Plateglass" did not catch on (流行) in the same way as "redbrick," and it is unusual to hear 1960s foundations described in this way today.

The phrase *New University* formerly appeared as a synonym for the *Plateglass* institutions. Today, the term specifically relates to any of the former polytechnics, Central Institutions or colleges of higher education that were given the status of universities by John Major's government in 1992—as well as colleges that have been granted university status since then. These institutions may also be described as post-1992 universities or modern universities.

For those who miss the opportunity for higher education at the age of 18 can obtain it through the Open University, founded in 1971, which offers extension courses taught through correspondence, television and radio programs, and videocassettes. It also sponsors local study centers and residential summer schools. The purpose of the Open University is to reach people who may not ordinarily be qualified for university study.

London has its own great schools. University of London was founded in 1836 as an examining and degree-giving body. Teaching functions were not added until 1898. It comprised at first University College (which had been founded in 1826 as the Univ. of London) and King's College (founded 1829 by adherents of the Church of England). Now it has 19 self-governing colleges, including the Royal Holloway, Goldsmiths, the Royal Academy of Music, King's College, and the London School of Economics. Also part of the University of London system is the School of Advanced Study, which includes some 10 institutes. With an enrollment of about 130,000 students, University of London is among the oldest and largest universities in the UK. In 1878 it became the first university in the UK to admit women. Its Senate House, built in Bloomsbury on the former Duke of Bedford's estate, was completed in 1937 to hold the university's central administration offices.

Sources of University Income

All British universities are partially funded by central government grants, except Buckingham University, which is the only private university in the whole country. Government funding is provided mainly through the four funding councils in England, Wales, Scotland, and Northern Ireland. The rest comes from various other channels. Tuition fees, donations (捐款), company contributions are all important sources of university income. Britain's universities are legally independent and enjoy complete academic freedom. The administrative of a university alone is responsible for the university's maintenance and development.

Types of University Degree

An undergraduate degree normally takes three years to complete. Types of undergraduate degree include:
- BSc (Bachelor of Science) — a science degree
- BA (Bachelor of Arts) — an arts degree
- BEng (Bachelor of Engineering) — an engineering degree
- Undergraduate Masters degree (e.g. MEng) — an enhanced four year undergraduate degree including extra subjects studied at a deeper level

Students who receive good grades in their undergraduate degrees may choose to take a Masters degree, which takes a minimum of one year to complete. Types of Masters degree include:
- MSc (Master of Science)
- MA (Master of Arts)
- MEd (Master of Education)
- LLM (Master of Law)
- MBA (Master of Business Administration)

If you would like to continue to study for a PhD, you will have to conduct a minimum of two years' research after the award of your MSc. In some subject areas, a student may transfer from BSc /BA/ BEng to PhD so that they follow a three year research program for PhD without first obtaining a Masters degree.

Top 10 Universities in U.K.
(According to Good University Guide, Times Online, 2009)

1	牛津大学	Oxford University
2	剑桥大学	Cambridge University
3	伦敦大学帝国理工学院	Imperial College of Science, Technology & Medicine
4	伦敦大学伦敦经济政治学院	London School of Economics & Politics Science (LSE)
5	圣安德鲁大学	University of St. Andrews
6	华威大学	University of Warwick
7	伦敦大学学院	University College London
8	杜伦大学	Durham University
9	约克大学	The University of York
10	布里斯托大学	Bristol University

IV British Literature

In the course of more than 1500 year's history, British literature, along with the development of the society, has been always the reliable witness meanwhile romantic interpreter of changes of society. Its contributions to diversity of world literature and upgrading of human civilization cannot be too emphasized. Today, famous English poets, playwrights, and novelists are quoted, translated, and loved throughout the world. So a glimpse of literature will definitely help deepen the understanding of the British society and culture. This brief pilgrimage to British literature will follow the following outline:

- Old and Medieval English Literature
- Literature in the Renaissance
- Literature in the seventeenth century
- Literature in the eighteenth century
- Romanticism in England
- The Victorian Age
- Literature in The Twentieth century

Old and Medieval British Literature (5th century A.D.—1485)

English descends from the language spoken by the north Germanic tribes, known as Angles, Saxons and Jutes, who settled in England from the 5th century AD onwards. They had no writing until they learned the Latin alphabet from Roman missionaries. Old English literature is mostly chronicle and poetry—lyric, descriptive but chiefly narrative or epic. Of the earliest heroic poetry, the most important poem now preserved is *Beowulf*, the first long poem in English (altogether 3,183 lines), which is considered the national epic of the English people. In the poem, the unknown poet expresses a hope that the evil should be punished, and the righteous will be rewarded. King Alfred's *The Anglo-Saxon Chronicles* (编年史) (Alfred lived during 848—901) is another famous work in Old English.

Middle English literature is a combination of French and Anglo-Saxon elements. Literature that the Normans brought to England with their conquest of England in 1066 is remarkable for its bright, romantic tales of love and adventure, while Anglo-Saxon literature is somber and serious. These features can be easily seen in Romance (传奇文学), the most prevailing kind of literature in medieval England. Geoffrey Chaucer was the first great name in English literature as well as the greatest English writer of the Middle Ages.

Literature in the Renaissance (late 15th century—early 17th century)

The Europe-wide Renaissance, having its origin in north Italy in the 14th century revived the study of Roman and Greek classics and marked the beginning of bourgeois revolution and liberation of human mind. Scholars and educators claimed themselves as Humanists and began to emphasize the capacities of the human mind and the achievements of human culture, in contrast to the medieval emphasis on God and contempt for the things of this world. The English Renaissance also encouraged the Reformation of the Church, eventually leading to the separation from Roman Catholicism and establishment of the Church of England, i.e. Protestantism.

The movement set England on the road of fast developing in terms of politics, economy and culture. During this period, England enjoyed stability and prosperity and at the end of it England became the strong power of the world and the ruler of the seas. This social circumstance undoubtedly stimulated the prosperity of literature. In fact, English literature in the Renaissance Period is usually regarded as the highlight in the history of English literature. Major literary genres, such as drama, poetry and prose, developed into their delicate maturity. Thomas Moore, Edmund Spenser, Christopher Marlowe, William Shakespeare and Francis Bacon are the outstanding

figures of the English Renaissance.
Literature of the 17th Century
The seventeenth century is an eventful one: the English Revolution (1642), the founding of the English Commonwealth (1649), the Restoration (1660), the Glorious Revolution (1688) and the King William's signing The Bill Rights. Henceforth, England has become a country of constitutional monarch.

With these social upheavals, literature of the era was undoubtedly of characteristic of the English bourgeois revolution, and meanwhile of pro-king, such as the Cavalier poets (骑士派诗人), who put their main interest in depicting the court life, or of mystery and fantasy, such as the Metaphysical poets (玄学派诗人). John Milton and John Bunyan were two greatest writers of revolutionary enthusiasm while John Donne was representative of the Metaphysical poets and Ben Johnson (1573—1637) of the Cavalier poets. Another figure we dare not forget to mention is John Dryden (1631—1700), who is regarded as the most important poet, playwright and literary critic of the Restoration period.

Literature of the Eighteenth Century
Socially, the 18th century saw the firm establishment of capitalism in England, the compromise between the aristocracy and the bourgeoisie in their joint rule over the people, the development of the industrial revolution, the rise of England as a big industrial and colonial capitalist power. Intellectually, the eighteenth-century England is also known as The Age of Enlightenment or The Age of Reason. The Enlightenment was a progressive intellectual movement throughout Western Europe in the 18th century and celebrated reason (rationality), equality, science and human beings' ability to perfect themselves and their society. These chief political, social and intellectual events that took place in England in the 18th century formed the important background for the development of the literature of this period.

Under these conditions, the popular press flourished, producing a succession of newspapers and literary periodicals in the manner of the two famous magazines *Tatler and Spectator*, edited by Richard Steele (1672—1729) and Joseph Addison (1672—1719). Owing to the flourishing of popular press, prose had a rapid development and novel flourished accordingly in this century. Swift, Defoe, Richardson, Fielding are among the major novelists of the time. In their novels, characters were no longer kings and nobles but the common people and satire was much used in writing. In terms of poetry, Alexander Pope (1688—1744), the representative of the neo-classicism (新古典主义), most popular poetic form of the time advertising reason and regularity, gained the highest exclamation for his mastery of heroic couplets (英雄双行体), poetic lines of iambic pentameter with the same rhyme at the end of every two lines. Richard Brinsley Sheridan (1751—1816) was the best dramatist of the era, known for *The School for Scandal*.

Literature of the Romantic Age (1798—1832)
The American Revolution (1776) and the French Revolution (1789) ignited the rapid spread of national liberation movements and democratic movements across the European countries and England was no exception. Under this political and social influences, a new literary movement called romanticism came to Europe and then to England. It was characterized by a strong protest against the bondage of neo-classicism, which emphasized reason, order and "elegant wit." Instead, romanticism gave primary concern to passion, emotion, imagination, inspiration and natural beauty. This movement appeared on the literary arena of England from the publication of *Lyrical Ballads* by Wordsworth and Samuel Coleridge (1772—1834, known for his *The Rime of the Ancient Mariner and Kubla Khan)* in 1798 to the death of Sir Walter Scott in 1832.

The Romantic Age is an age of poetry, during which a batch of first class English poets were produced, such as William Blake (1757—1827, famous for his *Songs of Innocence and songs of*

Experience), Burns, Wordsworth, Coleridge, Byron, Shelley and Keats. In terms of achievements of novels, Jane Austin offered us her charming descriptions of everyday life in her enduring works, and the greatest historical novelist Scott (1771—1832) impressed us with his masterpiece—*Ivanhoe*, which combines a romantic atmosphere with a realistic depiction of historical background and common people's life. Romantic prose of the period was represented by essayist Lamb.

Literature in Victorian Age (1832—1901)

During Queen Victoria's long reign (1837—1901), England grew from an agricultural country into an industrialized one and became the workshop of the world as well as its financial and political center. British people, while enjoying the continued prosperity brought by the industrialization, were also plagued by evils of the existing institutions—the government, the law, the church, the education and penal systems, with their injustice, cruelty, hypocrisy and corruption. Romantic poetry of the previous times were found weak in reflecting the new reality and naturally gave way to a new literary trend—Critical Realism, which devoted to exposing and criticizing all the social evils. Novel was the dominant genre of the age and flourished with a galaxy of brilliant novelists, female novelist in particular, appeared on the literature scene. Dickens, Thackeray and female writers Charlotte Bronte (1816—1855, noted for her masterpiece *Jane Eyre*, the first important governess novel), Emily Bronte, Anne Bronte (although not as famous as her two elder sisters), Elizabeth Gaskell (1810—1865, also referred to as Mrs. Gaskell, known for her biography *Her Life of Charlotte Bronte*), George Eliot were most important critical novelists of the time.

Along with critical realism, there were novelists of other literary schools. The decadence and hypocrisy of Victorian life is best reflected in the works of Oscar Wilde (1854—1900), who advocates the theory of "art of art's sake." The pessimism of the last few decades in the 19th century is seen in Thomas Hardy.

Poetry, though not as glorious as in the Romantic Age in general, still produced some influential poets such as Poet Laureate Alfred Tennyson (1809—1892), Robert Browning (1812—1889, now remembered for his employment of dramatic monologue in poetry) and his wife Elizabeth Barrett Browning (1806—1861,also referred to as Mrs. Browning).

The social contradictions were also reflected in the prose of the time. The important prose-writers who criticized the evil, of the capitalist society were Thomas Carlyle (1795—1881), John Ruskin (1819—1900) and Matthew Arnold (1822—1888, also a poet).

Literature in the 20th Literature

By the end of the Victorian Age, the glamour of the British Empire was beginning to fade due to the awakening of people in British colonies struggling for national independence. The two world wars and internal problems caused Britain to lose its worldwide supremacy totally as well as losses of numerous lives and people's bitter sufferings, physically and mentally. The dire social situation set an unprecedented background for development of literature. Thus, besides the tradition of critical realism, of which Galsworthy and Bernard Shaw were most eminent practitioners, new literary schools or movements succeeded one after another, experimenting with new literary techniques.

Roughly speaking, the development of English literature in the twentieth century can be divided into two stages, that is, literature between the two World Wars, and literature after World War II. There are three main trends of literature are worth our attention. They are Modernism, The Angry Young Men, and The Theatre of the Absurd.

Modernism is a rather vague term which is used to apply to the works of a group of poets, novelists, painters, and musicians between 1910 and the early years after the World War II. The term includes various trends or schools, such as imagism, expressionism, stream of consciousness and symbolism. It means a departure from the conventional criteria or established values of the Victorian age. Alienation (陌生化) and loneliness are the basic themes of modernism. In the eyes of modernist writers, the modern world is a chaotic one and is incomprehensible. Human beings are helpless before this materially rich but spiritually barren world and no longer able to do things that their forefathers once did. The modern poets and writers find in symbol a means to express their inexpressible selves. Joseph Conrad, Virginia Woolf, James Joyce (see Lrish Literature) and D. H. Lawrence are most brilliant novelists under this category, while T. S. Eliot, William Butler Yeats(see Irish literature) and Wystan Hugh Auden (1907—1973) are most talented poets who set the tone for modern poetry.

During the fifties there appeared a group of young writers who were fiercely critical of the established order. They were called "Angry Young Men," a term taken from John Osborne's play *Look Back in Anger*, which first appear in 1956. Most of them came from working class families and lower middle families. They wrote about the ugliness and sordidness of life and exposed the hypocrisy of the genteel class. Their works were written in ordinary, sometimes dirty language. The writers belonging to this group are Kingsley Amis, author of *Lucky Jim* (1954), John Wain, author of *Hurry on Down* (1953), John Braine, author of *Room at the Top* (1957) and Alan Sillitoe, author of *Saturday Night and Sunday Morning* (1958).

The Theatre of the Absurd is a term applied to a group of dramatists who were active in the 50's. The absurdity of human conditions is the main theme of the plays of the school of the theatre of the absurd. In the plays the dramatists express that life has no pattern of meaning or ultimate significance and that no activity is more or less valuable than another. Samuel Beckett is the representative of the school.

In the late of the 20th century, William Golding, Iris Murdoch, John Fowles, V. S. Naipaul and Doris Lessing are major figures of literature. A new trend in the contemporary literature is the rising of the popular novels, which can be justified by the fact that J. K. Rowling's *Harry Porter* books sold millions of copies worldwide and dominated bestseller lists at the end of the 1990s and in the early 2000s.

Chapter 12 Understanding the Republic of Ireland

I A General Survey

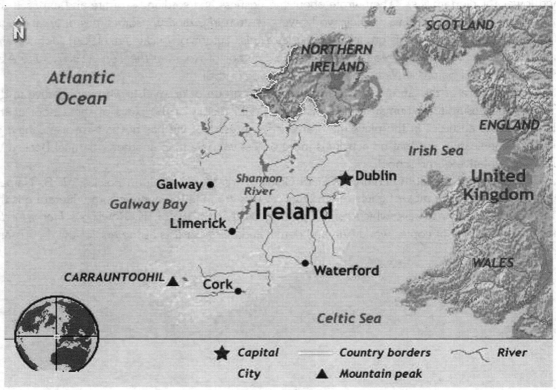

Map of the Republic of Ireland

Quick Facts about Ireland

Basic Facts	
Capital	Dublin
Area	70,273 sq km
National Day	17 March
People	
Population	4,062,235 (2006 estimate)
Population growth rate	1.15% (2006 estimate)
Population density	60 persons per sq km (2006 estimate)

Chapter 12 Understanding the Republic of Ireland

Largest cities, with population	
Dublin	505,739 (2006 estimate)
Cork	190,384 (2006 estimate)
Limerick	90,778 (2006 estimate)
Galway	72,729 (2006 estimate)
Waterford	49,240 (2006 estimate)

Languages	
English (official), Irish (official)	

Religious affiliations	
Roman Catholic	86.8 percent (2006)
Church of Ireland	3 percent 2 (2006)
Christian (unspecified)	0.7 percent (2006)
Presbyterian	0.6 percent (2006)
Nonreligious	4.4 percent (2006)
Other (including Muslim and Orthodox, etc)	4.5 percent (2006)

Health and Education	
Total Life Expectancy	77.73 years (2006)
Female	80.52 years (2006)
Male	75.11 years (2006)
Infant mortality rate	5.31 deaths/1,000 live births (2006)
Population per physician	357 people (2004)

Literacy Rate	
Total	100 percent (2005)

Government	
Form of Government	Republic and Parliamentary democracy
Head of State	The President
Head of government	The Taoiseach (Prime minister)
Legislature	Bicameral (两院制的) legislature
Voting Qualifications	Universal at age 18

Constitution	
The state operates under the Constitution of Ireland, adopted in 1937.	
Highest Court	The Supreme Court
Gross Domestic Product (GDP, in US $)	195.6 Billion (2005)
GDP Per Capita (U.S $)	$41,000 (2005)

Employment	
Number of Workers	2.154 million (2006)
Unemployment Rate	4.4 percent (2006)
Monetary Unit	
1 Euro = 100 eurocent	

The island of Ireland lies west of Great Britain across the Irish Sea and St. George's Channel. It is divided into two separate political entities: the independent Republic of Ireland, and Northern Ireland, a constituent (构成部分) of the United Kingdom. Dublin is the capital of the former, Belfast of the latter. The country is divided into four provinces: Leinster, Munster, Connaught, and Ulster. All of the first three and part of the fourth are situated within the Republic of Ireland. Ulster is made up of nine counties; the northeastern six constitute Northern Ireland. The area of the Republic of Ireland is 70,273 sq km, occupying almost 85% of the total land-mass of the island of Ireland, the second largest of the British Isles. Ireland means "Eire land." Eire is the Irish name for the country and is believed to mean "western land." Ireland's vivid green landscapes have earned it the title Emerald Isle (绿宝石岛). Traditionally, most Irish people made their living by farming the land.

The Capital and Major Cities

Dublin has been Ireland's capital city since medieval times. It is the largest city of the Republic of Ireland, and also the largest city on the island of Ireland. It is located near the midpoint of Ireland's east coast, at the mouth of the River Liffey and at the centre of the Dublin Region. It is the country's principal port and commercial and industrial center. Dublin City is the entire area administered by Dublin City Council. However, when most people talk about Dublin, they also refer to the contiguous (邻近的) suburban areas that run into the adjacent counties of Dun Laoghaire-Rathdown, Fingal and South Dublin. This area is sometimes known as "Urban Dublin" or the "Dublin Metropolitan Area." A person from Dublin is known as a *Dubliner* or a *Dub*. The population within the administrative area controlled by Dublin City Council was 505,739 at the census of 2006. Cork is the country's second largest city and major port. Other major cities and towns include Limerick, Galway, and Waterford.

Official Languages

The constitution provides both English and Irish (or Gaelic) as official languages. English is the main language used in Ireland (spoken with an Irish accent). The traditional Gaelic language is spoken mainly in areas along the west coast of Ireland. Ulster-Scots (or Ullans), used by some members of Ireland's Protestant community, is under consideration for special status. English is overwhelmingly dominant in almost all social, economic and cultural contexts. Irish was seen as a backward language. Irish was not allowed to be taught in schools and often children would be humiliated in front of the class if they spoke a word of Irish.

Religions

The major religions of Ireland are Roman Catholic and Protestant. Ireland, as the proverb goes, is the "Land of Saints and Scholars." The Republic of Ireland has one of the highest rates of regular and weekly church attendance in the Western World. However, there has been a major decline in this attendance among Irish Catholics in the course of the past 30 years. At the same time, the Roman Catholic Church in Ireland has experienced marked difficulties in recruiting clergy.

Protestant groups include the Church of Ireland (Anglican) and the Presbyterian (长老会的) and Methodist (卫理公会教派的) denominations (教派). The remainders claim no religious beliefs, or belong to the small communities of believers such as Muslims, Jews, Jehovah's Witnesses (耶和华见证会), and Orthodox (东正教). Ireland's constitution guarantees freedom of worship. St. Nicholas Anglican Church, the largest remaining medieval church in Ireland.

National Flag

The Republic of Ireland's flag is made of three equal-sized rectangles of orange, white, and green. The flag is twice as wide as it is tall. The green side is by the flagpole. It was first used in 1848. The green color on the flag represents the native people of Ireland (most are Roman Catholics). The orange color represents the British supporters of William of Orange who settled in Northern Ireland in the 17th century (most of whom are Protestants). The white in the center of the flag represents peace between these two groups of people.

National Emblems

Ireland is the only country in the world with a musical instrument as a national symbol. The mythical lore of Celtic harps makes them a very special emblem of Ireland's pride. In the 16th century King Henry VIII of England made the harp the official symbol of colonial Ireland by putting it on Ireland's currency and it became a recognized symbol of Ireland. According to the legend, the shamrock (三叶草) was used by St. Patrick, the patron saint of Ireland, in the fifth century to demonstrate the meaning of the Trinity (三位一体) when converting the Celts to Christianity. To this day it remains one of Ireland's most famous national emblems.

National Anthem

The Soldier's Song was written in 1907 by Peadar Kearney, but was not widely known until it was sung both at the General Post Office during the Easter Rising (起义) in 1916 and later at various camps where republicans were interned (拘留). Soon after, it was adopted as the national anthem, replacing God Save Ireland. The first edition of the song was published in 1916.

II Geography and History

A. Geography

Introduction

Ireland is on the western fringe of Europe. Its greatest length, from Malin Head in the north to Mizen Head in the south, is 486 km and its greatest width from east to west is approximately 275 km. The Republic of Ireland occupies a land area of 70,283 km² and the population is about 3.5 million. The terrain of Ireland is mostly level to rolling interior plain surrounded by rugged hills, low mountains and sea cliffs on west coast. The Emerald Isle is famous for its picturesque landscape with many beautiful lakes, hills and castles. From the gently rolling hills to the dramatic, windswept cliffs of Mayo, Clare, Donegal, and Galway, the landscape of this country is bursting with disparity (不同). It is comprised of a central plain enveloped by a rim of mountains and hills, and also holds beautiful mountain lakes. The country boasts semi-tropical bays warmed by the Gulf Stream, quiet sandy beaches, and rocky cliffs that comprise 3500 miles of coastline.

Rivers, Lakes and Mountains

Ireland is a country of many rivers and lakes, known as loughs. The principal rivers of Ireland are the Erne and the Shannon.

River Erne, in the Northwest of Ireland, rises from Lough Gowna in County Cavan, flows through County Fermanagh, and ends in Ballyshannon in County Donegal. The river is 120 kilometers long, and is very popular for trout fishing, with a number of fisheries along both the river itself and its tributaries. It is linked to the River Shannon by the Shannon-Erne Waterway. The river takes its name from a mythical princess named Éirne.

River Shannon is the longest river in both Ireland and Britain, and has influenced the military, social and economic history of Ireland since the beginning of time. It is rising in northwestern County Cavan and flowing for about 259 km in a southerly direction to enter the Atlantic Ocean via a 113-kilometre estuary below. It drains an area of 15,695 square km. Dividing Ireland almost in two and dominating the midlands landscape, the River Shannon has acted as a formidable barrier to movement from East to West while providing a marine highway from North to South. The River Shannon is now the backbone of a vast network of inland waterways, joined to the Erne via the newly restored Shannon-Erne link.

Apart from the Shannon, inland navigation largely depends on the remnants of a canal system built in the 18th and 19th centuries.

Major lakes include Ree and Derg on the Shannon and Mask, Corrib, and Conn in the west. In the mountains of the southwest are the three small and picturesque Lakes of Killarney, a popular resort area close to the town of Killarney, in mountainous County Kerry.

Among the principal mountain ranges are the Wicklow Mountains in the east, just south of Dublin, rising to more than 915 m above sea level. In the far southwest in County Kerry stand another mountain range, Macgillycuddy's Reeks. Stretching slightly over 19 km, they include the highest mountain in Ireland (*Carrauntoohil*, at 1,038 m), the two other 1,000 m peaks existing in Ireland (*Beenkeragh* at 1,010 m, and *Caher* at 1,001 m), and over 100 other peaks of over 2,000 ft.

Climate

Ireland's mild climate is a reflection of the fact that its shores are bathed by the relatively warm ocean waters of the North Atlantic Drift. Extremely high or low temperatures are virtually unknown. The average winter temperature ranges from 4℃ to 7℃, approximately 14 Celsius degrees higher than that of most other places in the same latitude. The average summer temperature of Ireland ranges from 15℃ to 17℃, or about 4 Celsius degrees lower than that of most other places in the same latitudes. Rainfall is heaviest on the westward facing slopes of the hills. The east is much drier. The sunniest part of the country is the southeast. The outstanding feature of the Irish weather is its changeability.

Natural Resources

Ireland's most valuable natural resource is its lowland soils. These soils support rich grasslands, which flourish across much of Ireland and provide extensive pasture for grazing animals. The soils also support a variety of cereals and root crops. Ireland has some natural mineral resources including deposits of zinc (锌), lead, gypsum (石膏), and alumina (氧化铝). Some natural gas deposits are found off the southern and western coasts. Peat, (泥煤：部分碳化的植物物质，通常指苔藓) from heaths (石南丛生的荒野) and bogs (沼泽) has long served as an important fuel source for homes and industry, and it is also used to improve soils for cultivation.

Peat is the first stage in the transformation of vegetation into coal. For hundreds of years,

Chapter 12 Understanding the Republic of Ireland

people have cut, dried, and burned it for heating and cooking.

Animals and Plants

Ireland's animal life does not differ markedly from that of England or France. Over many centuries of human settlement almost all of Ireland's natural woodlands were cleared, and indigenousanimals such as bear, wolf, wildcat, beaver, wild cattle, and the giant Irish deer gradually disappeared. However, the hardy and versatile Connemara pony, Ireland's only native pony breed, has been used by Irish farmers since prehistoric times. The great auk (大海燕) was exterminated in the 19th century. Small rodents (啮齿动物,如鼠或狸) living in forested areas and fields remain numerous across Ireland, as do numerous species of shore and field birds, including many types of gull. Birds of prey (猛禽) are rare. Ireland has no snakes; in fact, the only reptile found in Ireland is a species of lizard. Sedges (莎草,苔), rushes, ferns (蕨类植物), and grasses provide the dominant plant cover.

Connemara Pony

The Great Auk

B. History

An estimated 70 million people world-wide can claim Irish heritage. From before the arrival of Saint Patrick to the present day Ireland has had a history that could never be called quiet.

First Settlement

The first settlement of Ireland took place sometime around 6000 BC by hunters and fishers along the island's eastern coast, but we know very little about them apart from the fact that they built some fairly impressive monuments like Newgrange (爱尔兰中部古代巨石群纽格莱奇古墓,与巨石阵齐名) and Knowth Passage Tombs and that they fashioned beautiful items from gold and silver.

Newgrange is, without the shadow of a doubt, one of the most important archaeological sites of Ireland and what is more: it is the most important Corridor-Grave in the WORLD. While from a distance they look like round, grass-covered hills, they were in fact constructed in about 3200 BC as tombs. All three mounds, or cairns, are made from small stones layered with soil. They contain rock-lined passages with burial chambers known as "passage graves."

The Gaels

The Gaels (盖尔人:苏格兰、爱尔兰或马恩岛的说盖尔语的凯尔特人), a Celtic-speaking people from Western Europe, found their way to the island sometime between about 600 and 150 BC and subdued the previous inhabitants. They introduced many things that persist to this day, including their language, their games, their music, and a typically Irish attitude towards life. It appears that they were seen from the outside as a scary group of people, because the Romans gave them a wide berth (远避), despite their partial occupation of Britain during the 1st Century AD.

About the time of Christ the island was organized into five kingdoms, the traditional "Five Fifths of Ireland." By AD 400 seven independent kingdoms had evolved. The kings of these kingdoms often allied their armies to raid neighboring Roman Britain and the Continent. On one of these raids a lad of 16 was captured, returned to Ireland and sold into slavery. During his enslavement the boy turned to religion and some six years later at the age of 22 escaped. The young man studied theology in the Roman church and in 432 returned to Ireland, and began a lifelong quest of converting the Irish to Christianity. This was none other than Ireland's patron (守护神), Saint Patrick.

Christianity

Ireland is Christianized by St. Patrick in 432 AD. Very soon, the people of Ireland had taken the religion to their hearts. Christianity became the dominant religion of the entire island. In the wake of Christianity there was a flourishing of culture and learning connected with the churches and the monasteries. This early Christian culture helped account for the power of Catholicism in Ireland to this very day.

The Vikings

The Vikings from Nordic (北欧的) countries first attacked Ireland in 795. They looted (抢劫) monasteries (修道院) and took women and children as slaves. However the Vikings were not only raiders. They were also traders and craftsmen, and were the first to introduce the concept of money to the island. In the later 9th century they turned from raiding to conquest and founded Ireland's first towns, Dublin, Wexford, Cork and Limerick. They also gave Ireland its name, a combination of the Gaelic word Eire and the Viking word land. Eventually the Vikings settled down on the island, many became farmers and intermarried with the Irish and accepted Christianity.

The Normans

In 1168 the English invaded the island. These warriors were armed to the teeth and gave themselves the rather unimpressive name "Normans." From then on to about 1400, many Norman's moved to Ireland from England and settled the eastern areas, particularly around Dublin. They built imposing castles and constructed a few roads. Some became assimilated but strife (冲突) persisted between the native Irish and the colonists. This is the beginning of the Anglo-Irish conflict, which was to shape Irish history in the following centuries up until today. In 1367 a law was enacted to keep the two populations separate.

Religion and Class Conflicts

In 1495 **Henry VII** extended English law over the entirety of Ireland, and assumed supremacy over the existing Irish parliament. When **Henry VIII** became king of England, England broke with the Catholic Church (1536). He forced Ireland to break with the Catholic church too, and confiscated (没收) the land that the church possessed. The Irish, however, resisted. At this point the Catholic religion had been the religion in Ireland for a thousand years, and it constituted part of the national identity of the Irish. The Irish Catholic population was persecuted and the Protestant British oppressors took complete control. In 1541 Henry VIII becomes king of Ireland.

Queen Elizabeth continued the fight against the Irish Catholics, who kept resisting. There

Chapter 12   Understanding the Republic of Ireland

was particularly strong resistance in Ulster (乌尔斯特：原为爱尔兰一地区，在詹姆士一世统治时大部分被并入英国，今为北爱尔兰及爱尔兰共和国所分割). It was crushed by the English in 1607, and the Catholic leaders had to flee. The English crown confiscated their land, distributed it among 10,000 poor Protestants from Scotland, who were sent to Ulster to colonize the area. The original Irish population was forced off the land.

This is the starting point of the conflict between Catholics and Protestants in the North. These Scots were Calvinists, i.e. a form of Protestants. They quickly became economically and politically dominant, whereas the original population formed an underclass of laborers and tenant farmers etc. As Calvinists the Scots were hard working and very productive in trade and industry, Ulster developed differently from the rest of Ireland, which is largely agricultural.

English national politics continue to influence the situation in Ireland. In 1685—1688 James II became King of England. James was a Catholic, the Protestants in England were not satisfied with him and he was dethroned by William of Orange (William of Orange was a member of the Dutch aristocracy who ruled over England and Ireland as King William III from 1689 until his death on 1702. He ruled as joint monarch with his wife, Mary II, until her death on 1694, and then ruled as sole monarch). James fled to Ireland, where the Irish population supported him. William of Orange and his troops pursued him and they fought a battle, the Battle of the Boyne 1690, a key event in Irish history, where the forces of William defeated the forces of the Catholic King, James.

To this day Protestants in Northern Ireland celebrate this victory with parades and marches, and one of the leading Protestant organizations in Northern Ireland is called the Orange Order.

Penal Times and Rebellion

The first years of the 18th Century saw an attempt to rid Ireland of Catholicism, by implementing laws that restricted Catholic practice while making it extremely advantageous to become a Protestant. For example, they instituted the so-called Penal Laws 1691—1793. According to these laws the Catholic majority in Ireland cannot enter military service, hold public office, practice law, produce or print books, newspapers etc., own land, be ministers, be schoolmasters, pass on land to their children without dividing it, and thus impoverishing their descendants.

Throughout the 18th century this system of oppression was in effect. The Irish population was reduced to paupers (贫民), having to support themselves as tenant farmers, exploited by the British landlords, many of whom did not even live in Ireland but in Britain, and resources were drained from Ireland to Britain. In part this colonial exploitation helped finance the industrial revolution in England.

It wasn't until the end of the century that Irish people, both Protestants and Catholics this time, started to look for greater freedoms from England (it was the style of the time; just look at what happened in America). What unite them were the liberal ideas of freedom, equality, and brotherhood. These Irishmen saw clearly that their country could not develop economically and socially unless the colonial exploitation was brought to an end. In 1798 they rose in arms against the British. The rising was crushed by the British army and the leaders were hanged in public. The most famous of the leaders was Wolf Tone (a Protestant), who is considered as a national hero in Ireland to this very day.

The Potato Famine

On 1 Jan 1801, the United Kingdom of Great Britain and Ireland came into existence. Not surprisingly, the union in Ireland was highly unpopular and relations continued to deteriorate (恶化) between the Catholic and Protestant populations. In the 1830s, a movement began to repeal the union. It found little favor in Protestant Ulster, though, where growing prosperity kept many committed to the legislative union with Britain. Catholic areas of Ireland fared (进展)

less well and when the potato crops of the 1840s failed, a devastating famine resulted. The English government were so slow to react to the crisis that by the time the famine was over, an estimated one million people had died, and a further one million had left Ireland, arriving in the US and Britain, penniless and desperate. The Irish potato famine created a legacy of emigration from Ireland that did not stop until the late 20th Century. By 1960, the population of Ireland had dwindled to 4.3 million from an 1841 population of over eight million.

Partial Independence

Following the famine, strong, highly organized Irish political movements were born. Demand for national self-government came to the fore. The Catholics gradually gained parliamentary power and "home rule"(地方自治), a separate Irish parliament within the Union, gained popularity. Using their leverage (影响) in the British parliament, a home rule bill was enacted in 1914, but not put in effect until the end of World War I.

In the twentieth century, Ireland's situation has remained unsettled. In 1920, the British government passed the Government of Ireland Act. By it there would be 2 parliaments in Ireland, one in the north and one in the south. However both parliaments would be subordinate to the British parliament.

In 1921 a treaty between southern Ireland and Britain established the Irish Free State, a self-governing dominion within the British Commonwealth of Nations. This allowed the Northern Ireland Parliament to take the six northern counties out of the dominion. In the Free State it led quickly to a vicious civil war between both sides; those who agreed with the Treaty, and those who disagreed, but ultimately the treaty stood. The Irish Civil war accounted for 3,000 deaths on both sides. Most of today's political parties of the Irish Republic originate from this deeply divisive (造成不和的) political split.

The Republic of Ireland since the Split

In 1937 southern Ireland drafted and adopted a new constitution, which made an elected president head of state. Furthermore the name 'Irish Free State' was replaced with either Eire or Ireland. It remained formally within the British Commonwealth. Then in 1948 Ireland was made a republic and the last ties with Britain were cut.

In the north, the Protestants and Catholics continued their unsettled relationship with one another. In 1972, the Republic of Ireland joined the European Economic Community (EEC, now the EU), along with the United Kingdom and Denmark. Over the past few years it has integrated further into the European Union. That same year, the Northern Irish State was dissolved and the six counties were put under direct rule from London.

III Political System and National Economy

A. Political System

Politics of the Republic of Ireland take place in a framework of a parliamentary representative democratic republic. The Uachtarán (President) is the head of state. The Taoiseach (Prime Minister) is the head of government and of a multi-party system. Executive power is exercised by the government. Legislative power is vested in both the government and the Oireachtas (爱尔兰国家议会，由总统和两院组成), the bicameral national parliament. The Judiciary is independent of the executive and the legislature. While there are a number of important political parties in the state, the political landscape is dominated by two opposed and

competing Parties: Fianna Fáil and Fine Gael.
Government
Dublin Castle in Dublin, Republic of Ireland, is a major Irish governmental complex. Most of the complex dates from the 18th century. The Castle served as the seat of English, then later British government of Ireland under the Lordship of Ireland (1171—1541), the Kingdom of Ireland (1541—1800), and the United Kingdom of Great Britain and Ireland (1800—1922). Upon establishment of the Irish Free State in 1922, the complex was ceremonially handed over to the newly formed Provisional Government led by Michael Collins

Main office holders			
Office	Name	Party	Since
President	Mary McAleese	Fianna Fáil	11 Nov.1997
Prime Minister	Bertie Ahern	Fianna Fáil	26 June1997
	Brian Cowen	Fianna Fáil	14June 2007

Constitution
The state operates under the Constitution of Ireland, adopted in 1937. The constitution falls within the liberal democratic tradition. It defines the organs of government and guarantees certain fundamental rights. The constitution may only be amended by referendum(公民复决：对拟通过或已通过的法案进行的直接公民投票). Important constitutional referendums have concerned issues such as abortion, the status of the Catholic Church, divorce and the European Union.

Head of State
The head of state is the President of Ireland. In keeping with the state's parliamentary system of government the President exercises largely a ceremonial role but does possess certain reserve powers. The presidency is open to all Irish citizens who are at least 35. The President is elected to a seven year term of office; no candidate may serve more than two terms. In carrying out certain of their constitutional functions, the President is aided by the Council of State. There is no Vice-President in Ireland. If for any reason the President is unable to carry out his/her functions, or if the Office of President is vacant, the duties of the President are carried out by the Presidential Commission.

Executive
Executive authority is exercised by a cabinet known simply as the Government. Article 28 of the Constitution states that the Government may consist of no less than seven and no more than fifteen members, namely the prime minister, the deputy prime minister and up to thirteen other ministers. The prime minister is appointed by the President, after being nominated by the lower house of parliament. The remaining ministers are nominated by the prime minister and appointed by the President.

Legislature
The parliament of the Republic of Ireland is the Oireachtas. The Oireachtas consists of the President and two houses: Dáil Éireann and Seanad Éireann (also known as the Senate). The Dáil is by far the dominant House of the legislature. The President may not veto bills passed by the Oireachtas, but may refer them to the Irish Supreme Court for a ruling on whether to comply with the constitution.

The Four Courts in Dublin
It is the Republic of Ireland's main courts building. The Four Courts are the location of the Supreme Court, High Court, and Central Criminal Court of the Republic of Ireland.

Dáil Éireann: Members of the Dáil are directly elected at least once in every five years from mulit-seat constituencies. Membership of the house is open to all Irish and UK citizens who are at least 21 and permanently resident in Ireland. The electorate (有选举权者) consists of all Irish and UK citizens resident in Ireland over the age of 18. Members of the Dáil are known as Teachta Dála or TDs.

Seanad Éireann: The Senate is a largely advisory body. It consists of sixty members called Senators. An election for the Seanad must take place no later than 90 days after a general election for the members of the Dáil.

Judiciary

The Republic of Ireland is a common law (普通法,习惯法,判例法:来源和发展于英国的法律系统,以法院决议为基础,根据在这些决议中隐含的学说以及习惯和用法,而不是基于编纂的书面法律) jurisdiction. The judiciary consists of the Supreme Court, the High Court and many lower courts established by law. Judges are appointed by the President after being nominated by the Government and can be removed from office only for misbehavior or incapacity, and then only by resolution of both houses of the Oireachtas.

The final court of appeal is the Supreme Court, which consists of the Chief Justice and seven other justices. The Supreme Court has the power of judicial review and may declare to be invalid both laws and acts of the state which are repugnant (不一致的) to the constitution.

Political Parties

A number of political parties are represented in the Dáil and coalition governments are common. Neither of the two largest parties, *Fianna Fáil and Fine Gael*, strongly identifies itself as either a left or right-wing group. The third largest party in the state is the centre-left *Labour Party*. Labour is joined on the left by the Green Party and on the far-lleft by *Sinn Féin and the Socialist Party*. The right is represented by the Progressive Democrats who are classical neo-lliberals with regard to economic policy. Independent TDs (MPs) also play an important role in Irish politics.

B. National Economy

An Overview

The economy of the Republic of Ireland is modern and trade-dependent with growth rate averaging 10% from 1995 to 2000. Agriculture, once the most important sector, is now dwarfed by industry. Although exports remain the primary engine for the Republic's robust growth, the economy is also benefiting from a rise in consumer spending and recovery in both construction and business investment. House price inflation has been a particular economic concern. Unemployment is very low and incomes have been rising rapidly. Dublin, the nation's capital, was ranked 16th in a worldwide cost of living survey in 2006. Ireland has been reported to have the second highest per capita income of any country in the EU next to Luxembourg (卢森堡:欧洲西北部一国家), and the fourth highest in the world.

Agriculture, Forestry, and Fishing

About 17 percent of the total area of Ireland is cultivated, and much of the rest is devoted to pasture. Raising livestock is the chief agricultural activity, and meat products are among the most important agricultural exports. The trade in live animals, notably horses, and dairy products is also important. The principal field crops are wheat, barley, oats, and potatoes. The most fertile farmlands are found in the east and southeast.

Ireland has little productive timberland. As a result, the government has implemented reforestation programs in an effort to reduce the country's dependence on timber imports and to provide raw material for new paper mills and related industries. In 2005 forests occupied 10 percent of Ireland's total land area; the output of timber was 2.5 million cubic meters.

The fishing industry expanded in the late 20th century. However, the waters around Ireland and much of Europe have been heavily overfished, and annual fish catches are now subject to quotas (限额) established by the EU. Ireland's catch in 2001 was 417, 244 metric tons. Fish farming, both in freshwater and saltwater environments, is becoming more important as natural catches drop.

Tourism

The Irish government actively promotes the tourism industry, which has grown increasingly important to the economy. Dublin, in particular, has become an important tourist destination, in part because of the rapid growth of low-cost air services linking the city to the United Kingdom and mainland Europe. However, the most popular destination for tourists is the rugged west coast, where numerous peninsulas and bluff cliffs provide a dramatic contrast to the rain-hazed loughs of the interior. Many visitors choose to explore the countryside on foot. Horseback riding, cycling, golfing, and boating along Ireland's rivers and loughs are also popular tourist activities.

Currency and Banking

The monetary unit of Ireland is the single currency of the European Union (EU), the Euro (0.81 euros equal US $1, 2004 average). Ireland was among the first group of EU member states to adopt the Euro. The Euro was introduced on January 1, 1999, for electronic transfers and accounting purposes only. Ireland's national currency, the Irish pound, was used for other purposes. On January 1, 2002, Euro-denominated coins and bills went into circulation, and the Irish pound ceased to be legal tender (法定货币).

One Irish Euro Coin

There are not any €1 bills, just €1 coins. Euros are not produced in Ireland except for the €1 coins which feature the nation's symbol: a harp.

As a participant in the single currency, Ireland must follow economic policies established by the European Central Bank (ECB). The ECB is located in Frankfurt, Germany, and is responsible for all EU monetary policies, which include setting interest rates and regulating the money supply. On January 1, 1999, control over Irish monetary policy was transferred from the Central Bank of Ireland to the ECB. After the transfer, the Central Bank of Ireland joined the national banks of the other EU countries that adopted the Euro as part of the European System of Central Banks (ESCB).

IV Society and Culture

People of Ireland

Ireland's population is predominantly of Celtic origin, but ancient tribes had inhabited Ireland for thousands of years when Celtic peoples settled the island in the 4th century BC. Over the centuries Ireland absorbed significant numbers of Vikings, Normans, and English. More recently, Ireland's membership in the European Union (EU) has increased the number of citizens of other European countries living in Ireland, and small communities of ethnic Chinese and Indian people also have been established.

Since 1996 Ireland has received small numbers of refugees and asylum seekers from Eastern Europe, Africa, and Asia. Ireland also has a small indigenous minority known as Travelers. The number of Travelers is approximately 25,000. They move and camp across the Irish countryside in small groups in enclaves (少数民族聚集地) within cities.

Ireland's economic growth in recent decades has reversed a long trend of emigration, which initially was to escape the famine and later to seek employment and better lives. In the 1960s and 1970s emigration fell sharply. By the 1980s Ireland's population was growing at an annual rate of about 0.5 percent, and in the 1990s immigration began to exceed emigration. In 2002 Ireland's population grew at an annual rate of 1.15 percent, one of the highest rates in Western Europe.

Customs of Ireland

● *Marriage and Family*

People usually marry in their early to mid-20s. Most weddings are performed in a church, but a minority is also performed in a registry office. After marriage many people in rural areas stay close to their family's home and visit frequently. Many couples, particularly in the cities, live together before or instead of marriage.

Typically, the bonds between siblings in an Irish family are especially strong. In rural areas, extended families often live near one another, and family members who have moved to Dublin or overseas in search of work often return for Christmas and other family celebrations or funerals. Traditionally, women have not worked outside the home except to help on the family farm, but in Dublin and other cities the majority of women now have jobs. Salary levels for women still lag behind those of men, but gender discrimination is illegal. The Irish have elected two consecutive (连续的) women presidents since 1991.

● *Eating*

As an agricultural country, Ireland produces many fresh vegetables. Fresh dairy products, breads, and seafood are also widely available. Potatoes, once eaten at every meal, are still regularly served, but the Irish have embraced other foods such as pasta and rice. Apples, oranges, and pears have long been integral (必备的) to the Irish diet, but are now joined by a wider variety of fruit that have become available since Ireland joined the European Union (EU). Oysters and other shellfish are popular, and smoked salmon is considered an Irish specialty, as are Irish stew and Irish lamb. Irish breads include soda bread and brack (果子面包), a rich, dark loaf containing dried fruit and traditionally served at Halloween.

The traditional cooked breakfast consists of any or all of the following: bacon, sausages, grilled or fried tomatoes, mushrooms, eggs, white and black pudding and toast or bread fried in fat or oil. Fewer people now eat such a morning meal, however, preferring a lighter breakfast. In recent years, the Irish, particularly those in urban areas, have become much more adventurous in their diet, and now eat a wide variety of European and ethnic food. Pubs (public houses) and cafés serve both snacks and full meals.

The Irish generally eat three meals a day. The midday meal is usually referred to as lunch and the evening meal as dinner or, when it is less formal, as supper. But some rural people call the midday meal dinner and the early-evening meal tea. Many people, particularly in Dublin, no longer eat more than a light meal or snack in the middle of the day. Those who have an early-evening meal sometimes have another snack—sandwiches, cakes, or biscuits—at around 9 PM.

Tea and coffee are popular drinks in the home, and Dublin is rapidly developing a café culture. Pubs can be found in nearly every Irish town, where people gather to talk with friends, relax, listen to music, and have a drink. Beer is much beloved in Ireland, especially the dark stout(烈性啤酒) varieties. Renowned local stouts include Guinness, Beamish, and Murphy's. Irish whiskey is also a popular alcoholic beverage.

● *Housing*

In cities and towns, most Irish people live in houses, although apartments are growing in popularity as urban densities increase. In the countryside, traditional farmhouses constructed of stone or dried peat and covered with thatched roofs have been largely replaced by modern dwellings. Today, most homes are made from concrete, brick, or mortared stone and have tile roofs (瓦屋顶). In rural areas peat is still cut and dried for use as fuel for cooking and heating.

● *Socializing*

The traditional Irish greeting *Céad míle fáilte* literally means "A hundred thousand welcomes." However, the Irish greet one another with common English phrases such as "Hello" and "How are you?" or more casual greetings such as "How's it going?" The most typical Irish greeting is Dia dhuit, which means "God be with you." Goodbye is expressed with Slán (roughly "Go safely") or the warmer *Slán agus beannacht* ("Go safely, and blessings be with you"). Greetings are generally accompanied by a firm handshake, although in cities and among younger people it is not unusual for women to be kissed on the cheek when greeting. The use of first names is now widespread.

Unless one knows someone well, it is usual to telephone before visiting. Rural people are more likely than urban dwellers to drop in on friends unannounced, as was common practice in the past. People like to meet for conversation in pubs, which are important centers of social life.Visiting in the home takes place during holidays, especially between Christmas and New Year's Day, which is also the time when young people living abroad usually come home to visit. Parties are also popular during holidays.

Sports

The Irish are sports-oriented, and most weekends include some sporting activities for the family or the individual. Popular sports include the two national pastimes: Gaelic football and hurling (爱尔兰式曲棍球), both strictly amateur sports. The women's version of hurling is called camogie. The All-Ireland semifinals and finals, sponsored by the Gaelic Athletic Association (GAA), are highlights of the hurling and Gaelic football seasons.

Soccer, rugby, sailing, cycling, golf, and horse and greyhound (快速汽船) racing are also favorite activities. Soccer has become a particularly popular spectator sport in the 1990s, reflecting the enthusiasm surrounding the national team's successes during the first half of the decade.

Fishing is also a common recreational activity, featuring mainly trout and salmon fishing. Rugby internationals played at Dublin's Lansdowne Road stadium are considered high points of the sporting year. Enthusiasts of horse racing flock to the Galway Races in the summer and early fall.

Holidays and Special Days

Public holidays are observed in the Republic of Ireland on:
- New Year's Day, 1 January
- St Patrick's Day, 17 March
- Easter Monday, moveable

220 Understanding U.K. & Ireland

St. Patrick riding on a snake in St. Patrick's Day parade

- Labor Day/May Day, the first Monday in May
- June Bank Holiday, the first Monday in June
- August Bank Holiday, the first Monday in August
- October Bank Holiday (sometimes called the Halloween holiday), the last Monday in October
- Christmas Day, 25 December
- St Stephen's Day, 26 December

The most recent public holiday to be added was May Day (Labor Day). This holiday, taken as the first Monday in May, was introduced in 1994. Recently, senior politicians have been considering the addition of one or two extra public holidays in order to bring the number of such holidays in Ireland closer to the European average.

● *St. Patrick's Day*

Saint Patrick's Day (March 17), which honors the patron saint of Ireland, is the most important national holiday and is marked by parades, shamrock decorations, Irish songs and jigs (吉格舞) and sometimes the wearing of green (the national color) to represent the lushness of Ireland—the Emerald Isle. Today St. Patrick's Day is celebrated by the Irish as well as many Americans, Canadians and English people.

The Story of St. Patrick

St. Patrick was born about 389 A.D. in Northern Wales, which at that time may have been part of England or Scotland. He had an adventurous life and was captured by pirates at the age of 16. The Irish pirates brought him to Ireland to tend the flocks of a chieftain(酋长) in Ulster. Six years of slavery made him a devoted Christian. He escaped to France and became a monk. In 432, a vision led him to return to Ireland as a missionary bishop. He brought Christianity to Ireland and taught there for 29 years. Legend has it that resourceful Saint Patrick used the shamrock, a 3 leaf clover, as a diagram to explain the Holy Trinity to his uneducated congregation (圣众). St. Patrick founded 365 churches, baptized over 120,000 people and consecrated(使就圣职) 450 bishops. According to some Irish writings, St. Patrick died on March 17, 461 A.D. The anniversary of his death is celebrated as St. Patrick's Day.

Education

The Republic of Ireland's education system is quite similar to that of most other western countries. There are three distinct levels of education in Ireland: primary, secondary and higher (often known as third-level or tertiary) education. In recent years further education has grown immensely.

The Department of Education and Science, under the control of the Minister for Education, is in overall control of policy, funding and direction. Other important organizations are the National Qualifications Authority of Ireland and the Higher Education Authority; on a local level Vocational Education Committees are the only comprehensive system of government organization. There are many other statutory (法定的) and non-statutory bodies which have a function in the education system.

All children must receive compulsory education between the ages of six and fifteen years. The Constitution of Ireland allows this education to be provided in the home. In 1973 the requirement to pass the Irish language in order to receive a second-level certificate was dropped. Certain students may get an exemption (免除) from learning Irish; These include students who have spent a significant period of time abroad or students with a learning difficulty. English is the primary medium of instruction at all levels, except in schools in which Irish is the working language and which is increasingly popular. Universities also offer degree programs in diverse disciplines (学科),

taught mostly through English, with some in Irish.

University education in Ireland began with the founding of the University of Dublin, or Trinity College, in 1592. The National University of Ireland, established in 1908 in Dublin, has constituent university colleges in Cork, Dublin, and Galway. The college in Galway, although now a secular (非宗教的) institution evolved from Saint Patrick's College, founded in 1795 as Ireland's primary Roman Catholic seminary (神学院).

The university system was further extended in 1989 when the University of Limerick and Dublin City University (DCU) were accredited; both schools emphasize technical subjects. Ireland also has several state-supported training colleges and various technical colleges in the larger communities.

The University of Dublin, also called Trinity College, is the oldest institution of higher learning in Ireland. It was founded in Dublin in 1592 by Elizabeth I, queen of England and Ireland.

Ireland earned a reputation as an education and cultural center in the early middle Ages. From the 6th to the 8th century, when Western Europe was largely illiterate, nearly 1,000 Irish missionaries traveled to England and to continental Europe to teach Christianity. Irish missionaries founded monasteries (修道院) that achieved extensive cultural influence, which is especially well known for its contributions to education and literature. Classical studies flowered in ancient Ireland. Distinctive also at the time were the bardic (吟游诗人的) schools of writers and other intellectuals who traveled from town to town, teaching their arts to students. The bardic schools, an important part of Irish education, were suppressed in the 16th century by Henry VIII, king of England.

The University of Dublin

Literature

For a comparatively small country, Ireland has made a disproportionate contribution to world literature in all its branches. Irish Literature encompasses (包括) the Irish and English languages. The island's most widely-known literary works are undoubtedly in English. Particularly famous examples of such works are those of James Joyce, Oscar Wilde, and Ireland's four winners of the Nobel Prize for Literature: William Butler Yeats, George Bernard Shaw, Samuel Beckett and Seamus Heaney. Three of these were born in Dublin (Heaney being the exception, who has lived in Dublin but was born in County Londonderry), making it the birthplace of more Nobel literary laureates than any other city in the world.

George Bernard Shaw is an Irish-born British playwright. A founder of the Fabian Society, he wrote plays of iconoclastic (打破旧习的) social criticism, including *Arms and the Man* (1894), *Pygmalion* (1913), and *Saint Joan* (1923). He won the 1925 Nobel Prize for literature.

William Butler Yeats is the Irish writer who is considered among the greatest poets of the 20th century. A founder of the Irish National Theatre Company at the Abbey Theatre, Dublin, he wrote many short plays, including *The Countess Cathleen* (1892). His poetry, published in collections such as *The Winding Stair* (1929), ranges from early love lyrics to the complex symbolist works of his later years. He won the 1923 Nobel Prize for literature.

The novels and short stories of James Joyce are distinguished by their keen psychological insight and use of literary innovations, most notably the stream of consciousness technique. The stories in Dubliners, his only collection of short fiction, are generally regarded as models of the genre. His works include *Ulysses* (1922) and *Finnegans Wake* (1939).

In 1937 Irish-born writer Samuel Beckett settled in Paris and began writing in French. Although it was not his native language, French enabled Beckett to create some of his most enduring literary achievements. In perhaps his most famous work, *Waiting for Godot* (1953), Beckett explored the human need for hope and companionship. Beckett used sparse dialogue, clipped conversations, and an absence of plot to symbolize the inconsistencies of language and emotions. He died on December 22, 1989, in Paris, where he had lived for many years.

Seamus Heaney won the Nobel Prize in literature in 1995. Born in rural Northern Ireland, he left his native land to avoid political and religious violence, but his poetry remained centered on the people and places he encountered during his early years in the countryside. Although his poetry appears simple in its language and flow, its structure and references are often complex.

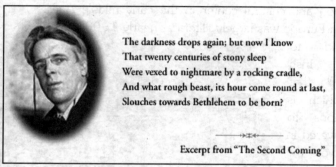

The darkness drops again; but now I know
That twenty centuries of stony sleep
Were vexed to nightmare by a rocking cradle,
And what rough beast, its hour come round at last,
Slouches towards Bethlehem to be born?

Excerpt from "The Second Coming"

Ireland's oldest literary traditions are found in the Irish language. Indeed, Irish has the third oldest literature in Europe (after Greek and Latin) and the most significant body of written literature of any Celtic language. Furthermore, the historic influence of Irish language traditions, such as a strong oral tradition of legends and poetry, has helped make much English Literature in Ireland quite distinctive from that in other countries.

From the older tradition, many Irish writers in English inherited a sense of wonder in the face of nature, a narrative style that tends towards the deliberately exaggerated or absurd and a keen sense of the power of satire. In addition, the interplay between the two languages has resulted in an English dialect, Hiberno-English that lends a distinctive syntax and music to the literature written in it.

Understanding Australia and New Zealand

A General Survey of Australia

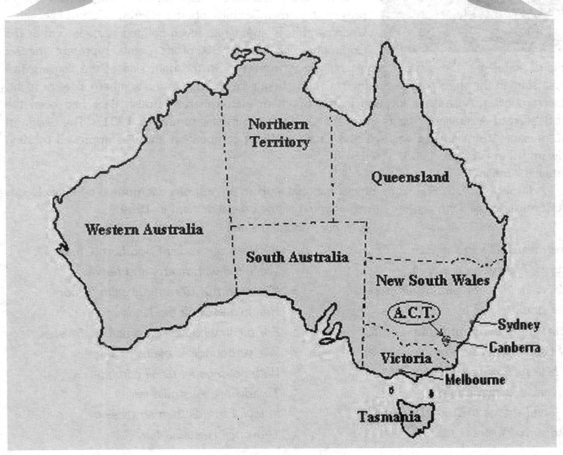

Map of Australia

I A General Survey

Australia is an island that is also a continent. It consists of two land masses: the mainland and Tasmania. In area it is the 6th largest country and the smallest continent. Its area is 7,682,300 square kilometers, about the size of the mainland states of the United States, excluding Alaska, and approximately 24 times the size of the British Isles.

Location

Australia lies southeast of Asia between the Indian and Pacific oceans. The name "Australia" comes from the Latin *australis* meaning "of the south." For its location in the southern hemisphere, Australia is often called "the land down under" in the West.

224 Understanding Australia and New Zealand

Capital

Canberra, specifically built as a capital city, is located in the Australian Capital Territory (A.C.T.) which is totally enclosed by the state of New South Wales. The A.C.T. is approximately 2,400 square kilometers in area with urban Canberra sitting in the north eastern quarter of the territory. The city is 281 kilometers from Sydney and 660 kilometers from Melbourne.

National Flag

The Australian flag is dark blue with the Union Jack (the flag of the United Kingdom) in the upper corner of the hoist. This symbolizes Australia's historical links with Britain and its present-day membership of the British Commonwealth. Underneath is a large white seven-pointed star, known as the Commonwealth Star. Six of its points represent the six original states and the seventh represents the territories. On the right side of the flag are five white stars in the shape of the Southern Cross, bright star groups in the southern skies at night. This symbolizes Australia's location in the Southern Hemisphere. British flags had been the official flag of Australia for years when the Commonwealth was formed in 1901. The design of the present Australian flag was selected after an official competition and was approved by King Edward VII in February 1903.

National Anthem

Advance Australia Fair is the official national anthem of Australia. Composed by Peter Dodds McCormick in the 19th century, it was adopted as the official anthem in 1984.

Advance Australia Fair

Australians all let us rejoice,
For we are young and free;
We've golden soil and wealth for toil,
Our home is girt by sea;
Our land abounds in Nature's gifts
Of beauty rich and rare;
In history's page, let every stage
Advance Australia fair!
In joyful strains then let us sing,
"Advance Australia fair!"

Beneath our radiant Southern Cross,
We'll toil with hearts and hands;
To make this Commonwealth of ours
Renowned of all the lands;
For those who've come across the seas
We've boundless plains to share;
With courage let us all combine
To advance Australia fair.
In joyful strains then let us sing
"Advance Australia fair!"

God Save the Queen/King, the national anthem of the United Kingdom, is the royal anthem of Australia, to be played at formal ceremonies attended by the Queen or members of the Royal family.

Coat of Arms

The Commonwealth coat of arms is the official emblem of Australia. It was granted by King George V in 1912. The central focus of the coat of arms is a shield, on which are the badges representing the six States. They are, from left to right, New South Wales, Victoria, and Queensland in the upper half and South Australia, Western Australia, and Tasmania in the lower half. The six badges are enclosed by an ermine border, symbolizing the federation of the States into the Commonwealth. The shield is hold by a red kangaroo on the left and an emu

(鸸鹋) on the right, two animals native to Australia. They stand on ornamental rests. As neither animal can move backward easily, they symbolize progress and a nation advancing forward. The crest (顶部) consists of a Commonwealth star, symbolic of national unity, on a gold and blue wreath. In the background of the coat of arms are sprays of golden wattle (金合欢树), with a scroll at the base bearing the word "Australia."

Floral Emblem

Golden wattle (金合欢) is the national flower of Australia. The floral emblem grows naturally in New South Wales, Australian Capital Territory, Victoria and South Australia. It reasonably tolerates frost and drought and grows widely in temperate regions. Today wattle symbolizes hope, opportunities and the natural wealth of Australia. September 1 is National Wattle Day in Australia, an occasion to inspire national sentiment (感情).

Golden wattle is an ornamental accessory (附加物) to the shield on the Australian Coat of Arms. It can also be found on some honorary medals and stamps.

Green and gold, resembling those of golden wattle, are the national colors of Australia. They are popular and widely accepted in sporting events. Almost all Australian national teams wear these two colors.

Population

Australia is the 53rd most populous country in the world. Its population, by estimation, amounted to 21 million on June 29th, 2007 and 90% lives in cities and major towns. Approximately 1.5% of the population is Aborigines(澳大利亚土著居民) or part Aborigines.

Australia is a country of migrants. Today, 22% of the population was born overseas; 18% of Australia-born people have at least one parent born overseas. Until the 1960s most of the migrants came from UK and Ireland but today a growing percentage come from Europe and Asia.

Languages

With hundreds of aboriginal languages and dialects spoken by indigenous people, English is the predominant and official language of Australia. As a variety of English, Australian English has an accent similar to dialects of the South-East of England. Its grammar and spelling are largely the same as those of British English.

Australians use many words that they consider unique to Australian English. A frequently quoted example is *Outback* (内地), meaning a remote, sparsely-populated area. Some words of aboriginal languages have found their way to Australian English, mainly names for plants, animals and places. Immigrants bring into Australia their native tongues. The most common foreign languages spoken at home are Chinese (Cantonese 1.2%, Mandarin 1.1%), Italian, and Greek.

Religions

Australia has no state religion. Freedom of worship is guaranteed by the constitution. The population is primarily Christian; of those 26.6% are Catholic, 20.7% Anglican, and 20.7% other Christian denominations. The number of people who say they have no religion is on the rise. Hinduism, Buddhism, Islam and Judaism numbers are increasing.

Currency

The unit of currency is the Australian dollar which is divided into 100 cents.

The notes are: $5, $10, $20, $50, and $100.

Coins: 5c, 10c, 20c, 50c, $1 and $2.

II Geography

Australia is one of the oldest continents; the effects of over 250 million years of erosion have turned it into a flat, low lying and stable land mass. It has a wide variety of landforms. Much of the flat inland is desert. At one time this was a fertile area with many lakes and marshes. Some of these old lakes survive today as salt lakes like Lake Eyre in South Australia, with the lowest elevation of 16 meters below sea level (it occasionally fills with water). The highest peak is Mt. Kosciusko, in New South Wales, which is 2,228 meters above sea level.

While Australia is often thought of as a dry thinly populated land, this is only true of the inland (or outback) areas. The eastern coast is more heavily populated. The huge interior is hot and dry with vast expanses of sandy desert or stone plains giving way to shrub savannah or mallee (澳大利亚南部产小桉树) scrub. The main mountains are along the eastern coast, known as the Great Dividing Range, which has an average altitude of less than 910 meters above sea level. In coastal regions the environments range from tropical rain forest in the north, to pastoral lands and forest in the east and the south east, to alpine country in the Snowy Mountains and central Tasmania.

Australia's deserts are as vast as the Sahara, the snowfields huge and picturesque. The surfing beaches are among the best in the world. Australia is the only continent without current volcanic activity—the last eruption took place 1,400 years ago at Mount Gambier.

Topography(地形学)

Australia is the flattest and lowest land mass with the average elevation of about 330 meters. It can be divided into three major topographic regions: the Eastern Highlands, the Central Lowlands and the Western Plateau (高原).

● *Eastern Highlands*

In the east the Great Dividing Range, or Eastern Highlands, separates the east coast from the vast interior plains. This mountainous region comprises of a series of plateaus and mountain ranges dotted with gorges, canyons, valleys and plains. The Range averages about 1,200 m in height and runs more than 3,500 km along the eastern coast from Cape York in the north to Western Victoria in the south. Tasmania is also a part of this massive range. The range is the source of mountains in Australia and also the main watershed (分水岭) in eastern Australia, dividing streams and rivers which flow directly into the Pacific Ocean on the eastern coast of Australia from those which flow westerly through the interior plains.

● *Great Western Plateau*

The enormous western half of Australia comprises the Great Western Plateau, which is a vast desert and semi-desert region that covers almost 66% of the land area and consists of ancient rocks similar to those of Africa. The Western Plateau has an average elevation of 305 meters. Located on the plateau are the country's four major deserts—the Gibson, Great Sandy, Great Victoria and Simpson. The region is generally flat, broken by various mountain ranges, such as the MacDonnell Ranges in central Australia, the Kimberley Plateau Region in the northwest, the Hamersley Range in the east and the Darling Range near the southwestern corner.

Uluru Rock, a World Heritage Site

● *Central Lowlands*

The vast, rolling plains between the Eastern Highland and the Western Plateau comprise the

Central Lowlands. This narrow region contains, from north to south, the Carpentaria Basin, the Lake Eyre Basin and the Murray-Darling Basin. The region has the richest pastoral and agricultural land in Australia but its west-central part is a barren, sandy desert.

Beneath the Central Lowlands is the Great Artesian Basin (大自流盆地), the largest artesian basin in the world. It underlies approximately one-fifth of the entire continent and functions as a life line through the interior of eastern Australia. The basin provides underground freshwater for drinking, irrigation, cattle raising and industry.

Long Coastlines

As the world's largest island bordering two oceans, Australia has a coastline of 25,760 km. according to the CIA World Factbook. Such a long beach is broken up by dramatic cliffs, headlands, inlets, rivers and waterways.

Plants and animals

● *Plants*

For nearly 50 million years the continent drifted alone over the ocean, separated from the rest of the world. This long-term isolation allowed the plants and animals on the continent to evolve independently into new species. Many amazing animals and flora occur only on this landmass and cannot be found anywhere else. Australia accommodates about 20,000 to 25,000 different native plants. Most of them are well adapted to the challenging environments of drought, fire, soil infertility and other harsh conditions. Eucalyptus (桉属植物)and acacia are the two dominant kinds in tree flora.

Eucalyptus

Members of the eucalyptus genus (种，类) make up over 75% of Australia's tree population. There are more than 700 species and most of them are native to Australia. Eucalypts are economically important for their use for ornament, construction, pharmacy (制药业), oil yield as well as paper production.

A mature eucalypt may be a tree over 60 meters in height or a low shrub called mallee (澳洲油桉) seldom taller than 10ms.

Acacia

Acacia, commonly known as wattles, is the second largest genus in Australia. Acacia shrub lands are common in semiarid and arid regions. Golden wattle is the national floral emblem of Australia.

Numerous types of wild flowers grow in the bush country. Each Australian state and territory has chosen a flower native to its region as an official floral emblem.

● *Animals*

The continent's long isolation from other land masses allowed native animal species in Australia to evolve into large populations.

Marsupials (有袋动物) are mammals carrying their newborn babies in a pouch (育儿袋) near their belly until the infants are old enough to survive on their own. The best known marsupials of Australia are kangaroos and koalas.

Kangaroo

Kangaroos are the only large animals that travel by hopping on their large, powerful hind legs and use their long muscular tail for balance. Different kangaroo species live in a range of different environments. Some make nests, some live above ground in trees and larger species tend to shelter under trees or in caves and rock clefts. Kangaroos live on grasses, leaves and other plants. They are shy and retiring by nature, and in normal circumstances present no threat to humans.

Koala

Koalas have soft dense fur that is grey or brown in color and a pale yellow or white belly. They have a large hairless nose, round, fluffy ears and almost no tail. The comical "teddy bear" appearance often gave them a name "koala bear". In fact, they have no relationship to the bear family. Koalas eat the leaves of certain kinds of eucalypts and rarely drink water, getting most of their fluid intake from the food. Eucalyptus leaves are poisonous to most animals, but koalas' digestive system is capable of detoxifying (解毒) the poison. The Koala lives nearly solely in the upper branches of his feeding tree. Strongly he enfolds (拥抱) the trunk of the tree with his powerful legs, whereupon his sharp claws of his toes drill into the bark. As a night active animal he spends all day sleeping in a crotch (分叉处). At night he climbs the upper branches to eat the leaves.

Koala

Platypus (鸭嘴兽) and Echidna (针鼹鼠)

The Duck-Billed platypus and echidnas are among the oldest and possibly strangest looking mammals. They are found only in Australasia and are the only mammals to lay eggs. Echidnas and platypus belong to a small order of animals called Monotremes (单孔类动物), of which they are the only surviving members. They have a total of 3 species: the Duck-Billed Platypus and 2 echidnas, the Long Beaked Echidna and the Short Beaked Echidna.

The Duck-Billed Platypus is an Australian and Tasmanian original. In fact there was a time when it was not believed to be real anywhere else. The platypus has had an enormous impact on the scientific world since it was first discovered in 1796. Its ducklike bill and furry mammalian coat appeared so strange it was difficult to classify it. The platypus is covered in short, brown fur and has a dense undercoat (绒毛) which helps it to maintain its body temperature. It is highly adapted to semi-aquatic (半水栖的) life and relies on its sensitive bill to locate food. Unlike that of a duck, its bill is soft and flexible, made of moist sensitive skin, and is rich in nerve endings.

Echidnas live in New Guinea and Australia. They are named after a monster in ancient Greek mythology. Echidnas seem to be very solitary creatures except when mating. They are very shy and, due to their good sense of hearing, also very alert. They run quickly, climb well, and run away from unusual noises, so are rarely seen. When threatened the echidna will roll into a ball, sometimes burying itself so that all is visible is a little pile of dirt and some spines (刺) sticking up. Although echidnas are pretty adaptable, they lack sweat glands (腺) and cope poorly with heat, dying quickly at temperatures above 35 degrees Celsius. They avoid these high temperatures by digging deep burrows and emerging only after dusk. They eat termites (白蚁), ants and other small insects.

Emu (鸸鹋产于澳洲的体型大而不会飞的鸟)

Australia is home to nearly 800 bird species. The most impressive is the emu, the world's second largest bird after the ostrich (鸵鸟). An adult emu has hairy, grey feathers, stands 1.5—2 metres in height and weighs an average of 60 kilograms. Emus can be found throughout the continent, except in rain forests and very arid areas.

Though unable to fly, emus can run very fast at speeds of up to 60 kilometers per hour. They travel long distances in pairs or small groups, searching for water sources and food. Emus are very docile and curious, and are easily tamed in captivity. They feed on leaves, grasses, fruits, native plants, insects and other small animals.

Climate

Australia is a flat landmass without high mountain ranges and is surrounded by mostly warm oceans. The Tropic of Capricorn (南回归线) runs through the northern part of the country. Such geological features help prevent extremes of cold temperatures. In summer the average temperature is 29℃. Winter averages 13℃ for the country as a whole. Generally, coastal and highland areas, especially in the southeast, are cooler than interior locations, and the northern two-thirds of the continent, particularly the northwestern coast, is the hottest region. Australia is the driest of all the inhabited continents. Over 80 percent of the continent has an annual rainfall of less than 600 mm; the arid deserts, less than 250 mm. In most years, large portions of the continent are subject to droughts.

Long periods of dry, hot weather, high winds and natural vegetation that burns easily make Australia particularly vulnerable to bushfires.

● *Climatic Zones*

Despite regional variations, the climate of Australia is broadly divided into three zones.

Tropical Climate in the North

Northern Australia is highly influenced by ocean currents and has essentially two seasons: a hot, wet period with heavy rainfall mainly in February and March, when the northwestern monsoons (季风) prevail, and a warm, dry interval characterized by the prevalence of southeasterly winds. Average maximum temperatures range from 30℃ to 39℃. This region enjoys much greater annual precipitation than central and western Australia. Many points have average annual rainfall of 1,500 mm.

Arid Climate in the Inland

The huge inland areas (or Outback) are hot, dry and thinly populated. It receives the least amount of rain, from 120 to 1,000 mm annually. Thunderstorms are relatively common and occasional torrential downpours can cause widespread flooding and fill the usually dry inland salt "lakes" like Lake Eyre. Snow never falls in any Australian desert.

The maximum temperature ranges from 24℃ in the southern deserts to over 36℃ in the northern grasslands. The differences between day and night temperatures and also between summer and winter are much bigger than along the coasts.

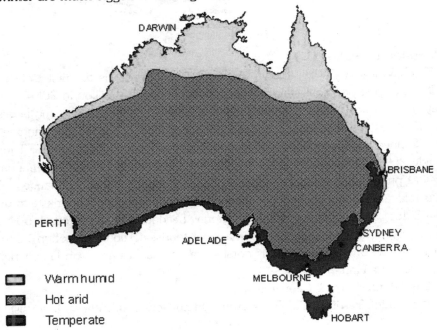

Understanding Australia and New Zealand

Temperate Climate in the South

The climate here is very moist and mild, receiving anywhere from 500 to 3,200 mm of rain annually. The average maximum temperature ranges from 12 to 27°C. In Australia, going south means traveling to a cooler region.

There are four distinct seasons. Because of its location in the Southern Hemisphere, seasons in Australia are opposite to those in the Northern Hemisphere. Summer, from December to February, is warm with occasional hot spells and mild nights. Winter, from June to August, is cool and showery although there are still plenty of sunny days.

III States, Territories & Large Cities

Australia has six states (Western Australia, South Australia, Queensland, New South Wales, Victoria and Tasmania) and two territories (Australian Capital Territory and Northern Territory).

New South Wales and Sydney

New South Wales (NSW), known as the Premier State, is the first British settlement in Australia. It is the most populous state with a population of 6.73 million in 2004.

Sydney, the state capital of New South Wales, is the country's oldest and largest city. It was founded in 1788 as the first European colony in Australia. Despite its beginning as a convict settlement, Sydney has grown into the economic powerhouse of the nation. The city provides approximately 25% of the country's total GDP and serves as the center for retail and wholesale trade as well as public administration and finance. The Australian Stock Exchange and the Reserve Bank of Australia are located in Sydney, as are the headquarters of 90 banks and more than half of Australia's top companies, and the regional headquarters for around 500 multinational corporations. Sydney is also a major international tourist destination, often referred to as the international gateway of Australia, and is notable for its beaches and twin landmarks: the Sydney Opera House and the Harbor Bridge.

Australian Capital Territory & Canberra

Australian Capital Territory (ACT) is surrounded by New South Wales. It consists of the inland part containing Canberra and Jervis Bay. Canberra is the state capital of the Australian Capital Territory and the federal capital of Australia. With a population of over 332,000, it is Australia's largest inland city.

Canberra is unusual among Australian cities as an entirely purpose-built, planned city. The site, previously a New South Wales rural area, was selected for the location of the nation's capital in 1908 as a compromise between Sydney and Melbourne, the two largest cities. Construction began in 1913 and the federal government moved to Canberra on 9 May, 1927, with the opening of the Provisional (临时的) Parliament House. Although the planned development of Canberra was hindered by the World Wars and the Great Depression, it emerged as a thriving city after World War II and has continued to expand. Canberra houses many breathtaking landmarks and heritage buildings, such as Parliament House, new and old, the High Court of Australia and federal government departments. There is also the Australian War Memorial and the National Gallery.

Queensland & Brisbane

Queensland (QLD), nicknamed the Sunshine State, is Australia's top tourism destination, well-known for its year round sunshine, magnificent coastline, endless sandy beaches, lush tropical rainforests and the natural wonder of the Great Barrier Reef.

Brisbane was founded as a penal (刑事的) colony in 1824. In 1859 it was declared the capital of Queensland. During World War II, General Douglas Macarthur directed the Allies' Pacific Campaign from the downtown headquarters. Today Brisbane is Australia's third largest city, a busy port, the hub of rail lines, and highways, and the business and cultural centre of Queensland.

Victoria & Melbourne

Victoria (VIC), the garden state, is the most densely populated and highly urbanized in Australia.

Melbourne is the capital city and most populous city of the State of Victoria, and the second most populous city in Australia with an approximate population of 4 million as of 2009. It was established in 1835 (47 years after the European settlement of Australia) as a pastoral township and was named in honor of William Lamb, the 2nd Viscount Melbourne (the Prime Minister of the United Kingdom during the reigns of King William IV and Queen Victoria) in 1837. Melbourne was declared a city by Queen Victoria in 1847 and became the capital of the newly-declared Colony of Victoria, when it was created from the Colony of New South Wales, in 1851.

When gold was discovered in the area during the 1850s (which sparked the Victorian gold rush), Melbourne was transformed into one of the largest and wealthiest cities in the world by the 1880s. Upon the federation of Australia in 1901, it served as the national capital and the seat of government for the newly-established Commonwealth of Australia until 1927—while the planned national capital of Canberra was being constructed.

The city is notable for its mix of Victorian and contemporary architecture, extensive tram network, Victorian parks and gardens, and diverse, multicultural society. Since 2002, Melbourne has been consistently ranked amongst the World's Most Livable Cities by The Economist magazine. It is also classified as a City of Literature by UNESCO, and is ranked as one of the top five university cities.

Melbourne has played host to a number of significant international and national events, including: the first sitting of the Parliament of Australia in 1901, Commonwealth Heads of Government Meeting in 1981, World Economic Forum in 2000, 2006 Commonwealth Games and G20 Summit in the same year. Melbourne is Australia's comedy capital, and hosts the world's second biggest comedy festival outside Edinburgh. In a country that is often labeled "sports mad", Melbourne has a reputation among Australians for being the national sporting capital, hosting a series of major sporting events such as the Melbourne Cup, the Australian Formula 1 Grand Prix, the Australian Open Tennis, the Australian Rules Football grand final and the 1956 Summer Olympics.

South Australia & Adelaide(阿德莱德)

Known as the Festival State, South Australia (SA) hosts over 500 festivals every year.

Adelaide, the capital of South Australia, is noted throughout Australia for its well-planned city streets and civic parks and gardens. Hosting festivals for everything from arts, wine and food to roses, car races and horse trials, the city has well established itself as the festival capital of Australia.

Western Australia & Perth(珀斯)

Western Australia (WA), the state of excitement, is the largest and most sparsely populated state. It offers an amazing variety of environments from the lush green forests in the south to the dry barren land in the north.

Perth, the state capital of Western Australia, is one of the most isolated cities in the world and contains around 70% of the state's residents.

Northern Territory & Darwin

Northern Territory, the Outback State, is a land of contrasts, ranging from fertile wetlands at the "Top End" to the arid and desert-like landscapes of the "Red Center."

Darwin is the state capital of Northern Territory. The city is notable among the capital cities for its history of major disasters. During WWII, Darwin was bombed 64 times by Japanese aircraft. It was the only locality in Australia to have come under substantial air attack. Darwin is also regularly subjected to heavy thunderstorms of its tropical climate. The city was almost completely destroyed by cyclone (飓风) Tracy in 1974. It was extensively rebuilt. Modern Darwin is a prosperous, cosmopolitan city, a booming tourist destination and an important military base for northern Australia. It serves both as the front door to Australia's northern region and as Australia's gateway to Asia.

Tasmania (塔斯马尼亚州) **& Hobart** (霍巴特)

Tasmania (TAS), the smallest state in Australia, is separated from the mainland by Bass Strait. The island, often called the holiday isle, attracts both Australians and overseas visitors with its unspoiled wilderness landscapes.

Hobart, the capital of Tasmania, is Australia's second oldest capital city after Sydney. It is small but full of 19th century buildings. Sandstone warehouses from the port's whaling days and houses of Georgian and Victorian eras have been remarkably well preserved.

Chapter 13 History, Politics and Economy of Australia

I History

The continent of Australia has been inhabited for over 40,000 years by Indigenous Australians. After some visits by fishermen from the north and by European explorers and merchants starting in the 17th century, the eastern half of the continent was claimed by the British in 1770 and officially settled as the penal colony of New South Wales on 26 January 1788. As the population grew and new areas were explored, another five largely self-governing Crown Colonies were successively established over the course of the 19th century.

On January 1, 1901, the six colonies federated and the Commonwealth of Australia was formed. Since federation, Australia has maintained a stable liberal democratic political system and remained a Commonwealth Realm. The current population of around 20.4 million is concentrated mainly in the large coastal cities of Sydney, Melbourne, Brisbane, Perth, and Adelaide.

Prehistory

The first human habitation of Australia is estimated to have occurred between 42,000 and 48,000 years ago. The first Australians were the ancestors of the current Indigenous Australians; they arrived via land bridges and short sea-crossings from present-day Southeast Asia.

There were no written records of human events in Australia before European colonization. The ancient traditions of Aborigines have been handed down orally through generations. The traditional way to educate about the history, culture and laws is storytelling, combined with art forms such as painting, singing and dancing.

European Colonization

The first definite sighting of Australia was in 1606 by the Dutch navigator Willem Janszoon. This date may be taken as a convenient starting point for the written history of Australia. Between 1606 and 1770, an estimated 54 european ships from a range of nations made contact with Australia. European voyagers charted parts of the north, west and south coasts of the continent which was then known as New Holland. However, no attempts to establish settlements were made.

In 1770, Englishman Lieutenant (海军上尉) James Cook sailed along and mapped the Australian east coast, which he named New South Wales and claimed for Britain. Very quickly Britain extended its claim to cover the whole of Australia. Given that Cook's discoveries would lead to the first European settlement of Australia, he is often considered its European discoverer.

The expedition's discoveries provided impetus (推动力) for the

Captain Cook

establishment of a penal colony there following the loss of the American colonies that had previously filled that role. The British then turned to Australia as a place to deport criminals. On May 13, 1787, the 11 ships of the First Fleet set sail from Portsmouth, England to Botany Bay in New South Wales under the command of Governor Arthur Philip. The party actually landed a short distance away at Sydney Cove, where the penal settlement was established on Jan. 26, 1788. The date is now celebrated as Australia Day and those convicts (罪犯) and marines (水手) on board are acknowledged as the Founders of Australia. The settlement was named Sydney after Britain's home secretary, Lord Sydney, who was responsible for the colony. Phillip became the first governor of the colony and encouraged exploration of the neighborhood.

Convicts worked as assigned laborers after their arrival in the colony. Unfortunately, few of them had farming or trade experience, nor did they understand the new environment. As a result, their initial attempts at farming failed. Through the 1790s the whole settlement faced perpetual food shortages. Natural food sources were largely limited to fish and kangaroo. The colony nearly starved and life was extremely hard for the first few years.

Some relief arrived with the 2nd fleet in 1790. It also brought to Sydney two men who were to play important roles in the colony's future. One was William Wentworth, who became a leader of the movement to abolish convict transportation and establish representative government. The other was John Macarthur, one of the founders of the Australian wool industry, which laid the foundations of Australia's future prosperity.

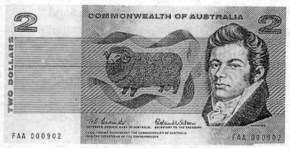

John Macarthur and the wool industry featured on the front of the $2 note

Gradually, the colony grew enough food to feed itself and the standard of living for the residents improved. From about 1815, the colony, under the governorship of Lachlan Macquarie, began to grow rapidly as free settlers arrived and new lands were opened up for farming. In 1813 a route was opened up through the Blue Mountains, west of Sydney, and westward settlement of New South Wales was begun.

Expansion of Colonization

Throughout the 19th century, Australia underwent the major processes that laid the foundation for its present society. The most prominent ones were the establishment of new colonies along the coasts and the opening up of the interior for sheep and cattle raising. European settlement of the continent proceeded gradually from the eastern coast toward the center.

The Indigenous Australian population, estimated at about 318,000 to 750,000 at the time of European settlement, declined steeply for 150 years following settlement, mainly because of infectious diseases combined with forced resettlement, brutal mistreatment and cultural disintegration. In 2006, 455,028 Aboriginal and Torres Strait Islander people were counted in the Census, representing an increase of 11% between the 2001 and 2006 Censuses.

Gold Rush

In 1851, Edward Hargraves (1816—1891), an immigrant from England, found gold near Bathurst in New South Wales. Word quickly spread. Within a week there were hundreds of people digging there for gold. Edward can never have imagined that his discovery would mark the beginning of the Australian gold rush. Shortly afterwards gold was discovered in even greater abundance in the newly formed Victoria. Later significant deposits were uncovered in other states except South Australia. From 1851 to 1861, Australia exported more than 124 million pounds worth of gold alone. By the turn of the century it had become the world's largest producer of gold.

There is no doubt that the gold rushes had a profound impact on the development of Australia's economical, political and social systems. Since 1851 many adventurers were attracted to Australia from all over the globe. The total population of Australia increased from 430,000 in 1851 to 1.7 million in 1871. Within a few years new arrivals outnumbered the convicts transported in the previous 70 years. They began to demand trial by jury, representative government, a free press and the other symbols of liberty and democracy.

Among all the foreign gold diggers, the biggest faction was Chinese. The Chinese immigrants referred to the Australian gold fields as "Xin Jin Shan". The Californian gold rush was in decline by the 1850s and had become known as

The 1850s gold rush attracted many Chinese people to Australia in search of a fortune.

"Jiu Jin Shan". Motivated by racism and by the fear of fiercer competition, miners and colonists launched campaigns to oust(驱逐) the Chinese from the goldfields. In 1856 Victoria restricted the entry of Chinese. Eventually, the exclusion of all but European settlers gave the colonies a "White Australia" policy.

The gold rushes were followed by rapid economic expansion. The goldfield towns grew quickly and sparked a huge boost in business investment and stimulated the market for local produce. The thriving economy also spurred the development of state infrastructure. The 1850s witnessed the construction of the first railway and the operation of the first telegraphs.

Federation

Before 1900, there was no actual country called Australia. The six colonies on the continent, having individually gained responsible government between 1855 and 1890, managed most of their own affairs like six separate countries while remaining part of the British Empire. The Colonial Office in London retained control of some matters, notably foreign affairs, defense and international shipping. On 1 January 1901, federation of the colonies was achieved after a decade of planning, consultation and voting, and the Commonwealth (联邦) of Australia was born, as a Dominion of the British Empire. The Australian Capital Territory (ACT) was formed from New South Wales in 1911 to provide a location for the proposed new federal capital of Canberra (Melbourne was the capital from 1901 to 1927). The Northern Territory was transferred from the control of the South Australian government to the Commonwealth in 1911.

Australia in Two World Wars

The First World War began when Britain and Germany went to war in August 1914. As part of the British Empire, Australia sent some 330,000 soldiers (out of a population of only about 4,500,000) overseas during the war. Troops were sent to take possession of German New Guinea and some other islands and many more to fight at Gallipoli, on the Turkish coast, in France and in the Middle East. Both Australian victories and losses on World War I battlefields contributed significantly to Australia's national identity.

In 1939 Australia entered World War II again as an ally of Britain. In 1940—41, Australian forces played prominent roles in campaigns against Germany and Italy in Europe, the Mediterranean and North Africa, as well as against Japan in south-east Asia and other parts of the Pacific. At the peak of its war effort in 1943, Australia's armed forces numbered about 633,400—from a population of 7,300,000.

After Singapore fell in February, 1942, Japanese aircraft bombed towns in north-west

Australia and Japanese midget(小型的) submarines attacked Sydney harbor. With many of its troops fighting in North Africa, Australia was suddenly faced with the threat of Japanese invasion. With Britain preoccupied with her own fight for survival, Australia turned to the United States as a new ally and protector.

On 7 May 1945 the German High Command authorized the signing of an unconditional surrender on all fronts: The war in Europe was over. On the 14 August 1945 Japan accepted the Allied demand for unconditional surrender. For Australians, it meant that the Second World War was finally over.

For Australia, as for many nations, two world wars remain the most costly conflicts in terms of deaths and casualties. In 1914 the male population of Australia was less than 3 million, yet, 416,809 of them enlisted, of which over 60,000 were killed and 156,000 wounded, gassed, or taken prisoner. By the end of WWII almost a million Australians, both men and women, had served in the armed forces. 39,366 were killed and 23,477 wounded by enemy action during the war.

Postwar Australia

The years after the war brought increased economic activity and industrial expansion. The need for more farmers and industrial workers led to highly successful attempts to attract European immigrants. Since the 1970s and the abolition of the White Australia Policy, immigration from Asia and other parts of the world was also encouraged. As a result, Australia's demography(统计学), culture and image of itself were radically transformed.

The final constitutional ties between Australia and the United Kingdom ended in 1986 with the passing of the Australia Act 1986, ending any British role in the Australian States, and ending judicial appeals (上诉) to the UK Privy Council (枢密院). Australian voters rejected a move to become a republic in 1999 by a 55% majority, but the result is generally viewed in terms of dissatisfaction with the specifics of the proposed republican model rather than attachment to the monarchy. In its postwar foreign policy, Australia allied itself closely with the United States and participated in Asian affairs.

II Political System

The Commonwealth of Australia is a constitutional monarchy with a federal parliamentary system of government—"Constitutional" because the powers and procedures of the Commonwealth Government are defined by a written constitution, and "Monarchy" because Australia's Head of State is the monarch of the United Kingdom.

Constitution

The Constitution of Australia, which came into force on 1 January 1901, is based on British parliamentary traditions and includes elements of the United States system. It establishes the Commonwealth government, defining its structure, powers, procedures and the rights and obligations of the states in relation to the Commonwealth.

Other pieces of legislation that have constitutional significance for Australia are the Statute of Westminster 1931 and the Australia act 1986. Together, these Acts had the effect of severing all constitutional links between Australia and the United Kingdom. Therefore, even though the

Constitution was originally given legal force by an act of the United Kingdom parliament, the Australian Constitution can be amended only by Australian people through a national referendum (公民投票) in which all adults on the electoral roll must participate. Any constitutional changes must be approved by a double majority—a national majority of electors as well as a majority of electors in a majority of the states and territories (at least four of the six). The double majority provision makes alterations to the Constitution difficult, and since Federation in 1901 only eight out of 44 proposals to amend the Constitution have been approved.

Separation of Powers

Separation of powers refers to a model in which political powers and responsibilities are distributed among several, often three, branches: the legislature (立法的), the executive(行政的) and the judiciary(司法的). It is believed that separation of powers protects democracy and prevents tyranny. Under the Australian Constitution, the three arms of federal government are:

* Legislature: The Commonwealth Parliament
* Executive: The Queen, whose executive power is exercisable by the Governor-General, the Prime Minister, Ministers and their Departments
* Judiciary: The High Court of Australia and subsidiary Federal courts

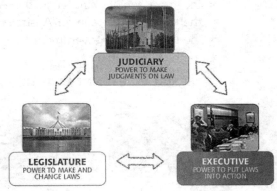

The diagram illustrates the principle of the separation of powers.

Each arm of federal government has separate and distinctive powers and areas of responsibility.

● ***Executive***

◇ Queen of Australia

As a member of the Commonwealth of Realms, Australia recognizes the British monarch as sovereign. Thus, Queen Elizabeth II has been the reigning monarch of Australia since February 6, 1952. She is officially called Queen of Australia when in Australia or performing duties on behalf of Australia abroad.

◇ **Republicanism**

Republicanism has always been there in the Australian background. It is a movement to change Australia's status as a constitutional monarchy to a republic. Republicans believe that their head of state should be an Australian citizen instead of the British monarch. In the 1990s the issue was bought to the forefront of national debate by the Australian Labor Party which first made republicanism its official policy. In 1999, Australians were asked to vote in a referendum to determine whether their nation would become a republic. The referendum was defeated and Australia decided to remain a constitutional monarchy. In recent years the prevailing mood towards the monarchy suggested by most polls is one of indifference or apathy (冷漠).

◇**Governor-General (总督)**

In Australia, the Queen is constitutionally represented by the Governor-General at the federal level and by the Governors at the state level. The Governor-General is appointed by the Queen on the recommendation of the Australian Prime Minister.

According to the Australian Constitution, the executive power of the Commonwealth is vested in the Queen and exercisable by the Governor-General as the Queen's representative. However, by convention, the Governor-General acts almost wholly upon the advice of the Prime Minister and parliamentary ministers. The role of the Governor-General is primarily symbolic and cultural. In practice, the Prime Minister and the cabinet are in control of government departments and run the business of government.

The Governor-General usually holds office for five years. He/She serves as a symbol of the legal authority under which all governments and agencies operate. Possibly the most important duty of the Governor-General is to encourage, articulate and represent those things that unite Australians as a nation.

◇ **Prime Minister & Cabinet**

The Prime Minister is:
* the most senior minister in the Australian Parliament
* the key spokesperson for Australia
* the leader of the government
* the head of Cabinet.

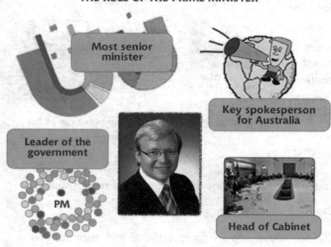

The diagram illustrates the role of Prime Minister.

In practice, the executive power is possessed by the Prime Minister and the Cabinet. But neither of the two is mentioned in the Australian Constitution. Their roles and functions derive constitutionally from their membership of the Federal Executive Council (联邦行政咨询委员会) and from convention.

The office of Prime Minister is in practice the most powerful political office in the Commonwealth. The Prime Minister is head of government for Australia and holds office on commission (任命) from the Governor-General. Except in rare circumstances, the Prime Minister is always the leader of the political party which has the most seats in the House of Representatives.

The Cabinet, a council of senior ministers presided over by the Prime Minister, is responsible for managing the policy directions and business of the government. Major policy and legislative proposals are decided by the Cabinet. The Prime Minister selects ministers for Cabinet positions. These ministers meet at least once a week to discuss vital issues without the Governor-General. Since the Australian Constitution does not recognize the Cabinet as a legal entity (实体), its decisions have no legal force. Decisions made by the Cabinet should be ratified by the Federal Executive Council, a body composed of the Governor-General and ministers. The Executive Council makes no real decisions, serving mainly to give formal approval to decisions of the Cabinet.

● *Legislature*

◇ **Bicameral Parliament** (两院制议会)

Federal legislative power in Australia is vested in a bicameral parliament, consisting of the Queen represented by the Governor-General, a Senate and a House of Representatives. The essence of a parliamentary democracy is that citizens elect representatives to make laws on their behalf.

The Senate consists of 76 members (12 from each state and 2 from each territory). Senators are popularly elected under a form of proportional representation; senators from states are elected to six-year terms and senators from territories are elected to three-year terms. According to the Australian Constitution, the House should have about twice as many members as the Senate. The number of members from each state is proportional to its population, but must be at least five. As of the 2001 elections the House has 150 members, all of whom are directly elected to three-year terms. Members of the House of Representatives reflect the interests of their electorates when they make speeches. They also assist people in their electorate to solve problems about such things as pensions, migration and taxation.

The two Houses have equal powers, except that there are restrictions on the power of the Senate to introduce or directly amend some kinds of financial legislation. The role of members and senators is to:

* set up parliamentary committees to examine government bills
* investigate how the government spends money in the budget by participating in estimates committees, which are held twice a year
* question the government each day in Question Time in both the House of Representatives and the Senate

Question Time

In Question Time, members and senators (the legislature) question and scrutinize the Prime Minister and ministers in the government (the executive).

◇**Functions of Parliament**

Parliament has three main functions: legislation, scrutiny (examining the government), and formation of government.

The most important function of Parliament is to make new laws and change or improve old ones. Laws and major policy decisions are made in the House of Representatives and reviewed in the Senate. A bill becomes a Law only after it has been passed in identical form by both Houses of the Parliament and has been approved by the Governor-General.

The government or executive implements the laws and other decisions of the Parliament. However, the Parliament likes to check or scrutinize what the government does, especially how the government spends money. The opposition plays an important part in the scrutiny activities of Parliament.

Another function of the Parliament is to provide the members of the Executive Government from its membership. After a general election the political party with the support of a majority of members in the House of Representatives becomes the governing party and its leader becomes the Prime Minister. The Prime Minister and his/her Cabinet are responsible to Parliament, and through it, to the people.

● *Judiciary* (司法系统)

◇**Law**

The law of Australia consists of statute law and common law. Although Parliament can override common law by passing legislation, this does not mean that Parliament is dominant over judges and the courts. The strict insulation of judicial power is a fundamental principle of the Constitution of Australia. The independence of the courts and judges, and their separation from the legislative and executive branches of government, is regarded as of great importance.

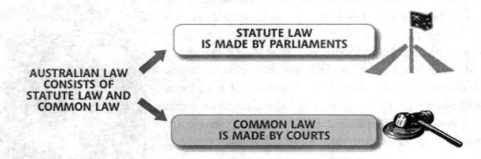

◇ **Courts**

The Constitution establishes the High Court of Australia and empowers the Commonwealth Parliament to create other federal courts including the Federal Court of Australia, the Family Court of Australia and the Federal Magistrates Court of Australia.

High Court of Australia

The High Court of Australia, the highest in the Australian court hierarchy, consists of a chief justice and six other justices, each of whom is formally appointed by the Governor-General. The functions of the High Court are to interpret and apply the law of Australia, to decide disputes involving acts of the federal parliament and to hear appeals from federal, state and territory courts. The Court is the final court of appeal for the whole Australia.

Three Levels of Government

The federal, state and local governments make up the 3 levels of government in Australia. Each level has different responsibilities.

The Federal Government passes laws affecting the whole nation. Its legislative power is limited to a few key areas, including coinage, taxation, banking, insurance, defense, foreign affairs, postal and telecommunications services, trade and immigration.

Although the six states federated to form the Commonwealth Government, they still have their own constitutions and retain the legislative power over matters not controlled by the Commonwealth. However, if a state law conflicts with a federal law, the federal law prevails. Each State has a Governor, who is appointed by the Queen on the advice of the Premier of that State. State governments have the same divisions of legislature, executive, and judiciary as the

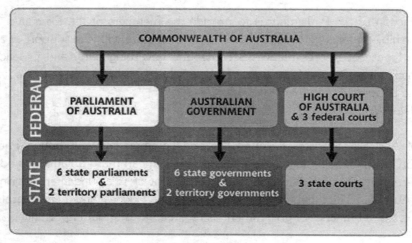

Australian Federation

Chapter 13   History, Politics and Economy of Australia

Commonwealth Government. The High Court of Australia acts as an umpire(仲裁人), interpreting the constitution and resolving disputes between the Commonwealth and the states.

Territories can be administered by the Commonwealth Government, or they can be granted a right of self-government.

Within each state or territory, hundreds of local governments are established to take responsibility for a number of community services. Local governments have a legislature and an executive but no judiciary. Local governments are usually referred to as councils.

Major Parties

Three political parties dominate Australian politics.

* **The Liberal Party of Australia (LP)** is a party of the centre-right which broadly represents business, the suburban middle classes and many rural people.
* **The National Party of Australia (NP)** is a conservative party which represents rural interests. In practice, the Liberal and National parties have frequently combined in coalition(联合) governments and opposition, at both the federal and state levels.
* **The Australian Labor Party (ALP)** is a social democratic party founded by the trade union movement and broadly represents the urban working class, although it increasingly has a base of middle class support.

III   National Economy

Currency	Australian Dollar ($A or A$, AU$ or $AU, AUD)
Exchange rates	Australian dollars per US dollar: 1.3285 (2006), 1.3095 (2005), 1.3598 (2004), 1.5419 (2003), 1.8406 (2002)
Trade organizations	APEC, WTO and OECD
GDP (PPP)	$674.6 billion (2006 est.)
Inflation (CPI)	3.5% (2006 est.)
Labor force	10.74 million (2006 est.)
Main industries	mining, industrial and transportation equipment, food processing, chemicals, steel
Agriculture products	wheat, barley, sugarcane, fruits; cattle, sheep, poultry
Export goods	coal, gold, meat, wool, alumina, iron ore, wheat, machinery and transport equipment
Import goods	machinery and transport equipment, computers and office machines, telecommunication equipment and parts, crude oil and petroleum products

Australia has a prosperous, Western-style market economy. Australia's annual GDP has been growing by an average of 3.3 percent since 1990, well above the rate of world growth and ahead of other developed economies. GDP in 2006 reached $674.6 billion. The stable economic growth is coupled with low inflation. Inflation rate in 2006 was 3.5 per cent.

Rich in natural resources, Australia is a major exporter of agricultural products, minerals, metals, and fossil fuels. Primary products account for 57% of the value of total exports, so a downturn (低迷时期) in world commodity prices can have a big impact on the economy.

The Australian economy is dominated by its service sector, yet it is the agricultural and mining sectors that account for 65% of its exports. The service sector of the economy, including tourism, education, and financial services, comprises 70% of GDP. Agriculture and natural resources comprise 3% and 5% of GDP but contribute substantially to export performance. Australia's largest export markets include Japan, China, the US, South Korea and New Zealand.

Agriculture
● *Crops*

Agriculture in Australia is a major industry and employs only 3.6 percent of the total workforce. The country is self-sufficient in almost all foodstuffs and is a major exporter of wool, meat, dairy products, and wheat. 80% of all agricultural production is exported. Although only 6.4 percent of Australia's total land area is arable (适于耕种的), this acreage is of great economic importance. In Australia, farm sizes range from relatively small part-time farms to operations of more than 5000 hectares. In general, farming is characterized by large scale, highly mechanized and efficient operations.

● *Horticulture (园艺)*

Horticulture is one of Australia's largest industries, and produces a wide variety of fruits, vegetables, nuts, nursery products and cut flowers. Major horticultural sectors include grapes, macadamias (澳洲坚果), garden plants, potatoes, tomatoes, citrus (柑橘类) fruits, apples, bananas and chestnuts (板栗). Australia is one of the few countries that produce licit (合法的)opium (鸦片) for medicinal purposes. This industry, centered in Tasmania, is subject to strict controls.

● *Livestock*

The arid and semiarid regions provide the most extensive type of soils through the Australia continent. These soils, with the recurrent (周期性发生的) droughts, are more suitable for light livestock grazing than for farming.

● *Sheep Industry*

Wool has been a staple(主要产品) of the Australian economy since the colonial period, and it was important to the development of agriculture as the country's largest industry. Australia remains the world's largest wool producer and exporter. The country usually produces more than 25 percent of the world's yearly output. Historically, up to 90% of Australian wool was exported. Lamb has become an increasingly important product as the sheep industry has moved its focus from wool production to the production of prime lamb. Live export of cattle and sheep from Australia to Asia and the Middle East is a large part of Australian meat export.

Although sheep are farmed Australia-wide, 36% of the flock is in New South Wales. About half of the country's wool is produced in New South Wales and Western Australia.

● *Beef Industry*

Australia is one of the world's leading producers of cattle and was the world's second largest exporter of beef after Brazil in 2004—05. Over 60% of its total beef production is exported primarily to the United States and Japan. The industry has benefited from the discovery of BSE (also known as mad cow disease) in Canada, Japan and the United States, as Australia is free of the disease. The country produces both beef and dairy cattle. Dairy products are Australia's fourth most valuable agricultural export. Australia accounts for 16 percent of world dairy product exports and is ranked third in terms of world dairy trade. Dairying is now mainly concentrated in Victoria and Tasmania.

Chapter 13 History, Politics and Economy of Australia

Forestry

Australia has the sixth largest area of forest in the world, 4% of the world's forests, with only Russia (20%), Brazil (12%), Canada (8%), the USA (8%) and China (5%) having more. There are 164 million hectares of forest in Australia—covering 21 percent of the continent. That's about 8.2 hectares of forest for each Australian, one of the highest areas per person in the world (the world average is 0.6 hectares).

About 13 percent of Australia's 163 million hectares of native forest are in conservation reserves, which compare favorably with a global average of 11 percent. Over 83,000 people are directly employed in Australia's forest industries. Over 80 percent of these employees work in the wood and paper manufacturing industries.

Fishery

Australia has the world's third largest fishing zone covering 11 million square kilometers and extending 200 nautical miles out to sea. The commercial fishing industry ranks fifth in value amongst Australian rural industries after beef, wool, wheat and dairy. Production focuses on high value export species. The export trade is dominated by five key products, rock lobster, pearls, prawns, tuna and abalone (鲍鱼).

Aquaculture (水产业), or fish farming, has grown rapidly in every state and territory since 1980, and income from this industry rose more than threefold during the 1990s. Pearls and trochus shells (有珍珠层的圆锥形螺壳) have been harvested off the northern coast since the 1800s. Darwin, Broome, and Thursday Island are the main pearling centers, Australia now produces around 62 percent of the world's South Pacific cultured pearls. The cultured pearl industry is dominated by Japanese-Australian ventures.

Mining

The mining industry has been an important factor in the social and economic growth of Australia. The gold discoveries of the 1850s were responsible for the first big wave of free immigration and for the settlement of some inland areas. The mining sector has expanded significantly since the 1970s, with major discoveries of iron ore, petroleum, coal, and natural gas. Today, Australia is self-sufficient in most minerals of economic significance, and in several cases is among the world's leading producers. The minerals industry in general is the country's largest export earner.

Australia is the world's largest producer of both gem or near-gem diamonds and industrial-grade diamonds, producing about two-fifths of the global total. Australia accounted for some 13 percent of the world's gold production in 1998, placing it third in the world rankings after South Africa and the United States. About three-fourths of the nation's output is mined in Western Australia.

About 96 percent of Australia's iron-ore production also takes place in Western Australia. Almost all of the iron-ore is exported to Japan; Australia is now Japan's major supplier. In the late 1990s Australia was the world's largest producer and second largest exporter of bauxite (铝矾土,铁铝氧石), the largest producer and exporter of alumina (氧化铝) and the third largest exporter of aluminum. (Aluminum is the world's most abundant metal, and it only occurs in compounds in nature. Most commonly it is extracted from bauxite which is found in brazil, Australia and Africa.)

Coal is the country's top export earner and coal mining is heavily concentrated in New South Wales and Queensland.

Manufacturing

Principal branches of the Australian manufacturing sector by value of production are metals and metal products, food products, transportation equipment, machinery, chemicals and chemical products, textiles and clothing, wood and paper products, and printing, publishing and recording media. Despite Australia's wealth of mineral resources, mineral processing is limited. Manufacturing facilities are concentrated in New South Wales (especially in Sydney and Newcastle), Victoria (primarily in the Melbourne metropolitan area), and secondarily in the state capitals and main provincial centers.

Tourism

As one of Australia's most important industries, tourism grew rapidly in the late 20th century, and it now represents one of the most dynamic sectors in the Australian economy, accounting for more than 500,000 jobs in the late 1990s. International tourism received a major boost from the highly successful Summer Olympic Games hosted in Sydney in 2000.

The strong growth in domestic tourism has tapped the expanding range of attractions in each state and territory-amusement and theme parks, zoos, art galleries and museums, certain mines and factories, national parks, historic sites and wineries. Some of the most popular attractions are Queensland's spectacular Great Barrier Reef, the Northern Territory's Kakadu National Park, and the famous beach resorts in the Brisbane, Cairns, and Sydney regions.

Banking & Finance

● *Banking System*

The first Australian bank was established in Sydney in 1817. The current banking system includes:

* the Reserve Bank of Australia
* Big Four banks: ① the Commonwealth Bank of Australia, ② the Australia and New Zealand Banking Group, ③ the Westpac Banking Corporation, and ④ the National Australia Bank
* a variety of credit unions, credit cooperatives, and building societies （建屋互助会） operating partly as banks, finance companies and money-market corporations, as well as some foreign banks.

Reserve Bank of Australia is Australia's central bank with responsibility for regulating monetary policy including the official interest rate. Although some 50 banks were operating at the beginning of the 21st century, more than half of the total banking assets were controlled by the Big Four institutions.

Australia has become a significant player in the global financial industry as a result of its strong domestic and international economic record. The country has the highest percentage of shareholders in the world. Almost 54 per cent of the adult population own shares in publicly listed companies. The Australian Securities Exchange (ASE) is the primary stock exchange in Australia. It is the product of the merger of the Australian Stock Exchange and the Sydney Futures Exchange in December 2006.

● *Currency*

Australia used pounds, shillings and pence until 1966, when it adopted the decimal system with the Australian dollar divided into 100 cents. The basic unit Australian dollar is often abbreviated to $, A$ or $A, $AU or AU$.

Australia's notes are printed on plastic (polymer 聚合体), a technology pioneered in Australia. These notes are more counterfeit-proof （防伪造的）, durable and cleaner than traditional paper money.

Brightly colored Australian notes, printed by Note Printing Australia, come in $100, $50, $20, $10 and $5.

Australian coins are produced by the Royal Australian Mint. There are $2, $1, 50 cent, 20 cent, 10 cent, and 5 cent units.

◇ *Coins*

The Australian dollar replaced the Australian pound on 14 February 1966. At the time of introduction, 1, 2, 5, 10, 20, and 50 cent coins were issued. $1 and $2 coins followed in 1984 and 1988 respectively. The one and two cent coins were discontinued in 1991 and withdrawn from circulation. All Australian coins have the portrait of Queen Elizabeth II on the front. The reverse of the:

$2 coin features an Aboriginal tribal elder, the Southern Cross and native grass trees.

$1 coin features kangaroos.

50c coin features Australia's Coat of Arms.

20c coin features the platypus (soon to be replaced with an image of Sir Donald Bradman).

10c coin features a male lyrebird (琴鸟) dancing.

5c coin features an echidna.

2c and 1c coins were phased out in 1990 and 50c coins frequently feature commemorative designs.

★ *Banknotes*

A brief monetary history:

British currency, till 1914

Australian Pound = 20 Shillings = 240 Pence, till 1966

Australian Dollar = (0.50 Pound) = 100 Cents, from 1966

Transport

Because of Australia's great size and its relatively small population, transport has always been a highly significant part of the infrastructure of the national economy. The total length of operating rail networks in Australia is almost 40,000 kilometers. The main lines were laid down in the second half of the 19th century. Australia's trains are clean, comfortable and safe, and for the most part service standards and facilities are perfectly adequate.

Australia has approximately 811,601 km of roads. About 40 percent of the overall length is bitumen- (沥青) or concrete-paved, including more than 16,000 km of state highway. Over 12 million vehicles (including motor bikes) are registered in Australia, including half a million trucks and more than 60,000 buses called "coaches." Australia has one national coach operator: Greyhound Australia (no relation to Greyhound in the US). Tasmania is serviced by Redline Coaches. While public transport remains important in urban areas, cars have increasingly provided the most convenient means of travel between home and work and to social and recreational activities. More than 14 million people have a driver's license.

A comprehensive network of airline services links major cities and even remote settlements. Domestic lines carry about 25 million passengers yearly. Because of the long distances between cities and the country's ideal flying conditions, Australians are especially accustomed to air travel. International airports are located near each of the mainland capitals and near Cairns and Townsville.

Ocean shipping is vital to the national economy. Australian companies retain a virtual monopoly on coastal interstate trade, but international shipping is nearly all foreign-controlled. Major ports include Melbourne, Sydney, and Fremantle (in Western Australia).

Chapter 14　Culture and Society of Australia

I　Culture

Multiculturalism is Australia's main social policy. At times people think of Australians as Anglo-Australians. However, a large number of people from a variety of other backgrounds are also Australians. This means people in Australia come from a wide variety of cultural, linguistic and religious backgrounds. Generally speaking, Australian culture belongs to Western culture. It has inherited English and European cultural tradition and contains aboriginal, Asian and American culture. Consequently, a multi-culture and multination cultural system came out.

● *Aboriginal Culture*

Australia is the land on which the Aborigines lived and developed generation by generation. Therefore its culture has been consequentially influenced by Aboriginal culture. The Aborigines made a great contribution to Australian culture. For example, the origin of many Australian place names is closely related with its society, economy, geography and history. The word *Kangaroo* came from Aboriginal language, later "kangaroo land" became the nickname of Australia.

● *Culture of English and European Tradition*

Since 1788, the primary basis of Australian culture until the mid-20th century has been Anglo-Celtic, although distinctive Australian features had been evolving from the environment and Indigenous culture.

Australia follows the English pattern and develops gradually from England's immigrants. In politics, Australia is the member of Commonwealth of Nation. In language, English is its parent language. In culture, Australia has inherited lots of traditions of Britain. Therefore, Australia is sentimentally attached to its mother land, Britain. This complex can be seen from its national song "Advance Australia Fair." Some of the lines are as follows: *Britannia then shall surely know; beyond wide ocean's rolls; her sons in fair Australia's land; still keep a British soul.* Due to the blood relationship and the traditional relations, in the Australian minds, Australia is still "a British inalienable part of empire." In an Australian heart, old land, old country, old home are all synonyms (同义字) of Britain. To visit England is to go home. The world famous harbor Sydney is nominated under the name of a British minister at that time. Some states' names such as New South Wales, Victoria, Queensland all have deep connection with its mother country, Britain.

The founding of Australia, 26 January 1788

● **Asian Culture**

Australian mainstream culture, in the key of English and European culture, has melted lots of Asian factors. In Australian towns, restaurants and shops run by Chinese, Vietnamese, Japanese and Koreans can be easily found. Chinese people have made great contribution to Australian culture. In Australian English, there are many words with Chinese characteristics: *Fang-tan*(源于中国的一种赌博);*Like a pakapu ticket*(源自19世纪后半叶来自广东的华人在澳洲使用的一种彩票,澳洲人看不懂,便称指为"不可思议的事物");*Yum cha*(广东话

的早茶); and *Dim-sim* (点心).

- **American Culture**

Over the past 50 years, Australian culture has been strongly influenced by American popular culture (particularly television and cinema). After World War I, American jazz, dancing and popular music was introduced to Australia and became predominant. Afterwards a lot of choreographic(舞台舞蹈的) and jazz music was widely accepted and became more and more popular as an anthem for the youth generation fighting for personal freedom. From the 1920s, a number of Hollywood films gushed into Australia. During World War II Australia was a popular holiday place for American soldiers.

With the coming of modern American culture, American English, as the carrier of its culture, was introduced into Australia. Some phrases reflect the admiration towards Americans. Australians who imitated the manners or speech of American soldiers on holiday are called *Woolloomooloo Yanks*; women who liked to accompany American soldiers are named *Yank-happy*; the word *widge* refers to women who behave wildly and like wearing American fashionable dresses. In the 1950s, some common American expressions were used by Australians too, such as *hi, so long, sure, wow, guy, see you*, etc. Even the name of Australian currency was changed to dollar and cent from pound and penny.

Plenty of immigrants from all over the world not only changed Australians' eating custom and living pattern, but also enriched their thought and culture. They brought their civilization to the Australian continent, and molded colorful Australian culture.

II Education

An Overview

Australia's educational institutions provide high-quality education to students from all backgrounds. Diversity and quality underpin (支撑) Australia's education services. Schools develop students' skills and confidence; university graduates are in many of the world's leading research, innovation and problem solving teams; and the vocational and technical education sector is competency-based and industry-led. In international education and English-language training, Australia has developed a reputation as a world leader.

The Constitution of Australia allocates primary responsibility for school education to state and territory governments. The Federal Government is mainly responsible for funding higher education and provides supplementary funding to the states. Education in Australia follows the three-tier (等级) model which includes primary education, followed by secondary education and tertiary education (高等教育). The school year varies between states and institutions, but generally runs from late January until mid-December. Most states and territories operate on a four-term per year system, with a short holiday between terms and a long summer holiday in December and January. Universities normally operate over two semesters and the academic year begins in mid to late February and ends in November.

Primary & Secondary Education

Schooling in Australia is compulsory for all children between 6 and 15 years of age (16 in Tasmania). Generally, schooling lasts for 13 years, with some variations across states and territories. It starts with a preparatory year followed by primary and secondary school.

The year before a child is due to attend primary school is the main year for pre-school education. Most Australian children attend pre-school centers, while actually pre-school in

Australia is not compulsory.

Children begin primary school at the age of five. Primary schools provide basic education for children up to 12 or 13 years of age, after which they transfer to a secondary school. The most common type of secondary school is the co-educational (男女合校的) comprehensive or multi-purpose high school, which offers a wide range of subjects.

Of Australian students attending primary and secondary schools, about two-thirds are enrolled in government schools, with the other third in independent schools, mainly Roman Catholic schools. Government schools are free and receive the majority of their government funding from state and territory governments, while independent schools, both religious and secular, charge fees and the majority of their government funding comes from the Federal Government.

Both government and independent schools are required to follow the same curriculum (课程) frameworks. All schools provide subjects in the eight key learning areas: English, mathematics, studies of society and the environment, science, arts, languages other than English, technology and personal development, health and physical education. At secondary level, choice and diversity are increased as schools are able to offer a wide range of subjects. Around nine out of every ten Australian secondary schools also offer vocational education programs in addition to the standard school curriculum.

Two options (选项) are open to students when they complete three or four years of high school. They may choose to receive further education at a technical or agricultural college or other training institutions. Students who choose to continue at the high school level undertake two more years of study before taking an examination coordinated by the state for the purpose of university entrance. Due to limited space, not every student can expect to obtain a university place. Entrance numbers are primarily based on the number of students for whom the Commonwealth authorities are able to provide financial support.

Tertiary Education: VET

There are two types of tertiary education programs: those offered by institutions and industry in the vocational education and training (VET) sector, and those offered by universities and other higher education providers.

Vocational education and training provides students with the skills required in a modern economy and delivers competency-based training that is practical and career-oriented. This sector is divided into two sections: a nationally recognized government system of Technical and Further Education (TAFE) and private providers. TAFE is the largest provider of tertiary education courses in Australia with about 250 institutes and over a million students including about 41,000 international students.

Industry training is common to all the VET programs. The vast range of courses under this category includes information technology, business and management, marketing and communications, health, science, design and the arts, television production and media, environmental studies and land management, sport and recreation, engineering and building, and hospitality and tourism. English language training and university preparation courses are also offered.

The awards in VET sector are certificates(证书), advanced certificates, associate diplomas (文凭), and diplomas. Studying at TAFE level is also described as a way of gaining entry to Australia's universities. Most TAFE institutes have arrangements with specific universities, enabling students to gain credit for a portion of their study undertaken at TAFE.

Tertiary Education: University

The Australian higher education system comprises (in 2007):

* 39 universities, of which 37 are public institutions and 2 are private;
* 1 Australian branch of an overseas university;

* 4 other self-accrediting(授权的) higher education institutions;
* non-self-accrediting higher education providers accredited by state and territory authorities.

The non-self-accrediting higher education providers form a very diverse group of specialized, mainly private, providers that range in size and include theological (神学的) colleges and other providers that offer courses in areas such as business, information technology, natural therapies, hospitality, health, law and accounting. Degrees in Australia can take from three to six years to complete and are divided into two distinct tracks: the ordinary degree and the honors degree. The ordinary degree varies in length by field and university. Arts subjects are typically completed in three years, sciences in four years, and medicine in five years. An honors degree is required for a student to advance to the master's level. After completion of the ordinary degree the university invites a student to complete the honors degree. The honors degree takes an additional year to complete and involves mainly independent study leading to a research dissertation.

Diversity and autonomy are central features of Australian universities. Each university has the freedom to specify its own mission and purpose, modes of teaching and research, constitution of the student body and the range and content of educational programs. The majority of students live at home and attend university in their home state. In all universities, students have substantial control of the student unions, councils and athletic clubs. Compulsory fees that support these activities are collected from students by the universities.

2009 Australia University Rankings from World Top 200

University	Aus rank	World rank
Australian National University （澳洲国立大学）	1	16
The University of Sydney （悉尼大学）	2	37
The University of Melbourne （墨尔本大学）	3	38
University of Queensland （昆士兰大学）	4	43
University of New south wales （新南威尔士大学）	5	45
Monash University （莫纳什大学）	6	47
The University of Western Australia （西澳大学）	7	83
University of Adel （阿德雷得大学）	8	106
Macquarie University （麦考瑞大学）	9	182

Distance Education

Australia is a huge continent and is home to some of the most geographically isolated and remote communities in the world. How do children living in these communities go to school? The answer is Community Government Schooling and the School of the Air (SOA). Community schools provide an opportunity for children to attend schools and to grow up in their communities.

The School of the Air is a general term for correspondence schools catering (满足……需要) for the primary and early secondary education of children in remote Australia. School classes were conducted via shortwave radio from 1951 through 2002. Today's SOA students use high frequency (HF) radio transceivers to receive their lessons. A transceiver is a special type of radio that allows the user to both send and receive messages. This means that students can talk to each other as well as the teacher during classes. SOA teachers also try to visit as many students as possible at least once a year. A SOA covers all the same curriculum as any other school in the state, so SOA students are not disadvantaged.

The Australian National University (ANU)
ANU is a public research university founded on August 1, 1948 and located in Canberra. The university is often ranked as leading university in Australia on a number of measures.

The University of Sydney
Founded in 1850, it is the oldest and one of the largest university in Australia with over 47,000 students, including nearly 9000 international students sourced from more than 80 different countries.

III Literature

Australian literature in English began soon after the settlement of the country by Europeans and reflects a range of influences, from English literary traditions to the storytelling of Indigenous Australians and the European settlers and convicts (罪犯) who arrived in Australia in the late 18th century. It has developed certain well-defined qualities: a love of the vast, empty land with its unique plants and animals, a compelling sense of the worth of the common people, and freedom from the bondage of European traditions. Today's writing also reflects the cultural diversity of contemporary Australian society.

Australian writers have produced a diverse range of internationally acclaimed (称赞) novels, drama, poetry and non-fiction. Their works have increasingly been recognized through international literary awards. Many prominent authors have sought inspiration in English and European literature, and these cultural relationships remain strong.

The oral storytelling of Indigenous Australians and convicts and settlers contributed to the development of distinctive Australian writing styles. Early authors explored themes of Indigenous and settler identity, alienation, exile and relationship to place.

Adam Lindsay Gordon (1833—1870) Australian poet, horseman, very popular with Queen Victoria. The only Australian poet commemorated in Poet's Corner of Westminster Abbey.

Australia's vast, dry landscape itself became a character in early Australian works of literature. Dislocated from their countries of origin in the early days of Australia's settlement, many writers struggled with notions of what it meant to be Australian. Strong sentiments of egalitarianism (平等主义)—a wish to be free of the old society of class and privilege—were born and surfaced in Australian literature from that time.

Some early stories were of the "ripping (极妙地) yarn" (故事,奇谈) variety, typified in Rolf Boldrewood's *Robbery under Arms* (1882). Most of Boldrewood's novels were romances and his lead characters English gentlemen, but his outback settings introduced the Australian environment to many readers. Likewise, the poetry of English settler Adam Lindsay Gordon (1833—70) helped foster understanding of Australian identity. Gordon's *Bush Ballads and*

Galloping Rhymes became so popular in England that he was represented in the Poets' Corner of Westminster Abbey (the only Australian to be so recognized). Moral debate about the treatment of convicts underpinned Marcus Clarke's melancholy masterpiece, *For the Term of His Natural Life* (1874). It is possibly the most famous 19th century Australian novel and is still published today.

New Nationalism

Gold rush migrants arrived in Australia in the 1850s, some pressing for democratic rights and freedoms. The second half of the 19th century saw rapid social evolution, great cultural enthusiasm and new-found nationalism in Australia. Universities, libraries and museums were established, and journals such as the *Bulletin*, the *Republican*, *Australian Town and Country*, the *Sydney Worker and Truth* published the short stories of aspiring authors. Among them was Henry Lawson (1867—1922), whose first collection of stories appeared in 1894, followed by *While the Billy Boils* in 1896, generally considered his best prose collection. Born in a tent on the goldfields in New South Wales in 1867 and raised in rural poverty and city squalor, Lawson wrote with compassion about the lives and struggles of Australian pioneers—the men and women of the bush. Lawson helped define an Australian character based on mateship (同伴之谊) and perseverance(坚定不移) in the face of adversity.

Joseph Furphy (1843—1912), an outstanding writer of Australian fiction before World War I, was also inspired by the country's new-found nationalism. His masterpiece novel *Such Is Life* (1903), a fictional account of the lives of rural Australians in the late 1800s, shifted Australian fiction away from the colonial romance genre and earned him the reputation of Father of the Australian Novel.

A Shift in Mood

Until the Depression in 1929, most novels were optimistic about the "lucky country," past and present. However, in the late 1930s the literary mood shifted and darker world views were explored. An important writer in the early 20th century was Miles Franklin, whose feminism set her apart in a time of conservatism. Her most famous novel is *My Brilliant Career* (1901), which was made into an acclaimed film in 1979. Franklin died in 1954 and her will provided for the establishment of an annual literary award. Today The Miles Franklin Award, the first and most prestigious literary award in Australia, celebrates Australian character and creativity and is awarded for the novel of the year that has the highest literary merit and presents Australian life in any of its phases. The Award this year is worth $ 42,000.

Statue of the Author of *My Brilliant Career*, Miles Franklin

Indigenous writers

The first written Indigenous works were translations of traditional myths and legends originally told in song and oral narrative. Aboriginal writing in English is a relatively new phenomenon, starting with David Unaipon (1872—1967), who made a significant contribution to literature and science and to the advancement of Aboriginal people. Unaipon's book *Native Legends* was the first to be published by an Aboriginal writer (in 1929). This was followed by *Myths and Legends of the Australian Aborigines* (1930). In 1989, the University of Queensland Press established the David Unaipon Award, which recognizes and provides publishing opportunities for new Indigenous writers.

Other well-known Indigenous authors include the playwright Jack Davis, the writer Mudrooroo and the poet Oodgeroo Noonuccal, whose *We Are Going* (1964) was the first book of published poetry by an Aboriginal Australian. Sally Morgan's *My Place* (1987) was considered a breakthrough memoir (文集) that brought Indigenous stories to wider notice. Since the 1960s,

David Unaipon (1872—1967), Preacher, Author and Inventor

Patrick White (1912—1990), an Australian novelist, short story writer, and playwright, was awarded the Nobel Prize for Literature in 1973 "for an epic and psychological narrative art which has introduced a new continent into literature."

there has been a marked increase in publications by Indigenous writers, including poetry, fiction, drama, biography and autobiography, and political and sociological writing. In 2007, Indigenous writer and land rights activist Alexis Wright won the Miles Franklin Award for her novel *Carpentaria*.

Post-World War II Literature

The demand for popular fiction continued to grow in the second half of the 20th century. Prominent authors included Nevil Shute (1899—1960), an Englishman who settled in Australia and wrote novels including *A Town Like Alice* (1950), and Morris West (1916-99), who wrote 29 novels, including *The Shoes of the Fisherman* (1963). Colin Thiele wrote around 100 works, including novels set in rural Australia such as *Sun on the Stubble* (1961), *Storm Boy* (1963) and *Blue Fin* (1969).

At this time, many writers sought to examine the relationship between people and the environment. For some, this included promoting reconciliation with Indigenous Australians and developing a greater appreciation of their relationship with the land.

In 1973, Patrick White (1912—90) became the first Australian to win the Nobel Prize for Literature. He published twelve novels, two short-story collections, eight plays, and works of non-fiction.

Since Patrick White, Australia has produced a steady stream of outstanding novelists. Many have set their characters and narratives in Australia, although some have also achieved success with stories based in Asia, Europe and North America.

Migrant Writing

Since the end of World War II, more than 6.5 million people from around 200 countries have settled in Australia, including 675,000 refugees. There is now a significant body of "multicultural literature" in Australia, written by or about migrants. The writing reflects the diversity of Australia's literary community and the diversity of Australia's culture in general.

Contemporary multicultural writings include works by Asian-Australian authors such as Beth Yaph, Sang Ye, Brian Castro, Adib Khan and Yasmine Gooneratne; Greek-Australian writers such as Angelo Loukakis, George Papaellinas and Christos Tsiolkas; European writers such as Arnold Zable, who writes about refugees, his Greek relatives and his strong Yiddish (意第绪语的,犹太人的)-Polish culture; and Italian poets and writers such as Luigi Strano, Enoe Di Stefano and Paolo Totaro. Books by or about refugees are also now emerging, such as Natalie Huynh Chau Nguyen's *Voyage of Hope: Vietnamese Australian Women's Narratives*. JM Coetzee, the South African writer who won the Nobel Prize for Literature in 2003, moved to Adelaide, South Australia, in 2002 and became an Australian citizen in 2006. He has published three works since moving to Australia, *Elizabeth Costello* (2003), *Slow Man* (2005) and *Diary of a Bad Year* (2007).

Australian literary awards

There are more than 30 literary awards in Australia, including major government-funded prizes and specialist competitions. The most well-known include the annual Miles Franklin Literary

Chapter 14　Culture and Society of Australia

Award and the Australian/Vogel Literary Award.

The Miles Franklin Award, now worth around $42,000, (Australian dollars, 下同) was bequeathed (遗赠) by the will of Australian novelist Miles Franklin for "a published novel or play portraying Australian life in any of its phases". The Vogel Award is Australia's richest award for an unpublished manuscript ($20,000) and has helped launch the careers of some of Australia's most successful writers. The Barbara Jefferies Award ($35,000), instituted in 2007, honors Australian novels that depict women in a positive light.

Four state governments—New South Wales, Queensland, Victoria and Western Australia—also fund annual literary prizes and the Australian Government has announced a Prime Minister's Literary Prize for fiction and non-fiction books, with each of the two annual prizes worth $100,000.

> **Quick Facts of Prize Winners**
> - Australian authors have won many international awards, including the Nobel Prize for Literature (Patrick White, 1973), the Man Booker Prize (Thomas Keneally, 1982; Peter Carey, 1988 and 2001; DBC Pierre, 2003) and the Pulitzer Prize for Fiction (Geraldine Brooks, 2006).
> - Adam Lindsay Gordon is the only Australian with a bust in Poets' Corner in Westminster Abbey.
> - Three Australians have received the Queen's Gold Medal for Poetry: Michael Thwaites in 1940, Judith Wright in 1991, and Les Murray in 1998.

IV　Sports

Australia is a sports-mad nation. Sport plays an important part in Australian culture, 23.5% Australians over the age of 15 regularly participate in organized sporting activities.

At an international level, Australia is a strong competitor in cricket, hockey, netball, rugby league (联盟式橄榄球,), rugby union (联合式橄榄球), and performs well in cycling, rowing and swimming. Nationally, other popular sports include Australian rules football, horse racing, football (soccer) and motor racing. Australia also boasts a particularly rich tennis tradition. Melbourne hosts the annual Australian Open, one of the four Grand Slam tennis tournaments.

Australia is one of the only three countries that have competed at every summer Olympic Games of the modern era, winning its first two medals in 1896, five years before it existed as a country. Australia hosted the 1956 Summer Olympics in Melbourne and the 2000 Summer Olympics in Sydney, and has ranked among the top five medal-takers since 2000. Australia has also participated in every Commonwealth Games. It hosted the 1938, 1962, 1982 and 2006 Commonwealth Games. Other major international events held regularly in Australia include annual international cricket matches and the Formula One Australian Grand Prix (一级方程式大奖赛).

V　Holidays and Special Days

Australia Day

Australia Day is celebrated as Australia's official National Day on the 26 January, commemorating the arrival of the First Fleet at Sydney Cove on January 26, 1788 and the founding of the first permanent European settlement in Australia. Australia Day is the biggest day of celebration in the country and is observed as a public holiday in all states and territories. The formal celebrations begin on the eve of Australia Day and continue all through the next day. The ceremony is marked by flag hoisting, community awards presentation (Each year as people around the nation celebrate what makes the country great, there are some very special Aussies being recognized for their great work. These awards are known as the Australian of the Year Awards) and citizenship ceremonies along with local events, breakfasts, and merrymaking. Parades and fireworks are also a common feature in the national day celebrations of Australia. The most popular site of concerts, festivities and lightshows is the lawns of Parliament House in Canberra, the Capital city of Australia.

Name	Date
New Year's Day	1 January
Australia Day	26 January
Good Friday	Easter
Easter Saturday	the Saturday following Good Friday
Easter Monday	the Monday following Good Friday
ANZAC Day	25 April
Queen's Birthday	2nd Monday in June
Christmas Day	25 December
Boxing Day	26 December or 27 December

Easter

Easter commemorates the resurrection (return to life) of Jesus Christ following his death by crucifixion (钉于十字架处死). It celebrates the promise of life in the face of death. Easter celebrations also reflect on peace and forgiveness. It is a time for thinking about suffering, injustice and hardship. During Good Friday services Christians meditate on Jesus' suffering and on his words spoken from the cross: *"Father, forgive them; for they do not know what they are doing."* In addition to its religious significance, Easter in Australia is enjoyed as a four-day holiday weekend starting on Good Friday and ending on Easter Monday. The Easter holiday, particularly Easter Saturday, is a popular time for christenings and weddings. Unlike other Northern hemisphere countries, where Easter falls in the springtime, Easter in Australia is celebrated in the autumn season.

Australia is the land of people from a number of cultures. For this reason, Australia has a different style of celebrating the Easter festivity. There are certain things that are specific to Australia. To say for example, in major part of Northern hemisphere, the Easter bunny (rabbit) is considered to be one of the most important symbols of Easter. But in Australia, rabbits, or bunnies, are seen as pests, which have cost Australian farmers a lot of money and damaged many landscapes. Owing to this, the Aussie people have found another alternative Easter symbol, namely Bilby. The Bilby is a small mammal with large ears that is native to Australia. For some people, it is now the Easter Bilby that brings chocolate and decorated eggs to children on an

Easter Sunday morning. Chocolate models of the Easter Bilby are sold to raise money to help preserve the Bilby population.

ANZAC (澳新军团) Day

ANZAC stands for Australian and New Zealand Army Corps. It commemorates the landing of Australian and New Zealand troops at Gallipoli on 25 April, 1915. The date, 25 April, was officially named ANZAC Day in 1916. The spirit of ANZAC recognizes the qualities of courage, mateship and sacrifice which were demonstrated at the Gallipoli landing. ANZAC Day is a time to remember the deaths and sufferings in war, the courage of fighting men and women, and the ever-present hope for the peoples of the world to live together in harmony and lasting peace.

Commemorative (纪念的) services are held at dawn on 25 April, the time of the original landing, across the nation, usually at war memorials. This was initiated by returned soldiers after the First World War in the 1920s as a common form of remembrance. The first official dawn service was held at the Sydney Cenotaph (衣冠冢,纪念碑) in 1927, which was also the first year that all states recognized a public holiday on the day. Initially dawn services were only attended by veterans who followed the ritual of "standing to" before two minutes of silence was observed, broken by the sound of a lone piper playing "the Last Post." Later in the day, there were marches in all the major cities and many smaller towns for families and other well wishers.

Queen's Birthday

The Queen's Birthday celebrates the birthday of Queen Elizabeth II who is not only Queen of the United Kingdom but also Queen of Australia. The day has been observed since 1788, when Governor Arthur Phillip declared a holiday to mark the birthday of King George III. Until 1936 it was held on the actual birthday of the Monarch, but after the death of King George V it was decided to keep the date at mid-year. Queen's Birthday is celebrated on the second Monday of June except in the state of Western Australia where the Queen's Birthday holiday is celebrated in late September or early October. Neither date marks the real birthday of the sovereign. The holiday also marks the start of the Australian ski season, though it is quite common that there is no skiable snow until later in the month.

Christmas

For the majority of Australians, Christmas down under has all the glitter, tinsel and razzmatazz (活力) of a Christmas in New York, London, Paris or Vancouver. The major difference is one of WEATHER. Whereas the northern hemisphere is in the middle of winter, Australians are baking in summer heat. It is no unusual to have Christmas Day well into the mid 30°C. The heat of early summer in Australia has an impact on the way that Australians celebrate Christmas and on which northern hemisphere Christmas traditions are followed.

● *Customs*

In the weeks leading up to Christmas, houses are decorated; greetings cards sent out; carols sung; Christmas trees installed in homes, schools and public places. Everyone is busily planning Christmas break-up parties. Children are writing letters to Santa Claus and delight in anticipating his visit. On Christmas Day family and friends gather to share love and friendship, exchange gifts and enjoy special Christmas food. It must be mentioned that for Australians Christmas is still a time for remembering the true meaning of Christmas and a time for

Kangaroo Santa

remembering the birth of Jesus and the spiritual meaning of Christmas. For many, Christmas begins with families attending a mid-night mass.

● Carols

The warm weather allows Australians to enjoy a tradition which commenced in 1937. Carols by Candlelight is held every year on Christmas Eve, where tens of thousands of people gather in the city of Melbourne to sing their favorite Christmas songs. The evening is lit by the candles held by the public singing under a clean-cut night sky. Sydney and the other capital cities also enjoy Carols in the weeks leading up to Christmas.

Some uniquely Australian Christmas carols have become popular and are included alongside the more traditional carols sung at carol services and at Christmas church services: John Wheeler's *The Three Drovers* is perhaps the best known of these. Many light-hearted Australian Christmas songs have become an essential part of the Australian Christmas experience. These include Rolf Harris's *Six White Boomers*, Colin Buchanan's *Aussie Jingle Bells* and *The Australian Twelve Days of Christmas*.

Instead of the usual image of a reindeer drawing Santa's sleigh, many Australians cherish the image of six white boomers (large Kangaroos) hopping the sleigh across the sky.

● Food

In Australia traditional Christmas meals have been replaced with family gatherings in back yards, picnics in parks or on the beach. Cold turkey and ham, seafood and salads are often served instead of the hot roast dinner. It has even become acceptable to serve the traditional Christmas plum pudding with cold custard (奶油冻), ice cream or cream (乳酪). Pavlova (奶油水果蛋白饼), a meringue (蛋白与糖的混合物) base topped with whipped cream and fresh fruit, and various versions of the festive ice-cream pudding have also become popular.

● Outdoors

Christmas time is "holiday time" in Australia, with the majority of Aussies taking Christmas / New Years holidays to bake themselves in the sun and to enjoy the great Australian outdoors. Schools also close for six weeks over the period, and many families head to their favorite seaside retreat to fish, surf and play. It has become traditional for international visitors who are in Sydney at Christmas time to go to Bondi Beach where up to 40,000 people visit on Christmas Day. However, many people enjoy celebrating Christmas Day in their backyards, sitting around the pool, watching the kids swim, having a few drinks, and enjoying the company of their friends and family.

● Major sporting events

The Christmas break is also an opportunity for sports fans to enjoy two major sporting events: the Boxing Day Test and the Sydney to Hobart Yacht Race. The 26 December is the opening day of the Boxing Day Test between the Australian Cricket Team and an international touring side at the Melbourne Cricket Ground. This has been well attended since the first match in 1950 and watched by many others on television. In Sydney one of the world's most prestigious ocean races, the Sydney to Hobart(霍巴特,塔斯马尼亚州府) Yacht Race, starts on Boxing Day from Sydney Harbor.

Spend Christmas in the Great Southern Land

Chapter 15　Understanding New Zealand

I　A General Survey

Map of New Zealand

　　New Zealand, a small island country located in the South Pacific Ocean and close neighbor to Australia, has a landscape renowned for its varieties, and in particular, its scenic snowcapped mountains and rolling green pastures. The culture of New Zealand is a synthesis(综合体) of home-grown and imported cultures. Modern New Zealand society is a fusion of Polynesian, Asian and European cultures. New Zealanders are recognized globally for their progressive humanitarian stance, liberal politics and world-leading social welfare. The country enjoys a high quality of life. Before we scrutinize (细看) the details of this nation, let's have a glimpse of some basics about it.

A Collection of Fast Facts of New Zealand

Basic Facts	
Capital	Wellington
Area	268,680 sq km
People	
Population	4,027,947 (2006 Census) (2006 estimate)
Population growth rate	1.1 percent (2006 estimate)
Population density	16.1 persons per sq km (2006 estimate)
Largest cities, with population	
Auckland	1,241,700 (2005 estimate)
Wellington	370,100 (2005 estimate)
Christchurch	367,800 (2005 estimate)
Hamilton	185,100 (2005 estimate)
Dunedin	114,800 (2005 estimate)
Ethnic groups	
European	78 percent
Māori	14.6 percent
Pacific peoples	6.9 percent
Asian	9.2 percent
Languages	
English (official), Māori 毛利语 (official), Polynesian languages	
Religious affiliations	
Protestant	24 percent
Anglican	21 percent
Roman Catholic	13 percent
Buddhist	1 percent
Nonreligious	13 percent
Other (including Jewish and Hindu)	28 percent

Health and Education	
Total Life Expectancy	78.8 years (2006 estimate)
Female	81.9 years (2006 estimate)
Male	75.8 years (2006 estimate)
Infant mortality rate	6 deaths per 1,000 live births (2006 estimate)
Literacy Rate	
Total	7.1p 99 percent (1995)
Number of students per teacher, primary school	18 students per teacher (2002-200)
Government	
Form of Government	Parliamentary democracy
Head of State	Governor-general, representing the British monarch
Head of government	Prime minister
Legislature	Unicameral legislature
	House of Representatives: 120 members
Voting Qualifications	Universal at age 18
Constitution	
No written constitution; political system closely modeled on that of the United Kingdom.	
Highest Court	Court of Appeal
Unemployment Rate	3.9 percent (2004)
Monetary Unit	
New Zealand dollar ($NZ), consisting of 100 cents	

Capital City—Wellington

Whatever else it may be, Wellington is first of all the capital of New Zealand and the geographical, cultural, commercial, cosmopolitan centre of the country. In population, it is New Zealand's second largest city. Being the nation's capital and the seat of its government, Wellington has transformed itself via its café, fashion, restaurant, nightlife and artistic culture into a New Zealand's hot urban destination in the past few years.

Ethnic Groups

New Zealanders of European descent, who are often known by the Māori name Pakeha (<新西兰>白种人), comprise about 75 percent of the population. They are usually described as the largest ethnic group, but in fact they are ethnically mixed.

Pacific Islanders and East Asians each account for about 5 percent of the population. Māori, the native inhabitants of New Zealand, are the largest non-European group. They are a people of Polynesian origin who, in 2000, constitute some 15.7 percent of New Zealand's population. More than 95 percent of Māori live on New Zealand's North Island. Many Māori live in the East Cape area, where they form the majority of the population. Others live in the large cities of New Zealand such as Auckland and Wellington.

Official Languages

English and Māori are the official languages of New Zealand. Māori became an official language in 1987. New Zealand English is close to Australian English in pronunciation, but has several subtle differences. Some of these differences show New Zealand English has more affinity（相似）with the English of southern England than Australian English does. Several of the differences also show the influence of Māori speech. The New Zealand accent also has some Scottish and Irish influences from the large number of settlers. Māori is only used in New Zealand and nowhere else in the world. In the 1840 *Treaty of Waitangi*, Queen Victoria promised the Māori that their language would be protected. At present, the Māori language is commonly used in the media and at school. In April 2006, New Zealand became the first country to declare sign language as an official language, alongside Māori and English.

Religions

The majority of New Zealanders are Christian. Anglicans traditionally have formed the largest single denomination（教派）. The next largest Christian groups are Presbyterians and Roman Catholics. Religious practice is stronger among Māori and Pacific Islanders than among Pakeha. The Māori Christian churches, the Ringatu Church (founded in 1867) and the Ratana Church of New Zealand (1918), have relatively small but consistently active membership.

Flag of New Zealand

The New Zealand flag is the symbol of the realm government and people of New Zealand. It is a defaced blue ensign（国旗）with the Union Flag in the canton, and four red stars with white borders to the right. The stars represent the constellation of Crux, the Southern Cross, as seen from New Zealand. The flag proportion is 1:2 and the colors are red, blue and white. Proportion and colors are identical to the Union Flag.

Six flags other than the New Zealand Flag are flown for official purposes in New Zealand. They are the Queen's Personal Flag for New Zealand, Governor-General's Flag, New Zealand Red Ensign（英国商船旗）, New Zealand White Ensign（皇家海军旗）, Royal NZ Air Force Ensign, and New Zealand Civil Air Ensign.

National Anthems

New Zealand holds a rare position in the world in that it has two national anthems of equal standing — "God Defend New Zealand" and "God Save The Queen." Both of these anthems have origins which have been inspired by the fire of patriotism yet were written under different situations.

Coat of Arms

The first quarter of the shield depicts four stars as representative of the Southern Cross, then three ships symbolizing the importance of New Zealand's sea trade; in the second quarter is a fleece representing the farming industry. The wheat sheaf, in the third quarter represents the agricultural industry, whilst the crossed hammers in the fourth quarter represent the mining industry. The supporters on either side of the shield consist of a Māori Chieftain(首领) holding a taiaha (a Māori war weapon) and a European woman holding the New Zealand Ensign(国旗). Surmounting the Arms is the St Edward's Crown which was used in the Coronation（加冕礼）ceremony of Her Majesty Queen Elizabeth II. The crown symbolizes

the fact that Her Majesty is Queen of New Zealand under *the New Zealand Royal Titles Act 1953*.
Kiwiana (objects and symbols regarded as national icons)

"Kiwiana" is the term used to describe items relating to New Zealand's unique culture and history. Some notable items of Kiwiana people will probably encounter on their trip to New Zealand are listed below.

● *National bird：Kiwi Bird (奇异鸟,鹬鸵)*

The Kiwi bird is the country's indigenous flightless bird. It occurs only in New Zealand and is a New Zealand Kiwiana icon—New Zealanders even take their nickname from the little critter.

● *National Flower*

New Zealand's impressive ponga, or tree fern(桫椤), can grow to a towering height of 15 meters. With more than 150 fern species growing in New Zealand, the plant has become a national symbol.

● *Kiwifruit*

Originally known as Chinese gooseberries, kiwifruit were first introduced to the country by early settlers. Since then they have become synonymous with New Zealand, and are a major export earner.

● *Sheep*

Being the back bone of the New Zealand economy for over a century, sheep were first introduced by English settlers in the 19th century. Merino sheep(美利奴绵羊) that are prized for their fine wool, cloak Alps' foothills.

II Geography and History

Geography
● *Land*

The total land area of New Zealand is 268,680 square km, about the same size as Japan or the British Isles. The North and South islands make up almost the entire area of the country.

The North Island, 113,729 square km in area, is one of the two main islands of New Zealand, the other being the South Island. Approximately 76%(3,148,400)of New Zealand's population lives in the North Island. Several important cities are in the North Island, notably New Zealand's largest city, Auckland, and Wellington. Snow-capped Mount Ruapehu is one of the world's most active volcanoes and the largest active volcano in New Zealand. It is the highest point in the North Island.

The South Island is the larger of the two major islands of New Zealand with an area of 154,951 square km. The South Island is often called the Mainland (somewhat humorously) because it existed first according to Māori legend, and is larger than the North Island. The South Island only has a resident population of 991,100, about a quarter of New Zealand's four million inhabitants.

Map of North Island   Map of South Island

● *Natural Resources*

Land is one of the country's most valuable resources. More than half of the land area is either cropland or pastureland. Most of the arable land is found on the east coasts of both islands, in particular the Canterbury Plains. Pastures for livestock grazing dominate in north-central and western North Island and southern South Island.

About 31 percent of the land area is forested. The country has 6.4 million hectares of old-growth forest, much of which is designated for preservation. In addition, some forests are plantations of imported species such as the radiata pine. New Zealand rivers and lakes are an important natural resource as the source of hydroelectricity. Mineral resources are limited, with some reserves of coal, gold, iron ore, and limestone. Significant stocks of natural gas and less plentiful reserves of oil are located both offshore and in the western region of the North Island.

● *Climate*

New Zealand is located in the Southern Temperate Zone, south of the tropics. It has a mild climate with four seasons. The warmest months of summer are January and February and the coldest months of winter are June and July. Inland areas have cooler winters and warmer summers than coastal areas, where the moderating influence of the ocean creates a more temperate climate.

History

The first inhabitants of New Zealand, the Māori, are thought to have arrived over 1,000 years ago, traveling on canoes from a South Pacific homeland. Māori named the land Aotearoa ("Land of the Long White Cloud") and developed a very successful society.

The first European to sight New Zealand was Abel Tasman, a Dutch navigator who saw the South Island's West Coast in 1642. Although he never set foot on New Zealand soil, he annexed it for Holland under the name "Staten Landt"—later changed to New Zealand by Dutch mapmakers.

In 1769, Briton Captain James Cook was searching for a southern continent when his cabin boy sighted land near Gisborne (吉斯伯恩，新西兰北岛东岸港市) in 1769. Cook circumnavigated (环航)and mapped the country. He established friendly relations with some Māori. European migration began soon after and by

1839 there were an estimated 2,000 Europeans in New Zealand.

On February 6, 1840 representatives of Britain and Māori chiefs signed *the Treaty of Waitangi*, at Waitangi in the Bay of Islands, establishing British law in New Zealand while guaranteeing Māori authority over their land and culture, and granting the Māori British citizenship. Although there are continuing debates about the proper interpretation of the Treaty, it is considered New Zealand's founding document. After the signing of the Treaty numbers of British migrants increased enormously. A gold rush during the 1860s attracted even more migrants from around the world, yet Britain remained the "homeland" for most settlers and the majority of New Zealand's infrastructure was built on British models. Independence from Britain was formally proclaimed in 1947 and since that time New Zealand has increasingly developed its own unique culture: a mix of those that have settled the country throughout the centuries.

From the beginning, the country has been in the forefront in instituting social welfare legislation. New Zealand was the world's first country to give women the right to vote (1893). It adopted old-age pensions (1898); a national child welfare program (1907); social security for the elderly, widows, and orphans, along with family benefit payments; minimum wages; a 40-hour workweek and unemployment and health insurance (1938); and socialized medicine (1941). In recent years, New Zealand has introduced extremely liberal social policies. In June 2003, parliament legalized prostitution and in Dec. 2004, same-sex unions were recognized.

III Political System and National Economy

Political System

The politics of New Zealand takes place in a framework of a parliamentary representative democratic monarchy. The basic system is closely patterned on that of the Westminster System, although a number of significant modifications have been made. New Zealand's head of state is the Queen of New Zealand, currently Elizabeth II, but actual government is conducted by a Prime Minister and Cabinet drawn from an elected Parliament.

The New Zealand monarchy has been distinct from the British monarchy since *the New Zealand Royal Titles Act of 1953*, and all Elizabeth II's official business in New Zealand is conducted in the name of the Queen of New Zealand, not the Queen of the United Kingdom. In practice, the functions of the monarchy are conducted by a Governor General, appointed by the monarch on the advice of the Prime Minister. New Zealand was the first country in the world in which all the highest offices were occupied by women, between March 2005 and August 2006: the Sovereign Queen Elizabeth II of New Zealand, Governor-General Dame Silvia Cartwright, Prime Minister Helen Clark, Speaker of the New Zealand House of Representatives Margaret Wilson and Chief Justice Dame Sian Elias.

National Economy

● *Economy & Industry*

New Zealand has a mixed economy, dominated by an export-focused agricultural sector, together with significant manufacturing and service sectors. The economy is strongly trade-oriented with food and beverages representing a large proportion of exports. New Zealand has developed a world-wide reputation for top quality produce, from meat (New Zealand lamb is particularly renowned), to dairy products, seafood, fruit and vegetables, and boutique wines. Service industries, including tourism, consultancy and education, are also extremely significant to the New Zealand economy.

- *Currency and Banking*

The New Zealand dollar (currency code NZD) is the currency of New Zealand. It is normally abbreviated with the dollar sign $, or alternatively NZ $ to distinguish it from other dollar-denominated currencies. It is often informally known as the "Kiwi (dollar)" and is divided into 100 cents. (NZ$1.51 equals U. S. $1; 2004 average).

The Reserve Bank of New Zealand (founded in 1934) has the sole power of issue. It acts as a wholesale distributor to the trading banks, and manages the design and manufacturing of the currency. It also withdraws damaged or unusable notes and coins to manage the quality of currency in circulation

IV Society and Culture

Culture

New Zealand has a unique cultural identity, quite unlike anywhere else in the world. Decidedly multi-cultural, modern New Zealand society is a fusion of Polynesian, Asian and European cultures.

The earliest cultural tradition in New Zealand was that of the Māori, who developed a rich and diverse Polynesian culture in geographic isolation from the other cultures of Polynesia. European settlers brought with them their own traditions, which eventually dominated the country's cultural life. Since the 1950s the cultural fabric of New Zealand has become increasingly diverse with the immigration of peoples from the Pacific Islands and Asia.

- *Pakeha Culture*

Cultural activity among people of European descent, who are known as Pakeha in New Zealand, has long been strong, but until recently tended to follow British models. Cultural output was high in both quality and quantity. It was complicated by strong links with Britain, however, because London was in many respects the cultural capital of New Zealand. The most acclaimed New Zealand artists produced their famous works as expatriates (移居国外的人) in England. Artists and writers who stayed in New Zealand tended to feel alienated from, and unappreciated by, overseas European society. Even expatriate artists, however, explored their New Zealand roots. In the second half of the 20th century, Pakeha culture developed in its own right, producing many notable writers and artists whose works draw on the New Zealand experience.

- *Māori Culture*

In most Māori communities, men hunted and plowed, while women weeded, wove, and cooked. Group activities included food gathering, food cultivation, and warfare. Individuals specialized in different arts: poetry, oratory, tattooing(纹身), and the carving of wood, bone, and stone. Traditional Māori culture is expressed in song, dance, oratory, woodcarving, weaving, and architecture. Māori artists also bring Māori perspectives to canvas painting, fiction and poetry writing, and other art forms. The Māori have made a concerted effort to preserve their culture. In the 1980s they initiated a revival of their language and other traditions. By that time many Māori had assimilated into the predominant European culture. The majority of Māori had become urban dwellers, and younger Māori did not know the Māori language. Today Māori culture thrives in both traditional and reinvented traditions.

Customs

● Marriage and Family

Weddings are often followed by a sit-down meal and dancing. Among those of European origin, families tend to be small, and most own their homes. Many young adults leave for several years to travel and work in other countries (often the United Kingdom). This time abroad is commonly referred to as Overseas Experience, or OE.

Among the Māori, the extended family remains important, and several generations may live in the same house. Also important to the Māori is the community center, called the marae, a Māori community facility which consists of a carved meeting house, a dining hall and cooking area as well as the marae atea (sacred space in front of the meeting house). The marae is a symbol of tribal identity. It is a meeting place where people can discuss and debate various issues, and in which Māori customs are given ultimate expression. On the marae, official functions such as celebrations, weddings, christenings, tribal reunion, funerals take place.

● Eating

Traditional British-style big breakfasts and hearty meals of meat and potatoes have gradually given way to a more diverse and health-conscious diet. New Zealanders have long eaten beef, pork, mutton, and fish, and are now eating more poultry.

Fruit is plentiful, as are dairy products. New Zealand produces fine wines, and beer is a popular beverage. Popular takeout foods at lunchtime include meat pies, sandwiches, and filled bread rolls. Chinese food, pizza, hamburgers, and fried chicken are all available for a takeout dinner, in addition to the more traditional fish and chips and lamb roast. In the main cities, restaurants serve a wide range of cuisine, including Thai, Malaysian, Chinese, Indian, Greek, and Mexican.

New Zealanders generally eat three meals a day, and many still enjoy the British traditions of a morning cup of tea and afternoon tea at about 3 or 4 PM. The main meal is usually in the evening between 6 and 7 PM, although when dining out it is more likely to be around 8 PM.

● Socializing

New Zealanders usually shake hands when meeting someone (in formal circumstances, a man normally waits for a woman to offer her hand first), and first names are commonly used after an initial introduction. Informal greetings include the New Zealand version of "Good day," pronounced Gidday, or a simple "Hello" or "Hi." The Māori may greet each other with a hug or the traditional hongi-pressing noses together with eyes closed and making a low "mm-mm" sound. The Māori greeting "Kia Ora", which is a wish for good health, is now becoming far more widely used among the population in general (and in the tourism industry in particular). "Kia Ora" may be answered with the same.

New Zealanders frequently entertain in the home, and barbies (barbecues) are especially popular on summer weekends. There are few formal codes of etiquette, and social relations are generally casual. New Zealanders have a reputation for genuine hospitality toward visitors, and often invite people into their homes soon after making their acquaintance.

● Recreation

New Zealanders are keen sport participants and fans. Many will get up in the middle of the night to watch a broadcast of their team playing abroad. Rugby Union football is traditionally the favorite national sport. The All Blacks are New Zealand's national rugby union team. Rugby League football, soccer, hockey, cricket, softball, netball (a form of basketball), water sports, and track and field are also popular. Women participate actively in all these sports except professional rugby. New Zealanders take part in a variety of international sporting events, such as rugby, soccer, cricket, tennis, and sailing competitions. Popular leisure activities include beach swimming, fishing, skiing, and hiking. Other recreational activities include home improvements, gardening, watching television, and socializing at home or in a pub. New Zealanders may also spend weekends in their holiday homes or seaside cabins-known as bachs in the North Island and cribs in the South Island.

Holidays and Special Days

The official public holidays of New Zealand include New Year (the first two working days in January are public holidays), Waitangi Day (6 February), Easter (Good Friday through Easter Monday), Anzac Day (25 April), Queen Elizabeth II's Birthday (observed the first Monday in June), Labour Day (the fourth Monday in October), Christmas Day (25 December), and Boxing Day (26 December).

● *Waitangi Day*

Waitangi Day marks the occasion in 1840 when the United Kingdom signed *the Treaty of Waitangi* with the indigenous Māori. Under this treaty, New Zealand became a British colony. The Māori ceded sovereignty to the British in return for legal protection as British subjects. The Māori were guaranteed possession of their land, but with the limitation that they could sell only to the monarchy.

● *Anzac Day*(奥新军团日)

Anzac is an acronym(首字母缩略词) for Australia and New Zealand Army Corps. Along with Australia, New Zealand remembers its war dead every year on Anzac Day (25 April). It marks the anniversary of the 1915 landing on Gallipoli (加里波利), Turkey, of the Australian and New Zealand Army Corps (ANZAC). The landing was part of the ill-advised campaign, during the First World War, to capture the Dardanelles (达达尼尔海峡) and force Turkey, which was an ally of Germany, into submission. Thousands of Australian and New Zealand troops were killed before the campaign was abandoned.

Anzac Day is a day to remember the courage of the soldiers in this battle and the courage and sacrifice of all men and women who have served their country in times of war. A parade is held in many cities and towns.

Education

Education in New Zealand is nominally free for all primary, intermediate and secondary schooling. However, most schools also ask for a "voluntary donation" from parents, informally known as "school fees" or a "parental contribution."

● *Primary and Secondary Education*

Education in New Zealand is compulsory for all children aged 5 through 16. Disabled students with special educational needs can stay until the end of the year they turn 21. Students spend eight years in primary school, often transferring to specialized intermediate schools for the final two years. Secondary schooling generally takes five years, and it remains tuition-free for students under the age of 20. Most students attend public secular schools; only a minority attends private or church-affiliated schools.

● *Higher Education*

The system of higher education in New Zealand includes eight universities. The largest are the University of Auckland (founded in 1882), at Auckland, and Massey University (1926), with campuses at Auckland, Palmerston North, and Wellington. Other institutions of higher education are the University of Waikato (1964), at Hamilton; the Victoria University of Wellington (1899); the University of Canterbury (1873), at Christchurch; the University of Otago (1869), at Dunedin; Lincoln University (1990; formerly Lincoln Agricultural College), near Christchurch; and the Auckland University of Technology (2000, formerly the Auckland Institute of Technology). Several colleges provide teacher training, and polytechnic institutions offer degree programs, diplomas, and certificates in various technical and professional trades.

尊敬的老师：

　　您好！

　　为了方便您更好地使用本教材，获得最佳教学效果，我们特向使用该书作为教材的教师赠送本教材配套参考资料。如有需要，请完整填写"教师联系表"并加盖所在单位系（院）公章，免费向出版社索取。

北京大学出版社

教 师 联 系 表

教材名称	《英语国家概况》		
姓名：	性别：	职务：	职称：
E-mail：	联系电话：	邮政编码：	
供职学校：	所在院系：		（章）
学校地址：			
教学科目与年级：	班级人数：		
通信地址：			

　　填写完毕后，请将此表邮寄给我们，我们将为您免费寄送本教材配套资料，谢谢！

北京市海淀区成府路 205 号
北京大学出版社外语编辑部　李　颖
邮政编码：100871
电子邮箱：evalee1770@sina.com

邮 购 部 电话：010-62534449
市场营销部电话：010-62750672
外语编辑部电话：010-62767315